Britain 1895–1951

with Women and Suffrage c1860–1930 and Ireland 1914–2007

Derrick Murphy ■ **Graham Goodlad** ■ **Richard Staton**

Collins

Published by Collins
An imprint of HarperCollinsPublishers
77–85 Fulham Palace Road
Hammersmith
London
W6 8JB

Browse the complete Collins catalogue
at www.collinseducation.com

© HarperCollinsPublishers Limited 2008

10 9 8 7 6 5 4 3 2

ISBN 978 0 00 726872 6

Derrick Murphy asserts his moral rights
to be identified as the author of new
content in this work.

British Library Cataloguing in
Publication Data
A Catalogue record for this publication is
available from the British Library

Edited by Graham Bradbury
This edition commissioned by Michael
Upchurch
Original series commissioned by Graham
Bradbury
Design and typesetting by Derek Lee
Cover design by Joerg Hartmannsgruber,
White-card
Map Artwork by Tony Richardson
Picture research by Celia Dearing and
Michael Upchurch
Production by Simon Moore
Indexed by Ann Shooter
Printed and bound by Printing Express
Ltd, Hong Kong

ACKNOWLEDGEMENTS
Every effort had been made to contact
the holders of copyright material, but if
any have been inadvertently overlooked
the publishers will be pleased to make
the necessary arrangements at the first
opportunity.

B.T. Batsford Ltd for the extract from *The
Inter-war Economy: Britain 1919–1939* by
D. H. Aldcroft (1970). Cambridge
University Press for the extract from
Abstract of British Historical Statistics by
B. R. Mitchell and P. Deane (1962).
HarperCollins Publishers for the extract
from *Twopence to Cross the Mersey* by
Helen Forrester (1974). Macmillan for
the extracts from *The Edwardian Crisis,
Britain 1901–1914* by David Powell
(Palgrave Macmillan, 1996); *British
Political Facts* by David and Gareth
Butler (1994) and *Britain since 1789* by
Martin Pugh (Palgrave MacMillan,
1999). Orion for the extract from
Memoirs of a Conservative, 1910–37 by J.
C. C. Davidson (Weidenfeld &
Nicholson, 1969). Oxford University
Press for the extract from *England
1870–1914* by R. C. K. Ensor (Oxford
paperbacks, 1993). Paladin for the
extract from *The Decline from Power* by
Robert Blake (1986). Pearson for the
extracts from *The Shaping of the Welfare
State* (Longman, 1974) and *The Attlee
Governments* by Kevin Jeffreys
(Longman, 1992). Penguin Books for the
extract from *Divided Ulster* by Liam de
Paor (1971). Routledge for the extracts
from *Post-Victorian Britain, 1902–51* by
R. C. B. Seaman (1968). Bill Hamilton as
the Literary Executor of the Estate of the
late Sonia Brownell Orwell, Martin
Secker and Warburg for an extract from
The Road to Wigan Pier by George
Orwell, Copyright © George Orwell,
1937.

The publishers would like to thank the
following for permission to reproduce
pictures on these pages.
T=Top, B=Bottom, L=Left, R=Right,
C=Centre

akg-images 196; The Bridgeman Art
Library 23, 61, 166; Victoria & Albert
Museum, London, UK, / The Bridgeman
Art Library 30; Hulton-Deutsch
Collection / Corbis 103L; Getty Images
24, 26, 37, 39, 55, 60, 64, 74, 95, 100,
105, 123, 130, 136, 178, 186, 209, 231,
244, 247, 264, 282; Time & Life
Pictures/Getty Images 103R;
Popperfoto/Getty Images 203; AFP/Getty
Images 221, 295; Imperial War Museum
231; Punch Library 223L, 223R, 223C;
Unknown 45, 47, 78L, 78R, 117, 120,
131, 134T, 134C, 144, 148, 152, 273,
280, 286, 290.

Contents

This section of the book is designed to aid Sixth Form students in their preparation for public examinations in History.

- Differences between GCSE and Sixth Form History
- Extended writing: the structured question and the essay
- How to handle sources in Sixth Form History
- Historical interpretation
- Progression in Sixth Form History
- Examination technique

Differences between GCSE and Sixth Form History

- The amount of factual knowledge required for answers to Sixth Form History questions is more detailed than at GCSE. Factual knowledge in the Sixth Form is used as supporting evidence to help answer historical questions. Knowing the facts is important, but not as important as knowing that factual knowledge supports historical analysis.

- Extended writing is more important in Sixth Form History. Students will be expected to answer either structured questions or essays.

Structured questions require students to answer more than one question on a given topic. For example:

> (a) What problems faced Attlee when he became Labour prime minister in 1945?
>
> (b) How successful were the Labour governments of 1945 to 1951 in dealing with these problems?

Each part of the structured question demands a different approach.

Essay questions require students to produce one answer to a given question. For example:

> To what extent was the decline of the Liberal Party due to the First World War?

Similarities with GCSE

● **Source analysis and evaluation**

The skills in handling historical sources, which were acquired at GCSE, are developed in Sixth Form History. In the Sixth Form, sources have to be analysed in their historical context, so a good factual knowledge of the subject is important.

● **Historical interpretations**

Skills in historical interpretation at GCSE are also developed in Sixth Form

History. The ability to put forward different historical interpretations is important. Students will also be expected to explain why different historical interpretations have occurred.

Extended writing: the structured question and the essay

When faced with extended writing in Sixth Form History students can improve their performance by following a simple routine that attempts to ensure they achieve their best performance.

Answering the question

What are the command instructions?
Different questions require different types of response. For instance, 'In what ways' requires students to point out the various ways something took place in History; 'Why' questions expect students to deal with the causes or consequences of an historical event.

'How far' or 'To what extent' questions require students to produce a balanced, analytical answer. Usually, this will take the form of the case for and the case against an historical question.

Are there key words or phrases that require definition or explanation?
It is important for students to show that they understand the meaning of the question. To do this, certain historical terms or words require explanation. For instance, if a question asked 'how far' a politician was an 'innovator', an explanation of the word 'innovator' would be required.

Does the question have specific dates or issues that require coverage?
If the question mentions specific dates, these must be adhered to. For instance, if you are asked to answer a question on Britain's foreign policy it might state 'in the period 1937 to 1939'.

Planning your answer

Once you have decided on what the question requires, write a brief plan. For structured questions this may be brief. This is a useful procedure to make sure that you have ordered the information you require for your answer in the most effective way. For instance, in a balanced, analytical answer this may take the form of jotting down the main points for and against an historical issue raised in the question.

Writing the answer

Communication skills
The quality of written English is important in Sixth Form History. The way you present your ideas on paper can affect the quality of your answer. Therefore, punctuation, spelling and grammar, which were awarded marks at GCSE, require close attention. Use a dictionary if you are unsure of a word's meaning or spelling. Use the glossary of terms you will find in this book to help you.

The quality of your written English will not determine the Level of Response you receive for answer. It may well determine what mark you receive within a level.

To help you understand this point ask your teacher to see a mark scheme published by your examination board. For instance, you may be awarded Level 2 (10–15 marks) by an examiner. The quality of written English may be a factor in deciding which mark you receive within that level. Will it be 10 or 15 or a mark in between?

The introduction

For structured questions you may wish to dispense with an introduction altogether and begin writing reasons to support an answer straight away. However, essay answers should begin with an introduction. These should be both concise and precise. Introductions help 'concentrate the mind' on the question you are about to answer. Remember, do not try to write a conclusion as your opening sentence. Instead, outline briefly the areas you intend to discuss in your answer.

Balancing analysis with factual evidence

It is important to remember that factual knowledge should be used to support analysis. Merely 'telling the story' of an historical event is not enough. A structured question or essay should contain separate paragraphs, each addressing an analytical point that helps to answer the question. If, for example, the question asks for reasons why the Liberals won the 1906 general election, each paragraph should provide a reason which explains why this occurred. In order to support and sustain the analysis evidence is required. Therefore, your factual knowledge should be used to substantiate analysis. Good structured question and essay answers integrate analysis and factual knowledge.

Seeing connections between reasons

In dealing with 'why'-type questions it is important to remember that the reasons for an historical event might be interconnected. Therefore, it is important to mention the connections between reasons. Also, it might be important to identify a hierarchy of reasons – that is, are some reasons more important than others in explaining an historical event?

Using quotations and statistical data

One aspect of supporting evidence that sustains analysis is the use of quotations. These can be from either a historian or a contemporary. However, unless these quotations are linked with analysis and supporting evidence, they tend to be of little value.

It can also be useful to support analysis with statistical data. In questions that deal with social and economic change, precise statistics that support your argument can be very persuasive.

The conclusion

All structured questions and essays require conclusions. If, for example, a question requires a discussion of 'how far' you agree with a question, you should offer a judgement in your conclusion. Don't be afraid of this – say what you think. If you write an analytical answer, ably supported by factual evidence, you may under-perform because you have not provided a conclusion that deals directly with the question.

Source analysis

Source analysis forms an integral part of the study of History.

In dealing with sources you should be aware that historical sources must be used 'in historical context' in Sixth Form History. This means you must understand the historical topic to which the source refers. Therefore, in this book sources are used with the factual information in each chapter. Also, specific source analysis questions are included at the end of most chapters.

How to handle sources in Sixth Form History

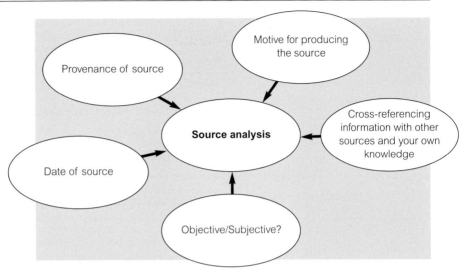

In dealing with sources, a number of basic hints will allow you to deal effectively with source-based questions and to build on your knowledge and skill in using sources at GCSE.

Written sources

Attribution or provenance and date

It is important to identify who has written the source and when it was written. This information can be very important. If, for instance, a source was written by Neville Chamberlain in 1938, this information will be of considerable importance if you are asked about the usefulness (utility) or reliability of the source as evidence of Britain's policy of appeasement.

It is important to note that just because a source is a primary source does not mean it is more useful or less reliable than a secondary source. Both primary and secondary sources need to be analysed to decide how useful and reliable they are. This can be determined by studying other issues.

Is the content factual or opinionated?

Once you have identified the author and date of the source, it is important to study its content. The content may be factual, stating what has happened or what may happen. On the other hand, it may contain opinions that should be handled with caution. These may contain bias. Even if a source is mainly factual, there might be important and deliberate gaps in factual evidence that can make a source biased and unreliable. Usually, written sources contain elements of both opinion and factual evidence. It is important to judge the balance between these two parts.

Has the source been written for a particular audience?

To determine the reliability of a source it is important to know to whom it is directed. For instance, a public speech may be made to achieve a particular purpose and may not contain the author's true beliefs or feelings. In contrast, a private diary entry may be much more reliable in this respect.

Corroborative evidence

To test whether or not a source is reliable, the use of other evidence to support or corroborate the information it contains is important. Cross-referencing with other sources is a way of achieving this; so is cross-referencing with historical information contained within a chapter.

Visual sources

Cartoons

Cartoons are a popular form of source used at both GCSE and in Sixth Form History. However, analysing cartoons can be a demanding exercise. Not only will you be expected to understand the content of the cartoon, you may also have to explain a written caption – which appears usually at the bottom of the cartoon. In addition, cartoons will need placing in historical context. Therefore, a good knowledge of the subject matter of the topic of the cartoon will be important.

Photographs

'The camera never lies'! This phrase is not always true. When analysing photographs, study the attribution/provenance and date. Photographs can be changed so they are not always an accurate visual representation of events. Also, to test whether or not a photograph is a good representation of events you will need corroborative evidence.

Maps

Maps which appear in Sixth Form History are predominantly secondary sources. These are used to support factual coverage in the text by providing information in a different medium. Therefore, to assess whether or not information contained in maps is accurate or useful, reference should be made to other information. It is also important with written sources to check the attribution and date. These could be significant.

Statistical data and graphs

It is important when dealing with this type of source to check carefully the nature of the information contained in data or in a graph. It might state that the information is in tons (tonnes) or another measurement. Be careful to check if the information is in index numbers. These are a statistical device where a base year is chosen and given the figure 100. All other figures are based on a percentage difference from that base year. For instance, if 1918 is taken as a base year for coal production, it is given the figure of 100. If the index number for coal production in 1939 is 117 it means that coal production has increased by 17 per cent above the 1918 figure.

An important point to remember when dealing with data and graphs over a period of time is to identify trends and patterns in the information. Merely describing the information in written form is not enough.

Historical interpretation

An important feature of both GCSE and Sixth Form History is the issue of historical interpretation. In Sixth Form History it is important for students to be able to explain why historians differ, or have differed, in their interpretation of the past.

Availability of evidence

An important reason is the availability of evidence on which to base historical judgements. As new evidence comes to light, an historian today may have more information on which to base judgements than historians in the past.

'A philosophy of history?'

Many historians have a specific view of history that will affect the way they make their historical judgements. For instance, Marxist historians – who take the view from the writings of Karl Marx the founder of modern socialism – believe that society has been made up of competing economic and social classes. They also place considerable importance on economic reasons in human decision making. Therefore, a Marxist historian of fascism may take a completely different viewpoint to a non-Marxist historian.

The role of the individual

Some historians have seen past history as being moulded by the acts of specific individuals who have changed history. Asquith, Neville Chamberlain and Churchill are seen as individuals whose personality and beliefs changed the course of British history. Other historians have tended to 'downplay' the role of individuals; instead, they highlight the importance of more general social, economic and political change.

Placing different emphasis on the same historical evidence

Even if historians do not possess different philosophies of history or place different emphasis on the role of the individual, it is still possible for them to disagree because they place different emphases on aspects of the same factual evidence. As a result, Sixth Form History should be seen as a subject that encourages debate about the past based on historical evidence.

Progression in Sixth Form History

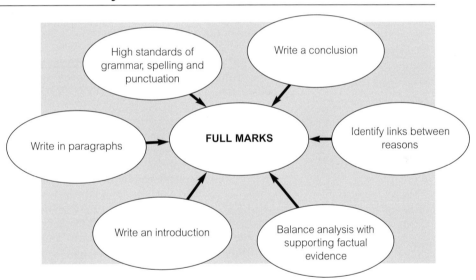

The ability to achieve high standards in Sixth Form History involves the acquisition of a number of skills:

● Good written communication skills

● Acquiring a sound factual knowledge

● Evaluating factual evidence and making historical conclusions based on that evidence

● Source analysis

● Understanding the nature of historical interpretation

● Understanding the causes and consequences of historical events

● Understanding themes in history which will involve a study of a specific topic over a long period of time

● Understanding the ideas of change and continuity associated with themes.

Students should be aware that the acquisition of these skills will take place gradually over the time spent in the Sixth Form. At the beginning of the course, the main emphasis may be on the acquisition of factual knowledge, particularly when the body of knowledge studied at GCSE was different.

When dealing with causation, students will have to build on their skills from GCSE. They will not only be expected to identify reasons for an historical event but also to provide a hierarchy of causes. They should identify the main causes and less important causes. They may also identify that causes may be interconnected and linked. Progression in Sixth Form History will come with answering the questions at the end of each sub-section in this book and practising the skills outlined through the use of the factual knowledge contained in the book.

Examination technique

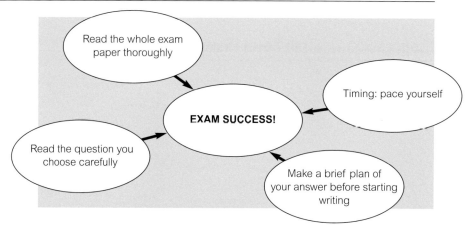

The ultimate challenge for any Sixth Form historian is the ability to produce quality work under examination conditions. Examinations will take the form of either modular examinations taken in January and June or an 'end of course' set of examinations.

Here is some advice on how to improve your performance in an examination.

● Read the whole examination paper thoroughly
Make sure that the questions you choose are those for which you can produce a good answer. Don't rush – allow time to decide which questions to choose. It is probably too late to change your mind half way through answering a question.

● Read the question very carefully
Once you have made the decision to answer a specific question, read it very carefully. Make sure you understand the precise demands of the question. Think about what is required in your answer. It is much better to think about this before you start writing, rather than trying to steer your essay in a different direction half way through.

Revision tips

Even before the examination begins make sure that you have revised thoroughly. Revision tips on the main topics in this book appear on the Collins website:

www.collinseducation.com

- Make a brief plan
  Sketch out what you intend to include in your answer. Order the points you want to make. Examiners are not impressed with additional information included at the end of the essay, with indicators such as arrows or asterisks.

- Pace yourself as you write
  Success in examinations has a lot to do with successful time management. If, for instance, you have to answer an essay question in approximately 45 minutes, then you should be one-third of the way through after 15 minutes. With 30 minutes gone, you should start writing the last third of your answer.

Where a question is divided into sub-questions, make sure you look at the mark tariff for each question. If in a 20-mark question a sub-question is worth a maximum of 5 marks, then you should spend approximately one-quarter of the time allocated for the whole question on this sub-question.

1 Britain 1895–1951: A synoptic overview

Key Issues

- How did Britain's position in international affairs change between 1895 and 1951?

- To what extent was the British economy and society transformed in the period 1895–1951?

- How far did the British political system change in the years 1895–1951?

1.1 An era of decline?

1.2 Why did the Commonwealth develop out of the British Empire in the period 1895 to 1951?

1.3 How far did British foreign and defence policy change between 1895 and 1951?

1.4 To what extent did Britain experience economic decline in the period 1895 to 1951?

1.5 How significant were changes in the mass media between 1895 and 1951?

1.6 How did British democracy develop in the period 1895 to 1951?

1.1 An era of decline?

Relative economic decline:
Although Britain's economy grew for most of the period from 1895 to 1951, Britain's share of world economic activity and trade declined, due to competition from other economies.

---

1. What do you regard as the most important change to affect Britain in the period 1895 to 1951? Give reasons for your answer.

In the period 1895 to 1951 Britain went through a period of major change. In 1895 Britain was the world's greatest sea power with the world's largest Empire. But by 1951 Britain's position had changed. In the intervening period Britain had fought two world wars and its position as a world empire and major military power changed. By 1945 two superpowers – the USA and the USSR – had emerged on the world scene, and by 1951 Britain had begun the process of decolonisation, which would see the British Empire shrink rapidly.

Britain also experienced major change in its economic position. In 1895 Britain was the world's biggest economy, but by 1951 it had been overtaken by both the USA and USSR. For most of the period Britain experienced **relative economic decline**.

Socially, Britain was transformed. By 1951 most Britons lived in urban areas. Primary and secondary education was free and, from 1948, Britons had free medical care through the National Health Service.

Finally, the party political system was changed out of all recognition. In 1895 British politics was dominated by the Liberal and Conservative parties, and a large third party existed in the form of the Irish Parliamentary Party. By 1951 the Liberals had been eclipsed by the rise of the Labour Party. In 1945 the Labour Party won a landslide victory, the first outright victory in its history. By 1918 the Irish Parliamentary Party went into rapid decline, to disappear with the creation of the Irish Free State in 1922.

1.2 Why did the Commonwealth develop out of the British Empire in the period 1895 to 1951?

In 1895 Britain possessed the largest empire in world history. It covered one quarter of the world's land surface and contained one third of the world's population. British colonial possessions were found on each continent and in every ocean. In 1895 Britain was involved in a dispute with two Dutch-speaking republics in southern Africa, the Transvaal and the Orange Free State. In 1899 relations deteriorated so badly that war ensued. Lasting from 1899 to 1902, the South African War was fought between the British Empire and two Dutch-speaking republics in South Africa, the Transvaal and the Orange Free State. By 1902 Britain had won the war and had absorbed the two republics into the British Empire. Victory meant that Britain controlled most of southern Africa – and most of the world's gold supply.

In 1895, parts of the British Empire already had internal self-government – Canada had become self-governing in 1867. By the outbreak of the First World War, in 1914, Canada was joined by New Zealand, Australia, South Africa and Newfoundland. In each case, self-government was granted to these areas' white populations. After the First World War, the Irish Free State (1922) and Southern Rhodesia joined what were known as the White Dominions within the British Empire. This was the beginning of the British Commonwealth.

A major landmark in the development of the British Commonwealth was the Statute of Westminster of 1931. This law granted full independence to the White Dominions, including control over foreign policy. But these dominions were still linked to Britain through a common head of state, the British monarch. The degree of independence now enjoyed by the White Dominions was demonstrated in 1939. On 3 September 1939, Britain and the Empire declared war on Germany. Canada declared war one day later to demonstrate it was a Canadian and not a British decision. Eire (the name for the Irish Free State from 1937) decided not to declare war and remained neutral from 1939 to 1945.

During the period 1895 to 1951 the British Empire faced the challenge of two political movements: nationalism and democracy. Ireland was one of the first areas to be affected. The Irish War for Independence (1919–21) led to the division of the United Kingdom, with the creation of the Irish Free State in 1922. By 1937 the Irish Free State became Eire, which was a republic 'in all but name'. However, Eire remained within the Commonwealth. In 1948 Eire became the Republic of Ireland, which left the Commonwealth in 1949.

More important for the development of the Commonwealth was India. British India was 'the jewel in the Crown', the most important part of the Empire. In 1886 the Indian National Congress was formed which demanded internal self-government for British India. In 1918 its leaders were demanding Home Rule for India. Under the guidance and leadership of M.K. Ghandi, the Indian National Congress used a variety of strategies to force Britain to accept Indian independence. Civil disobedience through strikes and non-cooperation with the British administration became central features of Ghandi's tactics. He also advocated self-reliance and the encouragement of Indian industry.

From 1909 to 1947 Britain tried a number of policies to limit the demand for independence. These included reforms of the Indian political system in 1909, 1919 and 1935. On each occasion more and more members of the Indian population were allowed to participate in the governing of British India. This policy was combined with repression and the imprisonment of nationalist leaders. The most notorious incident came in 1919, in Amritsar in the Punjab, where General Dyer ordered the massacre of unarmed demonstrators. Although Dyer was relieved of command, the incident created considerable bitterness against British rule.

By 1947 the British government had decided to grant Indian independence. Under the last **Viceroy** of India, Lord Mountbatten, British India was divided into two states, India and Pakistan. In the following year, 1948, independence was granted to Burma (now Myanmar) and Ceylon

Viceroy: The British monarch's representative in British India and the head of the British administration.

1. What were the main changes that affected the British Empire from 1895 to 1951?

(now Sri Lanka). These developments were a major turning-point in British imperial history. The Commonwealth now contained white and non-white dominions. Also the British withdrawal from India and South Asia began a rapid process of decolonisation of what remained of the British Empire.

1.3 How far did British foreign and defence policy change between 1895 and 1951?

Britain's foreign and defence policy was directly linked to its position as a world empire. From 1895 to 1951, Britain aimed to defend its empire, which meant, first, keeping command of the sea. As part of this global aim, Britain wanted to prevent any one state dominating the European continent. These inter-connected aims were the basis of British foreign policy in the nineteenth century and for the first half of the twentieth century.

In 1895 the Royal Navy had command of the sea. The Empire was linked by important naval bases, allowing the Royal Navy to operate around the globe. Gibraltar, Malta and Alexandria allowed the Royal Navy to dominate the Mediterranean Sea, and naval bases in eastern Canada, South Africa, Australia, New Zealand and Hong Kong allowed the Royal Navy to dominate the world's oceans. However, Britain's naval supremacy was under threat. Starting in 1898, Germany planned to build a navy to rival the Royal Navy. From that date until the outbreak of the First World War, in 1914, Britain and Germany were engaged in a naval arms race.

In 1914 Britain went to war with Germany to prevent it dominating the European continent – and threatening the British Empire. From 1914 to 1918 Britain suffered huge military casualties. Some 960,000 British and Empire troops lost their lives. However, by 1918 German military and naval power had been smashed and Britain retained its prominent position in imperial and naval terms.

In the inter-war period (1918–1939) the defence of the Empire was Britain's main consideration. This was the reason behind the construction of a major naval base at Singapore in South East Asia in the 1920s and 1930s. British military spending was limited, however, because of the weakness of the British economy, especially from 1930. By the mid-1930s the British Empire faced three major threats. Italy under Mussolini was planning to create an Empire in East Africa. In the Far East, Japan had attacked and occupied north east China (Manchuria) in 1931 and engaged in a major war against China from 1937. In Europe from 1933, German Chancellor Adolf Hitler wanted to destroy the Treaty of Versailles and make Germany the dominant European power.

The dilemma facing British policymakers during the 1930s was clear. Britain's lack of military and financial resources greatly limited its ability to meet the threats from Italy, Japan and Germany at the same time. To preserve peace and defend the Empire, British prime ministers Stanley Baldwin and Neville Chamberlain followed the policy of appeasement. Appeasement was used first with Italy. After Italy had invaded Abyssinia (now Ethiopia) in 1935 the Hoare–Laval Pact was a joint attempt by Britain and France to give Mussolini some, but not all, of Abyssinia. The Hoare–Laval Pact was never implemented, because of widespread opposition within Britain. The most notable example of appeasement was the Munich Agreement, Neville Chamberlain's concession to Hitler's Germany in 1938. Unfortunately, Chamberlain had little room for manoeuvre. Hitler threatened European war if the German-speaking part of Czechoslovakia, known as the Sudetenland, was not handed over to Germany. Fear of massive air raids on Britain by the German air force (and the belief that several White Dominions, such as South Africa, might not fight against Germany) forced Chamberlain to give way. Appeasement was eventually abandoned in the spring of 1939 when Germany occupied the Czech-speaking part of Czechoslovakia. The decision was made because it became clear to the British government that Germany wanted to dominate the whole of Europe, not just the German-speaking areas of the continent.

Britain's involvement in the Second World War (1939–1945) highlights the major problems facing British foreign and defence policymakers. Britain lacked the military resources to fight Germany and Italy alone from June 1940. Without considerable financial assistance and military material from the USA, through the Lend-Lease Programme, Britain would have gone bankrupt by the end of 1941. From December 1941 matters became worse when Japan rapidly conquered Malaya, Singapore and Burma and threatened British India.

By September 1945 Britain was victorious in her war against Germany, Italy and Japan. Britain made valuable contributions to the Allied war effort in Europe after D-Day in 1944, and in North Africa, Italy and Burma in 1942–45, but the major contributions to the defeat of Nazi Germany came from the USSR and the USA. In the war against Japan, the USA was the main Allied partner. Nevertheless, Britain was regarded as one of the 'Big Three' world powers in 1945. Britain participated in the Yalta and Potsdam conferences of 1945, along with the USSR and the USA. These conferences decided the post-war settlement.

At the height of victory, however, Britain's position in the world was in decline. The cost of war had virtually bankrupted Britain. Post-war Britain only recovered from the war through US aid, in the form of the Marshall Plan of 1947–52. The post-1945 world was to be dominated by two military and economic superpowers, the USA and the USSR. From 1945 onwards Britain was a secondary player in this bi-polar world. In the Cold War, Britain became a major base for US forces in Europe. In 1949 Britain joined the US-dominated North Atlantic Treaty Organisation (NATO), and in 1950 it sent troops as part of the UN force to defend South Korea (under the overall command of the USA).

1. In what ways did Britain's foreign and defence policy change from 1895 to 1951?

1.4 To what extent did Britain experience economic decline in the period 1895 to 1951?

A major feature of the period 1895 to 1951 was the relative decline of Britain's economy, which in 1895 was the biggest in the world. Britain was then the world's major manufacturing power. The area around Manchester, in east Lancashire manufactured approximately 60 per cent of the world's cotton textiles. Britain was also a major manufacturer of woollen textiles and engineering goods. In 1895 the most important energy fuel was coal, and Britain was the world's major producer, with South Wales exporting coal around the globe. Transporting British exports was the Merchant Navy, the largest in the world. Finally, London was the world's financial and banking centre.

How did Britain lose its economic dominance? Already by 1895 Britain faced major economic competitors. In Europe the German Empire, created in 1871, was a major rival in chemicals, engineering and coal production. By 1895 the USA, with its vast size, population and natural resources, was rapidly becoming the world's major economy, and by 1914 it had surpassed Britain. Also, during both world wars Britain lost important markets for its goods to rivals – to Japan in the case of the Far East markets, for example.

> **Demand Management Economics**
>
> *As put forward by the economist J.M. Keynes. It formed the basis of post-Second World War government economic policy until 1976.*
>
> Keynes believed that when the British economy faced economic depression in the 1930s this was due mainly to a lack of demand within the economy. Demand could be increased by the government spending money in the economy through financing factory building or improvements in the economy's infrastructure.
>
> This money would lead to an increase in employment. The newly employed workers would have money to spend, so this, in turn, would increase demand within the economy.
>
> Direct government intervention in the economy could, therefore, help to reduce unemployment. Through changing the amount of direct taxation and government spending the government could also affect the rate of inflation (a rise in prices).
>
> By these methods governments between 1945 and 1976 attempted to keep unemployment and inflation low. (Unfortunately, in 1973, the quadrupling of the world price in oil caused a large increase in business costs, which resulted in high inflation and growing unemployment. Keynesian economic policy was replaced by monetarist economic policy, which placed greater emphasis on using interest rates and a control of the money supply to achieve low inflation and unemployment.)

The historian Geoffrey Owen attributed Britain's economic decline to a lack of competition within industries. Weak management and poor industrial relations were both blamed for Britain's inability to compete effectively in international markets. The General Strike of 1926, for example, showed the scale of the problem. In addition, poor productivity and lack of investment in British industry were also important factors contributing to the decline.

By 1945 Britain had virtually exhausted itself economically in its fight against Germany, Italy and Japan. From 1941 Britain's war effort was kept going through massive aid from the USA. This continued in the period 1945 to 1951. Britain received a major loan from the USA in 1946, followed by Marshall Aid from 1947 to 1952. By 1951 Britain had just about recovered from the economic impact of the Second World War. However, the policy of rearmament introduced by the Labour government in 1950, to meet the threat of the USSR and to fight the Korean War, again dented Britain's post-war recovery. It wasn't until the late 1950s that Britain came to experience a consumer boom and a rise in the standard of living which the USA had experienced from the late 1930s.

1. Why did Britain experience relative economic decline in the period 1895 to 1951?

1.5 How significant were changes in the mass media between 1895 and 1951?

The first half of the twentieth century saw considerable advances in the mass media. The term 'mass media' includes books and film, but it is most closely associated with the press, television and radio. These are important institutions for spreading information about the political system. As a result, the mass media have helped form and influence people's opinions about politics.

Major factors in the development of the mass media have been the growth of literacy and the advance of technology. The Education Act of 1902 extended government involvement in education to cover secondary as well as primary education.

Newspapers

Until 1896 newspapers were read primarily by a small number of educated people. In that year Alfred Harmsworth (later Lord Northcliffe) founded the *Daily Mail*. At one halfpenny (0.2p), the *Daily Mail* became the first mass circulation newspaper with a daily sale of over 1 million copies. In 1900 it was followed by the *Daily Express* and, in 1904, the *Daily Mirror*.

With a wide readership, these newspapers began to influence public opinion. In 1898, for example, the so-called 'yellow press' in the USA were regarded as having whipped up popular opinion in favour of a war against Spain over Cuba. In the First World War, British newspapers took a strongly patriotic line, due, in part, to DORA (The Defence of the Realm Act, 1914) which censored newspapers.

In 1918 the *Daily Mail* ran a 'Hang the Kaiser' campaign supporting those candidates in the 1918 general election who embraced this policy. In 1924 the *Daily Mail* helped to defeat the Labour government by publishing the 'Zinoviev Letter', four days before the general election. This forged letter was supposedly from the Soviet-dominated Comintern Organisation to British communists asking them to engage in subversion against the British armed forces. This 'revelation' caused considerable distrust of the political left – Labour as well as Communist. In the years 1930 to 1931 the *Daily Mail* and *Daily Express* ran campaigns against the Conservative leadership of Stanley Baldwin. Baldwin complained that the press had 'power without responsibility', a claim that has lasted until the present day. But by 1937 daily newspaper circulation had reached 10 million.

In 1949 the first Royal Commission on the Press was established. One of its recommendations was the creation of a body to deal with complaints made against the press by the public – a 'Press Council' – which came into existence in 1953.

Radio and television

The development of radio led to the creation of the British Broadcasting Company in 1922. By 1926 the government enlarged its role by turning it into the British Broadcasting Corporation (BBC). Under the leadership of Lord Reith, who believed its role was to 'educate, inform and entertain', the BBC had a monopoly of public broadcasting within Britain.

The BBC began television broadcasts from Alexandra Palace in North London in 1936, though transmissions were subsequently interrupted by the war. Television technology was very limited in these early years, and television sets were very expensive. As a result, only a small minority of the population watched TV.

1. How did the mass media change in the period 1895 to 1951?

2. What do you regard as the most influential part of the mass media in forming public opinion, in the period 1895 to 1951?

1.6 How did British democracy develop in the period 1895 to 1951?

The right to vote

In 1895 the right to vote in national elections was limited to men over 21 years. However, registration and other restrictions meant that approximately 40 per cent of adult males did not vote. In addition, 'plural voting' was allowed – if an adult male owned property in more than one constituency, he had more than one vote. Joseph Chamberlain, the Colonial Secretary in 1900, had twenty-six votes! In addition, graduates of a number of universities – Oxford and Cambridge, for example – had an extra vote for their university seat in parliament.

The major change in democracy between 1895 and 1951 was the achievement of full democracy for all adult males and adult females. A significant feature of the political process before 1918 was the campaign for votes for women. Before 1914 much publicity was given to Suffragettes who took direct action to promote their cause. Their actions included attacking politicians opposed to votes for women, burning post boxes and chaining themselves to railings outside prominent buildings. In 1918 some women eventually received the vote. The Franchise Act of 1918 gave the vote to all adult males over 21 years and all women over 30 years. It took until 1928 for the vote to be extended to all women over 21 years. Women entered parliament, as MPs, for the first time in 1918 when Lady Astor was elected as Conservative MP for Plymouth. And in 1929 a Labour MP, Margaret Bondfield, became the first woman minister, as Minister of Labour.

Political parties

In 1895 national politics was dominated by the Liberal and Conservative parties. In addition a sizeable third party, the Irish Parliamentary Party dominated politics in most of Ireland. In 1918 the Irish Parliamentary Party went into rapid decline, to be replaced by the radical Sinn Fein Party. In 1922 the creation of the Irish Free State saw the loss of almost 80 per cent of Irish seats from the House of Commons. By 1951 the Labour Party had replaced the Liberal Party as the main political opponent of the Conservatives.

The decline of the Liberal Party was due to several reasons. One theory suggested that the Liberal government of 1905–1915 was beset by so many problems that it was on the brink of collapse when war broke out in 1914. Other historians have suggested that the impact of the First World War was the major cause of decline. In 1916 the Liberal Party split into two – those who supported Lloyd George (the Coalition Liberals) and those who supported Asquith (the Asquithian Liberals). Lloyd George replaced Asquith as Prime Minister in December 1916. Although Liberals reunited in 1923, their support for the minority Labour government of 1924 led to a collapse in Liberal electoral support in the 1924 general election.

The main beneficiary of the Liberals' decline was the Labour Party. In 1900 a Labour Representation Committee (LRC) was created to ensure that pro-trade union MPs were elected. In 1906 the LRC became the Labour Party. In 1914 the Labour Party had only 53 seats. But by 1924 it had overtaken the Liberals in MPs and votes cast. In 1924, and again from 1929 to 1931, the Labour Party formed the government with Liberal support. In 1931, however, the country faced a major economic crisis, and the Labour Prime Minister, Ramsay Macdonald, formed a national coalition government with the Conservatives and Liberals. The decision split the Labour Party, and in the 1932 election it fared disastrously, winning only 52 seats. It took the Labour Party the rest of the 1930s to recover. In 1940 the Labour Party joined Churchill's National government and played a major role in Britain's victory in the Second World War. In 1945 the Labour Party won a landslide victory in the general election.

From 1945 to 1951 the Labour government introduced major social and economic reform which included the creation of the NHS and nationalisation of many of Britain's major industries. The 1951 general election, which the Conservatives won narrowly, was almost a straight fight between Conservative and Labour.

The dominance of the House of Commons

In 1895 the House of Lords possessed considerable political power. Although it was unelected, it had an absolute veto on all legislation. It was dominated by Conservatives and tended to be supportive when the Conservatives formed the government. When the Liberals were in power, however, the House of Lords sometimes vetoed important legislation, the most important example being the Liberal Irish Home Rule Bill in 1893.

In 1909 the Lords took the unprecedented step of rejecting the Liberal government's Budget. This sparked a political crisis and two general elections on the issue in 1910. In 1911 the Liberals passed the Parliament Act, removing the Lords' absolute veto and replacing it with a delaying veto of two years. In the period 1911 to 1951 the Lords used their delaying veto only twice – on the Liberal Irish Home Rule Bill and the Liberal Disestablishment of the Anglican Church in Wales Bill, both in 1912.

The Parliament Act of 1911 confirmed the dominance of the House of Commons, and from 1902 to 1951 all prime ministers were MPs, rather than members of the House of Lords, which had been the common practice in the nineteenth century.

1. What do you regard as the most important change in British democracy between 1895 and 1951? Explain your answer.

2 The changing position of women and the suffrage question, c1860–1930

Key Issues

- How did the social and economic role of women change between 1860 and 1930?

- How important were the Suffragettes in the campaign for women's suffrage?

- How significant was the change in the political role of women by 1930?

2.1   The position of women in Victorian society
2.2   The campaign for women's suffrage before 1914
2.3   To what extent had the role of women changed within British society by 1914?
2.4   The impact of the First World War on the role of women
2.5   A position changed? Women 1918 to 1930

Framework of Events

1867	Failure of John Stuart Mill's attempts to include women's suffrage in the Reform Bill
1886	Repeal of the Contagious Diseases Act
1887	Married Women's Property Act
1903	Formation of the Women's Social and Political Union
1918	Representation of the People Act gives women over 30 the vote
1919	Lady Astor becomes first woman MP to sit in the House of Commons
1928	Equal Franchise Act gives women over 21 the vote
1929	Margaret Bondfield becomes the first woman cabinet minister, in the Labour government.

Overview

IN mid-Victorian Britain, although the country and Empire had a female monarch, Queen Victoria, women were second-class citizens. They could not vote for or stand in national elections. For most women, educational opportunities were limited to elementary education. Higher education was only for an elite few.

The prime role of women in society was child rearing – they were expected to get married and have children (and the main cause of death amongst women was childbirth). However, by 1930, the political, social and economic role of women had been transformed. In politics, they now had equal rights to men. They could vote and stand for Parliament – though women still formed a tiny minority of MPs. Educational opportunities had developed beyond recognition. Girls were educated to the same age as boys (though they still tended to be educated separately from the age of 12), and they could go to university. Women also became an important part of the workforce. In society, women found new freedoms which were reflected in their fashion and lifestyle – by 1930 many young women were 'flappers'. Yet life for most women, especially working-class women had changed little since the days of Queen Victoria.

2.1 The position of women in Victorian society

Second-class citizens

Women were second-class citizens – they had no independent political rights, and when they married they had no property. A woman's place was in the home, where they could fulfil their role in society as wives and mothers. They were expected to prepare for marriage and then, once married, look after the family home. This applied to working-class and middle-class women alike. Following marriage, women were expected to produce as many children as possible. In an era before effective birth control, it was not uncommon for women to have ten or twelve pregnancies. Queen Victoria had nine children and forty grandchildren! Medical knowledge and expertise of childbirth was limited, and the majority of the population could not afford professional medical care during birth anyway. As a result, many women died in childbirth. Many of the children too died within their first year, due to childhood diseases, such as measles, diphtheria, whooping cough and scarlet fever.

There were more women than men in the 1860s (1053 women for every 1000 men) and more than 2 million of the 10 million adult women in Britain did not have a husband. As a result, many women emigrated or engaged in domestic service.

Married women also suffered from the problem that, once married, all their wealth was automatically passed to her husband. Until 1887 married women had no rights over their own property. Although divorce was legal in mid-Victorian Britain, it was very costly and could only be afforded by the wealthy. In working-class districts, couples merely split up.

Although 'a woman's place was in the home' it did not mean that women did not work. The wealthy classes employed large numbers of domestic servants, such as kitchen maids, cooks, and cleaners, who tended to 'live in'. Another area for women's employment was prostitution, and virtually every Victorian town had brothels. To reflect the inferior social position of women, the Contagious Diseases Act, designed to protect soldiers and sailors against sexually transmitted diseases, was passed in 1864. This Act, which gave police the right to stop and medically inspect any woman suspected of being a carrier of such diseases, was seen, quite rightly, as a major affront to all women.

An important development in mid-Victorian Britain was the development of nursing. Before the Crimean War, wounded soldiers and sailors were looked after by amateurs – usually their sisters and mothers. As a result of the work of Florence Nightingale in that war, nursing developed as a recognised profession, which was the exclusive preserve of women.

In Victorian popular culture, women were 'the fairer sex' – weak, helpless and incapable of taking important decisions on finance or politics. Educational opportunities were extremely limited. Where they did exist, women were expected to learn the skills to become a successful housewife. Cooking, sewing, and cleaning rather than academic subjects were the norm for female education. An important book which was 'required reading' for all middle-class women was published in 1861 – *Mrs Beeton's Book of Household Management* – the essential guide for the budding housewife. The inferior position of women was also epitomised in literature. One of the most popular mid-Victorian novelists was Mary Ann

Evans, but her success was only possible because she published her books, such as *Middlemarch* and *The Mill on the Floss*, under a man's name – George Eliot.

Attempts at social reform

Parliament introduced several measures that attempted to improve the position of women. The Custody of Infants Act in 1839, for example, gave mothers of unblemished character access to their children in the event of separation or divorce. The Matrimonial Causes Act in 1857 gave women limited access to divorce but, while a man only had to prove his wife's adultery, a woman had to prove not only that her husband had committed adultery but also incest, bigamy, cruelty or desertion. In 1873 the Custody of Infants Act extended to all women their right of access to their children in the event of separation or divorce. In 1878, after an amendment to the Matrimonial Causes Act, women could secure a separation on the grounds of cruelty and claim custody of their children. Magistrates even authorised protection orders to wives whose husbands had been convicted of aggravated assault. In 1884 an important change was caused by an amendment to the Married Women's Property Act which made a woman no longer a 'chattel' but an independent and separate person. And in 1886, through the Guardianship of Infants Act, women could be made the sole guardian of their children if their husband died.

The repeal of the Contagious Diseases Act in 1886 not only removed an insult to women, it also marked a significant triumph for a political campaign led by a woman – Josephine Butler, the wife of the Headmaster of the independent school, Liverpool College.

Women in politics

In May 1867, at the height of the Reform Bill crisis, the Liberal MP, John Stuart Mill attempted to amend the Bill by granting an extension of the vote to a 'person' rather than a 'man'. The amendment failed by 194 votes to 73. However, the Reform crisis of 1865 to 1867 marked a turning-point in the issue of women in politics. In August 1867, Lydia Becker launched the Manchester Women's Suffrage Committee, which led to the creation of similar committees in Bristol and Edinburgh. Women's issues now began to emerge in national politics. Throughout the 1870s and 1880s several bills were submitted to Parliament calling for women's suffrage, but all attempts failed.

This did not mean women were prevented from playing any role in national politics. In 1883 the Conservative Party created the Primrose League to raise money and assist in electoral organisation, offering Conservative women an important role within the party. By 1891 the Primrose League had almost a million members. Women's Liberal Associations also developed along similar lines from 1881.

1. To what extent were women 'second-class citizens' in mid-Victorian Britain?

2.2 The campaign for women's suffrage before 1914

The campaign for the vote for women was only one element of a wider movement which saw the cause of women's emancipation slowly advance at this time. Hard-won legal rights had already been gained; women could vote in local elections and made valuable contributions on School Boards and as Poor Law Guardians. The next step, the campaigners thought, would be to enfranchise them in national elections. In 1867, John Stuart Mill had inserted an amendment into the Reform Act, which gave the vote to female householders. It was rejected. So many moderate activists began to establish local suffrage societies, coordinated by the National Union of Women's Suffrage Societies and campaigning for change by constitutional means.

When a Bill, introduced in 1897, also came to nothing, it was apparent to some women that more direct action was required. Recent evidence has shown that, in fact, the quiet work of the societies had convinced many people of the legitimacy of their claim for the suffrage. Historians have the advantage of hindsight – others at the time were not so convinced, hence the following trend towards a more militant approach. In 1903, after working for some years in the ILP in Manchester, Mrs Emmeline Pankhurst formed The Women's Social and Political Union (WSPU). This initially small group caught the public's attention when Christabel, one of Mrs Pankhurst's daughters, along with Annie Kenney, heckled Sir Edward Grey at an election meeting in 1905. They were both arrested and Christabel found herself in prison for refusing to pay the fine. Donations and support grew, mainly from upper- and middle-class women. In one sense, their initial financial contributions were valuable, although the failure to draw on wider working-class support hindered the WSPU's progress. Eventually, so did the Suffragettes' militant tactics, with which not all women agreed – in particular, the Suffragists who continued to use constitutional methods right up to 1914.

Liberal politicians were an obvious target of attacks. Here was an issue that the Liberals could support – political reform, espousing the rights of individuals, attacking injustices and disqualifications. However, Campbell-Bannerman's only achievement in this area was to pass the Qualification of Women Act (1907) which enabled women to serve on county and borough councils. WSPU militancy rose in response to inactivity from Westminster.

- Churchill was horsewhipped.

- Asquith had his doorbell rung constantly.

- Women chained themselves to railings, set fire to pillarboxes and slashed pictures in the National Gallery.

WSPU campaign stand, 1910.

- Politicians were interrupted at public meetings when speeches were heckled and banners were unfurled.

- Police and courts overreacted and when Suffragettes refused to pay fines, opting for prison instead, they started the tactic of hunger striking.

- The Government's tactics were heavy-handed – resorting to 'force feeding' to keep the women alive did nothing to enhance Liberal reputations.

The year 1910 started with a truce; so far the WSPU had brought their campaign to a point where an all-party group actually considered introducing what became known as a Conciliation Bill. This might have given a vote to female householders and those who qualified by occupation. It was never likely to succeed as Asquith was determined to oppose women's suffrage at all costs. Indeed, in 1911, Asquith was planning to introduce a Franchise Bill to extend male suffrage further and a Plural Voting Bill to stop a practice that so advantaged the Conservatives. It has been said that there was an intention that the Franchise Bill might be amended later to allow the female franchise. This seems unlikely given Asquith's attitude. He had been singled out for particular abuse – house windows broken, clothes torn; there was even a suggestion that his person was in danger. When the Speaker of the House ruled, in January 1913, that an amendment of the Franchise Bill could not be allowed as it would change it too much, Asquith wrote, 'The Speaker's *coup d'état* has bowled over the women for this session – a great relief'. His contribution to the failure of Suffragette militancy is of central importance.

The Government's response

Time had run out. It all coincided with a considerable increase in Suffragette violence, which in turn must have hardened attitudes against them. There is evidence that their tactics alienated men and moderate women who had grown tired of extremism and hysteria. These tactics included arson attacks, as well as the death of Emily Davison at Derby Day in 1913, when she threw herself under the King's horse. Arrests meant

Suffragette Emily Davison throws herself under King George V's horse.

hunger strikes to which the Government's answer was the 'Cat and Mouse' Act (the Prisoners' Temporary Discharge for Ill-Health Act), which allowed prisoners to be released and then re-arrested when they had recovered.

Christabel Pankhurst had been forced to flee the country and she tried to organise the campaign from Paris. Her book *The Great Scourge and How to End It*, an anti-male tract, tended to play into the hands of critics who could make out that the WSPU had lost all sense of proportion. There was much talk that women were too emotional, that they would lose their charm, that they suffered from numerous physical weaknesses – critics said that Suffragette behaviour confirmed how unreasonable they could be. Suffragettes were accused of abandoning lawful protest at a time when the rule of law was already being undermined – by the unions and in Ireland.

Indeed, the WSPU lost the sympathy of those who should have been its allies; the Liberal Party was the best chance they had and many Liberal politicians who were sympathetic at first (such as Lloyd George) discovered they too were under attack. Some women were profoundly anti-Suffragette; evidence, for example, the formation of the Women's National Anti-Suffrage League as early as 1908 – it was never as potent a force as the Pankhursts' group but it hinted at a body of critical opinion against it. It included Mrs Fawcett, leading Suffragist and President of the National Union of Women's Suffrage Societies, who claimed that the WSPU had done more harm than good. Mrs Fawcett's organisation had grown steadily from a membership of 6,000 in 1907 to 50,000 in 1913. Historian Martin Pugh notes that this growth was a reaction to the militancy of the WSPU and it was probably 'the one positive contribution of the Pankhursts to winning the vote'. Pugh hints that the Pankhursts' role has been much exaggerated but they did have an amazing ability to publicise themselves and their activities.

Most commentators are agreed that the Liberal Government's response to the Suffragettes also lies at the heart of the crisis. The Government which stood for social reform and justice was seen to be acting in an oppressive un-Liberal manner. What a contrast between the 'softly, softly' approach in Ireland and the forcible feeding of hunger strikers. As the historian L.C.B. Seaman comments:

> The attitude of the Government to middle-class Englishwomen demanding the right to vote, and reacting with violence to the Government's provocative and pointless delay, provides a sinister comment on the persistent Liberal claim to stand for a higher morality than other political parties. The Prisoners' Temporary Discharge for Ill-Health Act ('Cat and Mouse' Act) came strangely from a government which a few years before had been grieved so sorely by the hardships suffered by Boer women and children, and by Chinese coolies in the Transvaal.

1. How important in the campaign for women's political rights was the Women's Social and Political Union?

2. Did the Suffragettes provide a major political threat to the Liberal Government in the years before the outbreak of war in 1914?

Asquith, who had an unshakeable belief in constitutional processes, thus stands accused of forcing the WSPU into militant resistance outside the law. There were opportunities to pass legislation, all scuppered by the Prime Minister. In these circumstances, repeated efforts to introduce Private Member's Bills (in 1908, 1909 and 1913) were doomed. Asquith apparently believed that granting the vote to women on the same basis as men, under the property qualification rules, would mean that these would be better-off Conservative voters, thereby damaging Liberal fortunes. Asquith had no way of knowing if this was true. When war broke out in 1914, women were still without the vote – like the problems posed by union militancy, it was yet another issue that the Liberal Government had failed to settle.

Emmeline Pankhurst is arrested at a demonstration outside Buckingham Palace, 1914.

1. How far does this photograph suggest that the Police regarded Mrs Pankhurst as a militant campaigner?

2. How useful is this photograph as evidence of the Suffragette movement's militant campaign for 'votes for women'?

Source-based questions: The Suffragettes

SOURCE A

'We have tried every way. We have presented larger petitions than were ever presented before for any reform; we have succeeded in holding greater public meetings than men have ever had for any reform. We have faced hostile mobs at street corners, because we were told that we could not have that representation for our taxes that men have won unless we converted the whole country to our side. Because we have done this we have been misrepresented, we have been ridiculed …

Well, sir, that is all I have to say to you. We are not here because we are law-breakers, we are here in our efforts to become law-makers!'

From Mrs Emmeline Pankhurst's speech in front of magistrates in London, 1908.

SOURCE B

The vote was not sought for any practical object, but as a symbol of equality. They were obsessed by an inferiority complex. And similarly upon politics at large their militancy had more effect than their suffragism. The means mattered more than the end … the WSPU leaders proclaimed, by word and deed, that the way to get results was through violence. Such doctrines are always liable to become popular …

From *England, 1870–1914* by R.C.K.Ensor, published in 1936.

SOURCE C

There is a case for saying that by the early 1900s the debate over the general principle of enfranchising women had been largely won. This, however, by no means resolved the problem … politicians had yet to be convinced that women's suffrage mattered enough to the majority of women to justify devoting scarce parliamentary time to it. Up to a point Mrs Fawcett's non-militants helped to persuade them by mobilising more trade unions behind the cause, and by their shrewd electoral pact with the Labour Party in 1912; this put real pressure on the Asquith Government …. by encouraging a drift of Liberal women towards Labour. In addition, Fawcett's National Union of Women's Suffrage Societies at last began to grow … from under 6,000 in 1907 to over 50,000 by 1913. Many of the new members were women who had been aroused by suffrage activities; while they did not wish to be involved with militant methods themselves, they felt moved to show their support for the cause in a different way. This was probably the one positive contribution of the Pankhursts to winning the vote.

From Martin Pugh's article 'Votes for Women' (published in *Britain 1867–1918* by the Institute of Contemporary British History, 1994).

Source-based questions: The Suffragettes

1. Study Source A.

How does Mrs Emmeline Pankhurst defend her actions?

2. Study Sources A and B.

Compare the views of a suffragette (Source A) with those of a historian (Source B). Which gives the more reliable account to a historian studying the reasons for Suffragette violence? Give reasons to support your answer.

3. 'The impact of the Suffragettes on society before the First World War has been exaggerated.' Use the sources and your reading to explain whether you agree with this statement.

2.3 To what extent had the role of women changed within British society by 1914?

The historian Louise Black argues the case that a 'new woman' was to be seen by the turn of the twentieth century. Who was she? Well, she smoked, played hockey and tennis, went on shopping sprees, used trains and motor cars, and ate out at public restaurants. Almost certainly educated, upper or upper middle class, and single, the 'new woman' shocked Edwardian sensitivities in demanding equal pay, the right to enter the professions, equal rights in marriage and, of course, the vote. David Powell, in *The Edwardian Crisis: Britain 1901–1914* (1996), warns that while this stereotype may have been a 'literary and journalistic creation' there was some truth in it. He writes: 'Contemporaries were aware of the existence of a new generation of women for whom marriage was not necessarily the sole aim of life and who were, through education or employment, throwing off the shackles of a traditional home and upbringing ...'. The progress achieved by women in all areas of Britain's social and economic life was mixed; steps forward were taken in the face of ingrained attitudes which proved harder to change. For many, their lives were little changed from those of their mothers and grandmothers. Indeed, many women saw no reason to challenge the *status quo* as they accepted society's assumptions about their place in it. Other women, however, clearly felt they had far to go before achieving any measure of equality.

Changes were taking place in the world of work, in education, in the law, in public as well as private family life. Above all, though, it was the campaign for women's suffrage which attracted the most attention. The Pankhursts' claims that their tactics brought success sooner rather than later are open to question. The WSPU certainly galvanised support, but it also galvanised the opposition which was able to accuse women of being emotionally unbalanced and unfit to take a more active role in society. However, while the Suffragettes created what seemed like an atmosphere of crisis, their work was only part of a larger canvas.

Women, particularly from the middle class, were becoming more involved in politics. Beatrice Webb, for instance, was a leading member of the Fabians although female involvement in national policy and organisation was rare. It was at a local level where things advanced more dramatically. After 1894, women were able to sit on parish and district councils; in 1907, the Qualification of Women Act extended this right to county councils. To add to those who were elected to these bodies, there were hundreds more who sat on School Boards and who served as Poor Law Guardians.

Women at work

At work, class played as significant a part in determining women's employment as did gender. For working-class women, it was true that factory and mill conditions had improved and maximum hours had been fixed by statute – just as they had been for men. But it is difficult to accept that any progress had been achieved. Women provided cheap labour for employers and their work was often casual and temporary – for women of childbearing age their health certainly suffered from their annual pregnancies and too rapid a return to long hours of work following the birth. Hence the concern for the nation's health, in which the debate on 'National Efficiency' merely served to emphasise that only unmarried women should seek employment outside the home. Little effort or encouragement was made to help working-class women return to work after adding to the family because society accepted that the 'feminine' role for women was at home, bringing up the children and training their daughters to become, in their turn, mothers and housewives. This attitude so powerfully underpinned Edwardian views of women that it resurfaces continually, even in areas such as education where women had made more progress.

When women did work, it was assumed they would accept roles that did not detract from their 'femininity'. In 1911, 35 per cent – almost all from working-class backgrounds – were in domestic service, although this figure was in decline. The reasons for this are unclear; after 1870, more women had access to education and thereby different types of work in towns, rather than in rural areas. Perhaps there were fewer girls for the 'big house' to draw on. It is not inconceivable that some families could not afford as many servants. Whatever the reasons, unmarried working-class girls were increasingly becoming shop assistants or conforming to stereotypes (cooks, machinists or mill hands), while married women would spend long hours at home dressmaking, childminding or making cardboard boxes.

However, marriage to a skilled working man who could command higher wages brought altogether different social aspirations. Here, a wife could share her husband's pride in the fact that she would not have to 'take in' work and supplement the family income.

Three-quarters of all British women were kept in 'separate spheres' from men. Where they did work together, women were more poorly paid, had poorer chances of promotion and normally completed unskilled tasks. Men were seen as more skilled, adaptable and of managerial status. Even when occupied in the same job, women were paid less. Female clerks received only one-third the pay of male counterparts. Some trade unions disapproved of working women; only 3 per cent of women were unionised compared to 20 per cent for men in 1901.

It was difficult for a poor, single girl to remain 'respectable', and the historiography of women's movements documents how little progress was made to reduce prostitution at this time. The law was much criticised for the hypocritical attitude taken towards punishing the prostitutes when no action was taken against those men who exploited them. Christabel Pankhurst's moral blasts against men as carriers of sexually transmitted diseases (for example in her book *The Great Scourge and How To End It*) provoked hostility and deflected attention away from the campaign to criminalise the procurement of girls for prostitution.

Changes were more apparent for middle-class women by the 1890s. Birth control, while not entirely socially acceptable, was clearly being practised; middle-class women on average had three children compared with the six in working-class families. Superficial analysis might conclude that this released more time for careers or leisure activities. However, middle-class (and upper-class) women were still severely constrained by financial dependence on their father or husband and by stifling social expectations of decorous boredom, then a good marriage, maintaining a position in 'society' by the side of their husband, childbearing and, throughout it all, sexual inhibition. Bertrand Russell, who married his first wife in 1894, commented on how she had been taught to think that 'sex was beastly'.

Opportunities for young, unmarried middle-class women, though, were increasing. Lower-grade work was readily available; women clerks, typists, bookkeepers were in demand. Between 1891 and 1911, the number of women clerks in commerce tripled and 35,000 were employed as telephonists by the GPO (General Post Office; forerunner of British Telecom). Women were taken on as health visitors and even factory inspectors (after 1893). However, it was not untypical that women who became journalists were expected to write about cooking or fashion. Entry into the professions, stubbornly male dominated, would prove harder and relied on expanding educational opportunities.

Education

Certainly, doors were opening. Middle- and upper-class girls attended fee-paying schools or were educated at home. Education for working-class girls in the years after the passage of the 1870 Act gradually became more widespread, and was free and compulsory, although the curriculum reflected society's expectations of adult women's role in society. Universities were accepting women; colleges at both Oxford and Cambridge were established. Women such as Sophia Jex-Blake pioneered access to university medical schools, but it was still difficult to find sufficient places and even more difficult to secure a position in a hospital afterwards.

It is true that there were more dentists, midwives and pharmacists, but progress was slow. In 1881, there were 25 women doctors; by 1901, there were still only 212 (out of a total of 220,000). In 1910, women first took examinations to become chartered accountants. In contrast, 150,000 women teachers dominated the profession in 1891, but at lower rates of pay and with less scope for advancement than men. There were no women solicitors or barristers and only a tiny number had successfully negotiated the selection process for the Civil Service.

The law

Women's legal rights in marriage had made huge strides. They ended the century as the legal equals of their husbands, not just their 'property'. They could keep their own earnings and property – indeed they were free to manage their own property as they saw fit. Having already gained the right to receive maintenance payments, a landmark legal judgement in 1910 also gave divorced women substantial rights over the custody of children. Nevertheless, divorce for women was much more difficult than it was for men. A man only needed to prove adultery by his wife, whereas a wife needed an extra burden of proof, such as cruelty. Equality of treatment was not achieved until 1923.

Despite widening opportunities for women, society's attitudes proved difficult to shift. Married women were still expected to sit by the hearth or their husband's side; 'separate spheres' still determined gender roles. However, pre-war trends were recognisable, especially for younger women – a point which should not be overlooked by those who exaggerate the importance of the First World War in making the dramatic breakthrough by advancing women's position in the economy and society.

2.4 The impact of the First World War on the role of women

The First World War was a total war. Not only did Britain have to fight the Central Powers on land and on sea but it was also engaged in a war of production at home. So important was wartime production to victory that this aspect of the war effort was called the 'Home Front'.

The only women allowed into combat zones were nurses. Throughout the war nurses played a vital role, ministering to wounded soldiers. In 1915 a British nurse, Edith Cavell, was executed by the German authorities in occupied Belgium. Cavell had been caught trying to assist British prisoners of war to escape. The execution caused national outrage in Britain. An unarmed civilian – and a woman – had been put to death by the German army. It proved to be a major propaganda weapon, and was used against the Germans for the rest of the war.

Women in war work

Women played a key role on the Home Front. The mobilisation of millions of men for the army and navy left a huge gap in the labour market at home. This gap was filled by women, but not without controversy. Government attempts to use female labour met with opposition from the trade unions, who feared 'dilution' of skilled workers by the unskilled, thereby lowering wage rates. But by 1915 opposition could not stand in the way of using female labour. The *National Registration of Manpower Report* in August 1915 and the failure to recruit sufficient workers through the Munitions Volunteer Programme meant that the government had no choice but to recruit women if it wanted to field a continental-size army to fight the Germans. As a result, women employed in munitions work rose from 83,000 at the outbreak of war to 340,000 in July 1916. By the end of the war (November 1918), 947,000 women were involved in the production of munitions. The work was unpleasant and often dangerous, and more than 300 women lost their lives as a result of TNT poisoning and explosions in munitions factories.

Women also played important roles in other areas of the war economy, such as bus conductors, telephonists, secretaries, mechanics and waitresses. In 1914 there were 6 million women in full-time employment, many of them in domestic service. By 1918 the figure had risen to 7.3 million. The employment of women, therefore, was not new – it was the new type of employment that was significant.

'For Every Fighter a Woman Worker.' First World War YWCA propaganda poster.

1918: A turning-point in women's rights?

During the war the issue of extending the right to vote rose again. In 1915, a 'Speaker's Conference', convened by Asquith, the prime minister, discussed the subject of women's franchise. Although the Conference was unwilling to accept equal rights with men, it was willing to accept a compromise solution. As a result, many of its recommendations were included in the Representation Act, 1918, which gave the right to vote in national elections to women over the age of 30. The prime minister, Lloyd George, claimed that the decision was a fitting reward for the war service of women. The Act also introduced universal suffrage for men over 21 (but took the vote away from conscientious objectors).

Women were also allowed to stand for Parliament. The first woman elected in the December 1918 general election was Countess Markiewicz, MP for Dublin, St Patrick's Division, even though she was in Holloway Prison at the time. She was a member of the Sinn Fein Party, however, and refused to take her seat. Instead she joined the Irish Republican parliament, Dail Eireann, in Dublin in January 1919. The first woman to sit in the House of Commons was Nancy, Lady Astor, Conservative MP for Plymouth, Sutton Division, in 1919, after her husband, the sitting MP, became a member of the House of Lords.

Another important reform was the Sex Discrimination Act of December 1918. This opened up jury service, the legal profession and the position of 'Justice of the Peace' to women. The National Insurance Acts, 1918, 1920 and 1921 made women wage-earners eligible to National Insurance benefits. Nursing was also granted full professional status.

1918 also saw the publication of two significant books by Marie Stopes. In *Married Love*, Stopes offered to free women from ignorance in sexual matters, and in *Wise Parenthood* she outlined a guide to methods of contraception. In 1920, she opened the Mothers' Clinic for Constructive Birth Control, in Holloway, North London. (Yet, in 1919, the popular Sunday newspaper, the *News of the World*, was cheerfully offering a free tea tray for every 'proud mother of ten children'.)

1. How did the position of women change during the First World War?

2. A turning-point in the position of women? Assess this view of 1918.

Although these were important reforms, the position of women did not change overnight, and many prejudices against women remained. In addition, tens of thousands of women became war widows, and many more had to look after wounded husbands and sons.

2.5 A position changed? Women 1918 to 1930

The 1920s was a decade of great social change in Britain. Many women no longer followed the old tradition of marriage and motherhood. Women's fashions changed – and so did the length of their hair. The 1920s saw the rise in popularity of 'jazz' and new dances from the USA, such as the Charleston and the Black Bottom. At the end of the war, thousands of women lost their jobs in war work, but many others received employment in service jobs, such as secretaries.

Yet for most women – especially working-class women – the home and child rearing remained the norm, with the man still the 'breadwinner'. Manufacturing work was dominated by men, and so were the professions. And when women did get employment, it was usually at a lower rate of pay than men doing the same job.

In Parliament, Lady Astor was seen as a novelty rather than a normal MP, (although in 1923 the Intoxicating Liquor Act (Sale to Persons under Eighteen), introduced by her, became the first Act to result from a bill introduced by a woman). In the 1931 general election, only 67 women candidates stood, with 15 getting elected as MPs – out of a total of 648. The first three women MPs were all elected for seats which had been held by their husbands. Lady Astor (Conservative) was joined in the House of Commons in 1921 by Margaret Wintringham (Liberal), who was returned for the marginal constituency of Louth (even though, as a mark of respect to her dead husband, she had not spoken in public throughout her campaign). In 1923 Mabel Hilton Philipson, who as Mabel Russell had been a well-known musical comedy actress, took over as the Conservative Member for Berwick-upon-Tweed after her husband (a National Liberal) had been unseated because of the fraudulent practices of his agent. One of the first Labour women to be elected (in December 1923) was Margaret Bondfield who, in January 1924, became the first woman to hold ministerial office, after Baldwin's resignation and the formation of Ramsay MacDonald's government. She was appointed Under Secretary in the Ministry of Labour. Although she lost her seat at the general election later that year, she was returned again at a by-election in 1926, and in June 1929 she was appointed Minister of Labour, the first woman member of the Cabinet, and the first British woman politician to be admitted to the Privy Council. She held this position until her parliamentary career came to an end in 1931 when she (and Labour) lost in the general election.

1. In what ways did the lives of women change during the 1920s?

2. To what extent had women achieved equality with men by 1930?

Equal Franchise Act, 1928

Political equality for women finally came in 1928, when the vote was extended to all women over 21. This enfranchised 'the flapper vote' – young women in their 20s. A bill was introduced in March 1928 to give women the vote on the same terms as men. There was little opposition in Parliament, and it became law on 2 July 1928.

1. Which of the factors in the mind map do you regard as the most important in achieving greater equality for women? Give reasons for you answer.

2. In descending order of importance, how would you assess the other factors in bringing greater equality for women? Write a sentence next to each factor explaining your choice.

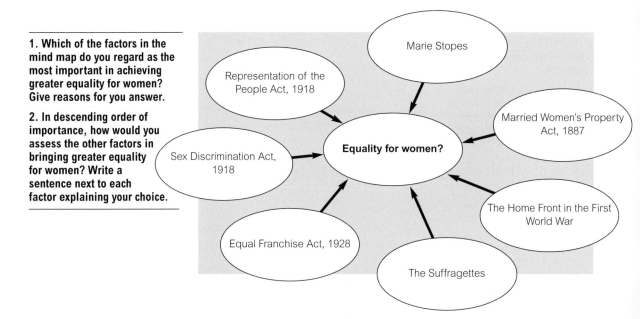

Further Reading

Texts designed for AS and A2 students

Women's Suffrage in Britain 1867–1928 by Martin Pugh (Historical Association Pamphlets, 1980)
The British Women's Suffrage Campaign: 1866–1928 by Harold Smith (Longman Seminar Studies, 2007)

For more advanced reading

The Women's Suffrage in Britain and Ireland by Elizabeth Crawford (Routledge, 2005)
The Militant Suffrage Movement by Laura Nym Marshall (Oxford University Press, 2003)
The Women's Suffrage Movement in Britain, 1866 –1928 by Sophia van Wingerden (Palgrave, 2003)

3 The era of Conservative domination and the rise of Labour, 1895–1906

Key Issues

- Why did the Conservatives, rather than the Liberals, form the governments between 1895 and 1903?

- Why did a distinct Labour Party develop during these years?

- Why did the Conservatives suffer a crushing defeat in the January 1906 general election?

3.1 To what extent were the Liberals in decline in the 1890s?

3.2 The origins of Labour representation in Parliament: what difficulties did the early pioneers face?

3.3 Salisbury's Third and Fourth Administrations, 1895–1902: was there any prospect of further reform?

3.4 How serious were the problems faced by Balfour's Government, 1902–1905?

3.5 How successfully did Balfour deal with these problems up to 1905?

3.6 Historical interpretation: Why did the Liberals win a landslide victory in January 1906?

Framework of Events

1895	General election returns Salisbury to power with a large majority
	Coalition between Conservatives and Liberal Unionists
1897	Workmen's Compensation Act
	Queen Victoria's Diamond Jubilee
1898	Campbell-Bannerman appointed Liberal leader
1899	The Boer War starts
1900	'Khaki' election returns Salisbury to power
	Labour Representation Committee is formed
1901	Queen Victoria's death; Edward VII becomes King
	The Taff Vale Judgement
1902	Balfour succeeds Salisbury as Prime Minister
	Education Act
	Treaty of Vereeniging ends the Boer War
1903	Tariff reform campaign starts Lib–Lab pact
	Suffragette WSPU set up
1904	The Report of the Inter-Departmental Committee on Physical Deterioration
1905	Balfour resigns; Campbell-Bannerman calls a general election
1906	January: General Election and Liberal landslide victory
	Labour Representation Committee renamed the Labour Party.

Overview

Conservative: Technically called the Unionist Party after the Liberal Unionists joined the Conservative Party in 1895.

I T is tempting to see politics at the turn of the twentieth century as a time of transition from the Victorian age, which closed with the ascendancy of the Conservative Party, led by Lord Salisbury up until 1902 (the last time the country was run by an aristocrat from the House of Lords), to the Edwardian age which began with such a sense of uncertainty about the future. Working-class movements and labour representation in Parliament reflected new forces at work in a Britain that felt threatened by international economic rivalry. Our position as 'workshop of the world' was no longer secure and concerns about the 'state of the nation' and 'national efficiency' were growing, particularly since it had proved so difficult to win the South African War against the Boers. The Suffragettes had been formed in 1903 although, as yet, there were only hints of their most militant campaigning.

This chapter ends with an astonishing Liberal election victory in 1906, which brought to an end Balfour's Conservative Government of 1902–05. Contemporaries may have felt unease about what was to come, but there were important elements of continuity as well as change throughout the period. The development of 'labour' was by no means certain, while the Conservative Party remained steadfastly in the hands of the **'Hotel Cecil'**. Many areas of the British economy continued to lead the world, although demands for reform to alleviate the effects of industrial society were growing. Under the Conservatives, however, social reform would not be a prominent feature of government. Why then did they occupy so dominant a position over domestic politics?

'Hotel Cecil': The nickname originated from Salisbury's 1900 Government, which contained many of his relations, including his nephew Arthur Balfour (who later became Prime Minister).

All the points mentioned in the mind map contributed towards the Conservative electoral defeat of January 1906.

1. What do you regard as the most important reason for Conservative defeat in January 1906? Give reasons for your answer.

2. In what ways were the following issues linked?: Taff Vale decision, 1901, Education Act, 1902, Lib–Lab pact, 1903.

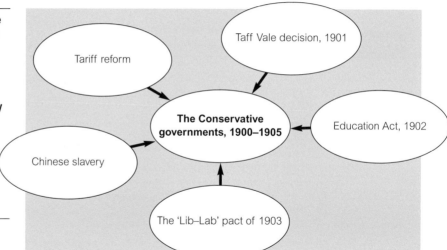

3.1 To what extent were the Liberals in decline in the 1890s?

In the 1895 general election, the Conservatives won 341 seats. When added to the 80 Liberal Unionist MPs, Lord Salisbury had secured a huge majority in the House of Commons. How serious was the collapse in Liberal fortunes? The seeds of Liberal decline were clear during their last Government because of the following:

● Their reliance on the support of the Irish Home Rule Party.

● The division in the party once the Marquis of Hartington and Joseph Chamberlain had led the Liberal Unionists across the floor of the House of Commons to join the Conservatives.

● The defeat of the 1893 Home Rule Bill which left them without a major cause to pursue.

- The results of the 1895 election which revealed their reliance on Welsh and Scottish votes, as they failed to gain a majority in England. Even worse was a failure to increase their share of the working class vote.

- Their prominent figures – Lewis Harcourt, John Morley and Lord Rosebery – who conducted petty quarrels and divergent policies which failed to keep the Party together.

Unity was never an easy matter as the Party consisted of many disparate elements. Gladstone had kept things together, but now there was generous scope for squabbling and in-fighting. Rosebery resigned in 1896, only to be replaced by Harcourt who also failed to give a firm sense of direction to the Party; witness his feeble attempts to discredit Chamberlain for his part in the Jameson Raid in 1896. Harcourt limped on until 1898, when Sir Henry Campbell-Bannerman replaced him. Campbell-Bannerman was solid, uninspiring, largely unknown outside Liberal circles and dwarfed by powerful Conservative figures such as Joseph Chamberlain and Lord Salisbury.

Was it clear to the voters what the Liberals stood for? The historian D.A. Hamer notes that once Home Rule had moved more into the background, 'Sectionalism re-emerged, rampant and uncontrollable'. Another historian, Paul Adelman, in *Gladstone, Disraeli and Later Victorian Politics* (1983), refers to this 'reversion to "**faddism**", with each Liberal section pursuing its own hare oblivious to the rest of the field'. What was it to be – temperance, land reform, Welsh disestablishment, or Liberal imperialism? The new strand here was Liberal imperialism which had its supporters like Lord Rosebery who wished to develop the Empire, without recourse to aggressive flag waving, and social reform at home.

The problem was that little of this cut much ice with working-class voters in the cities – the Liberals' loss of power in London and other major cities shows this. More recent research by John Vincent and D. Fraser has suggested that the Liberals should have addressed matters of closer interest to the working man – jobs and wages, not flag waving or controlling licensing hours. Local Liberal associations also contributed to the arguments in favour of an independent labour representation in Parliament by turning their backs on candidates from working-class backgrounds – Keir Hardie is a case in point. Men like him were losing faith in the Liberals.

Even more serious, in the short term, was the loss of leadership and money when the Unionists left in 1886. The Party had been unable to fight the Conservatives in 114 seats – not a situation they had been in at the previous election. In 1900, even more Conservatives were unopposed – a source of embarrassment made worse by the Liberal's opposition to the Boer War, which enabled the Conservatives to label many of them pro-Boer. There is, then, a strong case for saying that Lord Salisbury's ascendancy was the electorate's response to the absence of a credible alternative to the Conservatives.

One interpretation is that Liberalism was also being undermined by existing social trends which made their decline inevitable. This view regards the 1906 Liberal victory as merely a temporary, if spectacular, revolt against the Conservative/Unionist alliance. Crudely speaking, the middle classes were drifting to the Conservatives. Representatives of commerce were joining the landowning party, making the dividing line between these two economic groups increasingly blurred, as each invested in the other's interests. Many landowners, for example, were helping to develop railways, shipping and mining. The Conservatives were beginning to represent the fears of substantial elements of the propertied classes who had much to lose if Radical Liberals pandered to **militant trade unionism**

'Faddism': Many Liberals had their own sectional 'fads' or favourite causes, such as temperance reform (limiting the sale of alcohol) or disestablishment (depriving the Church of its connection with the State).

Militant trade unionism: Extreme and sometimes violent workers' action taken against capitalism.

or Irish nationalism. An expanding lower middle class – such as junior managers, white collar staff, foremen artisans who wished to protect their salaries and better houses in the suburbs, away from the slums – looked to the Unionists to guard their new status. This was 'villa Toryism' and it adds weight to historian J.P. Cornford's view that class increasingly decided voting patterns. In rural areas, the Anglican clergy and gentry continued to maintain their grip – but 'villa' Tories in the boroughs tipped the scales.

There is also a widely accepted view that Conservative organisation, run by Aretas Akers-Douglas and Captain R.W.E. Middleton, was very efficient. Most seats were fought, the number of party agents multiplied in the constituencies, while plural voting (property owners, businessmen, university graduates) running at 7 per cent of the total vote is generally reckoned to have helped the Conservatives.

The 1884 Reform Act also disadvantaged working-class voters – possibly up to 4 million. The registration system required 12 months in a tenancy before a person could vote. Since working men changed jobs and houses more often, they tended to disenfranchise themselves; anyway, they had weaker habits of political allegiance to any party. If the working class was inclined to apathy as far as political (as opposed to industrial) action was concerned, it made it more difficult for the Liberals to exploit their potential voting support.

The Redistribution of Seats Act of 1885 did much to help 'villa Toryism'. The Act divided voters into roughly equal constituencies with single members to represent them. Salisbury's hand behind this reform ensured that when the new boundaries were drawn, Conservative voters in the towns would not be swamped. It enabled middle-class suburbs to elect Conservative members. As a result, towns like Sheffield, Glasgow and Manchester were returning Tory MPs. The historian Martin Pugh highlights, in *The Evolution of the British Electoral System, 1832–1987* (1988), the powerful work done by the Primrose League. This was a Conservative social organisation that drew in these middle-class voters to a range of entertainments such as concerts, fêtes, shows and weekend tours. Such 'popular' activities helped to integrate people into the beliefs of the Party, adding to a groundswell of supporters. It helped to spread myths about the reforms passed by the Party. Leaflets such as 'What the Conservatives have done for the British people' effectively spread the message, although the reality lacked substance.

What is more difficult to explain is the support the Conservatives gained from sections of the working class – so-called 'slum Toryism'. Was it the patriotic appeal of Empire, Queen Victoria's jubilees and tales of imperial glory which appealed to the working class? The 'Khaki' election of 1900, called during the Boer War, returned 402 Conservatives and only 184 Liberal MPs to Westminster. The anti-war 'Little Englanders' among the Liberals compromised any chances they might have had, as they split with Rosebery's Liberal Imperialists who were in favour of the war. Such chaos rebounded in Salisbury's favour, and the timing of this election so early during the war must have made an impact of sorts. However, historian H. Pelling challenges the view that the Empire made any lasting impression on a working class more interested in material wellbeing – represented by jobs, prices and wages. If this is the case, then clearly the Liberal Party had little to offer.

Was there a groundswell of support for a new party that might give the working man a voice in Parliament? What progress did 'labour representation' make into the late Victorian political system?

1. What changes took place that enabled the Conservatives to increase their number of MPs?

2. Which was the most important factor in explaining the Conservative ascendancy after 1895? Give reasons to support your answer.

3.2 The origins of Labour representation in Parliament: what difficulties did the early pioneers face?

There was nothing inevitable about the origins and growth of a party that spoke up specifically for the interests of the working class. It grew out of a series of false starts and strangely 'incompatible elements', which came together in the 1880s and 1890s. From its beginnings, socialists found it difficult to decide what methods might be employed to achieve their aims. Competing voices called, at one extreme for a radical socialist programme which aimed for collective ownership of the means of production, distribution and exchange. At the other extreme was a more pragmatic programme that set its sights on getting broad agreement in Parliament for a number of limited, practical approaches to improve working conditions. These tensions were apparent as the early activists took their first steps towards political organisation.

Marxist: Belief in the ideas of Karl Marx, author of *Das Kapital*, often called the manifesto of Communism.

The Social Democratic Foundation (SDF) was formed by H.M. Hyndman, a Cambridge-educated stockbroker and **Marxist**, in 1884. He used the Labour Party mainly to spread revolutionary socialist ideas, although his high-handed and increasingly violent tactics employed when organising demonstrations by the unemployed in London (1886–87) led to quarrels between its prominent members. For instance, H.H. Champion, the editor of a socialist newspaper, *Justice*, was to leave at this time, as did John Burns and Tom Mann. These small groups of the Left were prone to self-destructive internal dissension. Nevertheless, the SDF was a potent force in London, drawing young activists into the movement.

The other important group, formed in 1884, was the Fabians – middle-class intellectuals such as George Bernard Shaw and Sydney and Beatrice Webb. The Fabians supported the virtues of state and municipal socialism, often called 'Gas and Water' socialism, introduced gradually, to moderate the evils of capitalism and usher in a socialist state. They were not alone in opposing the call for a new party to represent labour; they believed the best way forward was for their ideas to 'permeate' the leadership of existing parties. Some historians, such as P. Thompson and Eric Hobsbawm, dismiss claims that the Fabians had any lasting influence. Paul Adelman, in *The Rise of the Labour Party 1880–1945* (1986), gives them credit for being 'successful propagandists for the ideas of "evolutionary socialism"'. He does add, though, that there were fewer than 2,000 socialists in Britain by 1889, and many of them were middle class.

The 1880s also saw the rise of the 'new unions', and the expansion of the right to vote in 1884. How far either of these developments helped the socialist groups is difficult to say. The complexities of the 1884 Reform Act regularly meant that 40 per cent of the male population was unable to vote. It is true that nine working men had been elected to the House of Commons by 1886. As 'Lib–Labs', they shared the views of the old leadership of the Trades Union Council (TUC) in speaking for workers' interests whilst remaining resolute supporters of the Liberal Party. Henry Broadhurst was typical of this group.

James Keir Hardie, however, was not. He was a miner who worked tirelessly to encourage his fellow workers to vote Liberal, but who came to realise the need for a separate voice in Parliament for working men. In 1888, Hardie polled 614 votes at the Mid-Lanarkshire election, standing as an independent labour candidate. In 1892, he and two other independent labour candidates, John Burns and J.H. Wilson, were elected to Parliament. Hardie's victory at West Ham South (London) was far from his Scottish heartland and proved that working-class voters could be tempted away from the Liberals and Conservatives. The leadership of the trade unions was

Keir Hardie (1856–1915)
Hardie was a miner, nonconformist and founder of the Scottish Labour Party. He was the first 'Labour' MP, representing West Ham South in East London in 1892.

unconvinced. Despite the success of new unionism in organising unskilled workers, winning the dockers' and the matchgirls' strikes of 1889, their impact was short-lived. In the 1890s, employers began to undermine all unionised labour but the numbers in 'new' unions slumped badly to less than 10 per cent of total union membership. For the time being, the TUC was content, unlike Hardie, to keep the faith with Gladstone.

Why was the Independent Labour Party formed in 1893?

Hardie succeeded in bringing different socialist groups into some kind of 'alliance'. In January 1893, the Independent Labour Party (ILP) was formed at a conference in Bradford, attended by 120 delegates, including socialists from labour clubs, the SDF and Fabians. It drew on grassroots support from a number of regions:

● From Bradford, where prolonged, violent strikes against the Liberal factory owners of the Manningham Mills who were trying to cut wages, led to the establishment of the Bradford Labour Union.

● From Hardie's own Scotland, where the opposition to Irish Home Rule had sapped Liberal strength.

● From Lancashire, where energetic working-class Toryism in certain areas had made it difficult for the Liberals, who were often identified as the mill owners, to make electoral headway.

● In Manchester, where Robert Blatchford had started a popular weekly socialist newspaper, *The Clarion*, while in 1892 the Manchester and Salford ILP was formed.

The ILP proclaimed the socialist principle of collective ownership of the economy. In attempting to maintain as broad appeal as possible, the word 'socialist' was omitted from the title. Instead the 'Independent Labour Party' was chosen and, as historian David Howell notes, the balance was struck with having Labour in the title while trying to pursue distinctly socialist goals.

The ILP rapidly grew in popularity, with 35,000 members by 1895. It followed in the fairly liberal tradition of British trade union activity with none of the overtones of class warfare and revolutionary violence found on the continent. Activists were often ex-Liberals, such as Ramsay MacDonald who had a background in this 'reformist' tradition. Another strand in the ILP was nonconformity. Philip Snowden, then a young Yorkshire ILP worker, wrote in his autobiography that the new party 'derived its inspiration far more from the Sermon on the Mount than from the teachings of the economists'. Clive Behagg, a historian writing in *Years of Expansion, Britain 1815–1914*, agreed that 'many of its leaders were more familiar with the Bible than with Marx'.

Could the ILP develop a wide appeal, at a time when the Liberal Government of 1892–95 seemed to be giving up the ghost? Apparently not. In 1895, the ILP lost in all 28 constituencies where it had candidates. Keir Hardie also lost his seat, leaving the ILP with no representation in the Commons. In the absence of any finance worth speaking of, much now depended on the extent of trade union support – without a firm basis from established working-class organisations. The future looked bleak. Many of the leaders of the older unions, for instance the miners and craft associations, continued to oppose the ILP. However, the adoption by the TUC of central socialist ideas, such as the demand for an eight-hour working day, showed how socialism was slowly infiltrating the trade union movement. Burns and J.H. Wilson were elected onto the Parliamentary Committee of the TUC. The 'old guard' tried to stem the tide. They had no time for the

Block vote: A delegate would cast votes, which were equivalent to the numbers of members in the trade union he represented.

more provocative aspects of the socialist programme and the introduction of the **block vote** system was partly a response to fears that 'dangerous', minority elements might come to dominate the Parliamentary Committee.

However, by the end of the 1890s, significant shifts in trade union attitudes were taking place. There was dissatisfaction with the Liberals. They were clearly riddled with factionalism and seemed unenthusiastic about reforms such as the eight-hour day. Local Liberal associations were reluctant to adopt working-class candidates, as at Attercliffe in Yorkshire in 1894. Industrial competition led to a number of long-drawn-out disputes (e.g. the great engineering lockout of 1897) with employers who were extending working hours, using new machines to force redundancies, and drawing on non-union labour to avoid the 'closed shop'. Even the old established craft unions were under attack, making their leaders reconsider their views. In 1899, an Appeal Court ruling (Lyons *versus* Wilkins) limited unions' rights to picket peacefully. Against this managerial and legal onslaught, and with the Liberals offering policies such as Disestablishment and Temperance reform, it dawned on trade union leaders that independent labour parliamentary representation might have its advantages. Similarly, ILP leaders, Hardie, MacDonald, Snowden and Glasier too were recognising the realities of the situation – a deal with the unions might bring progress.

When the TUC met in 1899, the Amalgamated Society of Railway Servants, which was itself fighting against employers who refused to recognise the union, called for a conference to help improve representation for labour in Parliament. The resolution was only passed by 546,000 votes to 434,000, but it was sufficient. When the Conference met in 1900, the SDF, Fabians, ILP and 67 trade unions were represented. A Labour Representation Committee (LRC) was set up with an executive committee consisting of each socialist group but with the trade union members in the majority. The

1. What message is this cartoon trying to make about Labour Party links with the Liberal Party?

2. How reliable is the cartoon?

'Not a Wise Saw – Mr Keir Hardie wishes to make Labour representation entirely independent of the Liberal Party.' Cartoon from 1893 following the formation of the Independent Labour Party (ILP). The tree is the 'Liberal Party', the branch 'Labour' and the saw 'ILP'.

LRC, on Hardie's insistence, set out general aims rather than anything specific such as the cherished 'collective ownership', much to the SDF's anger, and they withdrew as a result.

In 1900, the LRC won only two seats in Parliament: Keir Hardie and Robert Bell (of the Railway Servants' union). There were eight 'Lib–Labs'. Once again, money was insufficient to support candidates during elections. Hardie knew that more dynamic trade union support was the only hope. It would be the Taff Vale Case (see page 42) which cemented the bond between unions and the new party, boosting the number of unions who supported the LRC (affiliations) by 168 between the start of 1901 and the end of 1903. It was quite plain that the Conservative Government would not reverse the House of Lords judgement, while Paul Adelman notes that the Liberals 'were either unenthusiastic for, or pessimistic about the outcome of, a new trade union Bill'. Hence the unions swung their support behind the LRC. Membership rose to about 850,000 and annual revenue had grown to £5,000 by 1903, which helped to finance elections and to pay existing MPs.

The LRC was now engaged in negotiations with the Liberal Chief Whip, Herbert Gladstone, to form an electoral pact. When it came to such matters as education and imperialism, the LRC and parts of the Liberal Party did tend to think along similar lines. Also, there was a danger of splitting the vote between LRC and Liberal candidates; for example at Lanark in 1901, when this very scenario enabled the Conservative to win. For both parties, precious party funds might be saved. The Liberals could see that they might win some working-class seats, while the LRC would certainly boost their numbers in Parliament. Hence, in certain constituencies, the Liberals would not oppose the LRC candidate, in return for support for the Liberals in Parliament. By 1905, they had agreed to support each other's candidates. For some LRC leaders, it seemed a logical development; others who still nursed their dream of a vigorous socialist programme, such as the SDF, were more uncomfortable. It neatly illustrates the internal dissensions which continued to thrive within the new party.

Despite this, the January 1906 general election saw 29 LRC MPs returned to Parliament. A month later, when they took their seats, they did so as members of the renamed Labour Party.

1. What were the aims of:

(a) the Social Democratic Federation

(b) the Fabians

(c) the Independent Labour Party?

2. How far was the period after the Taff Vale Case (1901–06) the turning point for the rise of the Labour Representation Committee?

3.3 Salisbury's Third and Fourth Administrations, 1895–1902: was there any prospect of further reform?

During his Third (1895–1900) and Fourth (1900–1902) Administrations, Salisbury achieved little in domestic affairs. Costs – that is, taxes and rates – were to be kept down. Chamberlain did have schemes for reform, such as the introduction of old age pensions, but he was increasingly drawn into the world of the Colonial Office. Indeed the Boer War brought plans for domestic reform to a grinding halt. Perhaps the Conservatives were fortunate that the economy was doing better and standards of living were rising. An Agricultural Ratings Bill lowered rates for farmers. There were isolated reforms in Ireland, such as the Land Act (1896) which increased the process of selling land to tenants. County Councils were introduced there in 1898.

Perhaps the two major pieces of legislation which Salisbury was persuaded to support in 1897 were:

● An Education Act which increased the State funding for Voluntary (Church) schools.

- A Workmen's Compensation Act which made employers liable to pay their employees compensation if they suffered an injury because of their work.

Chamberlain was able to squeeze some money out of the Treasury for some colonial reforms, but otherwise the *status quo* was defended with success.

The 'Khaki' election of 1900, as stated earlier, returned a massive Conservative majority. However, Salisbury was ill and not entirely at ease with those around him. He waited for the new King, Edward VII, to be crowned and then retired leaving the premiership in the hands of his nephew, Arthur Balfour. Salisbury had probably achieved what he had set out to do – limit reform, defend the interests of the landed classes and steer Britain safely through a difficult period when the Empire was growing apace and numerous agreements had to be reached to dissipate colonial tensions.

Would things change a great deal under Arthur Balfour?

Do you agree that Salisbury achieved little of lasting importance? Give reasons to support your answer.

3.4 How serious were the problems faced by Balfour's Government, 1902–1905?

Was Britain still in the ascendant?

Signs of decline alarmed contemporaries. There are many references to 'the condition of England' and 'national efficiency' in the literature of the period. There are numerous strands to the debate. Was it because Britain felt itself isolated in a hostile world? Or was it because Britain's economic lead over its rivals was being lost? Whether or not historians agree on the extent of a 'great depression' in industry and agriculture is beside the point. Contemporaries believed it and their perceptions were underpinned by a series of shocking investigations into poverty which appeared from the 1880s onwards. Charles Booth's massive study, the *Life and Labour of the People in London* (completed in 1903), found one-third of the population barely existing below the poverty line. His findings filled 17 volumes in all, meticulously detailing families who were poor not because they were lazy and feckless, but because of the size of their families. Seebohm Rowntree's study in York, *Poverty: A Study of Town Life* (published in 1899), came to similar conclusions. Unemployment or illness and old age were not the major causes of poverty. At the heart of the problem lay large families, low wages and the death of the main household wage-earner. These were 'scientific' studies, meant to inform rather than dramatise. Other titles, such as *Horrible London*, *The Bitter Cry of Outcast London*, or William Booth's *In Darkest England*, told much the same story. Social degradation, starvation, disease and poverty existed in the heart of Britain's cities.

How could British workers compete with those abroad? How could a country which sought to 'civilise' Africa turn its back on the awful reality which existed at home? They argued that the general health of the country should have been better. The picture of child health was particularly alarming. Infant mortality was as high as 202 deaths per 1,000 births reported in Sheffield, in 1901. Little wonder that a committee was set up in 1903 to investigate why so many volunteers during the Boer War were rejected because of their poor physical condition. In 1900, of 11,000 volunteers in Manchester, 8,000 were deemed unfit to carry a rifle and undertake training.

Here was a rising tide of social pity that demanded collectivist action –

state involvement to lessen the extreme effects of the free market economy. Would Balfour's Cabinet respond to the challenge?

Balfour's Premiership: why have his personal qualities been criticised?

Arthur Balfour seemed to be his uncle's 'natural successor', sharing many of his assumptions – he was cautious, suspicious of change, social reform and the 'masses'. There was no doubting his intellect or his awareness of the major issues facing the country in terms of 'national efficiency'. His ministry had its successes; but despite these, Balfour has been roundly criticised. Rich, cultured, aristocratic and aloof, his wit may have been appreciated in 'society' but to others he appeared uninterested, even bored with the tedium of government business. David Lloyd George was provoked to compare him to 'the scent on a pocket handkerchief'. Robert Blake, in *The Conservative Party from Peel to Thatcher* (1991), accuses Balfour of failing to recognise social changes taking place among the electorate, arguing that 'he made insufficient allowance for the unreason of the masses'. Austen Chamberlain realised that, 'He has no comprehension of the habits of his countrymen and no idea how things strike them'. Perhaps he was 'too clever, too cool' (Robert Blake).

Balfour's book *A defence of philosophical doubt* is cited as evidence that the new Prime Minister was more interested in intellectual games than putting his considerable abilities into government action which might address 'the condition of England'. There was no greater contrast than with Joseph Chamberlain who, despite a press campaign on his behalf, was never a real threat to Balfour becoming Prime Minister. Chamberlain knew that, as the leader of a small group of Liberal Unionists who had recently joined the Conservative Party, as well as being non-Anglican, he had little chance of the leadership, but he was willing to join the Cabinet. There must have been times when he was frustrated by a government which lacked drive and direction.

This is the critical view of Balfour and if the impending disaster which was to befall the Conservative Party is anything to go by, then much of it is justified. In Balfour's favour, however, one of his Government's earliest pieces of legislation was designed to improve educational standards, widely believed to be inferior to those, say, in Germany and one of the root causes of what was perceived as 'national decline'. There were other achievements but these were overshadowed by a succession of mishandled problems.

1. What problems faced Britain during Balfour's Administrations?

2. How far do you agree that Balfour was ill-equipped to deal with Britain's problems?

3.5 How successfully did Balfour deal with these problems up to 1905?

The Taff Vale Case, 1901

Trade unionists, not for the first time, felt that their legal rights were again under attack. In the 1890s, the Quinn *versus* Leathem case meant that anyone who organised a strike could be liable to civil action by the employer. Then in 1901, before Balfour had become Prime Minister, the House of Lords, acting as the final Court of Appeal, made their judgement in the Taff Vale Case. In 1900, there had been a strike against the Taff Vale Railway Company in South Wales. The Company took the union, the Amalgamated Society of Railway Servants, to court and won; the union had to pay £23,000 damages. The wider implications were clear: no union could strike without fear of being ruined when sued for damages.

Balfour's Cabinet preferred to set up a royal commission rather than reverse the Taff Vale judgement in law. The Labour Representation Committee (LRC) was a major beneficiary because of the boost to trade union affiliations to the new party (see page 40). It was not a coincidence that the political levy began in 1903. In the same year, the LRC came to an agreement with Herbert Gladstone, the Liberal Chief Whip: the LRC was allocated 35 constituencies where they could campaign for the anti-Conservative vote without the presence of a Liberal candidate too. In return, the LRC would not stand against Liberal candidates anywhere else in England and Wales. The arrangement continued right up to the First World War, and must have played a significant part in increasing the size of the Liberal landslide in 1906.

Balfour's record of helping the unemployed also proved inadequate. The Unemployed Workmen Act, passed in 1905, helped the urban unemployed find work through labour exchanges set up by local Distress Committees. These committees had no funds from the State that it could distribute as emergency relief. They were forced to rely on private charity for that. Once again, the Unionists appeared callous when faced with real need. Hence Robert Blake's view that 'Balfour was singularly insensitive to any save the most predictable reactions of the working class'.

Education

The 1902 Education Act, most commentators agree, was a considerable achievement as it established a new framework for secondary schools that would remain in place until the Butler Act of 1944. Unfortunately, the political storm it caused has been said to have eroded the Government's electoral position – but to what extent?

The Act dealt with the clear inadequacy of secondary school provision. The 1870 Act established provision from the rates for only elementary schools, but many **School Boards** were using their money to provide advanced courses for more senior pupils. In 1901, a case was successfully brought against the London School Board for providing this 'secondary' education. Robert Morant, a civil servant at the Board of Education, knew urgent action was required by the State to take responsibility for elementary and secondary education.

School Boards: Set up in 1870, these committees were elected by ratepayers to build and run elementary schools.

The 1902 Education Act

- The old School Boards were abolished.

- Local Education Authorities (LEAs) took over responsibilities for elementary and secondary education.

- Education was able to expand and Church schools (which were struggling through lack of funds) were to receive financial support from the rates for teachers' pay and education of a unified standard, while the Anglicans and Catholics provided the buildings.

- The numbers of schools and pupils in grant-aided secondary schools quickly increased (from 94,000 in 1905 to 200,000 by 1914) and many LEA grammar schools were developed to provide education for those with ability. Whether the academic education they provided was what Britain needed, given the shortage of graduate technicians, is debatable.

It was this final aspect which is held to have undermined some of the Government's popularity. Not unexpectedly, nonconformists hated what they said was 'Rome on the rates', as they had been looking forward to a time when Church school education might wither away. Nonconformists were now ferociously determined to use the Liberal Party to oppose the strengthening of the Anglican Church's position. Why did Balfour support the Act? Was it a way of dealing with 'national efficiency'? Was it a rational response to the fears that Britain was falling behind industrially because it was failing to provide quality technical education – as argued by K. Young, in *Arthur James Balfour* (1963)? For Robert Blake it was another one of Balfour's 'blind spots' – his failure to grasp the indignation the measure would cause. He soon faced a nonconformist revolt: 7,000 prosecutions of people who refused to pay their rates in 1903. Dr Clifford, a Baptist, helped to organise the opposition to the Act and it was in Wales where the battle raged most bitterly, particularly where nonconformists had to send their children to the only available school, which might be run by the Church. None of this made much sense as taxation had for many years been used to keep some denominational schools going – but in a way, because the subsidies were paid from rates, the impact on a locality was more obvious.

Whether or not the Act played a big part in losing the Conservatives electoral support is open to question. What is not open to question is the way it galvanised the flagging Liberals into a more united and dynamic force. Joseph Chamberlain realised a political mistake had been made as life had been breathed into a Liberal Party which had suffered from ineffectual leadership and divisions over the Boer War. The Act did much to heal the rift between pro-Boers such as David Lloyd George and Liberal imperialists like Herbert Asquith. Liberal energies seemed to be renewed in response to Balfour's persistent contribution to the misfortunes of his own party.

As a postscript, the Government produced a promising Licensing Act in 1904, which attempted to reduce the number of public houses in areas where they weren't needed. Once again, this constructive piece of legislation was used by nonconformists to castigate the Government for introducing a levy on the industry so that the brewers could receive adequate compensation for any losses they suffered.

Chinese slavery, 1902–1904

'Chinese slavery' proved to be another minefield which Balfour could have taken the trouble to avoid. With a little forethought, the Government might have recognised that the decision to send thousands of Chinese labourers to South Africa would provoke an outcry, which would undermine their electoral popularity. The British High Commissioner, Lord Milner, urgently wished to press ahead with rebuilding the economy of South Africa in the wake of the Boer War. The gold mines needed labour and these Chinese labourers were thought to be the answer. Milner's plan had been overruled once by Chamberlain who was more alive to the likelihood of a hostile public reaction. But in 1903 Chamberlain was not in the Cabinet, so Milner's plan was sanctioned. Coming so soon after Britain's embarrassment over the conduct of the Boer War, people were reminded of the 'concentration camp' mentality and 'methods of barbarism' (see page 45), when the Chinese workers were herded into labour camps. Not only were living conditions appalling (Milner was alleged to have agreed to flogging the Chinese as a punishment), but the close proximity of so many men struck many people as morally wrong as it might lead to 'nameless practices' – a lurid phrase which reflected nonconformist indignation. There was another more practical reason for white working-class anger: jobs were at stake and Chinese migrant labour was closing off any scope for white emigration to South Africa.

There was a sense of over-reaction here – the Liberals did protest too much, and their sense of outrage was somewhat overdone for political

The cartoon shows a rich Transvaal gold mine owner in the foreground. In the background are Chinese coolies working behind barbed wire.

(a) What message is the cartoonist attempting to convey about the reasons for the wealth of gold mine owners?

(b) Using information contained within this chapter, explain how the issue of Chinese labour in South African mines affected the popularity of the Conservative Government and the career of Lord Milner, the British administrator of the Transvaal.

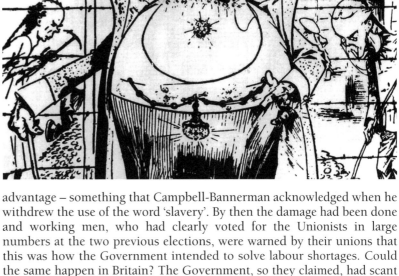

advantage – something that Campbell-Bannerman acknowledged when he withdrew the use of the word 'slavery'. By then the damage had been done and working men, who had clearly voted for the Unionists in large numbers at the two previous elections, were warned by their unions that this was how the Government intended to solve labour shortages. Could the same happen in Britain? The Government, so they claimed, had scant regard for the dignity of labour. Some of the indignation, though, sounded artificial and it is difficult to know how much damage was done. Historian L.C.B. Seaman argues that the Conservative defeat which came in 1906 'cannot be explained solely on rational grounds. Discontent with 20 years of Tory rule was deep-seated but incoherent … in the prevailing atmosphere of disillusionment after the Boer War, the public mind was more impressed by the issue of "Chinese slavery" …'

Combine this with reactions to the Taff Vale Case and it becomes easier to understand how the Government lost the support of the working class.

Joseph Chamberlain and tariff reform, 1903–1905

The worst was yet to come. Following the end of the Boer War, Joseph Chamberlain needed to breathe life into his career; the difficulty of defeating the Boers, the Education Bill and a string of poor by-election results (including the loss of North Leeds) exposed a flagging party. His solution was dramatic – tariff reform, based on **retaliatory tariffs**, **selective import controls** and **imperial preference**. It was a solution that proved to be an electoral disaster.

Chamberlain intended to challenge the orthodoxy of free trade, which had been an article of faith for both the Liberals and the Unionists for so long. Supporters of free trade were in no doubt that it meant cheap imports of food and raw materials. They had a point as Britain relied on a greater proportion of food imports from outside the Empire than within it. Supporters of tariff reform claimed that a number of countries – including major competitors such as Germany and the USA – had introduced protective tariffs, enabling their economies to expand, while Britain's was slowing down. Some protection, they argued, would give a boost to home industries. Again, such a case was difficult to sustain as it was based on assertion rather than firm evidence. Chamberlain made enthusiastic

Retaliatory tariffs: Import taxes placed on goods from a country which itself had imposed tariffs on goods entering its country.

Selective import controls: Tariffs at a lower rate for goods from the Colonies.

Imperial preference: Trade between the Colonies, such as food, to be given preference because it would attract lower tariffs compared with trade with the rest of the world.

claims, such as the three-quarters of a million extra jobs which would be created, while the stronger economy would generate more taxes for the introduction of old age pensions.

The arguments were not just about economics. Imperial preference would bind the Empire more closely together by favouring imperial trade, thus giving further impetus to the imperial idea. After the false starts of Chamberlain's proposals for an imperial free trade area (*Zollverein* – customs union) and *Kriegsverein* (an imperial navy had been suggested) at the Colonial Conferences of 1897 and 1902, imperial preference was greeted more warmly. The Premiers of Australia, New Zealand and Canada could see the advantage of protecting their fledgling industries and having lower rates of duty with Britain.

However, on his return from South Africa, where he had been engaged in postwar reconstruction, Chamberlain encountered obstruction from C.T. Ritchie, the Chancellor of the Exchequer. Ritchie's plans for the forthcoming budget, far from introducing further tariffs, were to abolish the existing duty on corn and thereby re-assert free trade. Balfour was not inclined to overrule Ritchie who had threatened to resign on the issue. Chamberlain, exhausted from his trip, was in no mood to fight. His biographer, Julian Amery, called this 'a fatal mistake'.

Chamberlain may have conceded, but it was only temporary. His speech arguing for preferential tariffs with the Colonies and questioning the benefits of free trade, delivered on 15 May 1903 in Birmingham, rocked the Party to its foundations. With characteristic fervour, Chamberlain's appeal to patriotic and imperial sentiments was clear: 'The Empire is in its infancy. Now is the time when we can mould that Empire.' But it was the economic case that drew most fire and if it was meant to incite opposition from within the Party, in particular from Liberal Unionists, it succeeded. By July, a Free Food League had been formed. Three dangerous factions began to divide the Conservatives: '**Whole Hoggers**', '**Free Fooders**' and '**Balfourites**'. Salisbury's son, Lord Hugh Cecil, organised a group of free traders, who became known as 'Hughligans'. Winston Churchill defected to the Liberals.

Balfour used his considerable skills to hide the split in their ranks, but matters had gone too far. Balfour might well have been personally sympathetic to tariffs, although perhaps limited to retaliatory duties and certainly not yet. His attempts to sit on the fence merely provoked ridicule as the split deepened. Chamberlain's Tariff Reform League directed the national campaign and with tensions becoming unbearable in the Cabinet, he resigned in September to take his arguments to the people. Balfour quietly agreed this was the best way out, especially if he was to keep the Liberal Unionists and the Conservatives together. Chamberlain agreed. It looked like another appeal for popular support over the heads of the Government. He had done the same in 1886 over Home Rule. Did he nurse any hopes of becoming leader? He probably understood that many Conservatives continued to be suspicious of him, hence his attempt to draw on his personal popularity among the voters. It would be unrealistic to think that Chamberlain had abandoned his hope of ever becoming Prime Minister. If Balfour called an election then it might well be 'Joe's victory'. A defeat might mean the end of Balfour, and Chamberlain could dispute the leadership.

Chamberlain's resignation was soon followed by another, much to Balfour's irritation. Lord Hartington, now the Duke of Devonshire, resigned in October 1903. He was a leading Liberal Unionist and Free Trader and his departure served to underline the deepening crisis. It also served to invigorate the Liberal Party, by uniting them in a zealous cause after so many years when they 'had been hopelessly divided on all the main political issues. This is quite an achievement for any campaign.' (Robert Blake)

Would food be dearer? Asquith was able to rouse Labour and the

'Whole Hoggers': Chamberlain's supporters who favoured tariff reform.

'Free Fooders': Supporters of free trade.

'Balfourites': These Conservatives who backed the Prime Minister.

A party election poster of 1906 attacking the Conservatives.

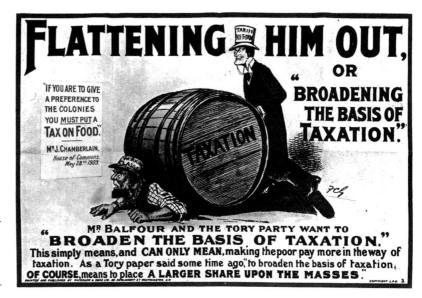

FLATTENING HIM OUT, OR "BROADENING THE BASIS OF TAXATION."

"IF YOU ARE TO GIVE A PREFERENCE TO THE COLONIES YOU MUST PUT A TAX ON FOOD."

Mr J. CHAMBERLAIN. *House of Commons. May 28th 1903.*

" Mr BALFOUR AND THE TORY PARTY WANT TO **BROADEN THE BASIS OF TAXATION.**" This simply means, and CAN ONLY MEAN, making the poor pay more in the way of taxation. As a Tory paper said some time ago," to broaden the basis of taxation, OF COURSE, means to place A LARGER SHARE UPON THE MASSES."

How useful is this poster to a historian studying why the Liberals won the 1906 general election?

working class by raising the spectre of expensive food – the legendary 'little loaf' of Chamberlain's making, compared with the Liberal 'large loaf'. There was considerable doubt as to whether the Conservatives were so keen on spending the alleged benefits of tariff reform on social reform, as Chamberlain said they were. Their record so far was unimpressive in trying to help those disadvantaged sections of society. This all helped to cement the electoral pact with Labour and did immense harm, which not even Chamberlain could reverse.

Balfour did his best to stagger on, putting off an election he thought he might lose and refusing to give his complete backing to Chamberlain's views. Joseph Chamberlain wanted an election hoping that the Liberals might self-destruct over Home Rule.

What did the voters think? It appeared that the more they heard, the less they liked. It was difficult to break the link between free trade and prosperity, which had served Britain so well for decades. It did not help that Chamberlain was never a wholehearted protectionist; he merely sought to give some temporary respite to the British economy.

Nevertheless, Chamberlain was convinced the case had been won in the Party, quoting only 27 MPs who might be called Free Traders. The strains were too great and when Balfour detected the whiff of Liberal internal dissension over Ireland (Rosebery made a speech criticising Home Rule), he took the chance to resign in December 1905. Balfour had convinced himself that divisions between the Liberal imperialists of the Liberal League and the Radicals might make it difficult for Campbell-Bannerman to form a government. Indeed, there was a plot of sorts. Three Liberal imperialists – Asquith, Grey and Haldane – had met at Grey's Scottish fishing lodge where they agreed to a compact. All three would not join the government unless Campbell-Bannerman ('C-B') went to the House of Lords and Asquith became Leader of the Commons. 'C-B' was having none of it; his offer to Asquith of the Exchequer was enough to break up the conspiracy and the others were to succumb to the lure of office and personal advancement too.

Campbell-Bannerman called an election for January 1906. The results were sensational. The Unionists were reduced to 157, the Liberals rose to 377. This gave the Liberals a huge majority, even bigger when their political allies were counted in – something of the order of 350 seats. While the Government did introduce some sensible legislation in the fields of education, licensing laws and Irish land reform, it was to no avail.

1. Why did

(a) the Taff Vale Case

(b) the Education Act, 1902

cause problems for Balfour's Government?

2. Put forward a set of ideas for and against the introduction of tariff reform in Britain.

3. Which set of arguments do you find most convincing? Give reasons to support your answer.

4. How far was Balfour responsible for the Conservative election defeat of January 1906?

3.6 Why did the Liberals win a landslide victory in January 1906?
A CASE STUDY IN HISTORICAL INTERPRETATION

The scale of the Liberal victory in 1906 continues to be the focus of debate. The overwhelming impression was that the Conservatives had been in power too long. Given 'Balfour's propensity to stir up a hornets' nest by his … methods of dealing with longstanding problems' (E.J. Feuchtwanger), the Conservatives looked not only like a party divided but also like one which seemed to misjudge the mood of the country and its own policies. The Liberals, on the other hand, appeared united and re-invigorated by a return to some of its traditional causes – primarily free trade, which proved to be the central feature of the election campaign.

What conclusions can be drawn from an analysis of the results?

The Conservatives slumped from the 402 seats won in 1900 to 157, its smallest number since 1832. The Liberals, however, increased from 184 to 377 (or 401 counting the 24 'Lib–Labs'). This reversal appears less dramatic when votes are taken into account. The Liberals gained just under 50 per cent, compared with 43 per cent for their opponents. Historians K.W.W. Aitkin and Robert Blake maintain that the number of votes per opposed candidate for the Conservatives was much the same in 1900 as in 1906; whereas there was a 25 per cent increase in the Liberal vote. This 'suggests … that the turnover of seats was not caused by a mass conversion from Conservatism to Liberalism but because a large number of people who had abstained in 1900 were stirred to vote for the Liberals – or – if one prefers it – against the Conservatives five and a half years later' (from Robert Blake's The Conservative Party from Peel to Thatcher). Recent analysis of Yorkshire constituencies adds weight to the view that an increased Liberal vote could have exaggerated effects because in many seats the winning margin was quite small in terms of numbers of votes. The **'first-past-the-post'** system translated into seemingly large gains of seats (for further discussion of this, see Simon Lemieux's article listed in 'Further Reading' on page 51).

'First-past-the-post': This electoral system, borrowed from horseracing, describes the situation where the candidate who gains the largest number of votes wins the election. Thus, someone would win in an election if they received 10,000 votes even if rivals all had 9,999 votes each.

What was the state of the Conservative Party and did it contribute to its own defeat?

Captain Richard Middleton had effectively oiled the Conservative Party machine up until 1903. His departure marked a decline in organisation, which undermined the Party's ability to fight an effective campaign. The historian E.J. Feuchtwanger has calculated that 27 Liberals were elected unopposed in 1906; whereas in 1900 the boot was on the other foot, when 143 Conservatives were elected unopposed. He also points out that 100 Conservative MPs retired, which probably meant a loss of 'personal' votes.

More serious was the loss of working-class support in once solid Conservative areas, such as Lancashire, London and the South-East. Why? The failure to reverse the Taff Vale decision was not the only issue. Chinese slavery and the 'small loaf' contributed to the conclusion that the Conservatives were unsympathetic towards working people, especially since the Government had been reluctant to introduce effective measures of social reform to alleviate living and working conditions. The historian Duncan Watts suggests that there was a momentum to the anti-government election swing. Since voting went on for three weeks, news of early swings to the Liberals in Lancashire spread elsewhere, which may have added further impetus to changes in voting.

Disenchantment with the Conservatives was apparent among the middle class too. Was this the effects of the Boer War and Chinese slavery which so badly tarnished the imperial dream? With the Conservatives so divided over tariff reform there seemed no objection to voting with the Liberals, who for once had managed to heal their differences. Neither was Home Rule such a prominent issue, so there could be no objections to voting Liberal on that score. Robert Blake argues that these factors partly explain how the Liberals were winning the central ground. His evidence for this was the drift of intellectual support (at the Universities) away from the Conservatives towards the Liberals.

Did the Liberals convince the voters that they should support a new party programme?

This is unlikely, as their programme was largely traditional. Opposition to food taxes, support for free trade, repeal of the Education Act of 1902 to please nonconformists, repeal of the Licensing Act of 1904 to satisfy the temperance lobby and the reversal of the Taff Vale judgement to please trade unionists. It was the usual message, but it did allow the temperance and nonconformist wings of the party to unite and present a vigorous front. Perhaps, then, it was this resurgence which did the trick rather than the substance of what was said. The Liberal programme on social reform, for example on old age pensions, was vague and there was no sign of that great wave of reform which began in 1908.

Did the Liberals rouse nonconformist support? Not especially, as H. Pelling discovered larger swings to the Liberals in areas outside the traditional nonconformist heartland. However, opposition to the 1902 Education Act certainly provided an opportunity for the Liberal Party to come together in the face of their opponents.

And what of the Labour Party?

1. Why have historians disagreed over the reasons why the Liberals won the 1906 election?

2. Do you agree that the Liberal victory of 1906 was a 'landslide' in name only?

The electoral pact with the LRC had been a success and it helped to establish Labour as a third force to undermine the Conservatives in key working-class seats.

L.C.B. Seaman targets the key issues when noting that 'The Liberals swept into power with sectarian prejudices on their Right flank, an angry trade union movement on their Left flank, and with their Centre marching triumphantly into the future behind the [free trade] ghosts of Cobden and Bright'.

Source-based questions: The rise of the Labour Party

SOURCE A

The ILP starts from the assumption that the worker should be as free industrially and economically as he is supposed to be politically … The men who are to achieve … reforms must be under no obligation whatever to either the landlord or the capitalist, or to any party or organisation representing these interests. Suppose, for the sake of argument, that 20 members would be returned to Parliament who were nominally Labour Members but who owed their election to a compromise with the Liberals, what would the effect be upon their action in the House of Commons? When questions affecting the interests of property were at stake, or when they desired to take action to compel social legislation of a drastic character, the threat would always be hanging over them that unless they… maintained party discipline they would be opposed. I have no desire to hold the seat on sufferance … I cannot agree to compromise my independence of action in even the slightest degree.

Keir Hardie commenting on the relationship between the ILP and the Liberal Party. Taken from Stewart J. Keir Hardie by William Stewart, published in 1925.

SOURCE B

… the LRC scored a string of by-election victories – at Clitheroe in 1902, and Woolwich and Barnard Castle in 1903. The significance of these developments has been much debated. It can be argued that the establishment of the LRC … was a vital staging post in the ideological as well as the organisational disengagement of the Labour movement from the tradition of Lib–Labism and that it represented a decisive move towards a more class-based system of 'industrial' politics in which the Liberal and Labour parties were bound to compete ever more fiercely for working-class votes. Conversely, it is possible to minimise the extent of the change that has occurred and to stress the basis for continuing cooperation between the two parties which were rooted in a common radical heritage. Despite the LRC's formal declaration of independence at its Newcastle conference of 1903, Liberal and Labour politicians were in agreement on most of the general political questions of the day. They were united in the 1900s by their opposition to the Unionist government and, insofar as they offered distinctive programmes to the electorate, their differences could be seen as complementary rather than competitive in their appeal. This last point is supported by the successful working of the secret electoral pact made between the Liberal chief whip, Herbert Gladstone, and the LRC secretary, MacDonald, in 1903 …

From *The Edwardian Crisis, Britain 1901–1914* by David Powell, published in 1996. The extract explains the historical strands that were the foundation of the Lib–Lab Pact of 1903.

SOURCE C

To the Electors –
This election is to decide whether or not Labour is to be fairly represented in Parliament.
The Trade Unions ask the same liberty as capital enjoys. They are refused.
The aged poor are neglected.
The slums remain.
Shopkeepers and traders are overburdened with rates and taxation, whilst increasing land values, which should relieve the taxpayer, go to people who have not earned them.
Wars are fought to make the rich richer, and underfed school children are still neglected.
Chinese Labour is defended because it enriches the mine owners.
The unemployed ask for work, the Government gives them a worthless Act …
Protection, as experience shows, is no remedy for poverty and unemployment.
You have it in your power to see that Parliament carries out your wishes.

From the Labour election manifesto of 1906.

---

1. Study Sources A and B.

How different are these sources in the views they express about the relationship between the Liberal Party and representation of labour in Parliament?

2. Study Source C.

How does the language and tone of Source C reflect the Labour Party's attempt to maintain a broad appeal?

Use the Sources and information contained within this chapter to answer the next two questions.

3. Was the electoral pact between the Liberals and the LRC the most important reason why the LRC was so much more successful at the 1906 election? Explain your answer.

4. Was the MacDonald/Gladstone electoral pact of 1903 the most important reason for the Liberal election victory of 1906?

Further Reading

Articles

In *Modern History Review*:
'A Rogue Result' by Simon Lemieux (Vol. 4 No. 2, November 1992)
G.D. Goodlad on Lord Salisbury (February 1996) and a series by Duncan Tanner
    on the rise of the Labour Party (November 1989, April 1994).

Texts designed for AS and A2 level students

On the Conservative Party:
Tories, Conservatives and Unionists 1815–1914 by Duncan Watts (Hodder &
    Stoughton, Access to History series, 1994)
Gladstone, Disraeli and Later Victorian Politics by Paul Adelman (Longman,
    Seminar Studies series, 1983)

As a general text:
Democracy and Empire, Britain 1865–1914 by E.J. Feuchtwanger (Edward Arnold,
    1985)

The following provide different interpretations:
The Conservative Party from Peel to Thatcher by Robert Blake (Fontana, 1985)
The Making of Modern British Politics 1867–1939 by Martin Pugh (Basil Blackwell,
    1982)

On the Labour Party:
The Rise of the Labour Party 1880–1945 by Paul Adelman (Longman, Seminar
    Studies series, 1986)
Labour and Reform, Working-Class Movements 1815–1914 by Clive Behagg
    (Hodder & Stoughton, 1991)

Biography:
Keir Hardie by Kenneth Morgan (Weidenfeld & Nicolson, 1975)

More advanced reading

Party and the Political System in Britain 1867–1914 by J. Belchem (Blackwell,
    1990)
The Rise of the Labour Party 1893–1931 by G. Phillips (Routledge, 1992)
Political Change and the Labour Party, 1900–24 by D. Tanner (Cambridge
    University Press, 1990)

4 The Liberals in power, 1905–1915

Key Issues

- Why and how far did the Liberals lay the foundations of the Welfare State?

- How far was the political crisis of 1909–11 a turning point in British history?

- To what extent had 'Liberal England' been undermined by a succession of pre-war crises?

4.1   What difficulties did the Liberal Government face under Campbell-Bannerman?

4.2   To what extent did 'New Liberalism influence government policy?

4.3   How far did the Liberals' social reforms lay the foundations of a Welfare State?

4.4   Why did the House of Lords' rejection of the 1909 Budget cause a political crisis between 1909 and 1911?

4.5   How successful were the Liberals in dealing with the political crises between 1909 and 1911?

4.6   Why were the Suffragettes a problem for the Liberal governments in the years before the First World War?

4.7   How successful was the Government in dealing with industrial unrest in the years 1910–1914?

4.8   Historical interpretation: The 'Strange Death of Liberal England'

Framework of Events

1905	December: Balfour's Conservative Government resigns
1906	January: Liberal victory at the general election
	Workmen's Compensation Act; Trade Disputes Act; School Meals Act
	Introduction of free medical inspection for schoolchildren
1908	Asquith becomes Prime Minister
	Old Age Pensions Act
1909	The People's Budget rejected by House of Lords
	Osborne Judgement
1910	General elections; constitutional crisis over powers of House of Lords; rise in militant trade union activity
1911	Parliament Act; National Insurance Act; Suffragette and trade union militancy
	Balfour's resignation; Bonar Law becomes Conservative leader
1912	Irish Home Rule Bill passes Commons, vetoed by Lords (became law in September 1914); Ulster Covenant; coalminers' strike
1913	Trade Union Act; Cat and Mouse Act; Home Rule Bill rejected; Triple Alliance of unions formed
1914	Decline in trade union violence; Triple Union Industrial Alliance formed; Home Rule Act passed but implementation delayed
1915	Asquith forms a National Government with Conservatives and Labour.

Overview

WHAT was the nature of the Liberal Party after their dramatic victory in the general election of January 1906? The figures suggested that the Party could sweep all before it:

Liberal MPs: 400, including 24 Lib–Labs
Conservative and Unionist MPs: 157
Irish Nationalists: 83
Labour MPs: 29.

The Cabinet headed by Sir Henry Campbell-Bannerman ('C-B') was not without talent. Its members had different opinions about the best way forward, but 'C-B' did manage to hold things together relatively successfully. The victory provided a majority of 130, which was even larger once political allies, such as the Irish Nationalists and Labour, were included. However, things were not as they seemed – there was little hint of that remarkable torrent of legislative reform which was to come after 1908. Few Liberal candidates had made specific references to social reform in their election addresses, although some had made vague references to the importance of introducing old age pensions. Instead, traditional Liberal ideas took their place at the head of the queue – such as ending the Church of England's hold on education, **temperance**, free trade, help for the unemployed, land reform, and perhaps some remedial help for the trade unions which were still paralysed by the Taff Vale judgement. Anyone attempting to identify a grand design of social reform would look in vain.

In many respects, it was 'business as usual'. Herbert Asquith, the new Chancellor of the Exchequer, kept the Treasury content with proposals for lower taxation and reduced expenditure. This was in line with old Gladstonian virtues of economies in government and *laissez-faire* individualism. Campbell-Bannerman was cautious, which may well have frustrated Radical Liberals and Labour members who were seeking more in the way of reform. John Burns, the first working man to take a Cabinet post – at the Local Government Board – was disappointing. Even someone who was recognised as a radical, David Lloyd George at the Board of Trade, had not yet seized the moment to take up progressive measures. These would come later, after 1908, during a remarkable period of social and constitutional legislation, which not only laid down some vital welfare reforms but also limited the powers of the House of Lords.

Temperance: The campaign to limit and then prevent the sale of alcoholic drink; associated with the pressure groups The Band of Hope Union and the United Kingdom Alliance.

1. Which of the issues mentioned in the mind map helped to lay the foundations for a future Welfare State? Give reasons for your choice.

2. Which issue mentioned in the mind map created the greatest problems for the Liberal governments of 1905 to 1915? Explain your answer.

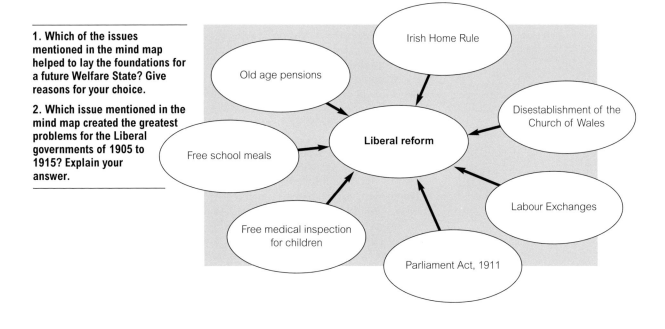

4.1 What difficulties did the Liberal Government face under Campbell-Bannerman?

Denominational schools: Those schools administered by a specific religious group such as the Church of England or Roman Catholic Church.

The new government's early legislation soon ran into difficulties. In 1906, an Education Bill which had in its sights Balfour's 1902 Act (see page 43) proposed that **denominational schools** should be taken into local authority hands and that the amount of religious instruction which could take place should be limited. The attack on the established Church of England would please nonconformists, but it failed to please their Lordships in the House of Lords. The Liberals discovered that the inbuilt Conservative majority in the House of Lords would again sabotage their programme – that of the newly elected government. It was a trial of strength which not only wrecked the Education Bill, but also two further bills. The Plural Voting Bill of 1906, designed to stop property owners voting several times, and the Licensing Bill, which aimed to limit the number of public houses (to satisfy pledges made to the temperance lobby), both fell in the Lords. The impression of a weak government which was beginning to stall or, as one contemporary put it, just 'ploughing the sands', is only countered by some worthy, if unspectacular (as far as the voters were concerned), measures to help children and workers.

The Trades Disputes Act of 1906 was a priority, given the call from Labour MPs for a reversal of the Taff Vale judgement. Campbell-Bannerman took an interesting line; faced with a cautious Liberal Bill, or a Labour Bill which would give the trade unions much more legal protection than they had enjoyed in the past, he chose the latter. The Act was passed and trade unions were made immune from having to pay compensation for damages caused by a strike. It was an important step which enshrined in law rights which were retained for over half a century. It was also a Bill that their Lordships were expected to reject, but did not, especially when there were so many working men's votes at stake. The Home Office, under Herbert Gladstone, rather surprisingly introduced some useful measures. Again, it was Labour influence which pressed for the Workmen's Compensation Act (1906). Employers would pay compensation not only when workmen suffered injury because of their work, but also for any diseases contracted through their employment. Payments would be made after only one week off work, instead of two. Mining MPs brought pressure to bear on the Government, who introduced a modest measure reducing miners' hours to eight and a half a day.

National Efficiency: A political view, popular among some politicians between 1899 and 1914, that if Britain was to maintain its position as a leading world power it had to improve the health and wellbeing of the British population.

The debate about **National Efficiency** continued following the 1904 report of the Interdepartmental Committee on Physical Deterioration, which had shocked the nation with reports of underfed children. A Labour MP introduced school meals, with government backing. The Education (Provision of School Meals) Act of 1906 did run into opposition from those who recognised that the State was taking a significant step forward in its provision. True, the scheme was voluntary, but critics saw it as 'socialism on the rates', and something parents should be responsible for anyway. Authorities only slowly introduced meals. The 1914 figure of 31,000 children receiving school meals sounds less impressive when it is remembered that only half the education authorities provided them at all. A further measure, in 1907, enabled medical inspections of elementary school children. Again it was not compulsory, but Sir Robert Morant, Permanent Secretary to the Board of Education, deserves credit for framing the legislation. Three-quarters of local authorities were providing medical treatment by 1914, and were clearly more active in this area.

For young lawbreakers, probation was introduced in 1907 to avoid their confinement with adult offenders. The Children's Act of 1908 went further. It brought numerous statutes together, banned prison for children under 14, introduced borstals for those under 16, and introduced special juvenile courts.

David Lloyd George, at the Board of Trade, was showing signs of initiating reform. His Merchant Shipping Act (1906) improved conditions of work for merchant seamen. He then managed to pour oil on troubled waters when he settled a threatened national railwaymen's strike.

The electors were unimpressed by the Liberal record as well as the trade depression which was beginning to make itself felt in industry. By-elections began to run against the Government. Ten were lost in 1907 and 1908, including Colne Valley, a Liberal stronghold snatched by an extreme socialist, Victor Grayson. Perhaps old age pensions would revive Liberal fortunes. A proposal to introduce this was long overdue, but had been delayed until the 1908 Budget. Asquith was preparing the measure when Campbell-Bannerman had a heart attack.

At 56 years of age, Asquith became Prime Minister of a talented Cabinet that, in the next three years, passed some remarkably successful legislation. Not that there were any signs of this in early 1908, when unemployment was rising, Labour allies were annoyed at the lack of progress on social reform and the naval arms race threatened the Budget surplus which was earmarked for pensions. Neither would the House of Lords look upon Asquith with any favour. Liberal legislation might again grind to a halt in the Unionist-dominated House of Lords.

1. What do you regard as the most important reform passed by the Liberals between 1905 and 1908? Give reasons to support your answer.

2. What reasons can you give for the electorate's disappointment with the 1905–08 Liberal Government? Explain your answer.

4.2 To what extent did 'New Liberalism' influence government policy?

Herbert Asquith (1852–1928)
Prime Minister 1908–16 and leader of the Liberal Party 1908–26. A firm advocate of Liberalism, but increasingly ineffectual as party leader in the 1920s.

'New Liberalism' was beginning to have a slow, if gradual, impact on sections of the Liberal Party, which was preparing the ground for its programme of social legislation – a programme which called for more government intervention to protect the weak, poorer elements of society. Mr Gladstone would not have approved. His *laissez-faire* attitude might have placed the emphasis on self-help and minimal government interference, but even moderate Liberals had recognised the need for more government action.

● The 'condition of England' question had made this more urgent. The decline in national efficiency had cast doubt on Britain's ability to maintain its position in the world.

● William Booth and Seebohm Rowntree had exposed and redefined the extent of poverty. They had shown that family size, low wages, unemployment, illness and old age, and the death of the family's wage earner were to blame for poverty – rather than lax working-class morality such as drunkenness and laziness. If adverse social and economic conditions were the root cause then there was a radical case for the State to provide a 'safety net' – a basic minimum benchmark of assistance.

● The poor state of industrial workers and army recruits made some Liberals wonder how Britain would compete effectively with the USA or Germany.

● The difficulties faced defeating the Boers in 1899 to 1902 had led Lloyd George to comment: 'The country that spent 250 millions to avenge an insult levelled at her pride by an old Dutch farmer is not ashamed to see her children walking the streets hungry and in rags.'

● In hindsight, the 'Great Depression' was perhaps not as severe as was once thought. However, it certainly undermined people's confidence at the time. It was no longer apparent that continued economic growth could solve the problem of poverty without more intervention from the State.

Collectivist: Opposite to *laissez faire*; describes the belief that government intervention in social and economic affairs can be of benefit to society.

● Public awareness of the trend to a more **collectivist** approach was growing after the passage of new measures such as the 1905 Unemployed Workmen Act (see page 43).

● Then there was the effect of having so many more MPs from the ranks of the working class – 53 in the 1906 Parliament. Were they so important in forcing the pace of change? Was the Liberals' response to the threat from the Left merely opportunistic? Historian Duncan Tanner (1994) has argued that 'Liberal theorists were developing their case for intervention long before the formation of the Labour Party in 1900. Very little (Liberal) legislation stemmed directly from labour pressure', although he admits that there were exceptions – trade union reform, school meals and payment of MPs. Nevertheless, the very existence of the Labour group must have crystallised the thoughts of Liberal reformers and 'Old Liberal' doubters alike – especially since there were vital working-class votes to be won. How might the Liberal Party adapt its traditional views and accommodate the rising expectations of the working class? Could 'Old Liberalism' adapt to the conditions of the age? Was 'new' Liberalism the answer?

'New Liberalism'

'New Liberalism' grew out of an intellectual tradition marked out by the teachings of Oxford philosopher T.H. Green, whose ideas were developed by L.T. Hobhouse and J. Hobson in the 1880s and 1890s. In 1893, the first meeting of the Rainbow Circle brought Hobson, radical Herbert Samuel (later a Cabinet Minister) and a number of prominent Fabian Socialists together. Government, they said, should take collective action to establish a national minimum standard of living. The arguments carefully built on traditional Liberal values of individualism. If people were impoverished, through no fault of their own, individual self-reliance was undermined. However, if the Government stepped in to guarantee a minimum standard of living, then the individual would be able to prosper. T.H. Green's idealism expressed it as the 'liberation of the powers of all men equally for contributions to a common good'. The Welsh nonconformist tradition brought a helping of social pity and a sense of Christian mission. The fruits of this activism could be seen when contemporaries spoke of 'municipal socialism'; local authorities were taking the initiative in education, sanitation, public health, poor relief – indeed a whole range of expanding services. There was, however, nothing remotely socialist in the programme of the young Liberals. If the socialists aimed to take over the wealth of the country, the Liberals wished to use that wealth to 'promote measures for ameliorating the conditions of life for the multitude' (Lloyd George).

Reforming 'New Liberals' could see the evolution of traditional party values. Nevertheless, tensions between the 'New' and the 'Old' Liberals remained. Were their differences ones of principle or strategy? Probably both. If the reformers stood for interventionism and a national minimum standard, they also stood for graduated taxation as a means to achieve it. Although still on a modest scale, taxation was seen as a way to shift wealth from the rich towards the poor.

The Cabinet, in 1908, remained unconvinced about the new course. Traditional Liberal values were still strong. However, the tide was turning. L.T. Hobhouse was campaigning strongly for 'collective action'; while, in

Gladstonian Liberalism: Its
principles were self-help, economies
in government, minimal state
interference and free trade.

1909, J. Hobson wrote that **Gladstonian Liberalism** had been replaced by a new 'commitment to a task which certainly involves a new conception of the State in its relation to the individual life and to private enterprise'. In other words, the emphasis on individualism and limited state interference was shifting towards more state activity so that people had 'equal opportunities for self-development'. Also in 1909, Lloyd George and Herbert Samuel began to argue for state intervention to protect individuals from the effects of unemployment, old age and sickness. Reviving the poor might stimulate business – such interests were close to Liberal hearts. Old Liberal individualism was changing its spots. However, the real influence of New Liberalism would not become apparent until Lloyd George and Churchill were in Asquith's Cabinet.

1. How did 'New Liberalism' differ from traditional Gladstonian Liberalism?

2. Which group was more supportive of New Liberal ideas, members of the Liberal Cabinet or grassroots Liberal supporters? Give reasons to support your answer.

Lloyd George's career, by any standards remarkable, coincides with these shifts in the Party. His historiography characterises him either as a social reformer and opponent of privilege or as a self-seeking opportunist who spoke of reform and used it to advance his career. Elements of both can be identified. His nonconformist energy would soon be harnessed to the crusading cause of radical reform, although there is little doubt that he recognised the political opportunities that presented themselves. At the same time, he made it more acceptable for the Liberal Party to embark on a new course. By 1909, the doubters in the Party were eclipsed – for the moment.

4.3 How far did the Liberals' social reforms lay the foundations of a Welfare State?

For mothers and children …
1906: The Education (Provision of School Meals) Act
1907: Notification of Births Act
    Medical inspections of all elementary schoolchildren
1908: The Children's Act

For the old …
1908: The Old Age Pensions Act introduced a non-contributory scheme, providing 5 shillings a week as a right to those over 70 years of age (7 shillings and 6d to married couples) as long as income did not exceed £31 a year. The full sum was only for those not earning more than £21 a year; between £21 and £31, pensions were on a decreasing sliding scale. The scheme, enacted through the 1909 Budget, cost between £8 million and £10 million.

For the sick and injured …
1906: The Workmen's Compensation Act forced employers to pay compensation to workers injured at work through accidents and related ailments.
1911: Part 1 of the National Insurance Act provided a payment of 10 shillings a week for a person who was off work because of illness. This lasted for 26 weeks, after which a disablement payment of 5 shillings a week was made. Treatment and medicines would be given free to the insured person but not to his family. A single maternity benefit of £1 10 shillings was paid on the birth of each child.
Who was to pay? For all workers earning up to £160 a year, the State would provide 2d, the employer 3d and the employee 4d – in this way it was claimed that the employee received 9d for 4d on an insurance principle – not charity. Low payments could lead to high benefit, given the balance of the insured risk.

For those out of work …

1905: The Liberal Government renewed the Unemployed Workmen Act. Distress Committees could be set up with grants to help provide work for the unemployed.

1909: a young civil servant, William Beveridge, inaugurated a plan for a national system of Labour Exchanges. By February 1910, 83 were open, and by 1913 this had risen to 430.

1911: Part 2 of the National Insurance Act helped about 2.5 million men in industries where the risk of unemployment was highest, e.g. shipbuilding, construction and engineering. An unemployed person received 7 shillings a week for a maximum of 15 weeks, as long as they had paid enough into the scheme beforehand. In context, the payments were quite low; they were a 'lifebelt' which might be added to any savings people might have.

And for the workers …

1906: Trades Disputes Act reversed the Taff Vale decision.

1908: Miners were to work a maximum of an eight-and-a-half-hour day.

1909: Trade Boards provided some protection for exploited workers in sweated trades, such as tailoring or box making. The Act enabled Trade Boards to fix minimum wages and maximum hours and for inspectors to report employers (who could be fined) who ignored the rulings.

1911: Shops Act granted a weekly half-day's holiday for shopworkers.

1913: Trade Union Act reversed the Osborne Judgement (which prevented members of unions from subsidising the Labour Party) by allowing unions, from a special political fund, to be used to support the Labour Party. People could opt out of the scheme if they chose not to make political payments of this sort.

Was this the 'foundation of a Welfare State'?

Definitions of the Welfare State vary from author to author. Some see it as a loose collection of social, medical and educational services provided by the State. Others see it as a comprehensive attempt not only to provide welfare but also to redistribute income, thereby serving the cause of social justice. By either definition, the Liberals fell short of providing a coherent welfare package – they muddled through, introducing changes which were modest by our standards. Such comparisons, though, are taken out of the context in which politicians found themselves at the turn of the century. A start had been made in the 1890s to establish a local structure of administration which proved invaluable as the Liberals studied other models of provision, mainly from Germany, and then started to make piecemeal reforms. All that Liberalism aimed for at this stage was to provide a basic minimum; it was always going to be a programme limited in its scope. On introducing old age pensions, Churchill declared that they never wished to take the 'toiler to dry land'. They sought only to 'strap a lifebelt around him'.

Whole areas remained unreformed – for example, housing was in short supply, and the dreaded workhouses would continue to have an influence for a number of years to come. Old age pensions and national insurance failed to go far enough. Pensions were not generous and not universal. Numerous people were left outside the scheme, such as ex-convicts and those who had not found employment for some time. The old, however, could emerge from the stigma of the Poor Law and a bold step had been taken. There is no reason to think that the statement 'God bless Lloyd George', recorded by Flora Thompson in *Lark Rise to Candleford*, was not widely shared. The achievement of passing the National Insurance Bills should not be underestimated either. Doctors had been dissatisfied with their level of remuneration, and insurance companies and friendly societies felt that their business was being threatened.

Labour Members of Parliament felt things did not go far enough and they had to be offered the payment of MPs before they swung in behind Lloyd George. Some workers felt that the exclusion of their families was unfair, although others resented the loss of 4d a week. Education continued to fall behind standards on the continent, particularly in Germany. For example, the amount spent on British universities lagged way behind German counterparts. Lloyd George and Churchill, the two moving forces, had been careful not to offend the wing of the Liberal Party which still held Gladstonian values. It is true that the extent of increased State, rather than local, interference was a new route for Liberals to take, but their view of collectivism involved the **insurance principle**. Recent research tends to imply that 'new' Liberalism had made inroads throughout the Party, but not as much as was once thought. Many rank-and-file members were true to traditional Liberal ideas.

Despite the lack of a long-term plan to fight poverty and despite the caution enshrined in the measures introduced, Liberalism was more dynamic and radical in reform than it had ever been. Many important principles had been established – a greater role for the State; the use of taxation and heavy expenditure to provide a basic minimum and help individuals to realise their potential. It is difficult to criticise the Liberals, who were making *ad hoc* (improvised) reforms to deal with specific problems, for reasons of both political gain and humanitarian concern. The Welfare State, with its commitment to Beveridge-style care 'from the cradle to the grave', is a much later concept. It should not be used to assess a Liberal programme, which never had anything as extensive as that in mind. Nevertheless, these early faltering steps were crucial to the later evolution of welfare services and the social service state. Churchill marked his satisfaction by writing: 'Beginnings are usually hard … but ten years hence all these bickerings will have been forgotten … We shall wonder how we ever could have got on without it, and a younger generation … will thank us for the grand achievement.' B.B. Gilbert explained the nature of this achievement, in The Evolution of National Insurance: 'They took British society into an entirely new field of activity, and although by no means solving the problem of the condition of the people, they settled the lines upon which the eventual solution would be found.'

Insurance principle: A form of self-help with State assistance to offset the worst effects of unemployment, sickness and old age.

---

1. Which group do you think benefited most from Liberal reforms:

(a) mothers and chiildren

(b) the old

(c) the sick

(d) the unemployed?

2. How far did the Liberal social reforms of 1906–14 lay the foundations of a 'Welfare State'?

4.4 Why did the House of Lords' rejection of the 1909 Budget cause a political crisis between 1909 and 1911?

Crossed the floor: Moved from one side of the House of Commons to the opposite side. In this instance, Churchill left the Conservatives to join the Liberals, on the opposition side in the House of Commons.

When Herbert Asquith became Prime Minister in April 1908, Lloyd George replaced him as Chancellor of the Exchequer, while Winston Churchill, who had **crossed the floor** of the House of Commons in 1903, occupied the Board of Trade. Both Ministers were prominent in a government remarkable for its vigour and pace of reform. Asquith tended to preside over this reforming Cabinet, rather than set matters in motion. It is generally accepted that he gave support, and helped to deal with administrative business with an extraordinary efficiency.

The Liberals faced a number of costly social and defensive problems. Old age pensions were a priority. 'Before this generation has passed away we shall have advanced a great step towards that time when poverty and wretchedness and human degradation which always follow in its camp will be as remote to the people of this country as the wolves which once infested its forests' (Lloyd George). But how would it be paid for?

Another concern was the German naval threat. Efforts to disarm at The Hague in 1907 had failed as was all too apparent when the Germans passed their Naval Law amendment in 1908. The race to meet this challenge by building a new generation of **Dreadnoughts** was given some urgency when George Wyndham, an opposition MP, coined the phrase which caught the popular imagination: 'We want eight and we won't wait.' This alone would cost £15 million.

So much depended on the success of the Chancellor's 'People's Budget' in 1909 – or what Lloyd George sometimes preferred to call his 'war budget' to fight poverty and squalor. However, Liberal legislation was vulnerable to the inbuilt Conservative majority in the House of Lords. Despite the Liberal view that an unelected House of Lords was undermining the democratically elected government, Balfour was not going to ignore the veto he had over government legislation. His often-quoted words confirmed that 'the great Unionist Party should still control, whether in power or opposition, the destinies of this great Empire'. Lloyd George replied by accusing the House of Lords of being 'Mr Balfour's poodle', although this should not suggest that the Unionists could act with any feeling of agreement. Racked by internal strife over tariff reform, they were able to agree that the new Budget and old age pensions were threats to an individual's rights over his or her own property. Would their Lordships veto the Budget? Custom suggested that the passage of money bills should not be interrupted.

Why did the Lords reject the Budget?

The Budget

The measures proposed would certainly, in Lloyd George's own words, 'hit the rich'.

David Lloyd George (1863–1945)
MP for Caernavon Boroughs 1890–1945, Chancellor of the Exchequer 1908–15, Prime Minister 1916–22 and Liberal Party Leader 1926–31. Lloyd George was both a radical thinker and wily political fixer.

● Income tax was increased from one shilling (1s) to 1s 2d for those earning over £3,000 a year.

● A new supertax of 6d in the £ was imposed on those earning over £5,000 a year. Combined, these taxes might only affect about 25,000 people in Britain, presumably few of them Liberal middle-income supporters.

● Increased duties were placed on spirits, tobacco, petrol; while a new road fund licence was introduced – some have regarded these as taxes targeted on the wealthy.

● However, the measures which proved to be most contentious related to increased death duties and the ownership of land; taxes which the moral wing of the Liberal Party had for long regarded would penalise income which had not been 'earned'. Workers laboured on the land or under it to create the wealth – the landowner merely spent the profits of other people's toil.

● This included a 20 per cent tax on the amount by which land had risen in value and half a penny in the £ on the increased value of land on which minerals were mined.

● These land taxes would require surveys of land ownership – literally, an intrusion into an individual's property holdings. Calculations were to show that the tax yield would be modest; the psychological impact on the propertied classes, however, was dramatic.

● Predictably, the Conservatives hated it. The Budget was defeated in the Lords by 350 votes to 75.

Historians have disagreed about Lloyd George's motives. Did he use the Budget to incite their Lordships so he could then diminish their powers, or

1. Why was the People's Budget introduced in 1909?

2. 'Hero or villain'. Which of these descriptions most suits Lloyd George during the debate over the People's Budget of 1909? Give reasons to support your answer.

did the drama unfold entirely by accident? It seems unlikely that the Chancellor engineered the Budget crisis and its outcome – such foresight might even have been beyond Lloyd George's control.

Was the budget inflated to guarantee its rejection? Again unlikely, as the costs of rearmament and pensions gave the Treasury some cause for concern. However, the possibility of the Lords rejecting the Budget must have occurred to the Chancellor. When they did so, he was alive to the possibilities. He grasped the moment to portray himself as a **philanthropist** – in a famous *Punch* cartoon Lloyd George was the highwayman, ready to hold up the rich with the words 'I'll make 'em pity the aged poor'.

4.5 How successful were the Liberals in dealing with the political crises between 1909 and 1911?

The significance of the Budget had gone beyond finance – the issue was now constitutional. The House of Lords had departed from established practice and rejected a money bill, but the next step the Government might take was not entirely clear. Asquith was cautious, Lloyd George less so, especially since by-election results seemed to indicate that an attack on the House of Lords might not be too unpopular. But if the powers of the Upper House were to be clipped, then how? Should a general election be called to place the activities of their Lordships in full public glare? For Asquith, this seemed a good moment to go to the country as the Conservatives were in something of a dilemma. Tory Lords did their case no good at all – for instance, the Duke of Beaufort was reported to have said that he would have liked to see Churchill and Lloyd George 'in the middle of 20 couple of doghounds'. If Balfour allowed the Budget to pass, it would look like surrender to the voters. And the tariff reformers, who were in no mood to surrender, would have probably split the Party. Reject the Budget, as they had decided to, and they stood accused not only of refusing to pay for Dreadnoughts and pensions but also of unconstitutional behaviour. Lloyd George seized on this: 'The question will be asked

Conservative election poster of 1910

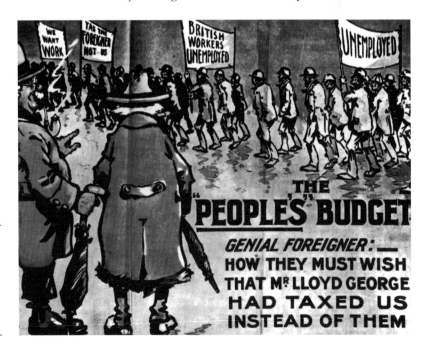

a) Is the poster for or against the People's Budget? Give reasons for your answer.

b) How useful is this poster to a historian as evidence of the public's view of the 1910 People's Budget?

whether 500 men … should override the judgement – the deliberate judgement of millions of people who are engaged in the industry which makes the wealth of the country. Who made 10,000 people owners of the soil, and the rest of us trespassers in the land of our birth …?'

A general election was called for January 1910. In a very high turn-out of 87 per cent, the result was close:

Liberals: 275
Unionists: 273.

The Irish on 82 and Labour with 40 gave Asquith his hold on power. John Redmond, the leader of the Irish Home Rule Party, had played his card powerfully, insisting that the Lords' veto should be scrapped, opening the way for a Home Rule Bill. The extent to which this 'no veto, no budget' threat was a real one is the subject of some controversy. For the time being, Redmond did support Asquith unconditionally – he had little choice.

The election also revealed that the growing tide of Labour gains had been stemmed. None of this was much comfort to the Cabinet, which was wavering and indecisive. Asquith gave no lead and it was at least two months before sufficient confidence had returned and the decision was made to proceed with a Parliament Bill.

● This would prevent the House of Lords from rejecting or changing a money bill.

● Other bills could only be delayed, becoming law if passed by the House of Commons three times (effectively a 'temporary' veto for two years).

● Parliaments were cut from seven years to five.

How would the Bill pass through the Upper House, as the Conservatives would be bound to reject it? Much depended on the attitude of the King. Asquith told the House that he would ask him to create sufficient Liberal peers to allow the Bill through. This would overwhelm the Unionist majority in the Lords. In the meantime, the Budget was pushed through the Commons and was grudgingly passed by the Upper House.

The progress of the attack on the Lords was suddenly halted by the death of King Edward VII, in May 1910. It placed the new King, George V, in a difficult position as he was reluctant to be involved in such a drastic political step so early in his reign.

The summer brought attempts at compromise. A Constitutional Conference brought the political leaders together. Nothing came of it. There was no escaping the stormy backdrop – the Budget, the Lords' veto, but most of all, Home Rule.

As the end of 1910 approached, the King did agree, in secret negotiations, that he would create sufficient Liberal peers, assuming that the contents of the Parliament Bill were put to the voters. The second general election of 1910 took place in December and produced similar results:

Liberals 272
Unionists 272
Irish Nationalists 84
Labour 42.

Attention turned to Balfour and Lansdowne, who now faced yet another uncomfortable choice – allow the Bill through and watch their powers be eroded or force the Government to ask the King to create about 250 extra Liberal peers. The Unionist position could hardly be described as harmonious; tensions continued to exist between those for tariff reform and those in the Party who were sceptical about its appeal to the voters. Once the

'Hedgers': They believed that the Government should give in because further opposition might mean the creation of so many Liberal peers that there would be a Liberal majority in the Lords, enabling the passage of at least Home Rule and anything else Asquith saw fit to put forward.

King's agreement to create Liberal peers had become widely known, the quarrelling among Unionists about how to deal with this erupted. On one side were the 'ditchers' who were willing to flex their muscles and oppose every part of the Parliament Bill – one writer characterised them as 'addicts of political machismo' (E.J. Feuchtwanger). They assumed that the Government would not carry out their threat and press the King into action. Facing them, were the '**hedgers**' who argued that if the Bill was passed then at least they would have some delaying powers left.

On 24 July, when Asquith told the Commons that the Bill would return to the Lords, there was such a barrage of abuse that he could not make himself heard for half an hour. Nevertheless, when the Bill reached the Lords for the last time, in August 1911, it scraped through by 131 votes to 114. The 'hedgers', who were boosted by the presence of the Anglican Church (in the form of 13 archbishops and bishops), had prevailed by voting with the Liberal peers – the Unionist dominance of the Lords remained intact but with only the power of delay. The Act proved to be a milestone for the Liberals and for the democratically elected Commons, although it had taken considerable effort, especially on Asquith's part. He had stuck to his task with determination and great political skill. If the Cabinet had sufficient energy left, the Liberal programme of reform and Home Rule could now be implemented. But it would be wrong to assume that a golden age of legislation and reform was about to dawn. 'Events' were to sap the Government as it faced turbulence from trade unions, Suffragettes and Ireland. For the Unionists, the three election failures to regain lost ground, particularly among the working classes, also exposed weaknesses in organisation as well as leadership. Balfour was no longer making the running and it was no accident that the slogan 'BMG' ('Balfour must go') was first heard among the tariff reform wing of the Party. In November 1911, Balfour decided to go, rather than wait to be pushed.

---

1. Why did it take so long to solve the political crisis caused by the ejection of the 1909 Budget?

2. How far were both the Liberal and Conservative Parties weakened by the constitutional crisis of 1909–11?

4.6 Why were the Suffragettes a problem for the Liberal governments in the years before the First World War?

The Suffragettes were militant campaigners who aimed to raise the profile of the women's suffrage movement through direct action. Reaching its height in 1913, the Suffragette movement attacked MPs who were opponents of women's rights to vote. Even the Prime Minister, Herbert Asquith, was attacked by an axe wielding suffragette when he visited Dublin. Suffragettes also engaged in other publicity stunts such as chaining themselves to railings outside the houses of prominent politicians and setting fire to pillar boxes. Acts which caused considerable public attention were the attempt to destroy the Rokeby Venus in the National Gallery, an oil painting of a nude woman and Suffragette Emily Davison fatally throwing herself under the King's horse during the 1913 Derby (see page 24). Even when arrested and imprisoned the Suffragettes carried on their campaign through hunger strikes.

The Suffragettes gained enormous publicity but had failed to convince a majority of MPs of their case by 1914.

For more information go to Section 2.2 on page 22.

4.7 How successful was the Government in dealing with industrial unrest in the years 1910–1914?

Along with Ireland and the Suffragettes, a period of bitter industrial unrest threatened the foundations of society and contributed to the end of liberalism, so it has been claimed. Socialist historians have attempted to identify worsening class conflict that manifested itself in the increasing number of violent strikes, which took place after 1908. They argue that the legal position of unions was threatened, especially after the Taff Vale case of 1902 – as was the rights of unionists to contribute to the Labour Party and have the voice of the working man heard in Parliament. According to left-wing theorists, this was the forerunner of the General Strike, which would challenge the Government and usher in a new form of society.

There is little evidence to support such claims. Much of it was either wishful thinking by comrades elsewhere, such as Vladimir Lenin who was observing events from afar or alarmists like the Mayor of Liverpool who asked that warships be stationed in the River Mersey during the Liverpool dock strike of 1911.

However, there was no doubting the ferocity and intensity of the wave of strikes with which the Government had to deal, although there is little evidence that class war was about to break out which would destroy Edwardian England.

Campbell-Bannerman's Cabinet had already taken steps to reverse the Taff Vale judgement (see page 42) and the years up to 1907 were remarkably quiet when compared with what followed. During that period, somewhere between 1.5 and 4 million days were lost each year through strikes. The figure jumped to over 10 million in 1908 and to 41 million by 1912. The catalogue of serious strikes began in July 1910. A railway workers' strike lasted four days, followed by cotton workers and boiler-makers. The worst outbreak was in South Wales where a simmering resentment boiled over into a riot in Tonypandy and at least one death. Winston Churchill sent troops to restore order; his reputation in the Welsh Valleys never really recovered from this. The dispute lasted ten months with victory for the owners who had resorted to using 'blackleg' miners.

The next year was no better. In June 1911, the sailors' and firemen's union went on strike and this led to 'sympathetic' strikes in the docks. Initially, this was unofficial but the National Transport Workers'

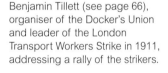
Benjamin Tillett (see page 66), organiser of the Docker's Union and leader of the London Transport Workers Strike in 1911, addressing a rally of the strikers.

Federation, formed in 1910 by Tom Mann, organised further disruption in the ports. The worst violence took place in Liverpool where two men were killed in clashes with troops. A national railway strike led to more deaths and Asquith only managed to head off a national strike when Lloyd George was brought in to handle the negotiations. He brought about a settlement by using the spectre of war against Germany to get the men back to work. The railwaymen gained much of what they set out to achieve and their unionised membership tripled between 1911 and 1914.

Three aspects of these disputes illustrate how organised unionisation still had a long way to go.

1. A common cause of the strikes was the refusal of employers to recognise the unions.

2. There was a remarkable degree of hostility shown to union leaders by their rank-and-file members; the latter were more militant than their leaders who tried to come to agreements with employers.

3. The Government was already showing how ready it was to intervene in disruptive disputes. At a time when there were no bargaining mechanisms, Liberals had to abandon *laissez-faire* principles in favour of helping employers and their men reach pragmatic settlements. It did not happen enough.

In 1912, the National Union of Railwaymen (NUR) was formed from three existing unions and this confirmed the move towards the creation of larger organisations. At the same time, the scale of stoppages also rose spectacularly – and alarmingly for the Government. The battleground moved to the mines where a million coal workers, by far the largest number so far, went on strike in support of their demand of a national minimum wage. The strike went on for three weeks before Asquith introduced a Bill that established a statutory minimum wage fixed by new District Boards, although it failed to satisfy union demands. The dispute was called off when a ballot of members fell short of the number needed to continue the stoppage. Not that there was any peace, because the dockers walked out next in London. This strike never gained any momentum, though, as the rest of the country declined to lend its support.

Ireland was not immune from union militancy, which must have added to the sense of crisis there. James Larkin, through the Irish Transport and General Workers' Union, organised transport strikes – the worst of which took place in Dublin in 1913. In the same year, the Triple Alliance was formed, comprising the Miners' Federation of Great Britain, the NUR and the Transport Workers' Federation. It looked like a formidable grouping of unions. Potentially, the Triple Alliance could organise stoppages that, if coordinated, would severely disrupt industry and the country. Was a general strike more of a possibility at the end of 1913 and the beginning of 1914? To answer this question, it is important to look at the causes of union militancy.

What lay behind the industrial unrest?

Was it the influence of **syndicalism**? Or was this period of strikes a response to prevailing economic conditions?

The syndicalist argument, which can be found in the writings of Cole, Halévy and Postgate, is partly based on an assessment of the impact of ideas – the ideas of Syndicalists such as Georges Sorel in France and Daniel de Leon from the USA. It does seem that important individuals were convinced by their arguments. One of the most famous was Thomas Mann, a key figure in the 1889 Dock Strike in London and the founder of the

1. Why did Britain have so many industrial disputes between 1910 and 1914?

2. How far was union militancy the product of a 'Syndicalist' revolt?

Syndicalism: Ideas that had spread from France which encouraged unions to combine in 'sympathetic strikes', supporting each other with direct action not only to win improved wages and conditions but also to undermine capitalism and governments so that a revolutionary state based on socialist principles might be set up.

Transport Workers' Federation. He published a journal called the *Industrial Syndicalist*, as well as forming an Education League to spread Marxist ideas. The movement managed to gain supporters in Ireland, with James Larkin, and in South Wales, where those miners who had been to Ruskin College Oxford (a seat of learning for working-class men) had been influenced by syndicalism. Groups such as the Central Labour College and the Plebs League spread the word and it was not a coincidence that it was in South Wales where 'The Miners' Next Step' was published. It called for one national union to call 'irritation' strikes so that profits would fall, enabling workers to take over all industries.

American syndicalists were particularly enthusiastic to see the creation of larger unions and the Triple Alliance of 1914 was seen as evidence of their influence.

On closer examination, many of these claims appear flawed. Syndicalism made few inroads into rank-and-file membership, which was more influenced by traditional liberal ideas and by economic conditions. 'The Miners' Next Step' of 1912 was followed in 1913 by a sharp decline in the number of days lost to strike action – down from 41 million to 10 million days. Things were equally subdued in 1914. Was this the expected revolution?

Tom Mann had not managed to gain nationwide support for the 1912 docks strike which had ended in failure. His claims of a rising tide of union violence leading to a general strike looked fragile. Neither did the Triple Alliance look too threatening despite the impact of mass, combined action. Its leaders were principally motivated not by thoughts of a general strike but by more practical ends. They wanted to strengthen their hand when bargaining for higher wages. They had strict rules for balloting members before a strike took place, probably in an attempt to prevent unofficial stoppages and so keep a grip on members. It is worth remembering that the militancy of union members was not always shared by the leaders, so the strikers fought them as much as the employers.

What other factors might explain the surge of union activity?

The 1906 Trades Disputes Act must have given unions the confidence to strike without the fear of being liable for damages. It could hardly be said to have provoked the militancy that exploded four years later. Might disappointment with the Labour Party be a factor? There is evidence that Labour was able to maintain its level of support although it was not in a position to make spectacular progress in Parliament or at the polls at the expense of the Liberals. It was seen as the junior partner of the Liberals, as a pressure group that had done solid, if not radical, reforming work. The Labour Party had lost a few seats in the 1910 elections, but this hardly constituted a disaster.

However, the impressions recorded by contemporaries was of a party which contributed little to the Liberal programme of reform except to vote for their legislation in the House of Commons. Ben Tillett wrote a pamphlet in 1908 called 'Is the Parliamentary Labour Party a Failure?' Labour seemed to be still searching for radical policies that would match those of the Liberals. The National Insurance Act was one case where Lloyd George was able to win over Labour's allies, namely the trade unions, and involve them in the operation of the Act. The historian Carl Brand concluded that Labour found itself 'dependent upon the Liberals, dissatisfied with its achievements, unsure of its aims, and apparently in decline'.

It is unlikely, however, that the industrial unrest was directed against the Labour Party, for two important reasons. Firstly, trade union members were more concerned about wages keeping pace with rising prices; secondly, the number of trade union affiliations to Labour rose by 50 per cent between 1906 and 1914. The miners had affiliated in 1909, deserting the Liberals. Labour might have been demoralised inside Parliament but support continued to rise for the Party outside Parliament (see also page 68) for Labour's success in local elections).

Was the Liberal Government to blame?

The Liberal Government was accused, for example, of not taking quick enough action to reverse the Osborne Judgement, which was certainly an embarrassment. Osborne, the secretary of the Amalgamated Society of Railway Servants, took his union to court for using part of his union fees to fund the Labour Party. This was called the 'political levy'. When the case reached the courts of the House of Lords in 1909, the levy was declared illegal. It effectively prevented trade unions contributing to Labour Party funds and election expenses – a situation not reversed until 1913. There was a feeling that the establishment was determined to undermine the Labour Party and the situation was made worse because MPs received no salary. This certainly had a disproportionate effect on working-class MPs and it was not until 1911 that Lloyd George granted all MPs a salary of £400. As the law had been turned on organised labour yet again, union activists were willing to turn to more extreme measures.

The George Dangerfield thesis – 'The Strange Death of Liberal England', published in 1935 – takes the view that the Government's failure to deal effectively with the industrial unrest is more proof that liberalism had been sapped of its strength and ability to cope with the pressures of class politics. This is now widely seen as an exaggeration of the Government's difficulties. It is true that, at times, the Government appeared uncertain and its response heavy-handed – hardly surprising given that unrest on this scale was a new phenomenon. Using troops against strikers was certainly inflammatory. But constructive work was done too. Lloyd George and Sir George Askwith were effective conciliators and, apart from passing a range of legislation to establish minimum wages and limit hours of work, the Government put in place mechanisms to settle disputes such as an industrial council and arbitration. If Liberalism was suffering a 'strange death', it seemed to have a remarkable amount of life left in it.

A far more convincing argument for the industrial unrest lies in economic factors. After 1909, wage rates were not keeping pace with rising prices. Inflation put workers into a position where they would have to defend their standard of living, at a time when people were concerned that Britain's economic supremacy was being challenged by powerful competitors overseas. Price inflation seems to have been worse in 1911 and 1912, coinciding with the period when wages fell most sharply behind the cost of living. Figures also show that it was manual workers who did particularly badly, earning a shrinking proportion of the national income. This is mirrored by the fact that those unions which were under pressure to defend wage rates were those who represented unskilled and low-paid manual workers.

Two sets of statistics require further explanation. A trade boom after 1910 soaked up the unemployed, and jobless totals fell from 8 per cent before this date to 3 per cent after it. Union membership also jumped from 2.5 million in 1910 to 4 million in 1914. The historian Pelling drew the conclusion that strike-breakers were in short supply as there were fewer unemployed, giving the rank-and-file more confidence to take action against their employers.

The current balance of opinion certainly favours these economic factors more than the 'political conspiracy' theories. Contemporaries were certainly alarmed by the unrest after 1910, just as they were sure that relative calm had broken out by 1914.

1. Why did people at the time think syndicalism was a major cause of industrial unrest?

2. How far was the Great Labour Unrest of 1910–14 the result of the Liberal Government's failure to deal with Britain's problems before 1914?

4.8 The 'Strange Death of Liberal England'
A CASE STUDY IN HISTORICAL INTERPRETATION

What was the condition of Liberalism at the point when the First World War broke out? In 'The Strange Death of Liberal England', George Dangerfield argued that Liberal decline could be traced to the period 1910–14 when a series of crises over the House of Lords, union militancy, women's suffrage and Irish Home Rule came together. They revealed a party which was unable to cope with, and adapt to, pre-war politics. Indeed, the decline of the Liberals was the inevitable consequence of the failure of the Party to alter views and articles of faith which were rooted in a different age.

Some historians have developed these views further. The 1906 election victory was regarded as a temporary revolt against years of Unionist rule; by 1910, with the loss of over 100 seats and a dependence on the Irish Nationalists to keep them in power, support was ebbing away. Asquith and his colleagues were, it is argued, unsuited to deal with challenges to the stability of the State and the Constitution. The Prime Minister, always a constitutionalist, was never able to understand the attacks made during the Home Rule or House of Lords crises.

Socialist historians such as Pelling claim that the problems created by union violence show that the Liberals were out of sympathy with the working class. In time, Labour would supplant the Liberals. Matthew, McKibbon and Kay show that, at local level, Labour was better organised and was making progress. In Leeds, for example, 14 Labour seats outnumbered the Liberals' 12. Labour was similarly successful in London County Council elections. Trade union membership was growing rapidly and it would give the Labour Party a politically aware base of support. The *Daily Herald* newspaper was founded in 1911 to spread and support the Labour message. Although the parliamentary party did struggle at this time, there is plenty of evidence of the vitality of the Party elsewhere.

A case has been made that 'new Liberalism' was making an impact with working-class voters. Peter Clarke's studies of Lancashire in 1971 found that Liberal social welfare was giving the Party a 'social democratic' face and a new appeal. Lloyd George's dynamism was the sign of a revitalised party that was holding Labour at bay. In 12 by-elections between 1910 and 1914, Labour failed to win one seat and lost three to the Liberals. It suggests a working-class base of support for the Liberals.

This view has not gone unchallenged. Pelling found that parts of the Liberal social welfare package failed to find favour with working-class voters. In 1986, Bernstein argued that even Liberals in particular regional areas were not as committed to 'new Liberalism' as they were to traditional articles of faith. He comments: 'Neither the new liberalism nor Liberal policies of social reform represented a fundamental re-orientation of the Liberal Party so that it could represent the interests of the working class rather than those of middle-class Nonconformists.' In a new study, G.R. Searle also questions whether the Liberal Party's reliance on business for finance fatally undermined its ability to appeal to the working class as a social democratic reforming party.

Duncan Tanner, taking a more balanced view, claims that neither side was making significant progress. 'A study of the Liberal reforms does not suggest that the Party was on the verge of collapse, but neither does it suggest that new Liberalism had effected its complete recovery.' As for Labour, it seemed unable to make inroads into Liberal support, remaining the 'junior partner' but with much potential. Had war not intervened, a new Lib–Lab pact was likely, enabling each to continue to draw on both middle-class and working-class support.

The last word should go to Trevor Wilson. In *The Downfall of the Liberal Party* (published in 1966), Wilson found that in 1914 the Liberals were showing strong signs of continued reform. But then it 'was involved in an encounter with a rampant omnibus (the First World War) which mounted the pavement and ran him over'. The war then led to a fatal split in the Party (1916–17), between the Lloyd George wing and Asquith's supporters. As Wilson comments, 'All that is known is that at one moment he was up and walking and at the next he was flat on his back, never to rise again; and in the interval he had been run over by a bus.'

If the war did the damage, were there signs of good health in 1914? On the one hand, Simon Lemieux believes that the Liberals in 1914 'cannot be given a clean bill of health; many worrying signs were there'. On the other hand, the worst of union militancy was over. The Suffragettes may have attracted considerable publicity but were hardly a threat to the foundations of the State. The House of Lords had been tamed by the Parliament Act.

Ireland had defeated the best efforts of politicians in the 19th century, but the Irish Problem became more acute after 1911 when Home Rule from Dublin was a real possibility. This led to the Ulster revolt as loyalists pledged that they would never submit to such a move. It brought Ireland to the brink of civil war. George Dangerfield drew on Asquith's failure to resolve this as evidence of disintegration of Liberalism as a political force. There are certainly valid arguments for criticising the policy of 'wait and see' and the policy of drift that contributed to the arming of Ulster and eventually of the Nationalist side. However, it is unreasonable to blame Asquith solely for not solving a complex and longstanding historical problem.

Had the Liberals 'run out of steam'?

Despite tensions between 'old' Liberals and 'new', Lloyd George was planning new initiatives. They included land reform, a minimum wage for agricultural labourers, security for tenants, and better rural housing. The war came and not too much changed. Voluntary recruitment swelled the Army, and emergency measures were taken, such as control of the railways and the Defence of the Realm Act. The Government ended its term in May 1915 after completing a spectacular period of legislation. This was hardly a sign of decline and defeatism.

---

1. Study the sections on the crisis with the House of Lords, the Suffragettes and the Great Labour Unrest in this chapter and the Ulster Crisis in Chapter 13.

What evidence is there to suggest that Britain faced a major social and political crisis in the years 1910–14?

2. Why do you think historians have offered different explanations for the social and political crises of the period 1910–14? Give reasons to support your answer.

Source-based questions: The Liberals, 1905–1915

SOURCE A

'I have one word for the Liberals. I can tell them what will make this ILP movement a great and sweeping force in this country – a force that will sweep away Liberalism amongst other things. If at the end of an average term of office it were found that a Liberal Parliament had done nothing to cope seriously with the social condition of people, to remove the national degradation of slums and widespread poverty and destitution in a land glittering with wealth ... then would a real cry arise in this land for a new party, and many of us here in this room would join in that cry. But if a Liberal Government tackle the landlords, and the brewers, and the peers ... then, the Independent Labour Party will call in vain upon the working men of Britain to desert Liberalism that is so gallantly fighting to rid the land of the wrongs that have oppressed those who labour in it.'

Lloyd George's speech in Cardiff in 1906 about the need for social reform.

SOURCE B

To many among the fathers of modern Liberalism, government action was something to be detested. They held, as we hold, that the first and final object of the State is to develop the capacities and raise the standard of living of its citizens; but they held also that the best way to do this was for the State to do as little as possible. Three causes combined to convert Liberalism from the principle of State abstention. The State's legislation was more competent and laws of regulation neither lessened prosperity nor weakened self-reliance as was foretold. It was realised that the conditions of society were so bad that to tolerate them longer was impossible, and that *laissez-faire* was not likely to bring the cure. And it was realised that extensions of law need not imply diminution of freedom, but on the contrary would often enlarge freedom.

Adapted from Herbert Samuel's writings in 1909.

SOURCE C

The outbreak of war in 1914 found the Welfare State in its infancy. The Poor Law was still the basis for the treatment of poverty, and unemployment benefits were low and limited in time. Treatment for ill-health, outside the Poor Law, was given to the worker and not to his family, and little was done for hospitals … In the wider sense of welfare, education was compulsory only up to the age of 14 … Housing still lagged behind even basic necessity, and social reform of all kinds was still inhibited by the old laissez-faire suspicion of state interference and still governed by the convenient permissive idea. Palliatives, rather than the radical programmes of reform, had been applied. Yet this kind of balance sheet tends to obscure real, if limited, achievement.

From *The Shaping of the Welfare State* by R.C. Birch, published in 1974.

1. Study Source A.

How useful is this to a historian studying the aims of the Liberal Party in 1906?

2. How far do Sources A and B agree about the reasons why the Government was taking a more active role in social welfare?

3. Study Sources B and C.

Explain how far the Liberal Government had laid the foundations of the Welfare State by 1914.

Further Reading

Articles

In *Modern History Review*:
Martin Pugh on votes for women (September 1990)
Ewen Green on the Parliamentary crisis of 1910–1911 (April 1996)
Paul Adelman on the decline of the Liberals (November 1989)
Simon Lemieux on the Liberals 1910–1914 (November 1992)
Duncan Tanner on 'New Liberalism' (November 1990)

Texts designed for AS and A2 level students

The Shaping of the Welfare State by R.C. Birch (Longman, Seminar Studies, 1974)
The Last Years of Liberal England, 1900–1914 by K.W. Aitken (Collins)
The Edwardian Crisis, Britain 1901–1914 by David Powell (Macmillan, 1995)
Lloyd George and the Liberal Dilemma by Michael Lynch (Hodder & Stoughton, 1993)
Democracy and Empire: Britain 1865–1914 by E.J. Feuchtwanger (Edward Arnold, 1985)
Lloyd George – The People's Champion by John Grigg (Methuen, 1978)
See also 'Women's Suffrage in Britain 1867–1928' by Martin Pugh (Historical Association, 1980) and *Electoral Reform in War and Peace 1906–1918* by Martin Pugh (Routledge & Kegan Paul)

5 The decline of the Liberal Party, 1910–1931

Key Issues

- How far was the Liberal Party in decline before the First World War?

- What impact did the First World War have on the decline of the Liberal Party?

- Was Liberal Party decline inevitable?

5.1 How strong was the Liberal Party in the period before the outbreak of the First World War?

5.2 How important was the First World War to Liberal Party decline?

5.3 Why did the Liberal Party decline after 1918?

5.4 Why did Lloyd George fail to revive Liberal fortunes in the 1920s?

5.5 Historical Interpretation: Was the decline of the Liberal Party inevitable?

Framework of Events

1910	Liberal Party wins two general elections in one year
1911	Parliament Act ends House of Lords' absolute veto on legislation
1912	Irish Home Rule Crisis begins
1914	Outbreak of First World War
1915	Liberals enter into coalition with other political parties
1916	Lloyd George replaces Asquith as Prime Minister
	Liberal party splits in two as a result
1918	Maurice Debate
	Franchise Act gives votes to women over 30 years
	Coupon Election
1923	Baldwin calls 'snap' general election
	Liberal Party reunites to fight election
1924	Liberals decide to support a minority Labour government
	Liberals suffer heavy defeat in general election
1928	Extension of franchise to include all women over 21
1929	Liberals again support a minority Labour government
1931	Political crisis: Labour prime minister, Macdonald, forms National government.
	Liberals split into pro- and anti-National government factions

Overview

O F all the developments in twentieth-century British politics, the rapid decline of the Liberal Party in national politics stands out as one of the most significant. By the outbreak of the First World War the Liberal Party had won three successive general elections, in 1906 and twice in 1910. A general election was likely in 1915 and the Liberal government felt confident it would win a fourth election victory. By 1931, however, the Liberal Party was a spent force in national politics – and was reduced to a small third party in the House of Commons.

The decline of the Liberal Party is linked inextricably to the rise of the Labour Party. It was the Labour Party, in the period 1910 to 1931, that eventually replaced the Liberal Party as the progressive party in British politics. What can explain such a change? Was the Liberal Party's decline inevitable or were specific events responsible for its fall. In the period 1910 to 1931 Liberal politics was dominated by two individuals – Henry Asquith (who died in 1928) and David Lloyd George (who died in 1945). Were these two politicians responsible, at least in part, for the Liberal party's declining political fortunes?

1. What do you regard as the *two* most important reasons for the decline of the Liberal Party?

2. Can you identify any links between the factors mentioned above in causing the Liberal Party to decline?

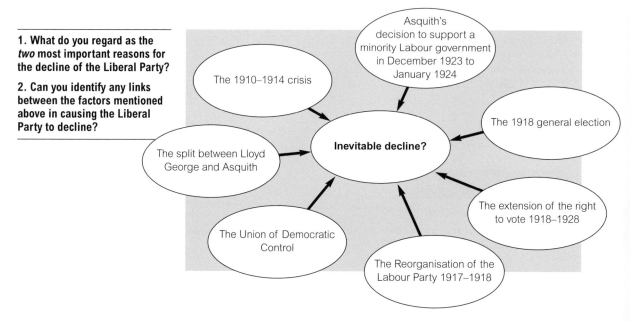

5.1 How strong was the Liberal Party in the period before the outbreak of the First World War?

In 1910 the position of the Liberal Party in national politics seemed very strong. By December 1910 the Liberal Party had won three successive general elections. As a result, the Liberal government was able to pass the Parliament Act in 1911, which brought about a major change in national politics. The Act removed the House of Lords' absolute veto on legislation, which had been a major problem for the Liberal government before 1911. The House of Lords was the unelected house – consisting of hereditary peers – which had a large Conservative majority. In the period 1906 to 1909 the House of Lords had vetoed important Liberal proposals on elections and licensing. In 1909 the House of Lords went so far as to reject the government's Budget, which sparked off a major constitutional crisis. It took two general elections in 1910 (January and December) to resolve it, and from 1911 onwards, the Parliament Act meant that the Liberals did not have to fear opposition from the Lords.

The major national opponent of the Liberal Party was the Conservatives. The Conservatives had been badly split from 1903 over the issue of tariff reform. This split had been healed by 1910, but the party lacked effective national leadership, and A.J. Balfour stood down as Conservative leader to be replaced by Andrew Bonar Law.

In his book *The General Elections of 1910*, Australian historian Neal Blewett pointed out that the Liberal government seemed to have a bright future. This view was supported by an important regional study by British historian P.F. Clarke, in *Lancashire and the New Liberalism*. The Budget of 1909 established the principle of progressive taxation. This meant that the rich paid more tax than the poor. The Conservatives supported tariff reform which planned to raise revenue by taxing food. This tax proposal would affect the poor much more than the rich. According to Blewett's and Clarke's views, British national politics was becoming 'class based' before 1914. In the long term this would mean that the Liberal Party would attract voters both from the poor and from the middle classes – a strong electoral base which should help the Liberals to remain a major force in national politics.

However, there were problems facing the Liberal government before 1914. In 1935 George Dangerfield wrote *The Strange Death of Liberal England*. He suggested that the Liberal government was on the verge of collapse when war broke out in August 1914. According to Dangerfield, the Liberals faced a number of inter-connected crises: the 'Irish Revolt, the Women's Revolt and the Labour Revolt'. The 'Irish Revolt' referred to the Ulster Crisis of 1912 to 1914 which brought Ireland close to civil war in 1914. The 'Women's Revolt' referred to the Suffragette campaign for votes for women. Finally, from 1910 to 1914 Britain faced major industrial unrest when miners, railwaymen and dockers launched national strikes.

Yet on closer examination the crises facing the Liberal government were less serious than Dangerfield suggested. The Suffragette movement made national headlines by their actions before 1914. However, by the outbreak of the First World War the Suffragette movement was in decline. The 'Cat and Mouse' Act, introduced by the government in 1914, dealt effectively with the issue of Suffragette hunger strikes in prison. Also the death of Emily Davison at the 1913 Derby, when she threw herself under a race-horse owned by the King, led to a fall in militant action.

The 'Labour Revolt' looked more serious. The outbreak of industrial unrest coincided with the arrival in Britain of radical socialist ideas from mainland Europe. The most significant new idea was syndicalism, which suggested that a social revolution could occur through concerted industrial action, which would be most potent in the form of a nationwide general strike. In 1914 three major unions, the railwaymen, miners and general workers formed the Triple Industrial Alliance. This alliance stated that if one of the three unions went on strike the other two would join them. This looked very much like the syndicalist general strike.

However, the main reason for industrial unrest was a rise in the cost of living (inflation), which led unions to go on strike to gain pay increases. The Triple Industrial Alliance aimed not to overthrow the government but to ensure that their strikes would be short and that the trade unionists would win.

The most serious crisis facing the Liberals before 1914 was Irish Home Rule. From 1910 the Liberals were kept in power because they were supported by the Irish Parliamentary Party. In return for this support the Liberals introduced a Bill to bring Home Rule for Ireland. As the House of Lords now had only a delaying veto for two years instead of an absolute veto, Irish Home Rule would become law in 1914. From 1912 to 1914 opponents of Home Rule (mainly in North East Ireland) protested against the measure. In 1912, they even formed their own army, the Ulster Volunteer Force, to oppose Home Rule by force if necessary. The pro-Home Rule faction in the rest of Ireland formed the Irish Volunteers to defend Home Rule. A potential armed conflict seemed likely by 1914. However, even before the outbreak of war in 1914, Asquith, the prime minister, was planning to exclude the six Ulster counties of North East Ireland from the operation of Home Rule, as a bid to diffuse the crisis.

Members of the Transport Workers Union at a mass meeting with a 'Daily Herald' banner.

Was the Labour Party a potential threat to the Liberal Party before 1914? The Labour Party had been formed in 1906, but by 1910 it had only 42 MPs. Although it was still a relatively small national party, it was split over what tactics to follow. Some Labour MPs wanted to offer general support to the Liberal government. Others wanted to support or oppose Liberal proposals on their merits. However, although small in number and internally divided, the Labour Party's future looked rosy. In 1908 the Miners' Federation of Great Britain, one of Britain's largest trade unions, switched support from the Liberals to the Labour Party. In 1911 the Liberals introduced payment for MPs, which greatly aided the Labour Party as many of its candidates were working men. In 1913 the Liberals passed the Trade Union Act, which allowed trade unions to use funds for political purposes, unless a trade union member expressly forbade the use of his funds for that purpose. This increased greatly funds available to the Labour Party. Finally, in 1912 the Labour Party launched two national newspapers, the *Daily Herald* and the *Daily Citizen*, which gave the Labour Party a national voice.

1. What was the most serious problem facing the Liberal government in the years 1910 to 1914? Give reasons for your answer.

2. Was the Labour Party a serious threat to the Liberals before 1914?

5.2 How important was the First World War to Liberal Party decline?

Britain declared war on Germany on 4 August 1914, after an intense debate in the House of Commons. At the time there was a fear that the Liberal government would split on the issue of declaring war. In the end, only one cabinet minister (John Burns) and two junior ministers (Trevelyan and Ponsonby) resigned. In her book, *Britain and the Origins of the First World War*, Zara Steiner suggests that the role of David Lloyd George was pivotal in keeping the Liberal government together. As Chancellor of the Exchequer, Lloyd George was the senior radical within the Liberal Party. He had vehemently opposed Britain's involvement in the South African War (Second Boer War, 1899–1902). Steiner believes that if Lloyd George had opposed entry into the war he would have split the Liberal government. In fact, Lloyd George became the most energetic and dynamic member of the government in prosecuting the war, being a great success as Minister of Munitions in 1915–16.

The impact of the war on Liberal principles

Entry into the First World War did, however, create a large number of problems for the Liberals. The need to mobilise the entire nation for war seemed to go against traditional Liberal principles. In 1914 the government passed the Defence of the Realm Act, which introduced strict censorship and gave the police the authority to arrest persons associated with anti-war activity. During the war, in a bid to maximise war production, the Liberal government had to take control over the coal mines and railway system. The most serious issue for Liberals, however, was the debate over the introduction of compulsory military service (conscription). Initially, the army could be filled with willing volunteers. However, by late 1915, the heavy casualties on the Western Front increased the demand for some form of compulsion. In October 1915 Lord Derby was appointed Director-General of Recruiting. He suggested an element of compulsion, which was introduced in May 1916. However, the huge losses sustained by the British Army at the Battle of the Somme (July–November 1916) led to the demand for full conscription. This issue was a major reason why Asquith was forced to resign as prime minister in December 1916, to be replaced by David Lloyd George. However, Asquith had never been comfortable as a war leader. In contrast, Lloyd George became 'the man who won the war'. He transformed traditional Cabinet government from December 1916, introducing an inner, 'war cabinet' for the more efficient management of the war. Lloyd George also recruited senior businessmen to run important aspects of the war effort, such as shipping. Finally, Lloyd George took over central direction of the entire war effort, both civil and military. His style of war leadership was emulated by Winston Churchill in the Second World War.

The Maurice Debate, 1918

Although Britain's direction of the war improved considerably with the appointment of Lloyd George as prime minister, the change of leadership had a devastating effect on Liberal unity. Asquith left the government and was supported by a large number of Liberal MPs. Meanwhile, Lloyd George led a coalition of Liberals, Conservatives and Labour. The split between Asquith and Lloyd George reached its height with the 'Maurice Debate' of May 1918. In March 1918 the Germans launched a last ditch offensive to win the war on the Western Front before the full might of the US army could be deployed. The German Army almost broke through the British forces of the 5th Army around Amiens. If they had succeeded they would have split the Allied Front in two. It was alleged that the British army lacked effective numbers of reserves to stop the Germans. Major General Maurice, a former Director of Military Operations, raised the issue in *The Times* and in the subsequent House of Commons debate Asquith launched a severe attack on Lloyd George. The debate was seen as a vote of confidence in the Lloyd George government. In the end the government won the vote, with 72 Liberal MPs supporting Lloyd George – but 98 Liberal MPs had supported Asquith. The war ended, but the split continued, and in the December 1918 election – the 'Coupon Election' – Asquithian Liberals and Lloyd George Liberals opposed each other.

A revolution in Irish politics

From January 1910 to the outbreak of the First World War the Liberals had been kept in power with the support of the Irish Parliamentary Party. In return for this support the Liberals introduced the proposal of Irish Home Rule. Events in the First World War shattered this relationship. At Easter

1916 a small group of Irish Republicans launched an uprising against British rule. Although the uprising itself was defeated easily, the execution of its leaders caused Irish public opinion to swing away from supporting the government and towards the radical Sinn Fein Party, which was associated with the uprising. However, the real turning point came in May 1918 when the British government attempted to extend conscription to Ireland. This united Irish opinion, with the Irish Parliamentary Party walking out of the House of Commons and joining Sinn Fein in an anti-conscription campaign. In the December 1918 election Sinn Fein won a landslide victory in Ireland, gaining 75 per cent of Irish seats, while the Irish Parliamentary Party lost most of its electoral support. In January 1919 most of the Irish MPs met in Dublin to declare an Irish Republic, and from then on the of majority Ireland's MPs did not sit in the House of Commons. Finally, in 1922, the Irish Free State was created, comprising three-quarters of the island of Ireland. The MPs from North East Ireland (Ulster) were predominantly Unionist and supported the Conservatives from 1922.

Labour reorganisation and development

In 1914 the small Labour Party in parliament was split. Some – mainly trade union-sponsored MPs – supported the war. Others, such as Ramsay Macdonald, the Labour Party Secretary, opposed it. The split widened in December 1916 when Arthur Henderson, a leading Labour MP, joined Lloyd George's coalition government. However, a turning point in Labour fortunes occurred in August 1917. A conference of socialists from across Europe was convened, aiming to devise a peace plan to end the carnage of the First World War. Henderson, as Britain's leading Labour MP, wished to go to the conference, which was in Stockholm in neutral Sweden, but he was prevented from doing so by Lloyd George. As a result, Henderson left the government. From then on he set about reuniting and reorganising the Labour Party, and in 1918 a new party constitution was approved. By December 1918, when the 'Coupon Election' took place, Labour had an effective nationwide organisation and was united around a strong socialist party programme.

During the war a group of disillusioned Liberals helped form the Union of Democratic Control. This group put forward the view that the war had been caused by secret diplomacy. It contended that if the populations of each of the belligerent states had been aware of their country's military and diplomatic commitments before 1914, then they would have openly opposed them. These views were adopted by most Labour MPs and, as a result, large numbers of disillusioned Liberal supporters joined the Labour Party. In many ways the rise of the Labour Party during the First World War had more to do with its views on foreign policy than its views on domestic issues.

The 'Coupon Election', 1918 – a turning-point?

All these changes had an impact on electoral support. In the 1918 election the Asquithian Liberals and Lloyd George Liberals opposed each other. The 159 Lloyd George candidates were issued with a letter of support signed by Lloyd George and Bonar Law, a letter which Asquith referred to as a 'coupon'. This 'Coupon Election' proved to be disastrous for the divided Liberals.

In the December 1910 election the Labour Party had attracted just 7 per cent of the vote. In 1918 this had risen to 22 per cent. By contrast, the Liberal share of the vote dropped from 43 per cent in December 1910 to 13.5 per cent for Lloyd George's Liberals and 12 per cent for the Asquithian Liberals in 1918.

1. What do you regard as the most important issue in the First World War which might explain the decline of the Liberal Party?

5.3 Why did the Liberal Party decline after 1918?

As the First World War drew to a close the conflicts within the Liberal Party intensified. Many of these were long-standing, but most arose immediately from the war itself. Several principles of Liberalism were victims of 'total war'. Censorship, for instance, offended the party rank-and-file. Conscription, both industrial and military, extended the coercive role of the state at the expense of Liberal belief in individual liberty. Asquith's reluctant acceptance of the need for military conscription provoked the resignation of his Home Secretary, Sir John Simon, early in 1916. **Free trade**, the guiding principle of 19th-century Gladstonian Liberalism, had also fallen foul of the war. McKenna's 1915 budget not only increased taxation, but introduced tariffs on luxury goods.

Free trade: International trade free from import or protective tariffs. Historically Liberals judged this vital both for the British Empire and to maintain peace.

Above all, tensions within the Liberal Party came to a head in December 1916, when Lloyd George replaced Asquith as Prime Minister. Along with many Conservatives, Lloyd George had long argued that Britain needed a more efficient, concerted war effort and that Asquith was not providing the necessary leadership. A historical view, blaming Lloyd George for conspiring with the Conservatives to remove Asquith and thereby splitting the Liberal Party into two factions, developed around the events of December 1916. Besides crediting Lloyd George with a foresight beyond even his undoubted skill at weighing up the political mood, this neglects both the extent to which parts of the party supported Lloyd George and the extent to which Asquith and his supporters were actively opposed to the government. While refusing to serve under Lloyd George and sitting on the opposition benches, Asquith initially promised the Coalition an attitude of 'general support'. Nonetheless, from 1917, as the historian Alan Sykes has argued, the Liberals were split between 'a leader who was no longer prime minister, and a prime minister who was not leader of the party'.

What impact did the 'Coupon' election of 1918 have on the Liberal Party?

When the first general election since 1910 was declared for December 1918, there were, effectively, two Liberal Parties in existence. The differences that emerged in 1916 had hardened into opposition. Broadly the Liberal idea of individual freedom was in conflict with the desire to fight the war effectively. During the war there were sharp clashes over the extension of duties on Indian goods, extending conscription to Ireland and excluding conscientious objectors from the franchise under the new Representation of the People Act. Most historians consider that the Maurice Debate of May 1918, when Asquith (for the only time) led opposition to the Coalition over the inaccuracy of War Office troop figures, cemented the divide within the party. Treating it as a vote of confidence in his government, Lloyd George won backing from 71 Liberals, but 98 voted against. In parliament separate **whips** operated for each group, but local Liberal Associations were increasingly partisan - mostly backing the Asquithians.

Whips: MPs of a party responsible for ensuring MPs support that party's position in the House of Commons.

The allegiance of the local associations was important in Lloyd George's calculations in 1918. With an electorate expanded threefold from 1910 to some 21 million, constituency organisation was essential. Despite some negotiations for reunion with the rest of the Liberal Party, the Prime Minister decided to continue the Coalition, issuing a coupon, signed by himself and Conservative leader Bonar Law, to approved candidates. Seats were divided between 374 Conservatives and 159 Lloyd George Liberals. In some seats Coalition Liberals backed Conservatives against Liberals and likewise Liberals backed Labour rather than Coalition candidates. In this election, with war having ended only a month earlier, the coalition won a landslide with 332 Conservatives and 133 Coalition Liberals returned. By contrast only 28 Asquithians won: John Simon, Reginald McKenna, Herbert Samuel and Asquith himself, in East Fife, were all defeated.

The Conservatives were the main beneficiaries of the 'coupon' election. However, the coalition programme had been radical in its proposals for social reform and reconstruction, and had gained Asquith's approval. Liberal ministers, notably Fisher at Education and Addison at Housing, acted on this programme and fought against the 'Geddes Axe' of 1922. This cut public spending after recession took hold late in 1920. As a result the position of the **'wee free'** Independent Liberals seemed uncertain. Even when Asquith returned to parliament in 1920 he provided only weak leadership. The differences between Liberals, to most voters, seemed more a question of personality than policy.

The electoral position of the Coalition Liberals was no more certain however. In Parliament they depended upon Conservative support and lacked real party and constituency organisation. Their successes in 1918 had come on a wave of patriotism at the victorious end of the war and by avoiding Conservative opponents in the election via the 'coupon'. These were conditions unlikely to last for long.

Lloyd George was aware of this problem. Through 1919 and 1920 there was discussion of a formal union with the Conservatives to form a 'centre party', a large anti-socialist grouping. This further split the Liberals. At the 1920 National Liberal Federation General Meeting in Leamington Spa, Coalition Liberals who attended were denounced and forced to withdraw. In the aftermath of Leamington Spa the Lloyd George constituency organisations, as many as 220, supported from the Prime Minister's own fund, were created. Competing magazines, the *Liberal Magazine* and *Lloyd George Liberal Magazine* were published. Division was now spread throughout the party.

'Wee free': Nickname of the Independent Liberal MPs after 1918 - opposed to the Coalition and its Liberal supporters.

1. What evidence is contained in the cartoons to suggest that Lloyd George was responsible for the decline of the Liberal Party?

2. Of what value are these cartoons to a historian writing about the decline of the Liberal Party in the early 1920s?

INTO THE LIMELIGHT.

THE COLOSSUS: A TALE OF TWO TUBS.

Two cartoons from *Punch* magazine from the early 1920s

Why did Liberal support erode?

This question needs to be addressed in relative terms and over the broad inter-war period. It was the party's failure to expand its support that was crucial and failure was often due to the number of candidates it could field. In the 1924 election (the third in three years) the party could only afford to run 346 candidates. In itself this suggested its third-party status. The party's proportion of the electorate fell dramatically, from 29 per cent in 1922 to 10.7 per cent in 1931. Only in 1929 did it receive more than 5 million votes, still a smaller volume than Labour in its heavy defeat of 1931.

The divisions within the Liberal Party were not solely responsible for the party's declining support. The expansion in the size of the electorate in 1918 meant effective local organisation was now vital for political parties. Compared with Labour, Liberal local organisation was poor. Labour in 1918 had reorganised its constituency structure and had the financial support of the trade unions. The organisational and financial strength of the Conservatives was also strong. Besides the lack of morale caused by divisions among the party leaders this lack of funds meant that fewer candidates could be fielded. Herbert Gladstone at the party HQ reported that organisers and activists were drifting away into the Conservative and Labour parties. Survival was achieved in cases such as Sheffield and Bristol through the creation of local alliances with Conservatives. Elsewhere Liberal local government representation, especially after the disastrous 1919 elections, went into rapid decline.

Without resources of finance and personnel the Liberals struggled to appeal to the new working-class and women voters. To many historians the rise of class politics in this period signalled the decline of the Liberals, caught between Labour and the Conservatives. Certainly, the Conservative and Labour votes were more geographically concentrated, in Southern and suburban, and industrial working-class constituencies respectively. This was vital in the first-past-the-post British electoral system. The Liberals had more even distribution.

The rise of Labour, especially in the industrial working-class areas, eroded the Liberal vote; it was against Labour opponents more than Conservatives that the Liberals struggled in the inter-war period. Mining areas which Liberals had held were solidly Labour by 1922. The Liberals were also less at ease with the growing influence of trade unionism than Labour. However, since the Conservatives also polled heavily among many of the new voters and Labour struggled in cities such as Liverpool and Bristol, class was clearly not the only factor behind voting behaviour.

Non-conformist: A Protestant who is not a member of the Church of England. Religious groups include Methodists, Baptists and Quakers.

1. What factors contributed to the divisions in Liberalism in the 1920s?

2. Why did Labour replace the Liberals as the main opposition to the Conservative Party?

Labour was increasingly able to pose as the alternative to the Coalition government. Lloyd George took a heavy-handed attitude. He used the force of the state against Labour unrest in the 1920 miners' strike. This contributed to the impression that Liberalism was neglecting the working class. On issues such as housing, unemployment, foreign and Irish policy, Labour benefited from the absence of distinctive Liberal leadership by Asquith. In by-elections against the Coalition, Labour picked up 14 seats between 1918 and 1922. The Asquith Liberals were not always able to field candidates and after 1919 only picked up two seats in Louth and Bodmin, the rural, **non-conformist**, Celtic fringes of Britain, which remained the party's only firm strongholds.

5.4 Why did Lloyd George fail to revive Liberal fortunes in the 1920s?

Sale of honours: Allowing individuals to buy hereditary peerages and knighthoods.

In 1922 the Conservatives withdrew from the Coalition. A central figure in this was Stanley Baldwin, the Conservative leader from 1923 to 1937. Baldwin was concerned that if the coalition continued the Conservatives would be associated with the corruption of Lloyd George's **sale of honours** (see chapter 7) and that Lloyd George might split the Conservatives just as he had done the Liberals. Baldwin's suspicion of Lloyd George's conspiring, historian Maurice Cowling has argued, led him to enter into a loose agreement with Labour leader Ramsay Macdonald to keep Lloyd George out of government.

The 1922 election exposed the weakness of the National (ex-Coalition) Liberals under Lloyd George. He was out of government for the first time in 16 years. The Liberals were reduced to 62 seats, despite the fact that most (and especially those in Scotland) were spared Conservative opposition. It also showed the divisions within Liberalism: National and Independent Liberals fought each other in several seats and in some there were even three Liberal candidates. The Independent Liberals increased their representation to 54, winning 32 seats from the Conservatives, but only one from Labour. Labour now outnumbered the Liberals and included some former Liberals within its ranks.

Reunion and revival?

The defeat of 1922 placed the possibility of reunion back on the agenda of Liberal politics. There were moves towards this, although they were strictly limited. This was due to Asquith's mistrust of Lloyd George and his overtures towards Labour and the continuing links between ex-Coalitionists and the Conservatives. By 1923, while the competing magazines had ceased publishing, Lloyd George was still reluctant to free up his fund for the Liberal Party or his separate HQ. What succeeded in uniting the Liberals was Baldwin's declaration in favour of protection at the end of 1923.

Liberal leaders were able to unite in defence of Free Trade. It says something about the condition of Liberal politics that it took a Conservative leader to achieve what two Liberal Prime Ministers could not. Local associations were revived by the old battle-cry of Free Trade. Substantial finance was forthcoming from the Lloyd George Fund. Despite this, Lloyd George allowed Asquith to lead the united party. This was because his supporters lacked a national constituency organisation. The Liberals defended the status quo and promised unspecified social reforms. Asquith argued that protection would push up food prices. Various schemes such as the extension of unemployment insurance and state investment in the economy were proposed to tackle unemployment. While Labour also defended Free Trade, Liberals criticised its ideas for the nationalisation (state ownership) of industry.

The Liberals won 158 seats, polling well in many of its traditional and nonconformist regions - the west country and the industrial north-west. Some 69 seats were won from Conservatives, but only 13 from Labour, with voting in northern England, South Wales and the Midlands (Derby, Leicester) demonstrating the Liberals' diminishing working-class support. Baldwin's protectionism had suffered a clear rebuff, with 258 Conservatives in the new parliament weighed against the Liberals and 191 Labour MPs after the Free Trade election.

The Liberal leadership was once more divided over its course of action. With the balance of power within the Liberal Party in Asquith's favour, the prospect of co-operating with the Conservatives was unpopular. Equally, outright alliance with the Labour Party was feared. Ultimately, a policy of independence was pursued, supporting Labour with the hope of influencing the policy of Macdonald's inexperienced administration. For such a strategy the Liberals required a united leadership to put pressure on Labour. Asquith adopted a rather passive attitude, awaiting Labour's failure. Lloyd George, on the other hand, while hoping that Labour would push reform (including electoral reform) forwards, was also hoping for an anti-socialist coalition with the Conservatives. Neither Baldwin nor Macdonald looked favourably upon such manoeuvring, and divisions between the Liberal leaders were reinforced. Yet the Liberal factions needed each other. Lloyd George and his supporters were increasingly aware that given limited prospects for coalition, they needed the party machine as a base. Under Asquith's control, the party organisation remained poverty-stricken and in need of the Lloyd George Fund.

The division meant that for the 1924 election (the third since 1922), Lloyd George was prepared to give only £50,000 to the party (compared with £160,000 for the 1923 contest). The upshot of this was that the Liberals fielded only 346 candidates, received less than 3 million votes and were reduced to a mere 40 MPs. Beyond the Celtic Fringe (North Wales, Scottish Highlands) the Liberals were decimated - losing 63 of the 67 English county seats won in 1923.

Lloyd George and new policies?

The 1924 result suggested that the Liberals were not seen as an alternative to Labour or the Conservatives. During the campaign, historian Chris Cook argues, 'the Liberals said nothing not being said already by Labour or Conservative'. The lack of a distinctive identity and original policies had blighted Liberal prospects since 1918. In 1923 this had been obscured by the defence of Free Trade, but by 1924 with the Conservatives abandoning protectionism and securing a landslide victory, the shortcomings of Liberal thinking and policy were more evident. Too easily Liberals in the 1920s resorted to outdated Victorian Liberal ideas in the absence of thoughts on the modern world. In addition, there was the lack of leadership provided by Asquith, who was defeated in 1924. Lloyd George, for good or ill, was a 'dynamic force' and one recognised as bringing ideas into the party, while being in no sense bound by them.

From 1921 the Liberal **Summer School movement**, founded by radicals like E. D. Simon and Ramsay Muir of the Manchester Liberal Federation, had served as a forum for debate and new policies within Liberalism. They had attempted to build upon pre-war New Liberalism and its belief in the positive, interventionist role of the state in securing the 'common good', an idea that came out of **John Stuart Mill**'s thinking. They also supported more traditional Liberal ideas of individual liberty and choice. The war had emphasised the more coercive role of the state. In the 1920s the competing interests of capitalism and labour (especially in industrial conflict and unemployment) made it more difficult for Liberal policy to claim to represent the 'common good'. New thinking was necessary to revive both the party and Liberalism itself.

From 1924 Lloyd George chose to appoint expert officials on inquiry panels to devise new policies. Such panels drew from the personnel of the 'summer schools'. The Land Inquiry Committee in 1925 published *Land and the Nation*. (Because of the colour of its cover it was known as the 'Green Book'.) It advocated state purchase of land. This would be leased to those who would use or cultivate it wisely and productively. *Coal and Power* (1924) had proposed a similar scheme for the mining industry.

However, re-thinking was inevitably linked to in-fighting within the Liberal Party. Such proposals were seen as too close to socialist nationalisa-

Summer School movement: A forum for Liberal policy discussion, independent of the party, founded in 1921. Intellectuals such as Keynes and Beveridge were among the participants. It was influential on Lloyd George's policy in the later 1920s.

John Stuart Mill: Liberal philosopher, 1806–73.

tion or too interfering on the part of the state for many Liberals. The fact that Lloyd George kept these panels independent of official Liberal organisation and funded them himself, also provoked opposition. Lloyd George was reluctant to release his fund to an inefficient party machine. To critics it seemed that Lloyd George, through these committees and organisations like the Land and Nation League, formed late in 1925, was creating a powerbase at the expense of the Liberal Party. As ever, lack of finances, after the failure of the 1925 'Million Fund', was central to Liberal problems. Lloyd George had offered to fund the party for three years in return for it adopting his land policy and this had deepened inner-party conflicts. By early 1926, when the land proposals were limited to acquisition of land for sale, some compromise had been reached.

However, by mid-1926 divisions had arisen once more. The Liberal position on the General Strike of May 1926 was to condemn the TUC for a constitutional challenge to the government. Lloyd George, now in more radical mood, argued that the government as much as the unions was worthy of condemnation and that a negotiated settlement was needed. Asquith turned on his old enemy. While Lloyd George's position as party chairman was secure, his position in the Liberal shadow cabinet was not. However, a stroke forced Asquith to resign as party leader in October and only Lloyd George had the qualities of leadership and wealth to help the party. With Lloyd George as leader, the old-guard followers of Asquith in the party, especially those who ran its organisation, such as Vivian Phillips, Herbert Gladstone, and Walter Runciman, withdrew. Herbert Samuel, not only an effective operator, but a neutral figure in party factionalism, was appointed chair of the organisation committee in 1927. Re-organising the party and promising to finance it for three years put the Liberal Party firmly under Lloyd George's control.

The Yellow Book and the 1929 general election

From 1925 the Liberal Industrial Inquiry, which included such luminaries as E.D. Simon, Ramsay Muir, Seebohm Rowntree, economist John Maynard Keynes, Herbert Samuel and Lloyd George himself, had been considering questions of industry and unemployment. In 1928 their conclusions, *Britain's Industrial Future* (the 'Yellow Book') were published. Its proposals were for government loans (more than £200 million) for public works such as electrification and road-building, a national investment board to direct resources into home industries, and expert staff to advise the government on economic matters. In terms of industrial relations, the hope was that a voluntary framework into which labour and management could enter would reduce conflict. Less than two years after the General Strike this did not, however, seem entirely realistic.

Broadly speaking, the state was to play a supervisory role, guiding and aiding, but not interfering with the economy. The document reflected the influence of the radical economics of Keynes in which the state acted to iron out the ups and downs of the trade cycle and unemployment. It also drew from Lloyd George's belief in the positive role and responsibility of the state, a theme of his pre-war New Liberalism that continued through the 1920s. Keynes had been a critic of Lloyd George's role in negotiating the Versailles treaty of 1919. That year he published *The Economic Consequences of the Peace*, arguing that the treaty was too harsh on Germany. But he was active in the 'summer schools' and owner of the influential Liberal magazine, *The Nation*.

Certainly Liberal thinking from the mid-1920s influenced what the historian Arthur Marwick termed 'middle opinion' in the 1930s. Figures like Harold Macmillan shaped moderate 'one nation' Conservatism.

Hugh Dalton and Hugh Gaitskill shaped moderate Labour thinking in the post-war world. Keynes and Beveridge (also involved in the summer schools) were responsible for shaping much of the post-1945 economic and social framework. Some historians, notably Robert Skidelsky, have judged *Britain's Industrial Future* a bold, radical document, addressing social problems and setting the agenda for future politicians. Others, like Sykes, consider the policy initiatives of the 1920s to have lowered the emphasis on Liberalism's popular, moral appeal to the strengths of individual character in favour of an emphasis on the technical management of the economy. This was understood only by an elite of experts.

In March 1929 *We Can Conquer Unemployment* (the 'Orange Book') put forward more concrete policy proposals. Politically, Lloyd George had always stressed the need to deal with the question of unemployment. *We Can Conquer Unemployment* proposed a self-financing two-year programme of road- and house-building that would reduce unemployment to 'normal' proportions, without leading to inflation. With Keynes as co-author of the accompanying *Can Lloyd George Do It?*, which explained the plans to solve unemployment, this was the centrepiece of the 1929 election campaign.

Hopes were high of Liberal success in 1929, prompted by a series of by-election victories (mostly in Conservative rural seats) through 1927 and 1928. *We Can Conquer Unemployment* had widespread support within the party and with the backing of the Lloyd George Fund there was an increase of no fewer than 167 candidates in 1924. The results were very disappointing. Only a mild recovery was registered, with 59 seats won. Mostly these had been rural Liberal strongholds prior to 1924, while further ground was lost to Labour in working-class areas like the north-east, East London and Lancashire. Only in South Wales did the plans for tackling unemployment win working-class constituency seats.

Despite these efforts, the Liberals found themselves (as after the 1923 election) supporting a minority Labour administration. If, as Trevor Wilson wrote in 1966, the Liberals had presented the most 'far-sighted and responsible party programme' put before British voters, why had it been rejected?

It seems doubtful that many voters considered the Liberal programme in such a light. After all, for much of the 1920s the Liberals had been more anxious to squabble among themselves than address the problems of the people. Having defended Free Trade in 1923 the party now seemed more pro-intervention, if not protectionist. Labour rather than the Liberals seemed in tune with working-class interests. For instance, *Britain's Industrial Future* showed a reluctance to side with the trade unions against employers. The state remained a force to be used against the unions and the stress put upon economic efficiency invariably seemed to favour management. Nor, in truth, was unemployment the problem in 1929 that it had been in the earlier 1920s or was to be by 1930. The programme was in many ways very technical, lacking in immediate popular appeal. It was also untried in practice, a set of theoretical ideas. This may well have prevented many voters taking an interest and put off (like those who voted against Baldwin's protectionism in 1923) many of those who did. Ideas could not win an election unless turned into popular policies. Caught as the third party in a two-party system (as Lloyd George feared in 1929), this was less a vote against Liberalism than against the Liberal Party and its track-record throughout the 1920s.

1. Was Lloyd George the Liberal Party's only hope for revival or the cause of many of its problems in the 1920s?

2. Why did the Liberal Party do so poorly in the 1929 election?

5.5 Historical Interpretation: Was the decline of the Liberal Party inevitable?

The decline of the Liberal Party, and its replacement by the Labour Party as the main progressive party in British politics was not inevitable. However, historians have differed in their views about what was the real cause of Liberal decline. George Dangerfield, in 1935, in *The Strange Death of Liberal England*, saw Liberal decline in terms of a cumulative domestic crisis that engulfed the Liberal government, in the years 1910 to 1914. To Dangerfield, the outbreak of the First World War brought a brief respite in Liberal fortunes.

Dangerfield published his book in 1935 at a time when Europe was being engulfed by dictatorships. Mussolini and Hitler were perceived as major threats to liberal ideas across the western world. Other historians have seen the First World War as the major event in destroying the Liberal Party as a national party. In 1966 the historian Trevor Wilson produced *The Downfall of the Liberal Party, 1914 to 1935*. He suggested that the strains of total war and the personality clash between Asquith and Lloyd George split the Liberals. This position was then exploited by the Labour Party in the 1918 election. The impact of the First World War was also seen as important by US historian Marvin Swartz in *The Union of Democratic Control and the First World War (1972)*. However, he emphasised foreign policy issues as a major factor in the switch from Liberal to Labour.

Clearly, in 1918 the Liberal Party was not as strong as it had been in 1910. This does not mean it was in terminal decline. Historian Maurice Cowling, in *The Impact of Labour* (1967), raised another issue. The 1918 Franchise Act gave the vote to all males over 21 years. This gave the vote to many working-class men. They were attracted to the Labour programme of domestic reform. The Act also gave the vote to women over 30 years. Cowling claims that Ramsay MacDonald, the Labour leader after the First World War, was very effective in his campaign to win support from women voters. In the period 1918 to 1923 Labour Party support rose from 22 per cent to 30 per cent in national elections. From 1918 to 1923 Britain had a three-party political system. The Liberals, Labour and Conservative parties all won large numbers of votes in national elections. However, poor Liberal party organisation, the continued split between Asquith and Lloyd George, and effective Labour campaigning meant that by 1924 Britain was reverting to a two-party race in national politics.

Yet on two occasions Liberal fortunes might have been reversed. The first came in 1918–19. With the growth of socialism across Europe and the triumph of communism in Russia, Lloyd George attempted to create a British anti-socialist 'centre party' party, out of the Liberals and Conservatives. In 1910, at the height of the constitutional crisis over the House of Lords, Lloyd George had also attempted to create a new national party of consensus from Liberals and Conservatives – at that time to meet the rising threat of Germany. In retrospect, Lloyd George's 1910 plan seemed over-ambitious. But in 1918, politics had changed dramatically from the pre-war days. From 1915 to 1922 Britain was ruled by a coalition government. Lloyd George hoped to turn the National Liberals (his supporters) and the Conservatives into a new national party. Any hope of such a policy came to an end in October 1922 when the Lloyd George coalition collapsed and the Conservatives again became an independent force in national politics.

The second occasion occurred in December 1923 and January 1924. This was highlighted in a 1971 article by historian P.F. Clarke entitled 'A Stranger Death of Liberal England?'. In December 1923 the Conservative prime minister announced that his party would abandon free trade as its economic policy. In its place it would introduce protection, based on import duties. The aim was to protect British industry from foreign competition. The decision helped reunite the Liberals. Defence of free trade was the one issue that united all Liberal MPs. Lloyd George and Asquith settled their differences and fought the general election as a united party for the first time since December 1910. The Liberals won four million votes, almost the same number as the Labour Party, but Labour won 191 seats to the Liberals 159. Asquith, as the leader of the reunited Liberals, now had the opportunity to reverse Liberal decline. He had a number of options. He could have demanded a coalition government between Labour and Liberals. He could also have demanded that this new non-Conservative government should introduce a new voting system, based on proportional representation. This would have guaranteed a three-party system in national politics. But Asquith missed both opportunities. He offered instead to 'support' a minority Labour government from January to December 1924. And in the general election of December 1924 the Liberals suffered for supporting Labour, losing a million votes and 119 seats.

Even after 1924 there was a chance that the Liberals might recover. In the general election the Liberals had put forward ambitious proposals to solve Britain's unemployment problems. These were contained in the book *Britain's Industrial Future*, popularly known as the 'Yellow Book'. It was written by the eminent economist John Maynard Keynes. In the 1929 general election the Liberals' national vote rose from 2.9 million votes to 5.3 million. However, the first-past-the-post electoral system meant that they only increased their seats from 40 to 59. In 1928 Asquith died, and Lloyd George returned as Liberal leader. However, as in 1924, the Liberals offered general support to another minority Labour government – another missed opportunity to participate in government. In August 1931 Britain was faced with a major crisis caused by the world economic depression. To meet the crisis, prime minister MacDonald formed a coalition government of Labour, Conservative and Liberal members. This National government, as it was called, pleased most senior Liberals. It was seen as a chance to permanently split Labour, as most Labour MPs opposed coalition. However, overall, the Liberals were as split as Labour on the issue. By 1931, in fact, the Liberal Party had split into three factions! In the general election, the National Liberals (who supported coalition) won 809,000 votes and 35 seats. Anti-coalition Liberals polled 1.4 million votes and won 33 seats. A separate Liberal group surrounding Lloyd George won 106,000 votes and 4 seats.

From 1931 Liberal support continued to decline. By the 1951 general election the Liberals won only 2.5 per cent of the vote giving them a mere 6 seats.

1. What do you regard as the most important factor in the decline of the Liberal Party?

2. Explain how differing historical interpretations have changed over time.

Source-based questions: The Liberal Party and the second Labour government 1929–1931

SOURCE A

We have every confidence that within three months of a Liberal government being in power, large numbers of men at present unemployed could be engaged on useful work of national development; and that within twelve months the numbers unemployed would be brought down to normal proportions. We should not, of course, rest satisfied with that, but should resume that policy which Liberalism was pursuing up to the outbreak of war, designed to reduce still further the burden of normal unemployment. To summarize: unemployment is industrial disorganisation. It is brought to an end by new enterprise, using capital to employ labour. In the present stagnation the Government must supply that initiative that will help to set going a great progressive movement.

From *We Can Conquer Unemployment* by David Lloyd George. This was the manifesto on which the Liberals fought the 1929 general election.

SOURCE B

At first Lloyd George aimed at a policy of parliamentary independence, judging Labour's proposals on their merits, and if necessary abstaining or even voting against them. Above all, party unity was to be maintained. This policy soon collapsed when the Parliamentary Liberal Party twice voted three ways over the government's Coal Bill in 1929–30. From mid-1930 Lloyd George began to move towards a policy of real cooperation with Labour in order to achieve an agreed policy on unemployment and electoral reform.

From *The Decline of the Liberal Party 1910–1931* by Paul Adleman, 1981.

SOURCE C

Broadly speaking the position is that the vast majority of the Party are working well together under Mr Lloyd George's leadership. Nevertheless there are certain members of the party – and among them some of the best known Liberals in the country such as Simon and Hutchinson – who are definitely bent on turning out the Government and those who follow them believe that they will have no Tory opponent at the next general election. They constitute a nucleus of disloyalty and disaffection in the Party; their interventions in debate and constant opposition in the division lobby weaken the influence of the Party in the House of Commons, while their criticism of our policy, as unprincipled as well as unwise, bewilders and discourages our supporters in the country.

From a letter by Sir Archibald Sinclair, Chief Whip of the Liberal Party, to H. A. L. Fisher, March 1931, during the second Labour government.

SOURCE D

Fresh splits completed the ruin of a once great party. As in 1924, how far to support a Labour government caused much soul-searching among Liberals. Lloyd George pushed for a comprehensive deal involving electoral reform to remove the first-past-post system. Sir John Simon and a group of Conservative-minded Liberals declared war on the Labour Government and denounced Lloyd George's dialogue in November 1930.

The crisis of August 1931 completed the fragmentation. Lloyd George was ill and Sir Herbert Samuel as acting leader of the party took the Liberals into the National Government that emerged. The party faced the 1931 election split three ways: Simonite Liberal Nationals who gained 35 seats; Samuelite Liberals who gained 33; and Lloyd George Independents who gained 4.

From *British Political History 1867 to 1990* by M. Pearce and G. Stewart, 1992.

---

1. Using information contained in this chapter explain the meaning of the phrases highlighted in the sources above:

a) using capital to employ labour (Source A)

b) electoral reform (Source C)

2. Study Source A.

Of what value is Source A to a historian writing about the Liberal Party and the 1929 general election?

3. Study Sources B, C and D, and use information from this chapter to assess 'To what extent was the decline of the Liberal Party between 1918 and 1931 due to internal divisions within the Party?'

Further Reading

Texts designed specifically for AS and A2 students

The Decline of the Liberal Party 1910–1931 by Paul Adelman (Longman Seminar Studies, 1981) – contains documents

The Liberal Party: Triumph and Disintegration, 1886 to 1929 by G.R. Searle (British History in Perspective, Macmillan, 1994)

Lloyd George by Stephen Constantine (Routledge Lancaster Pamphlets, 1992)

For more advanced reading

The Age of Lloyd George 1890 to 1929 by Kenneth O. Morgan (Allen & Unwin, 1978) – contains documents

A History of the Liberal Party 1895 to 1970 by R. Douglas (Sidgwick & Jackson, 1971)

The Liberal Democrats edited by Don McIver (Prentice Hall, 1996)

Lloyd George by Chris Wrigley (Historical Association Studies, Blackwell, 1992)

The Making of Modern British Politics 1867–1939 by Martin Pugh (Blackwell, 1992)

The Rise and Fall of British Liberalism, 1776–1988 by Alan Sykes (Stanford, 1997)

6 Social and economic history, 1918–1939

Key Issues

- Was decline or growth more significant as a feature of Britain's inter-war economic performance?

- What was the impact of government policy on the inter-war economy?

- How was the trade union movement affected by industrial conflict?

6.1 How serious were Britain's economic problems in the inter-war period?

6.2 What were the causes and consequences of the General Strike?

6.3 Historical interpretation: How severe was the impact of the Depression on British society in the 1930s?

6.4 Could the governments of the inter-war period have done more to alleviate the problems of the British economy?

Framework of Events

1919	Suspension of Britain's membership of the gold standard. Wave of industrial conflict; miners demand pay increase and seven-hour day. Sankey Commission recommends nationalisation (state ownership) of mines; rejected by Lloyd George government
1920	Collapse of post-war economic boom; slump begins. Unemployment Insurance Act extends cover for the jobless
1921	Black Friday: miners' strike defeated when rail and transport unions refuse support. Control of mines (transferred to the government in wartime) is returned to private hands
1925	Return to the gold standard: sterling restored to the pre-war exchange rate. Samuel Commission investigates problems of mining industry
1926	General Strike lasts for nine days in May. Miners' strike continues until November and ends in the miners' defeat
1927	Trade Disputes Act makes general strikes illegal and attempts to restrict trade union funding of the Labour Party
1929	October: Wall Street Crash in the USA signals start of world-wide economic depression
1930	Coal Mines Act reduces miners' working day and attempts to rationalise the industry
1931	Second Labour government breaks up over its failure to agree on cuts in unemployment benefit and is replaced by a Conservative-dominated National Government. Britain leaves the gold standard and spending cuts are introduced. Means test introduced to gauge eligibility for unemployment benefit
1932	Import Duties Act imposes general tariff of 10 per cent, except for food and raw material imports and imperial products entering Britain. 'Cheap money' – interest rates reduced from 6 per cent to 2 per cent. Ottawa agreements establish preferential trading arrangements for self-governing Empire countries
1934	Unemployment Assistance Act restores benefit cuts made in 1931. Unemployment Assistance Board set up. Special Areas Act tries to direct investment into designated areas of high deprivation
1935	Rearmament programme begins
1936	Jarrow Crusade – the best known protest march by the unemployed
1938	Nationalisation of coal royalties (mineral rights in mining areas)

Overview

A s a result of the First World War, Britain's role in international trade had diminished. This adversely affected the British economy. It was not merely that Britain had accumulated £1 billion of debt, owed mainly to the United States. During the war the disruption of trade had led former overseas customers to reduce the amount of imports they bought from Britain. In the Far East, markets for British goods had been penetrated by new competitors such as Japan. In the post-war years the problems of British exporters worsened as foreign countries protected their economies with tariffs (taxes on imports) and government subsidies.

These developments made life harder for Britain's old, established **staple industries** of coal, cotton, shipbuilding and iron and steel. This sector, which had formed the basis of the industrial revolution, was already vulnerable because of its dependence on ageing plant and technology, and its association with inefficient managerial methods and working practices. After a brief post-war **boom**, in 1920 a **slump** set in as world demand contracted. The result was large-scale unemployment in the regions (primarily northern England, South Wales and south-west Scotland) where the older factories, mines and shipyards were concentrated. This situation was appreciably worsened by the onset of world depression following the Wall Street Crash (the collapse of the United States stock market) in October

Staple industries: The older, heavier industries, on whose exports the British economy had traditionally depended – coal, textiles, iron and steel, shipbuilding.

Boom: A period when the economy expands and demand for goods and services is high.

Slump: A serious decline in demand for agricultural and/or industrial products, leading to a fall in prices and to business failures.

How useful is this map for a study of unemployment in the inter-war period?

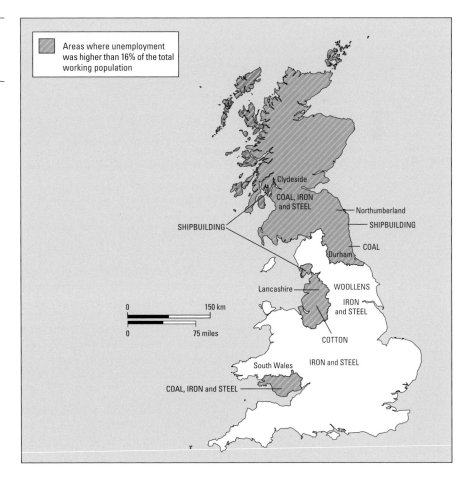

Areas where unemployment was higher than 16% of the total working population

The staple industries and regional unemployment in Britain in 1931

1929. Unemployment persisted in Britain's traditional industrial heartlands, even after the beginning of national recovery from the slump in the mid-1930s.

At the same time a number of newer industries and services managed to escape the worst effects of the depression and expanded in the 1930s, generating new jobs. These industries, which included electrical engineering and motor vehicle manufacture, were based mainly in the south-east and the Midlands. As a result inter-war Britain was a country of strong regional economic contrasts.

Another theme of this chapter is the changing fortunes of the trade union movement. Trade union membership had doubled during the First World War, increasing from just over 4 million to 8.3 million. The onset of mass unemployment, however, weakened the unions' bargaining power and membership grew very slowly during the 1920s. The decade also saw the most dramatic example of industrial conflict in British history, the General Strike of May 1926. The failure of the Strike forced union leaders to adopt a more moderate approach in their dealings with the employers for the remainder of the inter-war period.

1. What do you regard as the most important social and economic problems facing Britain between 1918 and 1939? Explain your answer.

2. Can you identify any links between the problems mentioned above? Give reasons for your answer.

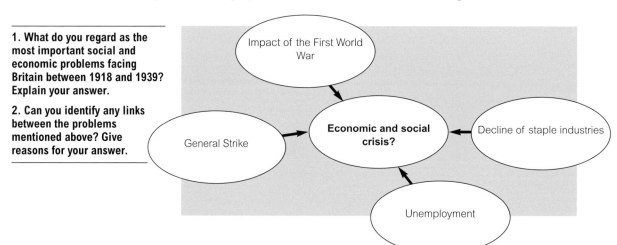

6.1 How serious were Britain's economic problems in the inter-war period?

The impact of war

The effects of the First World War upon the British economy can be divided into four main categories:

Physical losses

The First World War was far less physically destructive than the conflict of 1939–45, with the major exceptions of lost manpower (745,000 men were killed and 1.6 million were seriously wounded) and the sinking of approximately one-fifth of the merchant shipping fleet. Nonetheless one should also note the way in which the war increased the rate of depreciation of industrial plant. In wartime, key resources such as railways and mines were used more intensively, while their maintenance tended to be neglected.

Distortion of the economy

The war stimulated industries such as engineering, chemicals and shipbuilding, which had a direct relevance to the needs of the armed forces. Those that were less important in wartime (for example textiles and building) were relatively neglected.

Disruption of the export trade

Britain's staple industries, which relied heavily on exporting, found their old markets in Russia, the Far East and elsewhere closed to them during the war. Former customers for British coal, textiles or steel either developed their own industries or turned to new suppliers such as the United States and Japan. The contraction of trade during the war also reduced the income Britain traditionally derived from shipping. Before 1914 this had been a major component of Britain's 'invisible income' – earnings derived from services rather than goods, which had ensured a healthy **balance of payments** in peacetime. The decline of invisible income was a serious difficulty for a country facing an uncertain international financial situation.

War debt

To pay for the war the British government sold off foreign assets and borrowed heavily, both at home and abroad. This increased the size of the National Debt and had an **inflationary effect** in Britain. The accumulation of debt placed the country at a disadvantage in relation to its main creditor, the United States. The situation was compounded by the loss of investments in Germany, Austria-Hungary and Turkey (with whom Britain was at war) and in Russia (after the 1917 revolutions). The problems of wartime finance forced Britain off the **gold standard**, under which the value of the pound had been linked to gold. Post-war governments, supported by the orthodox thinking of the banking establishment, favoured a return to gold on the grounds that it was essential for the revival of financial confidence. It is now generally agreed that the 1925 return to the pre-war exchange rate of £1: $4.86 left the currency overvalued, and thereby damaged the prospects of Britain's export industries.

Boom and slump

In the immediate aftermath of the war the economy experienced a short-lived boom, as **speculative investors** responded positively to rising prices and to an optimistic assumption that pre-war 'normality' would return. By 1920, however, demand for goods had begun to decrease as overproduction caused prices to fall and government borrowing rates were raised in preparation for an eventual return to the gold standard. At the same time a world-wide fall in the price of primary products (food and raw materials) took effect. This meant that countries that were **primary producers**, concentrated in the British Empire, Latin America and the Far East, were in a weaker position for buying British manufactured goods.

A less favourable trading environment was bad news for Britain's traditional export-based industries. Exports of cotton textiles, for example, were less than half the 1913 figure in 1922. Coal exports were a third of the pre-war statistic. The world slump worsened the organisational and technological problems of heavy industries, which were dependent on outdated machinery and made extensive use of skilled labour. These industries badly needed to reduce excess capacity, to re-equip and re-locate to new areas. Yet these were costly undertakings for enterprises whose profit margins were falling because of adverse world conditions. Should the management of these old industries be blamed for failing to take strategic decisions in the interests of long-term survival? One possibility was for an industry to amalgamate numerous small, less efficient units and to scrap excess capacity. The leaders of the cotton industry were slow to do so in the 1920s, since they tended to believe that the slump would give way to a revival, in the manner of earlier fluctuations in the trade cycle. After 1929 the Bank of England sponsored the Lancashire Cotton Corporation and Combined Egyptian Mills, which undertook some **rationalisation** of spinning, but this did not go far enough. In the shipbuilding industry,

Balance of payments: The difference between a country's income from foreign countries and its payments to those countries.

Inflationary effect: An increase in the general level of prices caused by an event or situation.

Gold standard: A monetary system under which a national currency has a fixed value in gold.

Speculative investors: People who invest money in businesses, running risks because they expect to make an unusually large profit.

Primary producer: Producer of raw materials, e.g. raw cotton, coffee beans.

Rationalisation: Reorganisation of an industry in order to improve its efficiency.

reorganisation was hampered by weak management and by traditional ship-yard organisation, which protected counter-productive working practices.

The problems of the 'old staples' were intensified by the United States stock market crash of October 1929, heralding four years of economic depression during which world trade slumped by 35 per cent. In Britain the clearest indicator of depression was the persistence of unemployment at levels not seen prior to the First World War. Between 1921 and 1940 unemployment never fell below 1 million, or 10 per cent of the **insured population**, reaching almost 3 million in 1932–3, the worst point of the slump. Throughout the inter-war period the areas with the highest figures for joblessness were northern England, Scotland and South Wales – the parts of the country that depended most heavily on the traditional export industries. Nor did the recovery that began in the mid-1930s enable these trades to return to their pre-war levels of prosperity. Whereas Britain's share of world manufacturing exports stood at just under 30 per cent in 1913, it was little more than 22 per cent in 1937.

Insured population: Those workers covered by the National Insurance scheme, begun in 1911.

United Kingdom staple industries: exports, 1910–38

(Annual averages per decade, prices are adjusted to remove the impact of inflation.)

The exports of individual industries are shown in terms of their value (in millions of pounds) and as a percentage of total United Kingdom exports.

	Textiles		Iron and steel		Coal	
	£m	%	£m	%	£m	%
1910–19	200.2	40	62.9	12	50.0	10
1920–29	288.9	37	96.5	12	65.2	8
1930–38	106.0	24	54.1	12	37.7	9

(Source: *Abstract of British Historical Statistics* by B.R. Mitchell and P. Deane, 1962)

What do these statistics reveal about the fortunes of Britain's staple industries in the inter-war period?

Grounds for optimism?

In spite of this decline, historians have often emphasised the more positive aspects of the British economy's inter-war performance. It is noteworthy that on the eve of the Second World War, Britain's **gross domestic product** was half as great again as it had been in 1913. The steel industry, which had been hard hit in the 1920s by a combination of foreign tariffs and cheap imports from abroad, staged a convincing recovery in the ensuing decade. From 1932 British steel was protected by a 33.3 per cent tariff imposed by the government on foreign competition. Existing plant was improved, and efficient, **integrated steel works**, such as the one at Corby in Northamptonshire, were built. In the shipbuilding industry a modest revival of output was facilitated by a reduction of capacity, together with government subsidies and new contracts in the mid-1930s. The position of coal and textiles could be said to have stabilised by the end of the decade. Such developments allowed the historian John Stevenson, writing in *British Society 1914–45* (1984), to conclude that 'in spite of the problems of the traditional sectors, the inter-war years were marked by substantial economic growth, representing a significant improvement on the Edwardian era and in comparison with most other European countries'. The last point is particularly important. Historians such as R. Lewchuck, author of *American Technology and the British Vehicle Industry* (1987), have

Gross domestic product (GDP): The total value of goods and services produced within a country.

Integrated works: A factory where all parts of the production process are performed on a single site.

unfavourably compared British industrial performance with that of the United States. It should be noted that the greater size and purchasing power of the American population created a much larger internal market than in Britain, thus making large-scale capital investment possible.

It is the newer industries that provide the strongest case for an optimistic reading of the period. Industries such as motor-vehicle manufacturing, electrical engineering, plastics and artificial fibres (such as rayon) took advantage of the fact that, especially in the south and the Midlands, the majority of the population remained in work. A combination of steady wage levels and falling food prices meant that, for those who escaped the curse of unemployment, living standards tended to improve in inter-war Britain. Together with the availability of **hire purchase**, these factors created a buoyant market for consumer goods. Technical developments, such as mass production and the application of electricity, boosted the manufacture of cars and consumer durables such as radio sets. Goods were increasingly subject to standardised packaging and pricing. The growth of motor transport enabled new **chain stores**, such as Marks and Spencer, to receive supplies, while the local delivery van became a familiar sight in suburban and rural areas.

Government policy assisted the growth of some of the newer industries. By creating the Central Electricity Board in 1926, for example, it made possible the building of new power stations connected through a national grid of power transmission lines. The consequent fall in electricity prices had clear beneficial effects. Whereas in 1920 there were only 730,000 consumers, by 1939 there were almost 9 million. Similarly certain industries, such as motor vehicles and dyestuffs, gained from the selective imposition of protective tariffs during the First World War and the early 1920s. The aircraft industry, which had enjoyed only modest growth in the 1920s, was one of the main beneficiaries of rearmament in the late 1930s.

Inter-war economic developments

The newer industries managed to avoid some of the problems faced by the traditional export staples by exploiting the home market. Their success should not, however, be exaggerated. As Peter Dewey points out in his study, *War and Progress: Britain 1914–1945* (1997), the only 'new' industries with above average growth rates in the 1930s were motor-vehicle manufacturing, electrical engineering and rayon production. The enormous expansion of house building during that decade reminds us that the new, high technology industries were not the only ones to display evidence of vitality. Rising **real incomes**, together with cheaper mortgages, encouraged the building of 2,723,000 houses in England and Wales between 1930 and 1939. This should deter us from excessive generalisation about the contrasts between older and newer industries. Any study of the inter-war economy needs to recognise the great variety of experience during the period.

Hire purchase: A system that enables a customer to purchase an item by making payments in a series of instalments.

Chain store: One of a large number of shops, under the same ownership and located in different places.

Real income: The value of wages when set against changes in prices – i.e. an individual's purchasing power.

1. How did British industry change during the inter-war period?

2. To what extent were the problems of the 'old staple' industries due to poor management and organisation?

3. Explain why 'new industries' developed in inter-war Britain.

6.2 What were the causes and consequences of the General Strike?

The problems of one of the great staple industries, mining, were the root cause of the General Strike of May 1926. The events of that month stand alone as the only occasion in British history when the trade unions resorted to a general stoppage of work. Approximately 3 million people responded to an appeal from the **Trades Union Congress** (TUC) to strike in support of the coal miners, who were involved in a long-running dispute with their employers. Dockers, railwaymen, bus drivers and

Trades Union Congress: The central organisation in which Britain's trade unions were represented, established in 1868. The General Council was its governing body.

printers, together with workers in the building trade and the electricity, gas, steel and chemical industries, were among those who answered the call for working class solidarity. Stanley Baldwin's Conservative government treated the strike very seriously, condemning it as a challenge to constitutional government. With the help of the army and of civilian volunteers, the authorities operated well-laid emergency plans and managed to maintain the flow of essential supplies. After nine days, the General Council of the TUC called off the strike without securing assurances from the government as to the outcome of the miners' dispute. The miners alone remained on strike for another seven months before succumbing to defeat and returning to work.

Not surprisingly, the episode has attracted a great deal of interest among historians. The defeat of the unions has often been seen as a turning point in the development of the labour movement, a graphic illustration of the limitations of the strike as a weapon in industrial disputes. It is therefore important to be clear about the issues that led to the General Strike and the wider implications of these events.

What were the problems of the coal industry?

The dispute that developed into the General Strike had its origins in the problems of the coal industry. As we saw in Section 6.1, in the post-war period coal was one of the staple export industries worst hit by the adverse conditions of world trade. As new fuels, notably oil, increased in popularity, demand for coal grew at a slower rate than before 1914. The private owners, whose management of the industry had been interrupted by government intervention during the First World War, recovered their control in 1921. They have traditionally been viewed as exceptionally unimaginative and reactionary. In the memorable phrase of L. C. B. Seaman, author of *Post-Victorian Britain 1902–1951* (1966), 'the coal industry was certainly "**private**"; but it was not enterprising'. It is true that the owners were slow to amalgamate small colliery firms in the interests of greater efficiency. However, this view of the industry should not be overdrawn. The amount of coal cut by machinery increased from 8 per cent of output in 1914 to 14 per cent in 1921. Yet as Barry Supple points out in his *History of the British Coal Mining Industry* (1987), the benefits of mechanisation were offset by **deteriorating geological conditions**, a factor outside the owners' control.

Nonetheless the fact remains that the coal owners' most characteristic response to declining profits was to reduce the cost of production, primarily by cutting wages. The pressure to do so was increased by the Baldwin government's decision to return to the gold standard in 1925 at the pre-war exchange rate. The decision had the effect of making British exports more expensive and thus further weakened the position of the coal industry in world markets. In June 1925 the coal owners announced their decision to cut their employees' wages while requiring them to work for longer hours. The stage was set for a confrontation with the leaders of the miners' union, who were determined to defend the living standards of the workforce.

Why did the General Strike begin in 1926?

In 1925 the miners were led by an uncompromising president, Herbert Smith, and a union secretary with a militantly **Marxist** outlook, A. J. Cook. Their intransigent stand against the threatened pay cuts induced the TUC to approve an embargo on the movement of coal from the end of July. Rather than face industrial action, the Conservative government agreed on 'Red Friday' to appoint a royal commission under the Liberal politician, Sir

Private enterprise: Ownership of an industrial company by a private individual or group of individuals; the opposite of state ownership.

Deteriorating geological conditions: Physical problems in gaining access to deeper seams in the older coal mines.

Marxist: A follower of the ideas of the Communist thinker Karl Marx (1818–83), who argued that history developed through a series of struggles between social classes.

A. J. Cook (1885–1931)
General Secretary of the Miners' Federation of Great Britain from 1924. An inspiring speaker, he stood for a policy of refusing all concessions in dealings with the employers.

Events of the General Strike, 1926

1 May Miners are locked out by their employers, following breakdown of negotiations between the government and TUC representatives.

3 May The General Strike begins.

5 May In its first issue the government's official newspaper, the *British Gazette*, condemns the Strike as 'a direct challenge to ordered government'.

12 May The TUC leaders call off the General Strike following a meeting with the Prime Minister.

State subsidy: A grant of government money, awarded to support a particular industry.

Herbert Samuel, to examine the problems of the coal industry. It also announced a **state subsidy** to maintain the miners' current wage rates for nine months.

At the time, the Red Friday decision was greeted by the miners as a victory, and regarded by the coal owners as a surrender. In retrospect, it seems more likely that the government was seeking a breathing space in which to make preparations for a showdown with the miners, should a compromise settlement prove unattainable. It divided the country into areas under the authority of nominated civil commissioners, and established a body known as the Organisation for the Maintenance of Supplies to train volunteer strike-breakers. By the time the Samuel Commission reported in March 1926, the government was well equipped to resist a general strike. By contrast the TUC made few preparations, pinning its hopes on the Commission. The Samuel Report contained recommendations that were carefully balanced, condemning both the subsidy and the owners' demand for longer hours. For the longer term it proposed a reorganisation of the coal industry; in the short term, it accepted the need for

An armoured car escorts a food convoy through London's East End during the General Strike, May 1926

How useful is this source for a study of the General Strike?

wage cuts. The miners' leaders rejected these proposals, A.J. Cook summing up their position as 'not a penny off the pay, not a minute on the day'. When the subsidy ran out at the end of April, the coal owners locked the miners out.

The miners' case was now put to the government by the TUC General Council. Although they set up a committee to prepare a plan for strike action on 27 April, it seems that the TUC leaders believed that the government would give way. Large-scale industrial action began on 3 May, after the Cabinet abruptly broke off negotiations on the grounds that printers at the *Daily Mail* had refused to publish a leading article attacking the idea of a general strike. This has often been interpreted as an act of deliberate provocation, the work of Conservative ministers who were intent on facing down the unions. On the other hand, even if the talks had continued, it is unlikely that the miners would have agreed to any concessions on the issue of wages.

What were the consequences of the strike?

Although the response of working people to the strike call was an impressive achievement, the TUC had no reason to welcome a prolonged conflict. Their intention throughout was to put pressure on the government to re-open talks. A long strike would drain union funds and a resort to revolutionary violence was against their traditions. Indeed, with a few exceptions, the strike was remarkable for the orderly way in which it was conducted. The government, however, stood by its claim that the strike was an unjustifiable attempt to **overawe** legal authority. Its access to the broadcasting services of the BBC enabled it to win publicity for its position.

On 12 May the TUC leaders sought a settlement in return for calling off the strike. This was, in effect, an admission that they had been beaten by the government's superior organisational and financial resources. The TUC's failure to secure a definite commitment to the reinstatement of dismissed strikers indicated the extent of their defeat. This left the field open for the victimisation of strikers by their employers when the men returned to work. It took an unofficial resumption of the strike, the following day, to compel the government to intervene in the interests of fair play.

The General Strike did not help the miners, who stayed out until starvation drove them back to work on the owners' terms. By refusing to accept the Samuel Report's proposals, which Baldwin was prepared to implement, they unintentionally relieved the government of the obligation to persuade the owners to compromise. The result was an intensification of class feeling on the coalfields. In the long run, as A.J.P. Taylor argues in *English History 1914–1945* (1965), the owners' 1926 triumph sealed their fate. It made sure that, when the first majority Labour government was formed in 1945, nationalisation of the mines was an early priority.

The events of 1926 discredited the belief, common in trade union circles after the First World War, that employers and government could be coerced by means of large-scale direct action. The average number of workers involved in strikes and **lock-outs** in each of the years 1919–21, was 2,108,000; in 1926 it was 2,751,000. In each of the years 1927–39, it fell to 308,100. As Alan Bullock argues in the first volume of his *Life and Times of Ernest Bevin* (1960), union leaders came to appreciate the need to restrict the use of the strike weapon. The events of 1926 showed that industrial action on a national scale was likely to entail political conflict, of a kind that most leaders were not prepared to contemplate. The result was a move away from direct confrontation, towards a more pragmatic approach to industrial relations. An early example was the **Mond-Turner talks** of 1928–29, which

Overawe: To intimidate by fear or superior influence.

Lock-out: A tactic used by employers during an industrial dispute. Employees cannot enter the work place unless they accept the employer's conditions.

Mond-Turner talks: Discussions between the two sides of industry, led by Sir Alfred Mond, head of Imperial Chemical Industries (ICI) and Ben Turner, chairman of the TUC General Council.

Sympathetic strikes: A strike by workers in one industry in support of a strike by workers in another.

Political levy: A subscription to the Labour Party, paid by individual trade union members as part of their union dues. From 1913–27 a worker had to 'contract out' (i.e. positively to opt out of paying) if he did not wish to help fund Labour. 'Contracting in' meant that to contribute to the levy, a worker had to signify a positive wish to do so.

1. Which side was more to blame for the General Strike, the Baldwin government or the trade unions?

2. Why did the General Strike fail?

3. How significant was the General Strike for the future of the trade union movement?

involved employers and TUC representatives in discussions on improving the efficiency of industry.

On the other hand, the cause of reconciliation was not best served by the Baldwin government, which succumbed in the aftermath of the General Strike to pressures from the Conservative right. The 1927 Trade Disputes Act made **sympathetic strikes** illegal, banned civil servants from joining unions affiliated to the TUC and changed the system of trade union members paying their **political levy** to the Labour Party from one of 'contracting-out' to 'contracting-in'. The latter provision reduced Labour's income from affiliation fees by a third.

The General Strike was not a total defeat for working people. It played a part in discouraging employers from cutting wages in general (with the important exception of the mining industry) in the late 1920s. With hindsight the events of May 1926 appear as the final expression of a militant style of trade unionism, which was now being superseded. It is hard not to endorse A. J. P. Taylor's conclusion that 'the General Strike, apparently the clearest display of the class war in British history, marked the moment when class war ceased to shape the pattern of British industrial relations'.

6.3 How severe was the impact of the Depression on British society in the 1930s?
A CASE STUDY IN HISTORICAL INTERPRETATION

One, two or three Englands?

In 1934, as Britain began to emerge from the worst years of the inter-war depression, the celebrated writer J. B. Priestley published a travel book entitled *English Journey*. In this book Priestley related that he had seen not one but three distinct Englands in the course of his travels across the country. The first he termed 'old England', a place of picturesque countryside, inns and historic cathedral cities. The second was the smoky, depressed world of nineteenth-century heavy industry, typified by slum housing, mills, railway stations and Victorian town halls – 'this England makes up the larger part of the Midlands and the North … but it is not being added to and has no new life poured into it'. Thirdly, in southern England, he found a vibrant suburban world of 'arterial and bypass roads, of filling stations and factories that look like exhibition buildings, of giant cinemas and dance halls and cafés'. In this England a consumer culture modelled on American tastes had developed: here were 'miles of semi-detached bungalows and all with their little garages, their wireless sets, their periodicals about film stars, their swimming costumes and tennis rackets and dancing shoes'.

Historians continue to debate the enormous social contrasts that characterised 1930s Britain. The earliest accounts tended to emphasise the social deprivation of 'the devil's decade', a time of mass unemployment and of alleged missed opportunities on the part of successive governments. Since the 1970s, however, a more positive re-evaluation has taken place. Historians such as D. H. Aldcroft, author of *The Inter-war Economy 1919–1939* (1970) detected impressive growth in certain sectors of the economy. The most comprehensive statement of the 'optimistic case' has been *The Slump* (first published in 1977, re-published in 1994 as *Britain in the Depression*) by John Stevenson and Chris Cook. They stressed the rise in living standards for the majority of the population and drew attention to the limited nature of public support for a radical political solution to the depression.

This interpretation of the 1930s has not, however, gone unchallenged. Detailed research into the issues of health and nutrition has led some historians to question the extent to which the working classes escaped from poverty between the wars. Labour historian Jack Laybourn's 1990 study, the significantly titled *Britain on the Breadline*, shifts the focus back on to the human tragedy of large-scale unemployment and the waste of resources that it entailed.

It is important to be aware of the arguments on both sides, and of the passion with which the debate has often been conducted. This section presents some of the evidence for these contrasting interpretations.

What were the indicators of prosperity?

The main cause of stable or rising living standards was the fact that, for those in work, real incomes remained consistently higher than before 1914. Certainly, wages tended to fall during the depression and did not rise significantly until economic recovery was under way in the late 1930s. Prices, however, fell faster than wages during the slump. This was particularly true of food prices. As a result, the cost of living fell by more than a third between 1920 and 1938.

A further factor was the decline in average family size in inter-war Britain. Whereas a woman who married in the 1880s was likely to have an average of 4.6 children, by the late 1920s the equivalent figure was 2.19. This was partly due to the wider availability of artificial methods of contraception, which had been largely confined to the upper and middle classes before the First World War. Knowledge of birth control diffused down the social scale in the 1920s. At the same time, the official disapproval of contraception that had prevailed in Victorian and Edwardian times began to lift. This trend, which was to be continued after 1945, meant that a higher proportion of a family's income could now be spent on non-essential consumer goods.

Sir John (later Lord) Reith (1889–1971)
As Director-General of the BBC, from 1927–38, he insisted that public service broadcasting must not only entertain but also inform and educate its audience. Reith established a mixture of news, serious discussion, music and drama, which contrasted strongly with the 'lighter' output of commercial channels. He set the tone for the inter-war BBC by instructing announcers to wear evening dress, even in day time.

The main beneficiaries of inter-war prosperity were the salaried middle classes, whose financial security stimulated the great suburban house-building boom of the 1930s. The introduction of mass-production methods, together with low running costs, brought motoring within the grasp of many: the number of private cars rose from 1,056,000 to 1,798,000 in 1930–37. Radio sets were another consumer item that experienced an enormous surge in popularity between the wars. In 1922, the year that the British Broadcasting Company – forerunner of the British Broadcasting Corporation – was founded, 36,000 licences were granted. By 1938 that number had swelled to 8.97 million. As Peter Dewey reminds us in *War and Progress*, this was mainly due to the growth of middle-class purchasing power; in the 1930s a valve radio set would have cost the equivalent of two weeks' wages for an unskilled worker. Moreover the formal 'public service' ethos of the pre-1939 BBC, under its high-minded Director-General, Sir John Reith, may have limited its cross-class appeal.

Nevertheless it is clear that large sections of the working classes experienced a general rise in living standards. The expansion of the motor vehicle, chemical and electrical industries, and of the retail trade, led to the creation of better-paid jobs, especially in the south and the Midlands. Food processing, canning and pre-packaging brought access to a greater variety of foodstuffs. It seems clear that standards of nutrition and health were generally improving. Even John Boyd Orr, author of a critical 1936 study,

Food, Health, and Income, concluded that the national diet was better than it had been before 1914. Improvements in housing and sanitation helped to reduce the incidence of infectious diseases such as typhoid, which had been major killers in earlier generations. It is significant that a higher proportion of army volunteers was judged fit to fight in 1939 than in 1914.

On average, hours of work were reduced after the First World War, so that opportunities for leisure increased. For the first time day trips to the seaside came within the reach of large numbers of working people, as it became common to hire open-topped charabancs, the predecessor of the motor coach. It was less common, although by no means unknown, to take a week's holiday away from home. The first Butlins holiday camp was opened at Skegness in Lincolnshire in 1937. Professional football and cricket retained their mass appeal between the wars, aided by press and radio coverage. The presence of members of the royal family at the Cup Final match helped to enhance the image of football as a national game. The 1930s were also the golden age of cinema, which replaced the Edwardian music hall as a source of cheap entertainment. A survey of Liverpool audiences in 1937, for example, found that 40 per cent of the city's population went to 'the pictures' at least once a week. Cinema offered not only escapism from urban routine, but also a comfortable environment and opportunities for young courting couples to enjoy some privacy. The popularity of classless open-air activities such as cycling, hiking and rambling in the 1930s was another indicator of relative affluence for the many.

Index of wages, prices and real incomes in inter-war Britain

(The index for 1930 is 100)

	Weekly wage rates	Retail prices	Average annual real wage earnings
1920	143.7	157.6	92.2
1925	102.2	111.4	91.7
1930	100.0	100.0	100.0
1935	98.0	90.5	108.3
1938	106.3	98.7	107.7

Source: *The Inter-war Economy: Britain 1919–1939* by D.H. Aldcroft (1970)

How useful are these statistics for the study of living standards in inter-war Britain?

New leisure opportunities in inter-war Britain

Motor cars and coaches: These provided new opportunities for day trips and family holidays. By the 1930s the Bank Holiday traffic jam was an established part of national life. The first holiday camps were opened, with accommodation for half a million people by 1939.

Hiking and rambling: These became popular as townspeople discovered the countryside. The Youth Hostels Association and the Ramblers' Association were founded in this period.

Dance Halls: Influenced by developments in the United States, dance bands and 'big bands' became a popular form of evening entertainment. Radio broadcasts brought the music of well-known band leaders, such as Henry Hall and Lew Stone, into people's homes.

Popular reading: The first paperback books, Allen Lane's Penguin series, appeared in 1935. They were priced at sixpence each – said to be the amount a bank clerk could earn in 20 minutes.

Radio: The British Broadcasting Company was founded in 1922, becoming the British Broadcasting Corporation four years later.

Films: The arrival of 'talking pictures' in the late 1920s increased the popularity of the cinema. Between 1914 and 1939 the number of cinemas in Britain increased from 3,000 to almost 5,000.

A magnificent 1930s cinema. The interior imitated the luxurious surroundings of an ocean liner.

Gambling: This expanded in the inter-war years, with the organisation of national football pools and greyhound racing.

Football: The sport retained its pre-1914 popularity. The first Cup Final was played at the new Wembley Stadium in 1923. Other spectator sports, such as cricket and boxing, maintained a popular following, aided by press and radio coverage

The pessimistic case: the 'wasted years'

The persistence of mass unemployment is, of course, the main reason for a pessimistic reading of the social history of the 1930s. Indeed, as John Stevenson acknowledges in his study of *British Society 1914–45*, the problem of unemployment stands out because it has to be seen against a background of generally rising living standards for the majority. This is what made it appear so scandalous to many contemporaries, and it explains above all the lasting popular perception of the 1930s as 'the wasted years' or 'the devil's decade'.

It should be noted that it is hard to be precise about the extent of unemployment. Most statistics refer to those groups of workers who were covered by the **National Insurance** scheme, begun by the pre-war Liberal government in 1911 to cover workers in trades that were most vulnerable to unemployment. Although insurance provision was extended in 1920 to cover the great majority of manual workers, the self-employed, domestic servants and agricultural labourers remained outside the scheme. The latter were not included until 1936. For the greater part of the inter-war period, we are therefore dependent on estimates of the number of uninsured workers who suffered unemployment.

Unemployment was not a new phenomenon in Britain. Before the First World War it was quite common for workers to experience a number of short spells of unemployment in the course of their lives. This was particularly common for those engaged in trades such as building, which were affected by seasonal factors, or in industries such as shipbuilding, where employment depended on a firm receiving a contract. What made the inter-war years different was the sharp rise in longer-term unemployment. Stephen Constantine, author of *Unemployment between the Wars* (1980), notes that in September 1929, on the eve of the world slump, less than 5 per cent of applicants for relief had been out of work for more than a year. By August 1932 the figure had risen to 16.4 per cent, which was equivalent to more than 400,000 people. One month before the outbreak of the Second World War, there remained 244,000 long-term unemployed.

It was not the case that workers in the newer and generally successful industries were completely immune from unemployment. Seasonal unemployment affected the prosperous motor vehicle manufacturing towns such as Oxford and Coventry, where workers were sometimes laid off in winter, when demand for their products was lower. A regional analysis of Britain, however, reveals that unemployment was most persistent in northern England, South Wales and Scotland, where the older, declining staple

National Insurance: A scheme devised by Lloyd George as Chancellor of the Exchequer in 1911, intended to save certain categories of worker from the workhouse if unemployed. The idea was that weekly contributions by an employee, his employer and the state would build up a fund on which the former could draw for support when out of work. Benefit was limited to 15 weeks in any one year.

Unemployment in the United Kingdom, 1929–39

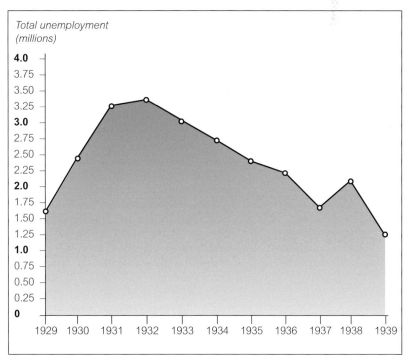

What are the strengths and weaknesses of graphs as a means of showing information?

industries were located. William Beveridge, author of the 1944 study *Full Employment in a Free Society*, calculated that 84.9 per cent of long-term unemployment was to be found in these areas. Although the rapidly-growing industries of the 1920s experienced unemployment during the slump, they recovered from it more easily than the old staples. To take two examples, in motor vehicle production, insured unemployment ran at 20 per cent in 1932 and at 4.8 per cent in 1937. The corresponding figures for shipbuilding were 62.2 per cent and 23.8 per cent. The underlying issue was one of structural unemployment – in other words, pools of localised but enduring unemployment associated with industries facing long-term problems of adaptation to economic change. For victims of this problem, the recovery of the late 1930s made sense only as a very relative concept.

What was the social and economic impact of unemployment on Britain?

Post-war governments recognised the problem of long-term unemployment by allowing claimants to draw benefit beyond the period to which they were entitled by their past contributions. These additional payments, known as 'uncovenanted' or 'transitional' benefits, showed an intention on the part of government to spare the unemployed the harshness of the **Poor Law**. From 1929 the administration of these benefits was placed in the hands of local authority Public Assistance Committees. As the financial crisis of 1931 deepened, the National Government decreed that applicants for relief must submit to a '**means test**' designed to gauge the level of need in individual households. The means test was widely resented by the unemployed for its perceived intrusiveness and lack of generosity. An unemployed man could find his entitlement to benefit – popularly known as 'the dole' – reduced if another member of his family was in work. Local variations in the way in which the rules were interpreted led the government to transfer responsibility for transitional payments to a central Unemployment Assistance Board in 1934. The idea was that the new body would ensure that uniform scales of relief would be applied, regardless of local political pressures. When the new scales were revealed, there was an outcry as these were often lower than the ones provided by local authorities. The government was obliged to intervene to maintain the old levels, delaying the introduction of the Unemployment Assistance Board until 1937.

As Stevenson and Cook point out in *Britain in the Depression* (1994), the dole enabled the unemployed to afford the necessities of life and thus helped to defuse popular discontent. Provision for the unemployed in 1930s Britain was more generous than in many countries at the time, including the United States. It is hard to generalise about the impact of unemployment on living standards. A great deal depended on whether a family unit contained dependent children or secondary earners, such as grown up children living with their parents. A number of social surveys were conducted in different areas during the slump, but the criteria for judging what constituted an unacceptable level of poverty varied considerably. Some studies, such as that undertaken by Dr M'Gonigle into mortality rates in Stockton-on-Tees, have been criticised for being based on relatively small samples. It is also difficult, when studying historically deprived areas, to isolate the effects of unemployment from more generalised poverty.

Even more subjective are the works of contemporary writers such as George Orwell, whose account of a visit to depressed north-west England, *The Road to Wigan Pier*, became a classic after its publication in 1937. In an important article in the journal *History* (July 1997), Robert Pearce has cast

Poor Law: The system of poor relief, dating back to 1834, under which able-bodied applicants for assistance were meant to enter a workhouse administered by a local Board of Poor Law Guardians. Conditions in workhouses were deliberately made unattractive to encourage the poor to be self-reliant.

Means test: An assessment of an unemployed person's economic reserves, carried out by the authorities to decide how much benefit the person was entitled to have.

serious doubt on the book's authenticity as a social document. By comparing the finished work with an unpublished diary kept by Orwell at the time, Pearce shows how the writer often lifted events out of sequence, exaggerated for dramatic effect and presented individual people and incidents as representative types without real justification. This underlines the fact that we should be cautious in appraising even the most prestigious of historical sources.

Nonetheless it is important to recognise the value of first-hand accounts of the effects of unemployment. A number of its victims wrote eloquent and moving memoirs depicting their experiences. Among the most widely read is Helen Forrester's account of Liverpool in the early 1930s, *Twopence to Cross the Mersey*. The book, first published in 1974, describes the descent into extreme poverty of a middle-class family, following the bankruptcy of the author's father. One of its strengths is its implicit acknowledgement of the greater psychological difficulties faced by a once-moneyed family in adapting to unemployment. The working-class people in whose company they found themselves were far more resourceful in coping with the problems of joblessness.

None of this should be interpreted as an attempt to minimise the suffering of the unemployed and their families in the 1930s. There can be no doubt of the very real hardship experienced by people whose horizons were determined by steadily diminishing expectations of a return to work. There is clear evidence that unemployment had an adverse effect on standards of nutrition, as families replaced relatively expensive foods with cheap 'fillers', producing an ill-balanced, unhealthy diet. Interviews with the unemployed, carried out by organisations such as the Pilgrim Trust,

What do these sources reveal of the social contrasts of 1930s Britain?

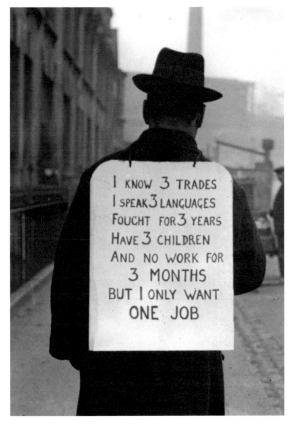

Depression and affluence: contrasting images of the 1930s

convey the equally serious psychological effects of their situation. The sense of powerlessness in the face of overwhelming economic forces, the gradual loss of hope and self-respect, are no less significant for being impossible to quantify. The most characteristic response to unemployment seems to have been a gloomy, fatalistic acceptance of one's lot. Thus a Carnegie Trust study of attitudes among young unemployed men in South Wales concluded that 'unemployment is not an active state; its keynote is boredom'. In the longer term the inter-war experience left a deep sense of waste and injustice, which led post-1945 planners to work for a better and more equal society.

Did the depression lead to political extremism?

The refusal of the unemployed to turn in large numbers to extreme remedies for their plight has often been noted. Sir Oswald Mosley's British Union of Fascists failed to make a major impact, even in the East End of London, where it concentrated its activities. Fascist violence and anti-semitism repelled the decent, law-abiding majority, while the movement's adoption of political uniforms seemed alien to British tradition. At the other end of the political spectrum, working-class support for Communism was limited to a handful of localities, such as the 'little Moscows' of the South Wales coalfields, where there was an historic tradition of militancy.

The one pressure group to concern itself exclusively with the problems of the workless, the left-wing National Unemployed Workers' Movement, was unable to overcome widespread apathy and suspicion of its Communist associations. Significantly, the organisers of the 1936 Jarrow Crusade, the best known demonstration by unemployed people in the period, refused to join forces with a NUWM protest. The Crusade, which was prompted by the closure of Palmer's shipyard, a major Tyneside employer, was a model of restraint. Supported by Jarrow's MP, Ellen Wilkinson, and by both Labour and Conservative councillors, the marchers went to London to present a moderately worded plea for state assistance in regenerating the local economy. After their appeal for an audience with government leaders was turned down, they quietly returned home. The episode drew public sympathy for the tragedy of mass unemployment, while underlining the fact that most of its victims were far from embracing revolutionary politics. The re-election of the Conservative-dominated National Government in 1935, together with the evident popularity of the monarchy, suggest that in broad terms the population shared similar values. The slump failed to undermine fundamental assumptions about constitutional government. In spite of the persistence of obvious contrasts, it seems that Britain in the 1930s remained a well-ordered and essentially cohesive society.

1. How and why have historians differed in their views of the British economy in the 1930s?

2. Why was there so little support for extreme political movements in Britain in the 1930s?

6.4 Could the governments of the inter-war period have done more to alleviate the problems of the British economy?

Treasury orthodoxy and the Keynesian alternative

The inter-war experience of unemployment and industrial stagnation has stimulated a lively debate about the policies pursued by the governments of the time. The post-1945 generation overwhelmingly took the view that the pre-war decade constituted a missed opportunity of tragic dimensions. Had the National Government undertaken an ambitious programme of public investment, the argument ran, Britain's recovery from depression

John Maynard Keynes (1883–1946)

A brilliant Cambridge economist, Keynes resigned his position as a Treasury civil servant in 1919 because he disagreed with the severity of the peace settlement with Germany. In the 1920s he became associated with the Liberal Party and developed radical ideas for government action against economic depression. He became a respected government adviser during the Second World War and was a major influence on the economic thinking of post-1945 British governments.

Bank rate: The interest rate at which the Bank of England lends to the commercial banking system

would have begun at an earlier stage. Such a policy would have increased the purchasing power of consumers and thus encouraged a revival of economic activity and employment. This approach was associated with the followers of the economist John Maynard Keynes, whose ideas found favour with governments after the Second World War. In the depression years, however, an expansionary economic policy was proposed by a mere handful of public figures. Those who advocated radical initiatives, such as Lloyd George and Oswald Mosley, were largely excluded from the corridors of power.

Instead, the inter-war political establishment remained wedded to a collection of ideas known as the 'Treasury view' and derived from Victorian traditions of public finance. This view placed great emphasis on the importance of a balanced budget, which was seen as vital to the maintenance of confidence in trade and industry. The aim of budgetary policy was to keep taxation at a relatively low level, so that it did not place an undue burden on productive enterprise. This placed limits on the permissible level of government expenditure. Orthodox thinking ruled out the idea of governments running a deficit to finance extensive programmes of state intervention. It was held that this would involve a risk of undermining private initiative and weakening business confidence. In conditions of depression, therefore, the natural tendency of governments was to abstain from large-scale manipulation of the level of demand in the economy. This was believed to be counter-productive and likely to exacerbate the contraction of economic activity.

Governments and the economy

There are two approaches that a government can take towards the economy. It can pursue a fiscal policy or a monetary policy:

Following a fiscal policy means a government raising revenue through taxation and deciding on the level and pattern of government expenditure. The budget, prepared by the Chancellor of the Exchequer, is an annual statement of government income and spending plans.

If a government pursues a monetary policy it regulates the level of money in the economy and thus the general level of economic activity. A government could use a reduction in the **bank rate** to make money cheaper (i.e. through lower interest rates, which lowers the cost of repaying a loan to a commercial bank) and thus encourage businesses to borrow and invest. Higher interest rates, on the other hand, make borrowing more difficult and are a means of restraining price rises. Decisions about fixing the rate at which one currency exchanges for another (or, alternatively, allowing them to find their own levels) are also part of monetary policy. These decisions will affect the balance between a country's imports and exports.

How could fiscal policy affect the problem of unemployment?

Since the 1970s there has been a greater awareness of the limitations of the 'Keynesian' approach to public finance. In particular, there has been a keener appreciation of the inflationary consequences of government spending – a dimension often ignored by those who have claimed that the governments of the 1930s could have done more. Moreover, historians now demonstrate a closer understanding of the constraints within which governments operated. One of the main arguments for government-funded public works was the concept of the 'multiplier', according to which demand would be generated as a multiple of the original expenditure. The idea would not, however, find

Classical and Keynesian views on managing the economy

- Classical economic ideas were well established in government and academic circles by the early twentieth century. Economists such as the Cambridge professor, Alfred Marshall, viewed the economy as a self-regulating mechanism, which did not need large-scale government intervention. It was subject to trade cycles, in which a period of downward movement in the level of output was followed naturally by an upturn or boom. Prices were determined mainly by the cost of labour (wages and in some cases National Insurance). In a slump, wages and interest rates would fall, bringing down the level of prices, until a point was reached at which businessmen would be able to start investing again. This would enable economic recovery to begin; prices would rise and full employment would return.

- Keynes argued that a general reduction of wages would have serious side effects. It would reduce wage earners' ability to consume (purchase) goods and services, thus keeping demand down. If interest rates continued to fall, there would be no incentive for people with spare money to invest it. The result would be a prolonged depression. Instead governments should focus on ways of increasing investment and consumption. They should spend money on public works schemes, to create jobs. Employed people would have money to spend on goods and services, which would stimulate economic activity.

- Classical economists argued that government spending on this scale would create a budget deficit (i.e. spending would exceed income). This was as bad for a government as it was for a private household. An unbalanced budget would hold up the revival of business confidence. Spending on government run public works would reduce the amount of money available for private investment.

- In response to these criticisms, by 1936 Keynes developed the concept of the 'multiplier'. According to this theory, a stimulus to demand could occur as a multiple of the original amount invested. By putting people back to work and increasing their purchasing power, the original investment would have a 'knock-on' effect on demand, encouraging activity in other areas of the economy.

- In the early 1930s Keynes likened himself to Cassandra, the prophetess in Greek mythology who was fated never to be believed. His ideas did not find wide acceptance until the Second World War. In the inter-war period, the 'Treasury view' was heavily influenced by the assumptions of classical economics.

full expression until Keynes' publication of his masterpiece, *The General Theory of Employment, Interest and Money* in 1936. The case for an expansionary programme of investment was not, therefore, fully formulated until recovery from the depression was well advanced. In any case, as the historian Ross McKibbin has pointed out, the small scale of pre-war British budgetary operations would have made such a strategy impossible. It would have called for a revolution in the machinery of government, to bring a greater volume of investment under state control, which would have been unacceptable to mainstream political opinion at the time.

The fact that governments did not use their fiscal (i.e. taxation) policies to 'prime the pump' of economic activity does not mean, on the other hand, that they pursued orthodox remedies with consistent rigour. A strict interpretation of the 'Treasury view' would have dictated a deflationary response to the depression – in other words, the raising of taxes and cutting of public spending, to reduce prices and costs, thus restoring **competitiveness**. In practice a balanced budget remained an unrealised ideal for both Conservative and Labour administrations. Philip Snowden, Labour Chancellor from 1929–31, raised taxation without reducing expenditure, to maintain the existing level of social provision for the unemployed. The onset of the 1931 financial crisis made necessary more restrictive measures, with the raising of direct taxation and of unemployment insurance contributions, together with cuts in public sector salaries. As the economic situation stabilised from the mid-1930s, there was a general liberalisation of government policy; income tax rates were reduced and the salary cuts were restored.

From 1937 increased spending on rearmament indicated a shift of emphasis, away from the pursuit of strictly balanced budgets. Nonetheless the National Government was reluctant to accept the need for borrowing as a means of financing rearmament. Traditional fears of the inflationary implications of government borrowing, and the need to reassure the financial markets, had a restraining influence. The eventual abandonment of these inhibitions was a measure of the seriousness of the international situation in the late 1930s. In short, inter-war fiscal policy was neither rigidly orthodox nor consciously radical, but a pragmatic response to changing pressures.

What impact did monetary policy and the gold standard have on the British economy?

The decision to return to the gold standard in 1925 at the pre-war parity has been widely blamed as a cause of economic hardship. As Chancellor of the Exchequer, Winston Churchill was formally responsible for re-establishing a **fixed exchange rate**. This was considered essential for the re-creation of conditions of pre-war 'normality'. The United States dollar was the only acceptable currency for a return to the gold standard, since it was the only one to have maintained its old parity unchanged. The price to be paid for restoration was a high one. To maintain the value set for the pound, interest rates had to be kept high. This made it expensive for businesses to borrow money from the banks. It also depressed the level of demand in the home market, with adverse consequences for both the manufacturing and the service sectors.

The case against the decision was put by Keynes in his 1925 essay on *The Economic Consequences of Mr Churchill*. According to Keynes, the Treasury had been misled by advice from the banking community into taking a step that left sterling overvalued by 10 per cent. Keynes predicted that this would reduce the competitiveness of British exports, leading to a general reduction of wages and to serious job losses in staple industries. The decision therefore sacrificed the interests of industry to those of the City of London as an international financial centre.

Historians such as Donald Moggridge, author of *The Return to Gold* (1969), have endorsed this critical attitude to the decision to adopt the pre-1914 exchange rate. They argue that post-war governments ignored the fundamental changes in Britain's world position that had occurred since the beginning of the First World War. The authorities had tied themselves to a single remedy and lacked the flexibility to change course in the late 1920s, when it became clear that British exports were lagging and

Competitiveness: The ability of an industry to produce goods at a price that will attract purchasers.

Fixed exchange rate: A set rate (or price) at which currency is exchanged for another or for gold.

unemployment remained at a high level. As Peter Dewey reminds us in *War and Progress: Britain 1914–1945*, policy makers failed to appreciate that British competitiveness had deteriorated during the war in relation to that of the United States. The exchange rate should have been determined by the realities of relative international efficiencies, and not the other way round.

In mitigation of the 1925 decision, it should be noted that there was nothing inherently unreasonable in wanting a system of fixed exchange rates, which would win the confidence of international traders and investors. British policy was based upon a widely anticipated rise in United States prices, which failed to materialise. Had this occurred, it would have reduced any gap between British and foreign prices and costs. Nor can the British authorities be held responsible for the fact that some countries, notably France and Belgium, returned to the gold standard after 1925 at much lower exchange rates than pre-1914. It is likely that these countries would have sought a competitive rate, regardless of the level chosen by the British authorities.

In his survey of *The British Economy since 1914* (1998), Rex Pope argues that an emphasis on government decision-making has distracted attention from more fundamental problems of British exporters. He identifies these as changes in global demand, continuing private investment in old technologies and a revival of competition following Germany's re-entry into world markets in the mid-1920s. This line of argument diminishes the responsibility of the government for economic difficulties.

Did 'cheap money' and the abandonment of the gold standard help the British economy?

It took the international financial crisis of July-August 1931 to force Britain off the gold standard. The National Government was formed to protect the position of the pound, after the second Labour government had failed to agree on a package of economy measures designed to achieve that end. Within a month of the new government's formation, a mutiny at the Invergordon naval base, sparked by news of spending cuts, caused a financial panic and compelled the abandonment of the gold standard.

It was ironic that it was the pressure of external events, rather than a deliberately considered government policy, that facilitated Britain's emergence from the 1931 crisis. The value of the pound stabilised at $3.40, thereby confounding the doom-laden predictions of those who had maintained that 'going off gold' would produce roaring inflation, on the scale of Germany in 1923. Instead the abandonment of the gold standard introduced a new flexibility to monetary policy, enabling a reduction of interest rates and thus helping to boost business confidence. The introduction of 'cheap money', with interest rates at 2 per cent, seems to have been at least

Permissive factor: A factor, which among others, allows an economic change to occur.

a **permissive factor** in the economic recovery of the 1930s. Although interest rates were irrelevant for many firms, whose investment was derived from reinvested profits, it certainly encouraged an expansion of the private house-building industry. The consequent growth of suburban Britain must have had a beneficial effect on other aspects of the economy by stimulating, for example, the road building and motor car industries. In this way government policy, modified by circumstances, had a generally positive effect.

Did the introduction of protective tariffs in 1932 help the economy?

Protective tariffs had been imposed on specific goods during the First World War to save shipping space when imports were menaced by German submarine warfare. In the immediate post-war period, measures such as the 1921 Safeguarding of Industries Act targeted certain industries which were deemed to be the victims of 'unfair' foreign competition. The success of the British dyestuffs and motor vehicle industries in the 1920s owed a great deal to the placing of tariffs on the products of overseas competitors.

Nonetheless, at the beginning of the 1930s more than four-fifths of imports remained untaxed. The defeat of the Conservatives, Britain's only major protectionist party, in the 1923 general election, indicated continuing popular support for free trade. The opportunity for a frontal attack on free imports was provided by the August 1931 financial crisis. The Conservative-dominated National Government's overwhelming electoral victory in October enabled it to introduce a general tariff of 10 per cent, with exceptions for Empire goods and food and raw materials. The duties therefore bore most heavily on manufactured goods produced by Britain's European competitors.

The government failed, however, to realise the vision of a system of imperial preference, to which a large section of the Conservative Party had become converted 30 years earlier. The idea was that Britain would sell its manufactured goods to the Empire countries, which in turn would sell their food and raw materials cheaply to the mother country. By raising tariffs against other producers, this would convert the Empire into a self-sufficient trading bloc. This dream did not correspond with the economic realities of the inter-war period. By then countries such as Canada and Australia had developed their own industries, and their priority was to protect them. Moreover in the 1930s the British government was committed to protecting its own farmers, which ruled out the free admission of large quantities of agricultural produce from the Dominions. Government subsidies enabled Britain's wheat farmers to enjoy guaranteed prices for their crops. Barley, oats and horticultural products were protected by import duties, while **marketing boards** were set up to aid other sectors. As a result the Ottawa agreements, negotiated in the summer of 1932, consisted of a series of **bilateral** deals and did not amount to an over-arching scheme of imperial protection.

Was protection worthwhile? It is hard to give a categorical verdict, since the effect on imports depended on the level of duty, the nature of demand for the product and the response of the overseas seller to its imposition. Protection helped to stabilise the position of the old heavy export industries such as steel, where the grant of a protective tariff was linked to an agreement to undertake reorganisation. Tariffs were a useful bargaining tool in negotiations to induce other countries to sign bilateral trade agreements with Britain. However, they were a blunt instrument that protected the inefficient and the efficient alike. The imposition of retaliatory tariffs by foreign competitors further limited the effectiveness of the policy.

What were the origins of government planning in the inter-war period?

The inter-war period also witnessed the first hesitant steps towards government planning for depressed industrial areas. The Industrial Transference Scheme, introduced by the Conservative government in 1928, was an attempt to improve the prospects of those living in areas of high unemployment, especially in the coal mining industry. The scheme's effect was marginal, largely because it failed to pay sufficient attention to aggregate demand for labour; in many cases miners were transferred to areas where unemployment was already problematic. The National Government devised a new regional policy in 1934, when it identified four 'special areas' – South Wales, north-east England, west Cumberland and Clydeside – where unemployment was particularly high. The intention

Marketing boards: These were set up after 1933 to help producers of specified products, by controlling prices and output. They covered milk, potatoes and bacon.

Bilateral: Involving two parties only.

was to encourage investment in these areas, although the level of funding allocated to the project was not high enough to have more than a limited effect on unemployment.

Governments fought shy of outright state ownership of industries, but were increasingly prepared to intervene where market forces failed to promote necessary rationalisation. For example in the late 1930s there were government initiatives to deal with over-capacity in the cotton industry. The chief effect of government intervention was to reduce competition, as in the case of civil aviation and road transport. The device of the **public corporation**, a compromise between private and state control, was used to establish monopolies in certain activities, for example in electricity generation and broadcasting.

However, neither these policies, nor the variety of subsidies and tax concessions awarded to industry and agriculture in the early 1930s constituted a coherent approach to economic planning. The machinery of government prior to 1939 was not adapted to a major expansion of the role of the state. The prestige and power of the Treasury enabled it to sustain its traditional function as a brake on government spending. The more 'interventionist' Ministries of Health, Labour and Transport, all relatively recent creations of the Lloyd George Coalition government, lacked the status to push for innovative policies. The result was that government aid and protection in the inter-war period tended to reduce competition and stabilise prices, without tackling the fundamental problems of the old industries, the twin challenges of inefficiency and excess capacity.

Conclusion

A comprehensive response to the problems of inter-war Britain would have entailed a planned overall approach to the stimulation of economic growth, migration of labour and location of industry. As Richard Middleton, author of *Towards the Managed Economy* (1985) has argued, this would have required a radical transformation of the existing political and administrative system. Perhaps the consequent erosion of democratic choice would have been too high a price to pay for the anticipated economic benefits. Instead, by the 1930s governments were moving in a pragmatic and piecemeal way towards greater intervention. Although this did not amount to a truly managed economy, it nonetheless provided a basis for more substantial departures in the field of planning after 1939.

Public corporation: A body run by a board nominated by the government, but operating largely on business principles and independent of day-to-day government control. The British Broadcasting Corporation, established in 1926, is an example.

1. What policies were available for governments to deal with Britain's economic problems between the wars?

2. What were the main differences between the Treasury and the Keynesian approaches to Britain's economic problems between the wars?

3. How damaging to the British economy was the return to the gold standard in 1925?

4. 'Cheap money and protection were vital to Britain's recovery from depression in the 1930s.' Do you agree? Use the information in this section to support your answer.

Source-based questions: Reactions to unemployment in the 1930s

SOURCE A

When people live on the dole for years at a time they grow used to it, and drawing the dole, though it remains unpleasant, ceases to be shameful. Thus the old, independent, work-house fearing tradition is undermined, just as the ancient fear of debt is undermined by the hire-purchase system. In the back streets of Wigan and Barnsley I saw every kind of privation, but I probably saw much less conscious misery than I should have seen ten years ago. The people have at any rate grasped that unemployment is a thing they cannot help. It is not only Alf Smith who is out of work now; Bert Jones is out of work as well, and both of them have been 'out' for years. It makes a great deal of difference when things are the same for everybody.

So you have whole populations settling down, as it were, to a lifetime on the P.A.C. And what I think is admirable, perhaps even hopeful, is that they have managed to do it without going spiritually to pieces. A working man does not disintegrate under the strain of poverty as a middle-class person does … Life is still fairly normal, more normal than one really has the right to expect. Families are impoverished, but the family-system has not broken up. The people are in effect living a reduced version of their former lives. Instead of raging against their destiny they have made things tolerable by lowering their standards.

From *The Road to Wigan Pier* by George Orwell, Copyright © George Orwell, 1937.

SOURCE B

Eventually I lived under a menacing cloud of fear that darkened my whole existence ?... There was no immediately obvious cause for it, no objective happenings or surroundings to which it could be immediately traced. It was a hellish brew, compounded of crushing despair, an abysmal sinking of the heart, and a mental distress so acute as to be well-nigh indistinguishable from physical pain.

I grew to an attitude of life that was entirely morbid. I sank deeper and deeper into a vortex of fear, depression and despair.

From *I was One of the Unemployed* by Max Cohen, 1945.

SOURCE C

One morning, however, the wait at the employment exchange was particularly long and chilly, and the ragged queue of weary men began to mutter rebelliously, and Father was drawn into sympathetic conversation with his fellow sufferers. They were, for the most part, respectable working men many of whose jobs were dependent upon the ships which went in and out of the port of Liverpool in normal times. They were curious about my father, because he spoke like an educated man ... They were friendly and, as Father met them again and again, they began to

fill him in on how to stay alive under almost impossible circumstances ...

There were agencies in the town, he was told, which would provide the odd pair of shoes or an old blanket for a child. There were regimental funds willing to provide a little help to old soldiers ... An open fire, he was assured, could be kept going almost all day from the refuse of the streets, old shoes, scraps of paper, twigs, wooden boxes, potato peelings ... One could travel from Liverpool to London by tramcar, if one knew the route, and it was much cheaper than going by train. Some of the men had done it several times in an effort to find work in the more prosperous south-east of the country.

From *Twopence to Cross the Mersey* by Helen Forrester, 1974.

---

1. Using the information contained in this chapter, explain the following terms:

a) the 'hire-purchase system' (Source A)

b) the 'P.A.C.' (Source A)

c) the 'employment exchange' (Source C).

2. Study Sources A and B.

How different are these sources in the impressions they give of working-class reactions to unemployment?

3. Study Source C.

How useful is this source as evidence for the impact of the Depression on people's lives?

4. Study all the sources and the information contained in this chapter. Do the sources give a complete picture of the effects of unemployment on British society in the 1930s? Give reasons to support your answer.

Further Reading

Articles

In *Modern History Review*
'The General Strike' by Margaret Morris and R.A. Florey (Vol.2 No.3)
'The General Strike: a bluff which was called?' by Joyce Howson (Vol.8 No.1)
'The Locust Years? Britain's inter-war economy' by D.H. Aldcroft (Vol.5 No.2)
'Perspectives: the 1930s – Britain in the Slump' by Ben Pimlott and John Barnes (Vol.1 No.3)
'Unemployment in inter-war Britain' by Joyce Howson (Vol.9 No.1)

Texts designed specifically for AS and A2 students

Britain: Industrial Relations and the Economy 1900–39 by Robert Pearce (Access to History series, Hodder & Stoughton, 1992)
The British Economy since 1914 by Rex Pope (Longman Seminar Studies, 1998)
Unemployment in Britain between the Wars by Stephen Constantine (Longman Seminar Studies, 1980)

For more advanced reading

Britain in the Depression: Society and Politics 1929–39 John Stevenson and Chris Cook, 2nd edn, (Longman, 1994)
British Society 1914–1945 by John Stevenson (Penguin, 1984)
The Development of the British Economy 1914–1990 by Sidney Pollard, 4th edn, (Edward Arnold, 1992)
War and Progress: Britain 1914–1945 by Peter Dewey (Longman, 1996)
The Working Class in Britain 1850–1939 by John Benson (Longman, 1989)

Documentary coverage

Democracy in a Depression: Britain in the 1920s and 1930s by Malcolm Smith (University of Wales Press, 1998)

7 The Conservative Party, 1918–1939

Key Issues

- Why did the Conservative Party occupy such a strong political position after the First World War?

- How did the Conservatives manage to hold office for most of the inter-war period?

- What part did Stanley Baldwin play in inter-war Conservative politics?

7.1 Why did the Conservatives fight the 1918 general election in partnership with David Lloyd George?

7.2 What factors brought about the disintegration of the Lloyd George Coalition in 1922?

7.3 Why did the Conservatives lose the 1923 and 1929 general elections?

7.4 Historical interpretation: Account for the Conservative Party's electoral dominance between 1918 and 1939

7.5 How can Stanley Baldwin's long tenure of the Conservative Party leadership be explained?

Framework of Events

1918	Conservatives agree to fight the December general election as members of a Coalition headed by David Lloyd George: 382 Conservative MPs are elected, together with 133 Lloyd George Liberals. They are opposed by 28 independent Liberals (followers of H. H. Asquith) and 63 Labour MPs
1920	March: proposals for the 'fusion' (amalgamation) of Conservative MPs with their Coalition Liberal partners are defeated
1921	March: Andrew Bonar Law retires as leader of the Conservative Party and is succeeded by Austen Chamberlain.
	November: the party conference at Liverpool approves the settlement of the Irish question negotiated by the Coalition government and Sinn Fein representatives
1922	October: growing backbench and junior ministerial opposition to Lloyd George's leadership culminates in a meeting held at the Carlton Club. The meeting votes, by a majority of 185 to 88, to end Conservative participation in the Coalition. A purely Conservative government, headed by Bonar Law, wins the ensuing general election: 344 Conservatives are elected, as against 142 Labour MPs, 53 Lloyd George Liberals and 62 Asquithian Liberals
1923	May: Bonar Law resigns as Prime Minister and is succeeded by Stanley Baldwin. The latter makes a surprise declaration in favour of a tariff policy at the October party conference, precipitating an election in December, at which the Conservatives lose their overall majority. With 258 seats, they are outnumbered in the Commons by 191 Labour MPs and 158 Liberals. This makes possible the formation of a minority Labour government in January 1924
1924	October: general election – the Conservatives return to office, with 412 MPs facing 151 Labour and 40 Liberal MPs. Baldwin forms a strong government, with Winston Churchill at the Exchequer, Austen Chamberlain as Foreign Secretary and Neville Chamberlain as Minister of Health
1929	The Conservatives lose the general election, winning 260 seats to 287 for the Labour Party and 59 for the Liberals. Ramsay MacDonald forms the second Labour government

1930	Baldwin's leadership is challenged by the 'United Empire Party', organised by Lord Beaverbrook, owner of the *Daily Express*, and Lord Rothermere, owner of the *Daily Mail*. Baldwin's moderate line on the future of Indian government also attracts the hostility of right-wing diehards in the Conservative ranks, led by Churchill
1931	March: the Beaverbrook/Rothermere campaign comes to an end. In August, a major financial crisis leads to the formation of a National Government with MacDonald as Prime Minister and Baldwin as his deputy. Conservatives work alongside Liberals and National Labour (former members of the Labour Party).
	October: general election – the National Government wins 554 seats out of 615. With 470 Conservatives returned, the party is the dominant force within the government. Labour wins only 52 seats
1932	The resignation of the free trade Liberal members of the government, in protest at its tariff policies, further strengthens the Conservatives' hold on power
1934	Baldwin defeats right-wing opposition within the Conservative Party to his policy on India.
1935	June: Baldwin succeeds MacDonald as Prime Minister.
	November: the National Government is confirmed in office, winning 429 seats (387 of these being Conservatives), to Labour's 154
1936	December: Baldwin achieves a final success, through his handling of the abdication of King Edward VIII. The King wanted to marry a divorced woman, Wallis Simpson; public opinion in Britain and the Empire countries will not accept her as Queen
1937	May: Baldwin retires and is succeeded as Conservative leader and Prime Minister by Neville Chamberlain
1938	The appeasement of Nazi Germany becomes a controversial issue within the party, with the debate over Chamberlain's Munich settlement in October
1939	September: Chamberlain takes the country to war, following Hitler's invasion of Poland. He is forced to give ministerial posts to the two most important critics of his appeasement policies, Churchill and Anthony Eden

Overview

B Y 1918 the Conservative Party had developed a distinctive identity and a broad base of support. In the second half of the 19th century it had evolved beyond its traditional land-owning roots, becoming the party of property in general – small as well as large, middle-class and urban as well as aristocratic and rural.

Conservatives believed in the following ideas:

● Free enterprise: The government was to interfere as little as possible in the economy. There were some exceptions to this: by the 1920s most Conservative

---

Leaders of the inter-war Conservative Party

November 1911 – March 1921	Andrew Bonar Law
March 1921 – October 1922	Austen Chamberlain
October 1922 – May 1923	Andrew Bonar Law (also Prime Minister)
May 1923 – May 1937	Stanley Baldwin (Prime Minister May 1923 – January 1924, October 1924 – June 1929, June 1935 – May 1937)
May 1937 – October 1940	Neville Chamberlain (Prime Minister May 1937 – May 1940)

Tariffs: Taxes on goods imported into a country. The opposite of the policy of free trade, followed by British governments from the mid-19th century to the early 1930s. Supporters of tariffs were known as protectionists.

politicians supported the introduction of protective **tariffs** against foreign competition. During the First World War, Conservatives had called for state intervention to organise manpower and materials for victory.

● Moderate social reform: Conservatives accepted the need to remove some of the hardships faced by the working population, partly in order to discourage support for the 'socialist' policies of their opponents.

● The defence of historic institutions: Conservatism was traditionally identified with the monarchy, the Empire and the Union with Ireland. Stability was the hallmark of British Conservatism; change was justified only when the alternative was judged to be worse.

Coalition government: A government containing representatives of more than one party.

The Conservative Party was the dominant force in British politics between the wars. Either on its own or as the most important element in a **coalition government**, it was in office continuously, with the exception of nine months in 1924 and just over two years in 1929–31. Even when the party lost a general election (in 1923 and 1929) its Labour opponents were denied a parliamentary majority. One of the main purposes of this chapter is to provide explanations for this remarkable success in apparently unfavourable conditions of mass democracy, unemployment and growing trade union organisation. One of the enduring themes of the period – and, arguably, of the party's whole history – is the Conservatives' ruthlessness in pursuit of political power. In 1918 the Conservative leaders judged that the party's interests would be best served by an alliance with the charismatic figure of David Lloyd George, who had made a reputation as a victorious war leader. Four years later the party was no less resolute in deciding to fight a general election independently of Lloyd George, whom it had come to regard as a political liability. In 1931 the Conservatives once again joined a coalition, when they entered a National Government with the Liberals and a small number of 'National Labour' MPs, led by Ramsay MacDonald.

The Conservatives proved resourceful and imaginative in campaigning for the votes of a democratic electorate. They were ahead of their opponents in exploiting the new media of radio and film to put across their message. They were also fortunate in the divisions that plagued their Labour and Liberal opponents. In Stanley Baldwin, who led the party for a total of 14 years, the Conservatives possessed a leader who was effective in generating a reassuring popular image and in maintaining unity through a series of crises and shifts of policy. Notwithstanding the conflicts over foreign policy issues under his successor, Neville Chamberlain, there is every reason to believe that, but for the political upheavals produced by the Second World War, the Conservative Party could have continued to hold centre stage. Most historians agree that there was little chance of Labour winning a peacetime election in 1939–40.

1. Place the issues mentioned in the mind map in order of importance in explaining why the Conservatives were so dominant in national politics in the period 1918 to 1939.

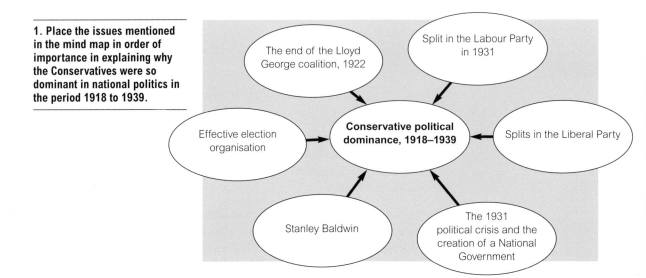

Leading Conservative ministers of the inter-war period

Lloyd George's Coalition Government, 1918–22

Andrew Bonar Law	Lord Privy Seal to March 1921
Austen Chamberlain	Chancellor of the Exchequer to April 1921; Lord Privy Seal to October 1922
A. J. Balfour	Lord President of the Council
Lord Birkenhead	Lord Chancellor
Lord Curzon	Foreign Secretary

Stanley Baldwin's Conservative government, 1924–29

Stanley Baldwin	Prime Minister
Winston Churchill	Chancellor of the Exchequer
Austen Chamberlain	Foreign Secretary
Neville Chamberlain	Minister of Health

Ramsay MacDonald's National Government, 1931–35

Stanley Baldwin	Lord President of the Council and also (from September 1932 to December 1933) Lord Privy Seal
Neville Chamberlain	Minister of Health, August to November 1931; then Chancellor of the Exchequer
Sir Samuel Hoare	Secretary for India

Baldwin's National Government, 1935–37

Stanley Baldwin	Prime Minister
Neville Chamberlain	Chancellor of the Exchequer
Sir Samuel Hoare	Foreign Secretary to December 1935; returned as First Lord of the Admiralty, June 1936
Anthony Eden	Minister for League of Nations Affairs to December 1935, then Foreign Secretary
Lord Halifax	(formerly Lord Irwin, Viceroy of India 1926–31) Secretary for War June to November 1935, then Lord Privy Seal

Neville Chamberlain's National Government, 1937–39

Neville Chamberlain	Prime Minister
Sir Samuel Hoare	Home Secretary
Anthony Eden	Foreign Secretary (resigned February 1938)
Lord Halifax	Lord President of the Council to February 1938, then Foreign Secretary

7.1 Why did the Conservatives fight the 1918 general election in partnership with David Lloyd George?

The political background

Andrew Bonar Law (1858–1923)
As party leader before the First World War, Bonar Law earned a reputation as a fierce opponent of the Liberal government's policy of Irish Home Rule. He accepted office in the Asquith Coalition in 1915 and served as Chancellor of the Exchequer and Leader of the House of Commons in the Lloyd George government. He was, in effect, deputy premier until poor health compelled his retirement in March 1921. In October 1922 he returned to active politics as a leading opponent of the Coalition. He served as Prime Minister until driven from office by terminal cancer seven months later.

From December 1916 Britain was ruled by a Coalition headed by David Lloyd George, the most dramatic personality in the Liberal Party. In forming this government Lloyd George had split his own party, causing a severe breach with the followers of the former Prime Minister, H. H. Asquith. The latter lost the premiership but retained the leadership of the Liberal Party. Lloyd George took charge of the country's destinies, supported by a minority of the Party's MPs. Between the followers of the two men no accommodation was possible. The new Prime Minister's political survival depended on the continuing co-operation of the Conservatives. They occupied three out of the five posts in the new, streamlined War Cabinet (the other two were Lloyd George himself and the leader of the Labour Party, Arthur Henderson). In the House of Commons, Lloyd George relied on the voting strength of Conservative MPs to maintain himself in office. It is therefore unsurprising that, as the war drew to an end in the autumn of 1918, he should seek to negotiate an agreement with their leaders to fight the coming general election together. Without such a deal he could not hope to continue as Prime Minister.

It is less easy to explain why the Conservatives should have wanted to continue their wartime arrangements with Lloyd George into the peacetime period. Why should they not feel confident of winning an election under one of their own leaders and thus having a chance of placing a Conservative Prime Minister in Downing Street? Before the First World War they had clashed repeatedly with Lloyd George, who had earned a reputation as a radical, high-taxing Chancellor of the Exchequer. With his relatively humble origins and Welsh nationalist background, he was an unlikely ally for the party of traditional institutions and inherited wealth. Yet in November 1918 he agreed a joint election **manifesto** with the Conservative leader, Andrew Bonar Law. Both leaders signed a letter of support – dubbed the 'coupon' by an embittered Asquith – addressed to Conservative and Coalition Liberal candidates of whom they approved. The ensuing general election was fought by the two groups working in close partnership.

Manifesto: A declaration of a party's intentions, published before a general election.

Lloyd George depicted in *Punch* as a conquering hero after the Paris peace settlement, 1919. He is attended by prominent Conservatives: Bonar Law and Arthur Balfour (in Roman helmets), Austen Chamberlain (the drummer) and Lord Birkenhead (with sponge and towel).

Of what value is this cartoon to a historian writing about the role of Lloyd George in British politics between 1918–22?

What did Lloyd George have to offer the Conservatives?

To a large extent the Prime Minister's image as a decisive and successful war leader compensated for his pre-1914 radicalism. Lloyd George had proved his underlying patriotism by working with the Conservatives to demand essential wartime measures such as conscription. In 1918 the Conservatives were reluctant to abandon a man who was popularly known as 'the man who won the war'.

Beyond this, it seemed likely that Lloyd George would have an open mind on controversial questions such as tariffs or Ireland. In spite of his pre-war image as a left-wing firebrand, at high political level there were clear indications that he could be flexible in practice, and that his attachment to Liberal ideology was superficial. He could be relied upon to adopt a realistic approach to issues of power politics.

Nor was this all. In the final year of the war all parties had agreed on a reform of the electoral system. The 1918 Representation of the People Act had given the vote for the first time, with minor exceptions, to all men over the age of 21 and to women over 30. The December general election was thus the first contest to be fought in truly democratic conditions. In the past the Conservatives had had to fight elections under a restricted franchise, which had excluded up to 40 per cent of the adult male population and the whole of the female population from the vote. In 1918 the size of the electorate was virtually trebled. In these circumstances many Conservatives despaired for their future as an independent political force. Bonar Law gloomily reflected that 'our party on the old lines will never have any future again in this country'. In contrast with the leaders of traditional Conservatism, Lloyd George was a **populist** politician who could speak to the working classes in their own language. It made sense to exploit his appeal and to cling to power through association with him.

Populist: Someone with a gift for winning the support of ordinary people.

The fear of Labour

Perhaps the most important concern for the post-war Conservative Party was the need to devise a strategy with which to meet the growth of **socialism**. According to the historian Maurice Cowling, author of *The Impact of Labour* (1971), British political history between 1920 and 1924 can be written in terms of the efforts of traditional politicians to resist this new threat to the established order. During the war trade union membership had increased from 4 million to 8.3 million and there had been worrying examples of **organised working class militancy**. In its 1918 manifesto the Labour Party had, for the first time, adopted a formal commitment to the state ownership of industry. When set against a background of Communist success in Russia's 1917 Bolshevik Revolution, the threat of social disturbance did not seem so exaggerated. The imminent **demobilisation** of hundreds of thousands of servicemen, coupled with the likelihood of further industrial disputes, provided powerful arguments for a united political front against Labour.

Socialism: The extension of the role of the state in the economy, with the intention of creating a more equal society. After 1900 socialism was associated mainly with the outlook of the Labour Party, although Conservative propaganda sometimes pinned the label on the party's Liberal opponents.

Organised working class militancy: Strikes by industrial workers, sometimes started without the approval of official trade union leaders.

Demobilisation: The process of returning servicemen to civilian life after a war.

For many Conservatives, then, partnership with Lloyd George was an essential guarantor of political survival. Bonar Law told his followers that he 'commands an amount of influence in every constituency as great as has ever been exercised by any Prime Minister'. To face the new challenges of the post-war world without him seemed an unjustifiably risky step to take.

A new partnership

It should be noted that enthusiasm for co-operation with Lloyd George was always strongest at the highest levels of the party. As John Ramsden, author of *The Age of Balfour and Baldwin* (1978) points out, most

Arthur James Balfour, Earl Balfour (1848–1930)
Prime Minister from 1902–5 and leader of the Conservative Party until November 1911. Balfour enjoyed a second political career as a member of the wartime coalition governments and remained a committed Lloyd George supporter until the downfall of the Coalition in 1922.

Lord Chancellor: Britain's most important judge. He serves also as a Cabinet minister and as chairman of debates in the House of Lords.

Conservative MPs accepted the advice of their leaders, that they should support the Coalition, but they did so in a detached way, without committing themselves to it permanently. Those who were most committed to the new regime were the party leaders, who tended to see the advantages of putting old party divisions behind them in order to tackle complex issues of peacetime reconstruction. Men such as A. J. Balfour, Foreign Secretary in Lloyd George's wartime administration, developed a personal regard for the Prime Minister through working with him in government. They came to envisage a new political environment in which sophisticated men of both the Conservative and the Liberal traditions could overcome their differences. Typical of this approach was the **Lord Chancellor**, Lord Birkenhead, who warned that the electors would reject 'those who try to marshal the dying forces of extinct controversies'.

In time this attitude would encourage some senior Conservatives to depend too heavily on personal association with Lloyd George, making them dangerously detached from the concerns and prejudices of the Tory rank-and-file. This approach therefore carried with it the seeds of the eventual disruption of the Coalition. In 1918, however, the attractions of an escape from pre-war party controversies seemed overwhelming.

1. 'An unnatural alliance.' Is this a fair description of the partnership between Lloyd George and the Conservative Party?

2. Was fear of Labour the main reason for the continuation of the Coalition Government in 1918?

General election results, 1918–1939

	Number of Conservative MPs	Share of total vote (%)
December 1918	382	38.6
November 1922	344	38.5
December 1923	258	38.0
October 1924	412	46.8
May 1929	260	38.1
October 1931	470	55.0
November 1935	387	47.8

7.2 What factors brought about the disintegration of the Lloyd George Coalition in 1922?

The continuation of party loyalties

In the first 18 months of the peacetime Coalition it was often suggested that the Conservative Party should permanently combine with the Lloyd George Liberals to form a new, dynamic centre party. Such a combination, it was argued, would be best equipped to tackle the challenges of the postwar economic and industrial situation and to exclude Labour permanently from power. Proposals for the 'fusion' of the two parties were not finally buried until March 1920, when Coalition Liberals voted against the idea.

Conservative Central Office: The professional organisation of the Conservative Party, established in London in 1870 and controlled from 1911 by a chairman appointed by the party leader. Its main role was to support the party organisation in the constituencies, to assist parliamentary candidates and provide publicity material and speakers.

Support for such a project was always strongest at governmental level, where the experience of working with former opponents had become an everyday habit by the early 1920s. Lower down the party structure the advantages were far less obvious. Rank-and-file Conservatives could not forget that, while their side provided 70 per cent of the Coalition's parliamentary strength, they occupied only 12 of the 21 Cabinet seats. Talented Conservatives such as Leopold Amery and William Bridgeman found their careers artificially halted at junior ministerial level by the need to find offices for their Liberal partners. **Conservative Central Office** loyally supported the party's participation in the Coalition, yet resented the need to stand aside at by-elections that they stood a good chance of winning outright.

Lloyd George as captain of the ship 'Coalition' with Conservative leader Bonar Law as his mate. March 1920.

WHAT'S IN A NAME?
Mate. "While we are doin' her up, what about givin' her a new name? How would 'Fusion' do?"
Captain. " 'Fusion' or 'Confusion' – it's all one to me so long as I'm skipper."

What does this Punch cartoon reveal about changing views of Lloyd George in the post-war years?

Party machine: A political party's organisational base.

MPs and party workers were well aware of the organisational weakness of the Coalition Liberals. They were cruelly but accurately described by the Conservative MP, J. C. C. Davidson, as a 'stage army' – a collection of prominent senior figures, such as Lloyd George and Winston Churchill, unsupported by a proper **party machine**. By contrast the Conservatives had a well-established and professionally-run national organisation. They enjoyed the advantage of a secure base in constituencies where more than 20 per cent of the population was engaged in farming or middle-class occupations. According to the historian Michael Kinnear in *The Fall of Lloyd George* (1973), throughout the 1920s the Conservatives had the support of 22.8 per cent of all agricultural constituencies and 43 per cent of the middle-class ones. Although this was not in itself sufficient for an independent majority, it provided a solid basis for negotiations with other parties. Knowledge of the strength of their grassroots support gave the Conservatives confidence in dealings with their Coalition partners.

Differences of policy and governing style

It was well known that many Coalition Liberals continued to think in terms of eventual reunion with the Asquithians, from whom they had been separated as recently as 1916. Their need to demonstrate their Liberal credentials antagonised the Conservatives. One example of conflict is the case of the Housing Minister, Christopher Addison, a radical Liberal who was later to join the Labour Party. He aroused Conservative anger through the high cost of his council-house building programme, forcing the Prime Minister to drop him in July 1921. The Addison case was part of a long-running concern about government expenditure, popularly known as 'waste', which underlined the differing priorities of social-reforming Liberals and economy-conscious Conservatives.

Local Conservative activists, whose collective voice was heard in the annual conference organised by the party's **National Union**, were most vocal in demanding that government policy be given a more distinctively Tory emphasis. The June 1920 conference heard demands not only for reduced government expenditure, but also for protective tariffs and reform of the House of Lords. The weakness of the latter had been an issue for Conservatives ever since the 1911 Parliament Act had deprived the Lords of the right to veto legislation. Rank-and-file Tories believed that it was essential to restore some effective power to the Lords in order to provide a defence against a future Labour government. This issue helps to explain the determination of the party chairman, Sir George Younger, and of the National Union's ruling executive, to frustrate Lloyd George's attempt to force the Coalition into a further general election in January 1922. Party organisers drew a clear distinction between support for the Coalition in the present and its indefinite continuation.

Conservatives admired Lloyd George's skill in resolving national problems, without really warming to him as an individual. His success in handling post-war industrial disputes persuaded many Conservatives that they no longer needed him as a barrier against left-wing revolution. At the same time his flexible approach to policy-making earned him a dangerous reputation for inconsistency. His response to the tangled problems of Ireland is a good example. At the end of the First World War British authority in Ireland faced a determined challenge from **Sinn Fein** and its armed allies in the newly-formed Irish Republican Army (see Chapter 13). Initially Lloyd George tried to defeat republican terrorism by force, reinforcing the British army with the violence of the Black and Tans. In the summer of 1921, however, he reversed the policy, embarking on negotiations with Sinn Fein representatives. The search for a settlement with open foes of the British Empire aroused the fury of the Conservative Party's right wing. It took all the authority of the Conservative Coalition ministers to persuade the party's November 1921 conference to accept the idea of a compromise solution. When Lloyd George sought to capitalise on his Irish settlement by holding a snap election, the Conservative Party organisation in the country rebelled. In this way the Prime Minister discovered the limits of his power as head of a mixed team.

In the autumn of 1922 Lloyd George's policy towards Turkey caused further offence to Conservative feeling. The Prime Minister and a handful of senior colleagues took Britain to the brink of war in order to resist the advance of a Turkish nationalist army towards the coast of Asia Minor. British forces at Chanak, a defensive point on the eastern side of **the Straits**, were instructed to stand firm after other European countries had withdrawn from the area. The policy ran counter to average Conservative opinion for a variety of reasons. Although the crisis was ultimately resolved without fighting, it seemed that Lloyd George had adopted a risky course. Bonar Law, who had retired as Conservative leader the previous year, sent a letter to *The Times* in which he declared that 'we cannot alone act as the policeman of the world'. Moreover the Prime Minister's support for Greek interests in the Mediterranean angered a party whose traditional sympathies lay with the Turks. The Minister of Agriculture, Sir Arthur Griffith-Boscawen, wrote that 'Conservatives generally would prefer to see the Turks there rather than the Greeks. A good understanding with Turkey was our old policy and it is essential having regard to the enormous Mahommedan [Muslim] population of the British Empire'.

Lloyd George's tendency, in the Chanak affair, to conduct policy with the assistance of a few like-minded individuals underlined another anxiety

National Union: Founded in 1867, this body represented the Conservative Party's voluntary membership outside Parliament. It did not have a direct influence on policy making but Conservative MPs could not ignore its views.

Sinn Fein: The Irish republican party, which at this period campaigned for the removal of Ireland from the United Kingdom. In 1921 the Lloyd George government reached a settlement with the Sinn Fein leaders, Arthur Griffith and Michael Collins. Southern Ireland, now known as the Irish Free State, would receive Dominion status – a form of self-government similar to that enjoyed by, for example, Canada and Australia. Northern Ireland would remain in the United Kingdom, with its own Parliament in Belfast.

The Straits: The narrow stretch of water between Europe and Asia Minor (modern Turkey), linking the Mediterranean and the Black Seas.

about his style of government. To many it seemed that he saw himself as a presidential leader rather than a traditional Prime Minister. His employment of a collection of unofficial advisers – the so-called Downing Street garden suburb – alarmed the conventionally minded. Moreover, in September 1921 he summoned the Cabinet to a meeting in Inverness Town Hall, in order to suit his personal convenience during a Scottish holiday.

Perhaps the most objectionable of Lloyd George's methods was his abuse of the political honours system. It was accepted practice for governments to offer titles in return for donations to party funds, and the Conservatives themselves benefited from such transactions. What caused offence was the cynical way in which Lloyd George allocated honours, with a price list apparently being circulated in the London clubs. Some of the proposed recipients were hardly suitable and in the summer of 1922 one of them, a shady South African financier named Sir Joseph Robinson, became the subject of a parliamentary debate. The air of corruption stained the Coalition's image, leading over 200 MPs to support a demand for all-party control of the honours system. It led a number of Conservatives, including the President of the Board of Trade, Stanley Baldwin, to feel that the government could not meet their expectations of high standards of honesty.

'Lloyd George's government was destroyed more by his style than by the content of his policies.' Is this a fair comment on the record of the post-war Coalition?

The growth of Conservative opposition

The most persistent Conservative opponents of Lloyd George came from the party's 'diehard' or traditional right wing. These people often had aristocratic or military connections and tended to view any liberal policy as a dire threat to national life. They had some success in 1921 when they became involved in a campaign run by the owner of the *Daily Mail*, Lord Rothermere, for the control of government expenditure. On their own, however, the diehards had little chance of unseating the Prime Minister. In *The Fall of Lloyd George* (1973) Michael Kinnear identified only 42 MPs who were unreservedly in their camp. Until the summer of 1922, when they found a more convincing spokesman in the form of Lord Salisbury, son of the Victorian Prime Minister, they lacked effective parliamentary leadership. Many of them held unreasonable and extreme positions, which prevented them from being taken seriously.

The revolt that brought down the Coalition in October 1922 succeeded because by then it extended far beyond the party's right wing. It involved the centre of the parliamentary party and was supported by the bulk of the Conservative organisation in the country. The fundamental issue was the determination of a cross-section of the party to recover its freedom of action. There was a growing feeling that, since Bonar Law's retirement from the party leadership in March 1921, the leading Conservative Coalitionists had become divorced from the feelings of their own supporters. They had fallen increasingly under the spell of Lloyd George and were accepting methods and policies that threatened the unity of the Conservative Party. The readiness of many Conservative candidates to run as independents at the next general election underlined their distrust of the Coalition government.

At the centre of the controversy was Bonar Law's successor as party leader, Austen Chamberlain. He allowed his judgement to be clouded by his loyalty to Lloyd George and by his personal belief that the survival of the Coalition was of overriding importance. He was a poor communicator, remote from his followers, who attended only three of the 26 major meetings of the party organisation held during his time as leader. As a result he tended to underestimate the depth of rank-and-file concern about the dominance of Lloyd George. The majority of Conservative MPs in 1922

Austen Chamberlain (1863–1937)
The elder half-brother of Neville Chamberlain. He had long experience of high politics, having first entered the Cabinet as Chancellor of the Exchequer in 1903. Apart from William Hague he was the only 20th-century Conservative leader not to become Prime Minister. His identification with Lloyd George put him in the political wilderness for a short time after the fall of the Coalition in 1922. In 1924–29 he served as Baldwin's Foreign Secretary. He was briefly First Lord of the Admiralty (in charge of the Navy) in the National Government of 1931.

Lord Birkenhead (1872–1930)
As F. E. Smith, he made his name before the First World War as a barrister armed with a devastating wit and later as a Conservative MP. He served as Attorney-General during the war and as Lord Chancellor from 1919–22, becoming a close personal associate of Lloyd George.

would have been satisfied had Chamberlain assured them that after the next election, the Coalition would be restructured to reflect their party's importance – in other words, that Lloyd George would be replaced by a Conservative Prime Minister. At times Chamberlain seemed to indicate his support for this position, but in the end he failed to persuade his followers that he would place the party's long-term interests first. The arrogant attitude of another member of the Prime Minister's inner circle, Lord Birkenhead, made the situation worse. One eye-witness, Lord Winterton, later recalled how Birkenhead taunted a gathering of junior ministers: 'Who is going to lead you to victory if you smash the Coalition? Some one like Bonar [Law] or Baldwin? You would not stand a chance.'

By September 1922 almost 200 MPs had informed their constituencies that they would stand at the next election as Conservatives pure and simple. Nevertheless, Chamberlain persisted in his preferred strategy of fighting the next election in partnership with Lloyd George and then attempting to determine the precise composition of the government. With the National Union conference scheduled for November, Chamberlain tried to stifle rank-and-file opposition by summoning a meeting of MPs at the Carlton Club on 19 October. He anticipated that the outcome of the Newport by-election, timed for the previous day, would support his claim that only the Coalition could halt the rise of Labour. With an independent Conservative running against the official Coalition Liberal candidate, he expected the anti-socialist vote to split, handing the seat to Labour. In fact Chamberlain's arguments were exploded by the result of the contest, where the independent Conservatives enjoyed a clear victory. In addition, the government's opponents found a convincing champion in the form of Bonar Law, who was now partially restored to health. He was persuaded to attend by the news that a meeting of almost 80 backbenchers had called for 'independent Conservative action, an independent programme and an independent leader'. Both he and Baldwin spoke at the meeting, concentrating on the threat posed by Lloyd George's leadership to Conservative unity.

The Carlton Club rebellion

Bonar Law (in top hat) emerges from the Carlton Club meeting in October 1922 at which the Conservatives voted to leave the Lloyd George Coalition

The Carlton Club gathering voted decisively to end the Coalition. Within hours Lloyd George had resigned from the premiership and Chamberlain from the leadership of his party. The events of 1922 highlighted the risks that lie in wait for government leaders who persuade themselves that they are indispensable. Some of those who attended the meeting considered that Chamberlain could have survived if he had accepted a compromise proposal, in favour of informal co-operation with the Lloyd George Liberals rather than outright coalition. D. H. Herbert, MP for Watford, later recalled that 'the uncompromising and somewhat aggressive attitude adopted by Austen Chamberlain surprised many of us, and even before Bonar Law's speech, tended to make us support the break up of the Coalition'.

The Carlton Club rebels were voting not to repudiate all notions of coalition government, but to recover the independence of their party from the stranglehold of this particular ministry. Baldwin's description of Lloyd George as 'a dynamic force ?... a very terrible thing', who had shattered the Liberal Party and might do the same to the Conservative Party, rang true. The vote marked the rejection of the style of government associated with Lloyd George and his cronies. Those who sided with Bonar Law showed that they valued honesty above brilliance, stability above unpredictability.

1. Draw a spidergram showing the main problems faced by Lloyd George's Coalition between the end of the First World War and the fall of the government.

2. 'A dynamic force can be a very terrible thing.' How far did the experience of Coalition government between 1918 and 1922 bear out Baldwin's description of Lloyd George?

7.3 Why did the Conservatives lose the 1923 and 1929 general elections?

1923: an unnecessary contest?

In order to understand the Conservative defeat in the December 1923 general election, it is important to be clear why the contest was held in the first place. Stanley Baldwin's dissolution of Parliament, only six months after he had inherited the premiership from the dying Bonar Law, puzzled contemporaries and has also been a source of historical controversy. The Conservatives had won a clear majority in November 1922, a month after the fall of the Lloyd George Coalition. Parliament had four years to run and the Liberal Party remained split between followers of Asquith and Lloyd George. Then, at the Conservative Party's Plymouth conference in October 1923, Baldwin announced that he was considering the introduction of a policy of tariffs, in order to protect industry and combat rising unemployment. Bonar Law had ruled out such a move the previous year and so a further appeal to the voters was needed before protection could be brought in.

The Plymouth announcement did not commit the government to an immediate election, but it took the party and the country by surprise and led to furious speculation about what would happen next. The result was that Baldwin called an election for 6 December. The Conservatives remained the largest party but lost their majority over Labour and the Liberals, who had unanimously declared themselves for the continuation of free trade. When Parliament met in January 1924 the Liberals, with 158 MPs, joined the 191 Labour representatives to turn the Conservatives out of office. Baldwin was widely criticised for having recklessly sacrificed a position of strength. His action had made possible the installation of the first Labour government. Only the fact that there was no agreed alternative candidate saved him from being ousted from the Conservative leadership.

In later years Baldwin devised his own justification for his behaviour in the autumn of 1923. He claimed that the tariff declaration had been a ploy to attract Austen Chamberlain and the other Conservatives who had remained loyal to Lloyd George in 1922. Protection was, he claimed, the one issue that could reunite the party. Even if the Conservatives lost the ensuing election, this was a price worth paying for having detached the pro-Coalition Conservatives from Lloyd George.

The main points of this rather subtle version of events were accepted for a long time by most historians, with the notable exception of A. J. P. Taylor. In *English History 1914–1945* (1965), he adopted the more straightforward explanation that Baldwin was seeking to tackle the problem of unemployment. By 1923 unemployment stood at more than one million, a figure equivalent to 12 per cent of the insured workforce, and it was thus becoming a serious political issue. The fullest study of the episode was published in the journal *Twentieth Century British History* (1992). In an article on 'Conservative reunion and the General Election of 1923', the historian Robert Self demonstrated convincingly that the re-absorption of the pro-Coalition Conservatives was not Baldwin's primary concern. He took up tariffs as a positive weapon with which to resist the Labour Party, and in order to pacify both right-wing diehards outside the government and more moderate protectionists within. Baldwin needed a new policy that would revitalise the government and give it a clear sense of direction. A close examination of contemporary evidence suggests that reunion with Austen Chamberlain and his followers became a serious consideration only in November, shortly before the decision to call the general election.

Self's study also makes clear how the Plymouth episode demonstrated Baldwin's inexperience as a leader. In making his announcement on tariffs, Baldwin seems to have believed that he could avoid committing the government to a general election before the following spring. Unfortunately the speech created such uncertainty that the only possible course of action was to dissolve Parliament at once. The decision took the party's grassroots by surprise. Local organisers had no time to prepare a professional campaign, and many MPs resented having to appeal to the electors little more than a year after the previous contest. Some had publicly committed themselves to free trade in 1922, and were thus highly embarrassed by the expectation that they should now support the opposite position. There had been no time to win over the press and the two most popular Conservative newspapers, the *Daily Mail* and the *Daily Express*, felt that Baldwin's statements on tariffs did not go far enough.

Key reforms of the 1924–1929 Conservative government

1925   Pensions for widows and orphans and for insured workers and their wives at the age of 65.
1926   Electricity Act transferred the distribution of electricity from numerous private companies to a Central Electricity Board. Creation of the British Broadcasting Corporation (BBC). (See Chapter 6, section 3.)
1928   Representation of the People (Equal Franchise) Act extended the vote to women aged 21 to 30.
1929   Local Government Act transferred responsibility for the poor from the old Boards of Guardians (created in 1834) to county and county borough councils. De-rating exempted agricultural land from rates (local authority taxation) and relieved industrial property and railways of three-quarters of the rate imposed on them.

One of the sharpest analyses of the defeat is by the historian Stuart Ball, writing in *How Tory Governments Fall* (1996), a collection of essays edited by Anthony Seldon. He argues that 1923 represented a serious failure of leadership on Baldwin's part. The policy was poorly worked out and left the Conservatives vulnerable to the charge that they would impose taxes on food. This claim had contributed to the Conservatives' loss of the 1906 election and was revived by a reunited Liberal Party in 1923. In defence of the historic Liberal principle of free trade, followers of Lloyd George and Asquith were able to come together for the first time since 1916. The accusation that the Conservatives planned to raise the cost of food for ordinary people in order to benefit the wealthy few also gave the Labour Party a useful card to play. In the circumstances, the Conservatives were fortunate not to lose more heavily. By entering an electoral campaign with a confused and unprepared party behind them, the leadership deserved to be beaten.

1929: the 'Safety First' campaign

The Conservative defeat of May 1929 is less easy to understand than that of 1923, since it came near the end of a full parliamentary term for Baldwin's second government and the party had plenty of time to prepare for it. Baldwin was personally popular and, although there had been clashes between ministers, he had led a remarkably united Government. The only resignation on a matter of policy (the Government's failure to achieve more extensive **disarmament**) had been that of Lord Cecil in 1927. He was a figure of marginal importance in the party. Moreover under the management of J.C.C. Davidson, Party chairman from 1926–30, Conservative organisation improved, with an expanding membership, healthy finances and new methods of publicity.

Nevertheless historians have generally been critical of Conservative preparations for the 1929 contest. According to John Ramsden's study, *The making of Conservative Party policy: the Conservative Research Department since 1929* (1980), little work was done on reviewing and formulating positive policies. Too much responsibility was handed to civil servants, who were not used to fighting elections. Partly because no alternative strategy had been worked out, and partly because Baldwin wanted to avoid potentially divisive issues, the party was forced to concentrate on attacking the programmes of Labour and the Liberals.

A great deal of criticism has focused on the Conservatives' electoral slogan of 'Safety First'. By contrast with Liberal proposals, in the so-called 'Yellow Book', for dynamic measures to deal with rising unemployment, it sounded unduly cautious and uninspiring. The Conservative campaign has received more generous treatment from the historian Philip Williamson, writing in *The Historical Journal* (1982). Williamson's article, '"Safety First": Baldwin, the Conservative Party, and the 1929 General Election', shows that the slogan was in fact a calculated attempt to exploit the strengths of the government's record. It was designed to contrast the solid performance of the government, and its reputation for responsibility, with the superficial glamour of opposition promises. Williamson points out that at the time this approach commanded broad support within the Conservative camp. Even Neville Chamberlain, the government minister most associated with constructive reform, regarded it as an adequate basis for electoral victory.

Nonetheless, the fact remains that the government did not convince the electorate that it had a clear sense of direction. By 1929 its most positive achievements, such as Neville Chamberlain's introduction of contributory pensions and benefits for widows and orphans, lay several years in the past. After the defeat of the General Strike in 1926, the Government had seemed to shift towards a more right-wing stance, thus losing its early appeal as a broad-based, moderate administration. The 1927 Trade Disputes Act, which attacked trade union funding of the Labour Party,

Disarmament: The reduction of a country's stock of weapons.

Neville Chamberlain (1869–1940)
Entered national politics in 1918, after a career in business and local administration in Birmingham. As Minister of Health from 1924–29, he earned a reputation as a social reformer. In the early 1930s he emerged as Baldwin's eventual successor, serving as Chancellor of the Exchequer from 1931–37 before becoming Prime Minister. He will forever be linked with the policy of appeasement, which reached its climax in the Munich agreement of 1938.

seemed vindictive. The severing of relations with the USSR, following a police raid in 1927 on Arcos, the Soviet trade delegation, marked a break with earlier moves towards conciliation abroad.

Conservative Party workers were not enthusiastic about the lead given by the government. In economic policy the government had not gone beyond a cautious policy of 'safeguarding' certain industries against foreign competition, so that full-blooded protectionists were dissatisfied. Changes such as the granting (in 1928) of the vote to women between the ages of 21 and 30 – popularly known as 'flappers' – were not calculated to stir Tory hearts. Many ministers, with the important exception of Baldwin himself, seemed old and tired. When the government revealed its master-plan in 1928 for dealing with unemployment, it came too late to take effect. De-rating – a proposal to reduce the rate burden imposed by local government on industry and agriculture – was intended to lower the costs of productive enterprise. Yet in the words of Cuthbert Headlam, a junior minister who sat for a marginal seat in north-east England, 'it is too complicated and revolutionary a series of proposals to be popular however good its effects may be going to be'. Moreover, shortly before the election, many householders found themselves facing rises in the rates that they were expected to pay.

In explaining the defeat Philip Williamson shifts the spotlight on to the increased scale of the Liberal challenge. Stuart Ball agrees with him in his essay on the 1920s in *How Tory Governments Fall* (1996). In 1926 Lloyd George had finally become leader of the Liberal Party, bringing with him not only new ideas about reviving the economy but also an influx of much-needed funds. As a result the Liberals were able to field 513 candidates, compared with 339 in 1924. There were no fewer than 447 three-cornered contests in 1929. In many cases this enabled the Liberals to take votes away from the government, allowing more Labour candidates to win. Labour was also a more convincing alternative to the Conservatives than it had been in 1924. It was no longer widely viewed as an extreme party – an image which the decline of industrial militancy, following the failure of the General Strike, had helped it to shed. With rising unemployment denting the government's claim to economic competence, Labour was in a position to make some gains. In Ball's words, Labour and the Liberals were 'the twin rocks upon which the Conservative vessel foundered'.

1. To what extent was the leadership of Stanley Baldwin responsible for the Conservative defeats of 1923 and 1929?

2. How far were the Conservative defeats of 1923 and 1929 caused by similar factors? Use all the evidence in this section to support your answer.

Source-based questions: The Conservative election defeat of 1929

SOURCE A

Proportion	Item mentioned
78.9%	Criticism of the de-rating policy and the reassessment of rateable values
73.6%	Absence of any 'positive', i.e. protectionist, policy, and criticism of the 'Safety First' strategy
57.9%	Criticism of the granting of the 'flapper' vote
57.9%	Attacks on the Party by a hostile press
42.1%	Leadership out of touch with the rank-and-file, and the ignoring of policy resolutions sent up through the Party organisations
36.8%	Intervention of a Liberal candidate
26.3%	Safeguarding not sufficiently emphasised
26.3%	Failure to modify the Defence of the Realm Act, and criticism of the Home Secretary
26.3%	Effects of the 'swing of the pendulum'
21.0%	Misrepresentation by opposition parties
21.0%	Failure to economise & reduce local and national government expenditure
15.8%	Failure to reform the House of Lords
15.8%	Criticism of the petrol tax
15.8%	Criticism of reforms in local government
10.5%	Criticism of the betting tax

The results of a survey of local Conservative Association opinions on the causes of the party's 1929 defeat. The survey was conducted by the Conservative National Union in July 1929. Quoted in Stuart Ball, *Baldwin and the Conservative Party: the crisis of 1929–1931*, 1988.

SOURCE B

I had originally contemplated an election in November 1928, but two factors affected the mind of the Cabinet. One was the large majority we still had in the House of Commons, which, having had since 1924, gave a sense of false security; and the other was a plot hatched by Neville Chamberlain and Winston Churchill by which they would scratch each other's backs on valuation and de-rating. Those of us who were in the professional side of politics knew perfectly well that the Labour local authorities would in March 1929 put in the new assessment figures in red ink on the return which they circulated to the ratepayers, and would feed the press with the news of the great increase of rates on small private people compared to the diminution [reduction] of rate on industrial concerns.

J. C. C. Davidson, Conservative Party chairman in 1929, quoted in Robert Rhodes James, *Memoirs of a Conservative: J. C. C. Davidson's Memoirs and Papers 1910–37*, 1969.

SOURCE C

The election was lost, not I think from any wave of resentment against the Govt. [Government] & certainly not against Baldwin, nor on any one particular piece of policy or legislation. Of the items which together produced our defeat I put the love of change common to all democracies or the swing of the pendulum as some call it as the first; after that the coincidence of reassessment with the derating bill which greatly prejudiced the latter, the cry of 'Safety First', the rather lukewarm action of past years in Safeguarding, the failure of most candidates to explain the Derating Bill, and put it forward as it ought to have been, as a winning card, and the wild promises of Liberals & Labour. Of course the money of L[loyd] George & his insistence on fighting every seat gave Socialism a victory which they could not have won, if arrangements had been made to avoid three-cornered fights where it was sure to lose the seat to a Socialist.

A diary entry for July 1929 written by W. C. Bridgeman, First Lord of the Admiralty from 1924–9 and a close friend of Baldwin. Quoted in Philip Williamson (ed.), *The Modernisation of Conservative Politics: the Diaries and Letters of William Bridgeman 1904–1935*, 1988.

---

1. Study Source A. Using information contained in this chapter, explain what is meant by the following:

a) the 'de-rating policy'

b) the '"Safety First" strategy'

c) the '"flapper" vote'.

2. Which is more useful to the historian of this period, Source A or Source B? Explain your answer.

3. Study Sources A, B and C and information contained in this chapter. Why did the Conservatives lose the 1929 election?

7.4 Account for the Conservative Party's electoral dominance between 1918 and 1939
A CASE STUDY IN HISTORICAL INTERPRETATION

The ability of the Conservative Party to retain power for so much of the inter-war period was not wholly due to the skill of its leaders or the devotion of its followers. External circumstances helped the party in this period to a quite unusual extent.

The electoral system after 1918

Although many Conservatives privately feared the arrival of full democracy, the extension of the vote in 1918 was balanced by the maintenance of some traditional features, which favoured the party of property. John Ramsden emphasises the importance of these in his study, *An Appetite for Power* (1998). He argues that technical changes to the electoral system denied Labour the chance of a parliamentary majority in 1929 and may have helped the Conservatives to remain the largest party in 1923. Plural voting enabled a businessman who lived in one constituency and owned property in another to have more than one vote. The university constituencies (including Oxford, Cambridge, London and the Scottish Universities), which were invariably won by the Conservatives and their allies, were not abolished until 1948. More importantly, the boundaries between constituencies were redrawn in 1918 to reflect population movements, giving middle-class suburbs a greater share of parliamentary representation. This alone was probably enough to give the Conservatives thirty more seats in 1918 than they had won in 1910.

Nor should the importance of changes in Ireland be underestimated. The Irish Nationalist Party, which had sustained Liberal governments in office since the days of Gladstone, was virtually wiped out in the 1918 election. Sinn Fein MPs, who won former Nationalist votes, refused to come to Westminster because of their extreme republican views, and thus played no part in British parliamentary politics. On the other hand the Unionist MPs, who dominated Northern Ireland, were firm allies of the Conservatives in this period. The 1921 Irish settlement guaranteed their position within the United Kingdom. Overall, Ramsden calculates that the Conservatives could count on approximately 200 safe seats, which gave them a solid advantage in the three party politics of the inter-war period.

The weakness of the opposition parties

The Liberals were plagued by splits within the parliamentary leadership and by weaknesses at grassroots level. Although Asquithians and Lloyd George Liberals reunited to fight the 1923 general election, the bitter split of 1916 had already done its damage. The Liberals were temporarily revitalised by Lloyd George after he took over the leadership of the reunited party in 1926, but even the 'Welsh wizard' could not reverse the party's long-term organisational decay. Many conservative-minded Liberal voters, who had been alarmed to see the party leadership support a Labour ministry in 1924, found a new and more appealing political home in Baldwin's moderate Conservative Party. Lloyd George's flirtation with the Labour government of 1929–31 encouraged a number of right-wing Liberal MPs to find common ground with the Conservatives. These '**Liberal Nationals**' became close partners of the Conservatives in the National Governments.

Although the inter-war years witnessed the steady growth of Labour, the party found it hard to win seats outside its traditional working-class

Liberal Nationals (later known as National Liberals): Liberal MPs who agreed with the Conservatives on the need for government spending cuts and tariffs to tackle the economic depression. A total of 35 Liberal National MPs were returned in the 1931 general election. Their leader, Sir John Simon, was successively Foreign Secretary, Home Secretary and finally Chancellor of the Exchequer in the National Governments. The party was formally amalgamated with the Conservatives from 1947.

industrial base. The second Labour government was badly divided over the August 1931 financial crisis (see Chapter 8, section 3). In the ensuing general election, it was vulnerable to accusations that it had 'run away' from making tough decisions on spending cuts.

The Conservatives themselves suffered from divisions in the inter-war period – over the Lloyd George Coalition in 1922–23, tariff policy in 1929–31, the advance towards Indian freedom in the first half of the 1930s and **appeasement** at the end of the decade. Yet, in spite of violent clashes between leading figures, none of these issues damaged the Conservatives fundamentally. In the end, however heated the argument, the Conservative instinct for unity reasserted itself. Over India, for example, the liberal line taken by the leadership was opposed by approximately one-sixth of the parliamentary party and by a strong movement in some of the constituency parties, especially in southern England. Right-wingers feared that an extension of self-government might lead to the end of British rule in India. However, the National Union Executive remained loyal to Baldwin and, at Westminster, the backbench **1922 Committee** helped to keep MPs in touch with the leadership. Whatever misgivings rank-and-file Conservatives may have felt about concessions to Indian nationalism, there was a general feeling that the issue was best handled by their own side. Baldwin and his colleagues could be relied upon to include safeguards for continued imperial control in the 1935 Government of India Act. In these circumstances the rebels, who had no spokesman of national standing apart from Winston Churchill, were bound to appear outdated and unnecessarily alarmist.

Appeasement: A policy, commonly associated with British governments of the 1930s, of making concessions to a potentially hostile power in order to secure peace. The 1938 Munich settlement, under which the German-speaking part of Czechoslovakia (the Sudetenland), was transferred to Hitler's Germany, is an example of appeasement in action.

The 1922 Committee: This began as a small club of MPs elected in the 1922 General Election. By the 1930s it had evolved into a committee whose membership consisted of all Conservative MPs who were not ministers. It provided a forum where Conservative leaders could meet their followers, in order to explain policy and gauge the opinion of the parliamentary party.

Winston Churchill (1874–1965)
Churchill had been a Liberal MP since abandoning the Conservative Party in 1904. He became a close associate of Lloyd George and held several Cabinet posts in the Coalition. In 1924 he returned to the Conservatives, serving as Chancellor of the Exchequer in Baldwin's second administration. He spent most of the 1930s as a backbencher because he disagreed with the party leadership's liberal line on India and its appeasement of Nazi Germany.

The Conservatives and Indian constitutional change

In 1929 the Viceroy of India, Lord Irwin (later Lord Halifax) responded to Indian nationalist pressure with a declaration that the sub-continent's destiny was to evolve towards Dominion status. In other words, it would become self-governing within the framework of the British Empire, like Canada, Australia and New Zealand. This line was supported by Baldwin and by the leadership of the Labour Party, but was violently opposed by diehards in the Conservative ranks. Churchill condemned it as a betrayal of Britain's imperial mission and resigned from the Conservative front bench team. The rebels staged a powerful show of opposition at the October 1934 party conference but were defeated two months later at a meeting of the Central Council of the Conservative National Union. They were unable to prevent the passage of the 1935 Government of India Act, which extended responsibility to Indians in the provinces and proposed a new federal authority at the centre.

Effective organisation

As Stuart Ball observes in *The Conservative Party and British Politics 1902–1951* (1995), 'the Conservatives were more truly a national party than either the Liberals or Labour'. The party had an organisational framework in all types of constituency and was particularly strong in rural, suburban and small town seats, where Conservative social events were an established part of the local fabric. The growth of a women's organisation was an encouraging sign. Apart from in 1922–23, funding was not a problem. The party was thus able to field more candidates than its opponents and to build up a network of professional constituency agents. Superior resources also enabled the party to distribute its publicity mate-

Using the new technology: Stanley Baldwin (on the left) making an open air broadcast during the 1931 general election with his National Government partners, Ramsay MacDonald (centre) and Sir John Simon (right)

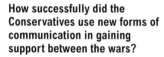

How successfully did the Conservatives use new forms of communication in gaining support between the wars?

rial widely and to exploit new methods of putting its message across to the electorate. For example, the Conservatives were the only party before 1939 to use cinema vans to attract audiences who might not have attended a traditional political meeting. They also developed close links with the commercial newsreel companies of the period. Although the latter were not mere tools of the party, in the 1930s the Conservatives and their National Government partners undoubtedly benefited from film coverage.

Policy formulation was another area in which the Conservatives developed a more professional approach between the wars. Under Neville Chamberlain's guidance the party leadership prepared carefully for the 1924 Election, establishing a policy secretariat to review options. The outcome was a document entitled *Looking Ahead*, the party's first comprehensive policy document. After the 1929 defeat a more permanent organisation, the Conservative Research Department (CRD), was created. The CRD proved its worth in gathering information for front bench figures, drafting speeches and helping to prepare the election manifesto. Thanks to the patronage of Chamberlain, the department acquired influence at the highest levels in the 1930s.

A reassuring image

Under Baldwin's leadership the Conservatives had remarkable success in projecting an image which was at once strong and moderate. In 1924 the party played on 'red scare' stories, contrasting itself with a Labour Government that seemed too friendly towards the Soviet Union. In 1931, participation in the National Government enabled the Conservatives to associate themselves with the theme of patriotic unity in the face of economic crisis. They offered a stable yet democratic alternative to the extremism of continental dictatorships. With the first signs of economic recovery by 1935, the Conservative-dominated National Government was well placed to win a further term of office. Prudent financial management, together with moderate reform in areas such as slum clearance and factory conditions, enabled the party to generate a responsible yet mildly progressive image.

As the historian Ross McKibbin argues in an essay on 'Class and conventional wisdom', published in *The Ideologies of Class* (1990), the

Sir Oswald Mosley (1896–1980)
A member of the 1929 Labour Government, Mosley resigned in 1930 and founded the New Party. In 1932 he started the British Union of Fascists, who imitated the authoritarian ideas and theatrical displays of Mussolini's Italian blackshirts. The BUF's activities were restricted by the 1936 Public Order Act, passed by the National Government to curb the wearing of political uniforms.

Conservatives strengthened their position by depicting Labour as the party of a particular sectional interest, the organised working class. By contrast the Conservatives persuaded a solid core of middle-class supporters, together with many uncommitted working-class voters, that they alone were fitted to rule in the interests of the nation as a whole.

On the political right there were no credible challengers. Sir Oswald Mosley's British Union of Fascists (BUF) remained a marginal party of protest, discredited by its attachment to 'un-English' political uniforms and violent methods. In Britain the impact of economic depression was never severe enough, over the country as a whole, to make people turn in large numbers to the radical right. A steady rise in living standards for those who were in work enabled a large section of the population, especially in the south and the Midlands, to benefit from the house-building boom of the 1930s and from the growth of new consumer industries (see Chapter 6, section 3.) Although diehard Tories might protest against 'liberal' National Government policies, few were prepared to support so obviously extreme and unconstitutional a movement as the BUF. Ingrained loyalty led the majority to stay in the Conservative Party, in the hope that they could influence it from within. Throughout the inter-war period the party included a broad range of views, with a secure hold on the centre-right of the political spectrum.

1. Why have historians disagreed about the reasons for Conservative electoral success between the wars?

2. Why did the extreme right prove such a failure in inter-war British politics?

3. How far was Conservative electoral success due to good party management?

Social reforms of the National Governments, 1931–1939

1933	Slum Clearance Act sets targets for local authorities to re-house people living in inner city poverty.
1934	Administration of unemployment relief is transferred from local authorities to a national Unemployment Assistance Board. Special Areas Act attempts to attract investment into areas where unemployment levels are highest.
1937	Factory Act reduces working hours for women and young people.
1938	Holidays with Pay Act extends paid holidays to 11 million workers.

7.5 How can Stanley Baldwin's long tenure of the Conservative Party leadership be explained?

The unexpected Prime Minister

In some respects it is surprising that Stanley Baldwin should have led the Conservatives for 14 years and have been able to stamp his own personality on the character of the inter-war party. H. Montgomery Hyde aptly subtitled his 1973 biography 'the unexpected Prime Minister'. Although Baldwin had been in the Commons since 1908, when he succeeded his father as MP for the Bewdley Division of Worcestershire, he had not had long experience of high office when he became Conservative leader and Prime Minister in May 1923. He had entered the Cabinet, as President of the Board of Trade, as recently as March 1921. He did not become a recognisable public figure until October 1922, when he spoke out against the Lloyd George Coalition at the famous Carlton Club meeting. The arrival in Downing Street of his patron and friend, Bonar Law, led to Baldwin's appointment as Chancellor of the Exchequer. Even then his succession to the premiership was not a foregone conclusion: in January 1923 he came into conflict with the Prime Minister over the terms of the American debt settlement, and revealed his lack of experience by disclosing the deal to journalists before it had been submitted to the Cabinet.

On several occasions there was a question mark over Baldwin's political future. It was his miscalculation that plunged the Conservative Party, without adequate preparation, into the December 1923 general election. In 1929–31, following a second electoral defeat, his leadership was threatened by a prolonged challenge from the two great newspaper owners, Lord Beaverbrook and Lord Rothermere. In early March 1931 key Shadow Cabinet colleagues prepared to abandon him and he came close to resignation. He was often criticised for not being sufficiently aggressive in opposition and the Conservative right wing never warmed to him. As Prime Minister he lacked a detailed grasp of many policy matters and seemed uninterested in the foreign and defence issues of the 1930s. In retirement during the Second World War, he was savagely criticised by many commentators for Britain's lack of military preparedness. How then are we to explain Baldwin's long period at the summit of British politics?

Good fortune

Luck, the simplest of explanations, takes us some way in analysing Baldwin's success. He gained the premiership in 1923 largely because the only credible alternative, Lord Curzon, was too difficult and pompous to be acceptable to his colleagues. Moreover it was generally accepted that, with Labour now the main party of opposition, it was inappropriate for the Prime Minister to sit in the House of Lords. Baldwin was fortunate in the timing of Bonar Law's retirement. It came too soon after the Carlton Club meeting for Conservatives such as Austen Chamberlain, who had been identified with the Coalition, to be considered. The lack of an obvious alternative also helped Baldwin to survive criticism of his leadership following defeat in the December 1923 general election.

Baldwin also benefited from the 'image problems' of his leading opponents in the 1930s. Churchill's attacks on his party leader over India were weakened by the violence of his language, which suggested that he was exaggerating his case for self-interested reasons. Memories of this episode also limited the impact of Churchill's warnings over Nazi Germany later in the decade.

A great communicator

Baldwin would not, however, have survived as long as he did without positive qualities of his own. Perhaps his greatest asset was a capacity to sense the public mood and to express it. He embodied his age in a way that few other politicians have done. With his baggy suits, country tweeds and trademark pipe, he was a figure with whom the general public could readily identify. His homely, down-to-earth style made it hard to remember that he was, in fact, both the inheritor of a large personal fortune and a highly-professional politician.

The titles of Baldwin's published collections of speeches give a clue to the nature of his appeal: *On England, Our Inheritance, This Torch of Freedom, Service of Our Lives, An Interpreter of England*. Through his public utterances, which were often addressed to non-political gatherings, Baldwin evoked a vision which was in tune with the instincts and feelings of his audience. He spoke nostalgically of a rural way of life which, by the 1920s, was fast disappearing. Sections of his 1924 address to the Royal Society of St George have become well known: 'the tinkle of the hammer

---

Sir Max Aitken, Baron Beaverbrook (1879–1964)
The owner of the *Daily Express*, Beaverbrook was a lifelong political intriguer. In 1929–31 he worked with Lord Rothermere, owner of the *Daily Mail*, against Baldwin's leadership. He held government posts in both world wars and was a close associate of Winston Churchill.

George Nathaniel Curzon, Marquess Curzon (1859–1925)
The most distinguished and experienced Conservative figure of the early 1920s. Curzon had served as Viceroy of India from 1898–1905 and had been a member of Lloyd George's five man War Cabinet. He was Foreign Secretary from 1919–23 and considered himself the inevitable choice for Prime Minister when Bonar Law retired.

Two photographs of Stanley
Baldwin

**What impression of Baldwin's
political style and image do
these photographs give?**

on the anvil in the country smithy, the corncrake on a dewy morning, the
sound of the scythe against the whetstone, and the sight of a plough team
coming over the brow of a hill?...' Linked to this romantic portrayal of the
English landscape were the enduring virtues of the national character: an
instinct for compromise, a basic kindliness and common sense, an ability
to reconcile freedom and individuality with order and responsibility.
Baldwin created an image of a nation at ease with itself, of a community in
which people of all backgrounds shared a common ideal of service. 'There
is only one thing which I feel is worth giving one's whole strength to,' he
declared in 1925, 'and that is the binding together of all classes of our
people in an effort to make life better in every sense of the word.'

In a country which had recently experienced the horror of the First
World War, and which now faced considerable economic and political
uncertainty, Baldwin's public image was immensely reassuring. As Neville
Chamberlain once acknowledged, he had a unique gift for communicating
with the politically uncommitted 'floating voter'. Baldwin's talent for words
was deployed to great effect, not only in traditional public meetings but

also through the new media of radio and film. He was the first major politician to grasp the importance of speaking to the radio microphone as if addressing individuals rather than a mass meeting. The introduction of sound newsreels in 1930 enabled him to reach a larger audience than ever before; at that time approximately 20 million people regularly watched cinema films. As John Ramsden observes in An Appetite for Power, Baldwin was 'the first British politician ever to become truly familiar to the voting public'. When he said, at the close of his 1935 general election broadcast, 'I think you can trust me by now', Baldwin was accurately reflecting the nature of the relationship that he had built with the ordinary voter.

A skilled politician

Baldwin's image as a plain-spoken countryman was deceptive. Churchill paid tribute to him as 'the greatest party manager the Conservatives ever had'; Beaverbrook, with more feeling, described him as 'the toughest and most unscrupulous politician you could find'. Although passive by nature, Baldwin could hit his opponents hard when the occasion demanded. The fact that he normally avoided excessive partisanship made him more effective when he chose to exert himself. His condemnation of the 1926 General Strike as 'a challenge to Parliament and … the road to anarchy and ruin' is a good example of his toughness in a crisis.

In the more subtle arts of political management Baldwin had few equals. In his 1924–29 administration, for example, he showed skill in maintaining the unity of a diverse ministerial team. He successfully combined keen protectionists such as Leopold Amery, the Colonial and Dominions Secretary, with the pro-free trade Winston Churchill. By offering the Exchequer to Churchill he surprised many observers, since the latter had so recently returned to the Conservative fold. Nonetheless the decision made sense politically, since the post absorbed the energies of a potentially troublesome colleague.

Baldwin's survival of the campaign orchestrated by Beaverbrook and Rothermere in 1929–31 showed him at his most skilful. The press lords' call for a policy of 'Empire Free Trade' struck a chord with large sections of Tory opinion. It was a re-packaging of the historic Conservative idea of imperial preference – the call for a comprehensive system of tariffs, designed to turn the British Empire into a self-sufficient trading bloc. With the 1929 electoral defeat a recent memory, Baldwin's position was vulnerable. The Express and the Mail possessed a combined daily circulation of 3.5 million and thus provided their owners with an influential platform. By 1930 Beaverbrook and Rothermere had formed their own United Empire Party, which opposed official Conservative candidates at by-elections. As the campaign increased in intensity, Baldwin showed flexibility in gradually moving closer to the Empire Free Trade position, while avoiding unqualified support for a policy which might prove an electoral liability. When the campaign against his leadership revived in the spring of 1931, he chose the right moment to retaliate against his press critics. Speaking in support of the official Conservative candidate in the St George's, Westminster by-election, he presented the issue as one of press versus people. In a famous phrase, he described the newspaper owners as aiming at 'power without responsibility – the prerogative of the harlot throughout the ages'. The attack helped to ensure the victory of the pro-Baldwin candidate, Alfred Duff Cooper, and to bring the Beaverbrook-Rothermere crusade to a close.

The Abdication Crisis, 1936

Edward VIII came to the throne in January 1936 on the death of his father, King George V. He was determined to marry his American-born mistress, Wallis Simpson. Already a divorcee, she was divorced from her second husband in the autumn of 1936. The government, together with majority opinion in both Britain and the self-governing Dominions, regarded her as an unsuitable choice. The King was the official head of the Church of England, which was opposed to divorce. Edward could not disregard conventional ideas of morality and expect to have Mrs Simpson as his Queen. The crisis was

Edward VIII with Mrs Simpson

resolved in December, with Edward's decision to abdicate the throne in favour of his younger brother. Edward took the title of Duke of Windsor and went to live in France, where he married Mrs Simpson in 1937.

Baldwin's handling of the issue was universally regarded as a personal triumph. As the King's first minister he avoided antagonising Edward, while ensuring that abdication was the outcome of the crisis. In so doing Baldwin demonstrated once again his feel for the middle ground of public opinion. Churchill and Beaverbrook, who attempted to start a movement in favour of Edward retaining the throne, were left in an isolated position. Baldwin was able to retire in May 1937, following the coronation of King George VI and Queen Elizabeth, in a glow of popular goodwill.

Conclusion

Lord Kilmuir, who served in the Conservative Cabinets of the 1950s, once described loyalty as the Tories' secret weapon. As Stuart Ball shows in *Baldwin and the Conservative Party: the crisis of 1929–1931* (1988), during the Empire Free Trade episode Baldwin strained that loyalty to the limit. In his anxiety not to commit himself to an electorally risky policy, he nearly alienatied those who most wanted a distinctively Conservative stance. He was fortunate that, as the Depression deepened in the course of 1930, protection became increasingly acceptable to business. This enabled Baldwin to adjust his economic policy to satisfy his own activists, without appearing to give in to pressure from the Empire Crusade.

Baldwin saw himself as educating his party in the need for a moderate, pragmatic approach to new problems. In his speeches he presented this as a characteristically Conservative position. As he declared in 1924, in tackling questions of social reform Conservatives were 'following the very traditions of Disraeli himself, adapted to the present day'. By generating a reassuring image of continuity, Baldwin persuaded the loyal centre of his party to accept change as a necessary part of life. This meant frustration for those who looked for a more confrontational style of politics.

The course of inter-war politics vindicated Baldwin rather than his critics. The creation of the National Government in 1931 isolated those who demanded a more aggressive Conservatism. Baldwin's instinct for consensus made him an ideal leader for the party at such a time. He was able to articulate a sense of national unity in face of the twin threats of economic crisis at home and political extremism abroad. In so doing he consolidated his hold on public opinion and made his position as party leader secure from further challenge. In 1937 he retired at a time of his own choosing, one of only three 20th-century Prime Ministers to leave office without being forced to do so by ill health, electoral defeat or a party revolt. This in itself was a considerable achievement.

'Baldwin owed his survival as Conservative leader solely to the absence of credible alternative candidates.' Do you agree? Use the information in this section to support your answer.

Further Reading

Articles

In *Modern History Review*
'The Conservative dominance 1918–1940' by Stuart Ball (Vol.3 No.2)
'Ditching the Goat: the fall of Lloyd George' by Graham Goodlad (Vol.10 No.4)
'Stanley Baldwin and the Conservative Party' by Derrick Murphy (Vol.9 No.4)

Texts designed specifically for AS and A2 students

Britain: Domestic Politics 1918–1939 by Robert Pearce (Access to History series, Hodder & Stoughton, 1992)
The Conservative Party and British Politics 1902–1951 by Stuart Ball (Longman Seminar Studies, 1995), also contains a useful selection of documentary extracts
Stanley Baldwin and the Search for Consensus by Duncan Watts (Personalities and Powers series, Hodder & Stoughton, 1996)

For more advanced reading

An Appetite for Power: a history of the Conservative Party since 1830 by John Ramsden (HarperCollins, 1998), Chapters 9 to 11
Baldwin by Philip Williamson (Cambridge University Press, 1999)
Bonar Law by R.J.Q. Adams (John Murray, 1999)
The Conservative Party from Peel to Major by Robert Blake (Heinemann, 1997), Chapter 7
How Tory Governments Fall: the Tory Party in Power since 1783 edited by Anthony Seldon (Fontana, 1996), Chapters 6 and 7
The Making of Modern British Politics 1867–1939 by Martin Pugh (Blackwell, 1982), Part 4

8 The Labour Party, 1918–1939

Key Issues

■ How did Labour change from being a trade union pressure group to a national party of government?

■ Did the Labour governments of the inter-war period achieve anything worthwhile?

■ What was the impact of the financial and political crisis of 1931 on the Labour Party?

8.1 How and why did Labour become a potential party of government after the First World War?

8.2 Did the Labour government of 1924 fail both the party and the country?

8.3 How far was the failure of the 1929–31 MacDonald government the result of fundamental fissures in the Labour movement?

8.4 Historical interpretation: Does Ramsay MacDonald deserve to be remembered as the great betrayer of the Labour Party?

8.5 How convincing was Labour's recovery from the disaster of 1931?

Framework of Events

1918	Labour adopts a new constitution, *Labour and the New Social Order*, containing a commitment to socialism for the first time. In the December general election, Labour wins 57 seats
1921	Trades Union Congress forms the General Council, which formally associates with the Labour Party in a new National Joint Council
1922	November: general election, Labour wins 142 seats, becoming the main alternative to the Conservative government
1923	December: general election, Labour wins 191 seats, and is able to take office for the first time with the support of the Liberals
1924	Ramsay MacDonald's minority Labour government holds office from January to October. It is then defeated in the House of Commons and in a further general election, losing 40 seats
1926	Failure of the General Strike. Conservative government's 1927 Trade Disputes Act inhibits trade union financing of the Labour Party
1929	May: general election. MacDonald forms his second minority government after winning 287 seats
1931	The Labour government breaks up because of divisions over how to respond to a severe financial crisis in August. It is replaced by a Conservative-dominated National government headed by MacDonald. Labour is heavily defeated in the October general election (46 seats compared with the government's 554). George Lansbury takes over as Labour Party leader
1935	Clement Attlee replaces Lansbury as leader of the party. Labour is heavily defeated in the November general election (154 seats, compared with 429 for the National Government)
1937	Labour's immediate programme outlines policies for a centrally planned economy
1939	Expulsion from the Labour Party of Stafford Cripps and other advocates of a 'popular front'. Labour supports the National Government's declaration of war on Germany

Overview

THE inter-war years witnessed Labour's replacement of the Liberals as the main progressive party in British politics. Labour gained only slightly more seats in the 1918 general election than it had done in the last pre-war contest in December 1910. Nonetheless, with more than two million votes, it had secured a larger share of the popular vote. Steps had been taken to lay the foundations of a more effective organisation and a new constitution had committed the party to the 'common [i.e. state] ownership' of industry as a long-term aspiration. These were significant developments for a party, created as recently as 1900 by a group of trade unions and socialist societies, to win parliamentary representation for working-class people.

Ramsay MacDonald, who was elected leader in 1922, was determined to establish Labour as a respectable and responsible party of government. In office in 1924 and 1929–31, this meant the deliberate pursuit of moderate policies to reassure the electorate that Labour was not a revolutionary faction. A clear-cut socialist approach, advocated by the party's left-wing associate body, the **Independent Labour Party**, was to be avoided. The fact that both administrations were minority governments, kept in office with the tolerance of the parliamentary Liberal Party, provided a practical obstacle to the adoption of a radical socialist agenda. In any case Labour's Chancellor, Philip Snowden, was firmly wedded to an orthodox understanding of finance based upon free trade, a cautious attitude towards public spending and the importance of a balanced budget. This effectively ruled out imaginative policies to tackle the problem of unemployment, which worsened appreciably following the onset of world depression in 1929.

In 1931 Labour faced a severe test of its credibility as a governing party. Faced with an international financial crisis, which threatened the stability of the pound, the second MacDonald government was unable to agree on a package of spending cuts. Acceptance of these was necessary if rescue loans from foreign bankers were to be obtained. The argument centred on the demand for a 10 per cent cut in unemployment benefit. A section of the Cabinet, led by the Foreign Secretary, Arthur Henderson, insisted that Labour's historic responsibility for working-class living standards should take priority. Rather than consent to the proposed cuts, nine ministers resigned, bringing down the government. MacDonald then caused lasting resentment in the Labour movement by accepting reappointment as head of a National Government, in which the Conservatives were the dominant group. He was joined by a handful of supporters, who took the label 'National Labour'.

Defeat in the ensuing general election and in the further contest of 1935 condemned the Labour Party to spend the remainder of the 1930s in the political

Independent Labour Party: Founded in 1893, this body advocated the 'common' [state] ownership of industry. In 1900 it joined with representatives of the trade unions and other groups to form the Labour Representation Committee, which took the name 'Labour Party' six years later.

Philip Snowden (1864–1937)
Snowden began his career as an activist in the Independent Labour Party in Yorkshire. His reputation as the Labour Party's financial expert earned him the post of Chancellor of the Exchequer in the first two Labour governments. He stayed with MacDonald when the latter formed the National Government in 1931, resigning a year later in protest at the abandonment of free trade.

Arthur Henderson (1863–1935)
The embodiment of Labour's trade union roots, Henderson served as party secretary for more than twenty years. He was the first Labour MP to acquire governmental experience, serving in both the Asquith and Lloyd George coalitions. After his resignation from the War Cabinet in 1917, he initiated a major overhaul of the party organisation. He was a key figure in the first two Labour governments.

wilderness. The 1931 crisis was a defining moment in the party's history, leaving a bitter memory of alleged betrayal by its leadership. Only the political transformation effected by the Second World War would make it possible for Labour to return to the corridors of power.

Leaders of the Labour Party, 1918–1939

1918–21   William Adamson

1921–22   J.R. Clynes

1922–31   Ramsay MacDonald

1931–32   Arthur Henderson

1932–35   George Lansbury (led the parliamentary party from 1931, after Henderson lost his seat at the general election).

1935–55   Clement Attlee

(The leader of the Parliamentary Labour Party was known as 'chairman' until 1922.)

---

1. Who or what was most responsible for Labour's successes in the 1918 to 1939 period? Explain your answer.

2. What do you regard as the most important turning-point in the history of the Labour Party in the period 1918 to 1939?

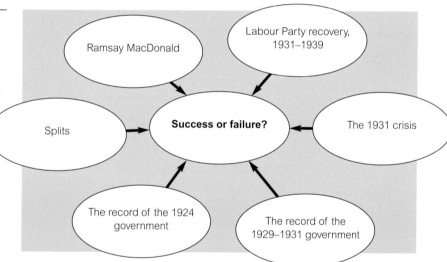

8.1 How and why did Labour become a potential party of government after the First World War?

The Labour Party was no less divided than the Liberals by the experience of the Great War. Ramsay MacDonald, the most outstanding of the pre-war chairmen of the Parliamentary Labour Party, had resigned his post in August 1914, in protest at Britain's involvement in the war. The majority of the party followed the new leader, Arthur Henderson, in qualified support for British intervention. A minority of Labourites outdid the Conservatives in passionate support for a vigorous prosecution of the conflict. Yet Labour emerged from 1914–18 united, with an increased parliamentary representation, ready to forge ahead as a potential party of government in its own right. By contrast the Liberal Party, which had been indisputably the senior partner in the pre-war progressive alliance, was weak, divided and in no position to provide national leadership. Why were the fortunes of Britain's two parties of the left so divergent?

The preservation of fundamental unity

The most influential study of this topic remains Ross McKibbin's *The Evolution of the Labour Party 1910–1924* (1974). McKibbin argued that Labour's emergence as a contender for power was a product of deep-seated socio-economic changes, which had begun before the First World War. The rise of the party reflected the growth of a strong sense of class consciousness among the industrial workforce, which found expression in the trade union movement. This meant that, far more than the Liberals, the party could claim to speak for the great masses of organised labour. Its foundation on the bedrock of class loyalty gave it an inherent strength, which divisions at parliamentary level could not seriously undermine.

Throughout the war Labour leaders maintained an essential unity on issues that affected the wellbeing of the working classes. The War Emergency Workers' National Committee, which concerned itself with everyday issues such as prices, rents and widows' pensions, was a practical example of this. Chaired by Arthur Henderson, it included MacDonald and other anti-war figures among its members. In any case, wartime differences of opinion in the Labour movement did not have the personal bitterness of the rivalry of Asquith and Lloyd George. The Liberal Party traditionally accorded a more prominent role to individual leaders and was thus harmed more seriously by divisions at high political level.

As his biographer, Chris Wrigley, has shown, Henderson's effectiveness as Labour leader derived largely from his capacity to reflect the consensus view of the Labour movement. His acceptance of Cabinet posts under both Asquith and Lloyd George enabled him to defend working people's interests at the highest level. Thus by declining to oppose military conscription in 1916, he was in a position to resist future moves towards compulsion in industry. His involvement in government enhanced Labour's confidence and laid down an important marker for the post-war period.

The growth of grassroots organisation

While the Liberal organisation contracted during the war, the Labour Party's began to expand and improve. In 1914 the Labour Party was still in essence a federal structure, whose membership was based upon affiliations through trade unions and socialist parties. This limited the party's ability to field candidates outside the small number of constituencies where it could rely upon the co-operation of a powerful affiliated body.

Henderson's resignation from the Lloyd George government in August 1917, following a dispute over his proposed attendance at an international socialist conference, provided an opportunity to overhaul this primitive organisation. Henderson encouraged the growth of local party branches, which, for the first time, would make possible large-scale individual membership. By 1924 only 19 constituencies lacked a branch of the Labour Party.

Nonetheless, one should not exaggerate the importance of this development. The continued growth of trade union affiliations was more significant for the party's electoral strength, since in most constituencies the unions remained the basis of local organisation. In the 1918 general election, no fewer than 25 of the successful Labour candidates were sponsored by the Miners' Federation of Great Britain. It was an accurate reflection of the unions' importance that, under the constitution adopted by the party in February 1918, they commanded 13 of the 21 places on the expanded executive body. Their continued control of party funding prevented the Labour leadership from carrying out a more equal distribution of resources across the constituencies. The overall result was that Labour consolidated its organisation in already winnable seats, which were typically in strongly working-class areas of the industrial north.

The franchise factor

The extent to which Labour benefited from the extension of the franchise, under the 1918 Representation of the People Act, remains controversial. The Act virtually trebled the size of the electorate, giving the vote to large numbers of women and working-class men. In an important article published in the *English Historical Review* (1976), H. C. G. Matthew, Ross McKibbin and J.A. Kay argued for the centrality of the 'franchise factor' in the post-war rise of Labour. They maintained that the Act's most important feature was the enfranchisement of a mass working-class population, whose predisposition to vote Labour could now find expression.

This view has not gone unchallenged. In 1983 Duncan Tanner, writing in *Bulletin of the Institute of Historical Research*, drew attention to the socially diverse nature of the new electorate. He pointed out that the pre-1918 voting rules had also excluded from the franchise middle-class sons living with their parents, domestic servants and soldiers resident in barracks. None of these groups could be viewed as automatic Labour voters. Moreover research into voting patterns among women suggests that they had exhibited a general tendency to vote in a Conservative direction.

Pacifist: A person who believes all war to be wrong.

As Martin Pugh points out in *The Making of Modern British Politics 1867–1939* (1982), the patriotic fervour of 1918 affected the outcome of the first post-war election. Those Labour candidates who won, such as the railwaymen's leader, J.H. Thomas, were often those who took a populist anti-German line. Those with a **pacifist** background, such as MacDonald and Snowden, suffered heavy defeats.

One incontestable reason for Labour success in 1918 was the straightforward fact that the party ran more candidates than in December 1910 – 388 as opposed to 78. This trend was continued in the post-war years; in the 1922 election there were 414 Labour candidates.

The drive towards independence from the Liberals

In the Edwardian period the relationship between the Liberal Party and Labour had clearly been one of patron and client. The latter had few distinctive policies of its own and had been heavily dependent on the goodwill of the Liberal administration for the passage of such measures as the trade union laws of 1906 and 1913 and the payment of MPs. In many respects the post-1914 Labour Party offered a safe haven to radical Liberals who had become disenchanted with the internal wrangling of their own party. Labour stood for free trade, internationalism and social reform in a manner wholly consistent with pre-war '**New Liberalism**'. The Union of Democratic Control, a wartime society that campaigned for a popular voice in foreign policy making, provided a forum in which representatives of both parties worked together. Its members included the idealistic Liberal, Charles Trevelyan, who was shortly to join the Labour Party in protest at the vindictive nature of the Versailles peace settlement.

New Liberalism: The social reforming ideas associated with the pre-1914 administrations of Campbell-Bannerman and Asquith. These governments took a more positive view than their 19th-century predecessors of the role of the state in society.

Nationalisation: The idea of state or common ownership of industry, expressed in clause four of Labour's 1918 constitution.

Capitalist: A supporter of the system of private enterprise.

Yet the younger party was also concerned with carving out for itself a new, clearly defined identity. This was one of the main reasons for the adoption, in its 1918 constitution, of a commitment to 'the common ownership of the means of production'. The espousal of **nationalisation** as a long-term aspiration for industry enabled the party to distinguish itself from the essentially **capitalist** Liberal Party.

National Executive: The Labour Party's governing body, especially important in periods of opposition, on which the trade unions, the constituency parties and the parliamentary party were represented.

---

1. Which of the factors discussed in this section do you think was most important in making Labour a potential party of government? Give reasons for your answer.

2. 'Labour's success in the period 1914–22 owed more to the mistakes of the party's opponents than to the skills of the Labour leadership.' Do you agree? Give reasons for your answer.

The drive to independent status was also reflected in the party's electoral strategy. Henderson's approach as leader was to contest by-elections wherever the local Labour organisation made a challenge feasible. Asked in December 1917 whether he would spare the seats of radical Liberals, he replied that 'discrimination would be difficult and that broadly he thought the policy would be to run a Labour candidate wherever there was a tolerable chance of carrying him'. This strategy was demonstrated in two Lancashire by-elections in the autumn of 1919. At Widnes, where he was a candidate, Henderson was happy to accept Liberal support. Yet shortly afterwards, in the Rusholme division of Manchester, a largely middle-class seat in which the Liberals had expected a free run, Labour's **National Executive** ran its own candidate.

Labour displayed its new-found ruthlessness most effectively in the 1923 general election, when the party ignored the fact that it shared obvious common ground with the Liberals on the central issue of the contest – free trade versus protection. With the possibility of power at last in sight, Labour's leaders could not afford the luxury of sentimentality towards their former partners. After 1918 they seized the opportunity to polarise politics between themselves and the Conservatives, so that the Liberals were gradually squeezed out as an effective rival.

8.2 Did the Labour government of 1924 fail both the party and the country?

J. R. Clynes (1869–1949)
He came from the party's trade union wing. Clynes served as Lord Privy Seal in 1924 and as Home Secretary in 1929–31.

J. H. Thomas (1874–1949)
A leading figure in the National Union of Railwaymen, Thomas was a friend of MacDonald. He served in both inter-war Labour Cabinets and in the National Government, until his disgrace in 1936 for revealing budget secrets. The cartoonist David Low invariably depicted him as 'the Rt. Hon. Dress Suit' on account of the enthusiasm with which he participated in high society.

The appointment of the first Labour government in January 1924 was widely regarded by contemporaries as an event of great political and social significance. King George V wrote in his diary, 'Today 23 years ago, dear Grandmama [Queen Victoria] died. I wonder what she would have made of a Labour government!' The new Prime Minister, Ramsay MacDonald, lacked the governmental experience of his predecessors and had risen from obscure origins, the illegitimate child of Scottish fisherfolk. One of the Labour ministers, J. R. Clynes, later recalled 'the strange turn in Fortune's wheel which had brought MacDonald the starveling clerk, Thomas the engine driver, Henderson the foundry labourer and Clynes the mill-hand' to the Cabinet room. Many on the political right expressed alarmist expectations of attacks on private property and established institutions. Among the more extreme predictions was a claim that women would be nationalised and free love proclaimed as official government policy. Winston Churchill, at that time shifting his allegiance from the Liberal Party to the Conservatives, wrote that 'the enthronement in office of a Socialist government will be a serious national misfortune such as has usually befallen great States only on the morrow of defeat in war'.

Notwithstanding such apocalyptic pronouncements, the government's behaviour proved to be so moderate that its most radical supporters were to be gravely disappointed. After less than ten months in office, no significant steps had been taken towards the achievement of socialist goals. The party suffered a heavy defeat in the general election of October 1924, winning 151 seats to the Conservatives' 419. Labour was not to form another government for almost five years. In the eyes of the left wing and

Leading members of the 1924 Labour Government

Prime Minister and Foreign Secretary	Ramsay MacDonald
Chancellor of the Exchequer	Philip Snowden
Home Secretary	Arthur Henderson
Colonial Secretary	J. H. Thomas

Members of the first Labour Government arrive at Buckingham Palace to receive the seals of office. Left to right: Ramsay MacDonald, J. H. Thomas, Arthur Henderson, J. R. Clynes (January 1924).

How important were Ramsay MacDonald and Arthur Henderson for the rise of the Labour Party between the wars?

of many trade unionists, the MacDonald administration had failed to justify the confidence placed in it a short time earlier. How are we to assess the record of that government today?

The decision to take office

The performance of the first Labour government was to be affected to a large extent by the circumstances in which it took office. It is important to remember that it was a minority administration, which had come to power because of the peculiar outcome of the December 1923 general election. Stanley Baldwin's Conservative government had dissolved Parliament in an abortive attempt to secure a mandate for the introduction of protective tariffs. Although the Conservatives, with 258 seats, remained the largest party in the Commons, they were outnumbered by the Liberals (159 seats) and Labour (191 seats), who had both campaigned in defence of free trade. Since the contest had turned on one issue, it could legitimately be argued that Labour, as the largest pro-free trade party, had the right to form a government. On the other hand, this would mean forming a ministry with the acquiescence of the Liberals, who could withdraw their support at any time.

In these circumstances Labour's term of office was unlikely to be more than a rather unsatisfactory apprenticeship in power. Some on the left were uneasy about the idea of taking office at all, fearing that the party would be hopelessly compromised by the institutions of capitalist society. The left-wing MPs elected for the Clydeside region of Scotland, supported by the Independent Labour Party, argued that MacDonald should deliberately court parliamentary defeat with an uncompromising socialist programme. The ensuing election would then enable the party to rally support in the country for a revolutionary transformation of society.

MacDonald risked the anger of committed socialists by declining to 'ride for a fall' in the manner recommended by the class warriors of the left. Instead he resolved that a policy of moderation was essential, to give the party a chance to prove its capacity to govern responsibly. If Labour was to establish itself as something more than a party of protest, it needed to win the confidence of the ideologically uncommitted outside the ranks of the movement. If Labour could exercise authority with dignity, it could consolidate its lead over the Liberals, which it had won since the end of the Great War. As MacDonald's biographer, David Marquand, points out, such an approach was dictated both by the circumstances of 1924 and by the nature of the Labour Party. Extreme care in demonstrating Labour's respectability was 'the price they paid for belonging to a working-class party which aspired to govern a class-divided and hierarchical society'.

The composition of the Cabinet was at one with this strategy. To compensate for his colleagues' lack of ministerial experience, MacDonald filled many posts with former members of the Conservative and Liberal Parties. The new ministers were schooled in constitutional practice by the Lord Chancellor, Lord Haldane, who had held the same office under Asquith. Only the Minister of Health, John Wheatley, was clearly drawn from the Labour left. Even in such an apparently minor area as the decision to wear traditional Court dress on ceremonial occasions, Labour's representatives emphasised their conformity to social convention.

The government's record

In domestic policy the government was consistent in its avoidance of radical departures. Perhaps its most creative action was Wheatley's Housing Act, which allocated state subsidies to local authorities, enabling them to build houses for rent. This was an extension of council housing policies initiated by Christopher Addison as Minister of Health in the post-war Lloyd George Coalition. On the central problem of unemployment, the Labour government offered no action beyond the uncontroversial funding of public works schemes. Faced with the threat of strikes by dockers and London transport workers, the government showed a readiness to use emergency powers bequeathed by the Lloyd George administration. MacDonald's insistence on the need to govern in the national interest effectively ruled out any particular sympathy for the trade union movement.

Continuity was also the hallmark of the government's imperial policy. Although work on the costly Singapore naval base was halted, there was certainly no indication that Labour stood for the abandonment of imperial commitments in general. Only in the field of foreign affairs could the government be said to have developed something approaching a distinctive line. Here Labour's emphasis on the reconciliation of post-war Germany bore fruit in negotiations for the withdrawal of the French army of occupation from the Ruhr. This was followed by MacDonald's chairmanship of a conference in London, at which the Dawes Plan, an attempt to alleviate Germany's reparations burden, was launched. This, the first successful attempt to mitigate the rigours of the Versailles settlement, set the tone for the policies of Governments of both parties over the next decade and a half. The emphasis was on making concessions to Germany, in the interests of wider European security. MacDonald's attempt, in the so-called **Geneva Protocol**, to widen the power of the League of Nations to settle international disputes, was less successful. The Protocol had not been ratified before the fall of the government and it was allowed to drop by the incoming Conservative administration.

Decline and fall

The manner in which the government met its end casts grave doubt on the political sensitivity of its leading figures. MacDonald's attempt to negotiate treaties with the Soviet Union gave the opposition parties a perfect opportunity to label the government as pro-Communist. The proposal to offer a loan to the Soviet regime, in return for a vague agreement to compensate British investors who had lost their claims in the Bolshevik revolution, was particularly damaging to Labour.

The government's mishandling of a law case involving J. R. Campbell, the acting editor of the Communist *Workers' Weekly*, gave Labour's opponents a

Geneva Protocol: A document promoted by MacDonald at the League of Nations. The signatories promised to accept a peaceful settlement of all international disputes and to disarm by agreement. They also agreed to offer support to each other if faced with unprovoked aggression.

further handle for criticism. After Campbell wrote an article calling on troops not to allow themselves to be used against strikers, the Attorney-General, Sir Patrick Hastings, started a prosecution. When the government decided to withdraw the charges, it laid itself open to opposition claims that it was being manipulated by extreme left elements. Conservatives and Liberals then united to defeat the government in the Commons.

In the ensuing general election campaign Labour was again identified in the public eye with the 'red menace'. This was through the publication of the notorious Zinoviev letter, an incitement to **sedition** apparently written by the president of the Communist International in the Soviet Union. The letter probably had a limited impact on the outcome of the election, which would have resulted in a Conservative victory even had it never appeared. In 1999 an official investigation suggested that the letter was forged by an exiled opponent of the Russian Revolution and leaked by members of MI5 and MI6, Britain's security services, to tarnish Labour's image. Historians agree, however, that the real significance of the letter was the way in which it gave Labour a plausible explanation for its defeat. Labour spokesmen maintained that it was a forgery and that they had been the innocent victims of a capitalist conspiracy. In this way the episode served to distract attention from an honest examination of the party's real weaknesses.

Sedition: An attempt, by speech or writing, to encourage disorder and disobedience to legal authority.

1924 and the future of Labour

Labour's defeat in the 1924 contest obscured the fact that the real losers were the Liberals, whose share of the poll had fallen from just under 30 per cent to less than 18 per cent since the previous contest. The strain of fighting three general elections in the space of two years had placed a considerable strain on the resources of a party denied the solid financial backing of the trade union movement. Moreover it seems likely that, influenced by the 'red scare' atmosphere of 1924, many moderate Liberal voters had turned to the more reassuring Conservative Party. By completing the destruction of the Liberal Party as a credible instrument of government, the election had fulfilled the most important purpose of MacDonald and his colleagues.

On the other hand, the experience of 1924 left many unresolved problems for Labour. In *The Making of Modern British Politics* Martin Pugh argues that MacDonald welcomed the coalescence of Conservative and Liberal opposition to the government in the autumn of 1924. Had the government not been released from office at that point, the passage of more time would simply have made the simmering conflict with the party's left harder to contain. Nine months was long enough to demonstrate Labour's capacity to govern. An extended term of office would have exposed the latent tensions within the Labour movement.

1. Did the Labour government of 1924 have any worthwhile achievements to its credit? Give reasons to support your answer.

2. 'The author of its own downfall.' Is this a fair verdict on the first Labour government? Give reasons to support your answer.

Two questions in particular would have to be faced if Labour were to have a chance of forming a more successful second administration. Serious thinking about unemployment, the dominant social issue of the decade, would have to be done. Further, the relationship between a Labour government and the trade unions would have to be properly defined. The real tragedy of 1924 was that a party that could claim to have been sabotaged by external forces was unlikely to undertake a thoroughgoing appraisal of its own shortcomings.

Source-based questions: The Labour government of 1924

SOURCE A

It would seem that the immediate future is now settled; that Baldwin is to resign and Ramsay to come in. I doubt whether either of them is right. Baldwin could easily have snapped his fingers at the no confidence amendment and announced that, as leader of much the largest section of the House, he had better moral authority than anyone else to carry on the King's Government until he was absolutely blocked, and Ramsay might well have declined to start the first Labour Government under impossible parliamentary conditions.

A letter from H.H. Asquith to a Liberal MP, W.M.R. Pringle, 10 January 1924. Quoted in *Asquith* by Roy Jenkins, 1964.

SOURCE B

It is possible for a Labour Government to exaggerate the limitation imposed upon it by the difficult position, to distrust its own power, and to forget that it has a far firmer hold on the mind of the country than on the mind of the House of Commons … the I. L. P. believes a minority Labour Government even now can advance Socialism by its legislative and administrative acts …. Why should we not at once devote the vast resources of the Government and the ability of its loyal and disinterested advisers, and of other representatives of the community to enquire into the application of Socialist principles to the reorganisation of industry and our economic life?

From Clifford Allen's chairman's address to the Easter conference of the Independent Labour Party, 1924. Quoted in *Clifford Allen: the open conspirator* by Arthur Marwick, 1964.

SOURCE C

It is no part of my job as Chancellor of the Exchequer to put before the House of Commons proposals for the expenditure of public money. The function of the Chancellor of the Exchequer, as I understand it, is to resist all demands for expenditure made by his colleagues, and, when he can no longer resist, to limit the concession to the barest point of acceptance.

From a speech by Philip Snowden in the House of Commons, 30 July 1924.

1. Study Source A. How useful is this source to a historian studying the circumstances in which the first Labour government took office?

2. Study Source B. In the context of this source, explain the reference to 'the application of Socialist principles to the reorganisation of industry and our economic life'.

3. Study Sources B and C. How and why do these sources differ in their respective attitudes to the aims of the first Labour government?

4. How complete a picture do Sources A to C give of the problems facing the first Labour government? Use the information in Section 8.2 to help answer the question.

8.3 How far was the failure of the 1929–31 MacDonald government the result of fundamental fissures in the Labour movement?

The period of recriminations following the fall of the first Labour government was short-lived. In the mid-1920s the grip of MacDonald on the party was confirmed. The failure of the General Strike in May 1926 seemed to endorse his moderate, constitutional approach to politics. The party's 1928 programme, *Labour and the Nation*, avoided specific proposals for progress towards a socialist economy.

In the May 1929 election Labour increased its representation in London and the industrial areas of England. The party won 287 seats, while the Conservatives won 260 and the Liberals 59. This meant that once again Labour took office as a minority administration. As Andrew Thorpe points

The caption reads:
Rt Hon Dress Suit (Checking the unemployment figures) – 1,739,497 – 1,739,498 – 1,739,499 – 1,739,501 !
J. H. Thomas, the minister responsible for unemployment policy, watches as Sir Oswald Mosley resigns from the second Labour government, following the rejection of his proposals for economic regeneration.

What does this cartoon reveal about the debate on unemployment during the second Labour government?

out in his *History of the British Labour Party* (1997), the party's success was partly due to the unusually high number of Liberal candidacies, which helped to split the anti-Labour vote.

Although the new government included the first woman Cabinet minister (Margaret Bondfield at the Ministry of Labour), its overall political complexion was similar to that of its predecessor five years earlier. At the Treasury, Philip Snowden's conventional outlook on financial affairs remained unchanged. Given that the fortunes of the ministry would be dominated by the onset of world depression in the autumn of 1929, this would prove to be MacDonald's most crucial appointment. Faced with rising levels of unemployment, the government resisted calls from Sir Oswald Mosley, a junior minister, for an expansionary economic policy based upon loan-financed public works, industrial protection and social reforms designed to reduce the size of the labour market. Mosley's resignation in May 1930 reflected the triumph of orthodox financial thinking.

In July 1931 a European banking crisis started a dramatic withdrawal of funds from the Bank of England, calling into question the position of the pound. These events coincided with the publication of a report from a government-appointed committee chaired by Sir George May, secretary of the Prudential Insurance Company. The May Committee predicted a budget deficit of £120 million and called for government economies amounting to £96 million, including a major cut in unemployment benefit. MacDonald and his colleagues accepted the broad thrust of this argument, that spending cuts were necessary to balance the budget. Only such a strategy could enable the government to secure credits from banks in New York and Paris, upon whose support the pound depended.

Retrenchment: A policy of reducing expenditure.

Acceptance of the principle of **retrenchment** did not, however, translate into Cabinet agreement on the level of the proposed cuts. Ultimately, it proved impossible to settle on a programme of cuts that would satisfy not

---

Leading members of the 1929–1931 Labour government

Prime Minister	Ramsay MacDonald
Chancellor of the Exchequer	Philip Snowden
Foreign Secretary	Arthur Henderson
Lord Privy Seal	J. H. Thomas (moved to Dominions Office, June 1930)

only Labour ministers but also foreign bankers and the Opposition party leaders, whose approval was necessary for the passage through Parliament of any proposals. The full Cabinet would agree on only £56 million of cuts, a figure well short of that demanded by the Conservative and Liberal leaders. On this issue the second Labour government broke up in August, to be succeeded by a National Government headed by MacDonald but dominated by the Conservatives.

Labour and the crisis of 1931

The collapse of the second Labour government has assumed a unique position in the history of the party. To Labour loyalists, the crisis of August 1931 has acted as a grim warning of the dangers of betrayal by untrustworthy leaders. According to this interpretation, Ramsay MacDonald and a handful of senior figures succumbed to the temptations offered by a manipulative capitalist establishment. Labour was undone by the treachery of its leaders, who placed the prospect of continuation in office ahead of their responsibilities for the rank-and-file of the movement. This interpretation perpetuates the sense of bitterness felt at the time by those who believed that a Labour government should resign rather than consent to economies, which would harm the unemployed masses. It reflects the contemporary belief that a capitalist conspiracy or 'bankers' ramp', assisted by the Conservative and Liberal leaders, had been allowed to prevail.

By focusing on the role of personalities, this view tends to divert attention from the deeper issues raised by the crisis. Could the final crisis of the government have been avoided, had different economic policies been pursued? How far did tensions within the Labour movement influence the options open to the government, and thus help to determine the events of 1929–31?

The views of historians

Scholarly debate on the policies of the second MacDonald government continues to be heavily influenced by the work of Robert Skidelsky in the late 1960s. His study, *Politicians and the slump: the Labour Government of 1929–1931* (1970), is a powerful presentation of the case for a radical alternative strategy to tackle the problem of mass unemployment. Skidelsky presents in a positive light the figure of Sir Oswald Mosley, whose unorthodox economic proposals bear comparison with the 'new deal' policies pursued by Franklin Roosevelt in the United States and with the interventionist outlook of Sweden's social democrat government. The rejection of the 'Mosley memorandum' in May 1930 is viewed as a tragically missed opportunity. The MacDonald government could have reversed the contraction of the economy with an imaginative programme of state investment, financed by deficit budgeting and designed to stimulate demand and generate employment. Instead, the Labour leaders' vague belief in 'socialism' as a future goal prejudiced them against the adoption of new initiatives to save the capitalist system. According to Skidelsky, in the circumstances of the slump 'socialism was impossible and capitalism was doomed: there was nothing to do but govern without conviction, a system [the Labour Party] did not believe in but saw no real prospect of changing'.

Skidelsky's work reflects assumptions widely held in the 30 years after the Second World War, when it was generally accepted that **Keynesian economic management** had made depressions avoidable. The reappearance of large-scale unemployment a generation after 1945 meant that it was now harder to see government manipulation of demand as a remedy. Attention was focused instead on underlying problems of competitiveness,

Keynesian economic management: Policies associated with the economist John Maynard Keynes. The idea was that governments could stimulate recovery from a depression by investing in public works schemes, thereby generating employment and reviving demand for manufactured goods. To finance such a policy, government would run a deficit – in other words, expenditure would be allowed to exceed revenue. In the inter-war period such thinking ran counter to the trend of orthodox opinion.

productivity and business management. This in turn promoted a more sympathetic view of the problems faced by the Labour government in 1929–31.

The most important contribution to the debate was by Ross McKibbin. In an article published in the journal *Past and Present* in 1975, he argued that the experience of the USA and Sweden in the 1930s indicates that expansionary economic policies were hardly an unqualified success. Moreover, the size of the British state's budgetary operations was too small to permit the kind of deficit financing advocated by Mosley and others. The level of government intervention necessary for the direction of investment would not have been acceptable to the conventional wisdom of the time. Only wartime conditions were capable of persuading the political and business world that such a revolution in the machinery of government was feasible. McKibbin's argument is a salutary reminder of the importance of seeing events through the eyes of contemporaries.

Decision-making in 1931

In any case, one should not exaggerate the extent to which the Labour government followed the strict principles of orthodox finance. Although Chancellor Snowden emphasised the importance of a balanced budget, the political and humanitarian need to protect the unemployed meant that the rules were bent in practice. Until the summer of 1931, he continued to allow borrowing from the Treasury to replenish the unemployment insurance fund, from which benefits were financed. He was persuaded to change direction by the need to restore confidence in sterling, in face of the financial crisis that began seriously to drain the Bank of England's gold reserves in July 1931.

It is possible to question the economic sense of the contemporary obsession with the value of the currency. Nonetheless, at the time it was almost universally agreed – even by Labour ministers who regretted its implications – that Britain must maintain its commitment to the gold standard. It was widely believed that the alternative would be a catastrophic collapse in the value of the pound, reminiscent of the German inflation of 1923. The former Labour minister, Sidney Webb, expressed amazement when the National Government later took Britain 'off gold': 'nobody told us we could do that'. In August 1931 the whole Labour Cabinet accepted the need to maintain the **parity of sterling**. To do so, the flow of gold from London must be staunched with the aid of credits supplied by foreign bankers. The only way to obtain these credits was for the government to provide hard evidence of its intention to balance the budget by means of spending cuts.

The argument within the Labour Party, then, was about the consequences of deciding to retain the current value of sterling. As was seen earlier, Labour ministers accepted the principle of spending cuts but failed to agree on the precise level. In particular, the fact that the unemployed would be called upon to bear a heavy share of the sacrifices aroused controversy. The idea of cutting unemployment benefit struck at the deepest instincts of the Labour movement. Historically the working classes had been seen as the victims of the capitalist system and as such they were considered entitled to 'work or maintenance'. In the summer of 1931 this case was put most forcibly by the leaders of the TUC General Council, who saw themselves as the legitimate spokesmen of the unemployed. The trade union bosses' conception of their role was essentially defensive; their responsibility was to prevail upon the Labour government not to allow the living standards of working people to be further driven down. Accordingly they mounted a campaign against the proposed cuts and made recommendations that would have penalised the

Parity of sterling: A fixed value for the pound against the United States dollar.

property-owning classes. They called for the replacement of unemployment insurance by a graduated levy, the taxation of fixed interest bearing securities and a possible revenue tariff.

Trade union pressure exercised a decisive influence on a section of the Cabinet led by the Foreign Secretary. For Arthur Henderson, a politician committed to maintaining the unity of the Labour movement, it was inconceivable to go against the explicit wishes of the party's trade union allies on such an issue. Rather than carry out an economy programme prescribed by bankers, Labour must leave office united and transfer responsibility for policy to the Conservative and Liberal Parties. The Lord Chancellor, Lord Sankey, noted in his diary on the day that the Labour Cabinet broke up, 'the result is due to Henderson changing his mind. At Llandrindod [where the two had met on holiday a few weeks earlier] he and I agreed to equality of sacrifice and cuts in the dole … The TUC won't agree so Henderson gave way.' Not surprisingly Sankey joined MacDonald in helping to form the National Government, whereas Henderson led the bulk of the Labour Party into opposition.

The nature of the rift revealed an underlying difference of priorities between the MacDonald and Henderson camps. The former believed that his long-term strategy of making Labour into a credible party of government required him to accept the advice of the banking community and the Opposition leaders. Labour must be seen to act in the national interest, as defined by the consensus view of informed opinion. Following the publication in 1977 of David Marquand's biography of MacDonald, it has become clear that the formation of a National Government was not for him a first choice. This option emerged only when it became clear that the Prime Minister was unable to find agreement among his colleagues on a package that could command broad parliamentary support. On the other hand, Henderson felt an overriding sense of accountability to the trade unions, with which the Labour Party was inextricably intertwined. In the summer of 1931 his sense of responsibility to the extra-parliamentary forces that had given Labour birth took precedence over other considerations. The crisis was more than a dispute over economic policy: it was a question of Labour's identity as a party and a movement.

1. What were the main problems facing the Labour government in the years 1929–31?

2. Were there realistic alternatives to the policies pursued by the second Labour government?

3. Is there any truth in the accusation of the Labour Party's opponents, that it 'ran away' in the crisis of 1931?

8.4 Does Ramsay MacDonald deserve to be remembered as the great betrayer of the Labour Party?
A CASE STUDY IN HISTORICAL INTERPRETATION

Rentier: One who lives on income derived from rents or investments.

The career of Ramsay MacDonald has been overshadowed by his role in the formation of the National Government. Former colleagues in the Labour Party viewed the events of August 1931 as an instance of gross misjudgement at best and as outright treachery at worst. Hugh Dalton, a junior minister at the time, scornfully told journalists that 'for a handful of panic he left us'. Clement Attlee, a man not given to exaggeration, characterised MacDonald's action as 'the greatest betrayal in the political history of this country'. In the wake of the crisis, many writers sympathetic to Labour began to question the whole of MacDonald's political record down to that date. Attention focused on his alleged insecurity, as an outsider to the establishment, which led him to succumb to the superficial attractions of high society. Sidney Webb, who served in the first two Labour governments, wrote ruefully that 'the willingness to use the weapon of seduction will be the last ditch in the defensive position of the British **rentier** class'. For more than a generation, MacDonald's name became a byword for vanity, snobbery and lack of fidelity to socialist ideals.

The process of rehabilitation began in earnest with the publication of David Marquand's biography, the first full-length study to be based on MacDonald's private papers and on Cabinet records. Marquand's scholarly approach did a great deal to correct the worst distortions of party political polemic. Nonetheless, an understanding of 1931 remains central to any appraisal of MacDonald's career. Even a commentator as judicious as the historian Kenneth Morgan concludes that 'in spite of everything, he remains doomed, perhaps damned, by his fatal miscalculation in August 1931'.

The case for MacDonald

Much of the positive work done by MacDonald for the Labour Party falls outside the confines of this book. He played a key role in the founding in 1900 of the Labour Representation Committee, the body which later evolved into the Labour Party. He exploited working-class dismay at the Taff Vale case in 1901, a legal judgement that left trade unions liable to be sued for damages incurred by strike action. The case enabled MacDonald, as secretary to the LRC, to obtain a significant increase in the number of trade union affiliations to Labour. Two years later he negotiated a pact with the Liberals, which gave the LRC a free run in 35 working-class constituencies. The deal made it possible for Labour to establish an electoral foothold in the contest of 1906. It also laid the foundations of the 'progressive alliance' between Labour and the Liberal governments, which set the agenda for politics up to the outbreak of the First World War.

As chairman of the parliamentary party from 1911–14, MacDonald was, by common consent, the most effective of Labour's pre-war leaders. He was a prolific writer and an inspiring speaker, both in the House of Commons and on the public platform. His principled opposition to Britain's entry into the war reinforced his radical credentials, giving him a standing with the Labour left that would not wholly dissipate until his second ministry. He sensibly avoided a division of the party, while building links with both Labour and radical Liberal figures through the anti-war Union of Democratic Control.

MacDonald's re-election as leader of the parliamentary party in 1922 enabled him to make his most important contribution to the rise of Labour: the creation of an image, respectable yet radical, that enabled the party to appeal beyond the ranks of its own faithful followers. MacDonald

More than a year before the formation of the National Government, the left-wing cartoonist David Low, suggests that Ramsay MacDonald is working along lines determined by the Conservative and Liberal Parties.

How useful is this cartoon as a source for studying the second Labour government?

saw that Labour now had an unprecedented opportunity to replace the divided and impoverished Liberals as the main party on the left of British politics. In 1929 the German writer, Egon Wertheimer, memorably described him as 'the focus of the mute hopes of a whole class'. By demonstrating Labour's competence to govern in 1924, and by maintaining a distance from the 'direct action' tactic of the General Strike, MacDonald helped to turn it from a party of protest into one of government. Although MacDonald personally would be attacked by his former comrades, this would broadly be the path followed by the Labour leadership in the 1930s. There are strong grounds for describing Labour's strategy in that decade, with its emphasis on parliamentary action, as 'MacDonaldism without MacDonald'.

In defence of MacDonald's economic policies in 1929–31, it should be recalled that few, if any, of his critics were capable of providing a coherent alternative strategy. A dramatic policy of economic **reflation** would merely have antagonised the business community and worsened the collapse of confidence in the pound. MacDonald's opponents in the August 1931 political crisis objected, not to maintaining the parity of sterling, but to the policies necessary to maintain that parity. Henderson and the eight other ministers who resigned had previously accepted the principle of spending cuts. Even if he was mistaken in his policies, MacDonald was at least consistent in his view of what constituted the national interest. He formed the National Government with reluctance, following strong appeals to his sense of duty from King George V. Far from actively plotting to abandon his Labour colleagues, he initially expected the National Government to be a temporary measure, designed to deal with an exceptional situation.

Reflation: A policy designed to increase economic activity by means of government expenditure. See Keynesian economic management, p. 149.

The case against MacDonald

MacDonald's excessive sensitivity to criticism, his clumsy handling of relations with senior colleagues and his inability to delegate limited his effectiveness as Prime Minister. In January 1924, for example, he almost denied Henderson a Cabinet post on the grounds that the latter would be better occupied in organising the party. This was a highly tactless way of dealing with Labour's second most important figure. Long before 1931, MacDonald's liking for aristocratic society had aroused the suspicions of many in his party, who came to feel that his radicalism was superficial. In his essay on MacDonald in *Labour People* (1987), Kenneth Morgan emphasises his subject's lack of an overtly passionate commitment to fighting social injustice. Personally aloof, he led the party as if from a lofty vantage point, a style against which his successors in the 1930s seemed consciously to react.

MacDonald must bear a large part of the blame for Labour's failure, while in opposition from 1924–29, to evolve a distinctive strategy for tackling unemployment. The party's 1928 statement, *Labour and the Nation*, was frustratingly vague. In *A History of the British Labour Party* Andrew Thorpe suggests that it was the production of a leadership that did not expect to win the next election. MacDonald's appointment of the intellectually limited J.H. Thomas as the minister responsible for unemployment policy in June 1929 was particularly uninspired. Even David Marquand acknowledges that MacDonald could have sought solutions with more energy and imagination. He did not try, for example, to introduce protectionist measures, which might have been a partial remedy and which would have commanded the confidence of business interests.

Before the 1931 crisis, MacDonald demonstrated a wish to put the search for consensus ahead of his loyalties to the Labour movement. On taking office in 1929, he appealed to the different sides in the House of

Commons to see themselves 'more as a Council of State and less as arrayed regiments facing each other in battle'. It is hard to resist the conclusion that this statement reflected MacDonald's personal preferences and was more than an acknowledgement of the second Labour government's minority status. In August 1931 he listened to the arguments of foreign bankers and of his political opponents, rather than seeking to understand the perspective of the trade union leadership. In the general election of October 1931 he widened the breach with his ex-colleagues by denouncing them for their alleged irresponsibility. The National Labour group that he led after 1931 proved to be a numerically weak parliamentary force, with a negligible grassroots following. Until his resignation in June 1935 MacDonald served as the uncomfortable figurehead of a predominantly Conservative administration. He ended his career isolated from his old party and with scant influence over the counsels of his new allies.

Conclusion

David Marquand considers that MacDonald's career demonstrates the need for a radical party to have not only 'high ideals and skilful leadership' but also 'intellectual coherence and a willingness to jettison cherished assumptions in the face of changing realities'. It was MacDonald's tragedy that his conception of Labour's role in the state led him into a position from which his reputation would never fully recover. Nonetheless it would be unfair to lay the blame for the party's 1931 debacle exclusively at his door. The fact that he was twice chosen as Labour's representative figure, in 1911 and again in 1922, says a great deal about the nature of the party. It can be argued that his tenure of the leadership reflects the structural and ideological weaknesses of the Labour movement as much as the limitations of one individual.

Which of the two cases, the one for or the one against MacDonald, do you consider the more persuasive? Use the information in the rest of this chapter to support your answer.

8.5 How convincing was Labour's recovery from the disaster of 1931?

Arthur Henderson gravely underestimated the significance of the events of August 1931 when he assured a Labour gathering that 'this is only an interlude in the life of the party, like the war'. Two months after this pronouncement, Labour suffered the greatest electoral defeat in its history. It lost 21 per cent of its 1929 share of the poll, winning only 46 seats to the massive 554 secured by National Government candidates. Most of Labour's leading figures, including Henderson himself, lost their seats: some would never return to the Commons again. A significant minority, including Ramsay MacDonald and his son Malcolm (himself a minister in the National Government) formed the National Labour Party. Their support for a Conservative-dominated administration ensured the permanence of the breach with their former colleagues. The memory of MacDonald's 'betrayal' of Labour in 1931 would haunt the party for a generation.

Although Labour recovered its standing a little in the November 1935 general election, winning 154 seats, the National Government enjoyed a majority of over 250. These results did not merely represent the cancellation of the tentative gains made by Labour in non-industrial areas during the 1920s. It was even more galling that many of the depressed parts of the country had declined to return Labour MPs. It was hard for the party to overcome the popular perception that it had 'run away' when faced in 1931 with financial crisis. With a Conservative-dominated administration firmly entrenched in power, and an electorate apparently impervious to Labour's appeal, the party's situation seemed bleak.

This section will assess the extent of Labour's problems in the 1930s. To do this it will examine the experience of the party in four key areas: leadership, organisation and discipline, the formation of policy and electoral prospects on the eve of the Second World War.

Leadership

The electoral holocaust of 1931 marked the effective end of Arthur Henderson's career as a front-line politician. After MacDonald's defection, he was a natural choice for the position of party leader, but his removal from the Commons made it impossible for him to perform the role adequately. By the time that he returned, as a result of a by-election in 1933, he was an ageing and increasingly irrelevant figure, with only two years to live.

The decimation of Labour's senior figures in the 1931 general election placed the leadership of the parliamentary party in the hands of the only ex-Cabinet minister to secure a place in the Commons. George Lansbury had served in a relatively modest capacity, as First Commissioner of Works, and in normal circumstances would never have been considered for the leadership. Although he stood out as a principled individual, with a strong ethical commitment to social improvement, he was ill-equipped for the exercise of the political arts. His leadership was abruptly terminated during the 1935 party conference, as a result of his uncompromisingly pacifist attitude towards Fascist Italy's threatened invasion of Abyssinia (modern Ethiopia). Publicly denounced for his conscience-driven politics by the movement's most important trade union figure, Ernest Bevin, Lansbury at once retired.

His successor was his former deputy, the almost equally unlikely figure of Clement Attlee. Like Lansbury, the new leader had been projected to the party's front rank by the events of 1931. Dry and uncharismatic, Attlee was widely viewed as a caretaker leader and had little opportunity to make his mark before the party was caught up in the 1935 election. Although Paul Adelman attributes his subsequent confirmation as leader to the feelings of trust that he inspired in the parliamentary party, it is also true that he benefited from the perceived defects of his two rivals. Arthur Greenwood was respected by the rank-and-file but not regarded as a potential leader. Herbert Morrison's inability to win the confidence of Labour's trade union wing made him an inherently more divisive figure.

Hugh Dalton, a junior minister in the 1929–31 government, commented acidly on Attlee's election in his diary, 'and a little mouse shall lead them'. This was a private comment by a notoriously prejudiced observer. Nonetheless it is true that Attlee failed to make a definite impression in the country at large before the outbreak of war four years later. It would take the experience of the war, during which he served as Deputy Prime Minister, to establish him as a potential national leader. Few people in 1935 could have predicted that he would lead Labour until 1955, becoming the longest serving leader of any major British political party in the 20th century.

Organisation and discipline

From an organisational perspective there were grounds for optimism in the 1930s. The continuing rise in individual membership, with some 419,000 members by 1935, was an encouraging sign.

Nevertheless this development brought its own problems for the leadership, with the growth of a constituency parties movement, intent on securing a greater say in policy making. An increased representation for the constituency section on the party's National Executive was pushed

George Lansbury (1859–1940)
The historian A. J. P. Taylor, in his book *English History 1914–1945*, described Lansbury as the 'leader of the emotional Left'. Lansbury had edited the Labour newspaper, the *Daily Herald*, in the early 1920s. He was popular in the Labour movement for his evident sincerity, but lacked governmental experience.

Ernest Bevin (1881–1951)
Bevin rose from humble origins to lead the Dockers' Union. He created and led the Transport and General Workers' Union from 1921–40. In Churchill's wartime coalition he served as Minister of Labour and National Service. As Foreign Secretary from 1945–51 he was one of the key figures in the Attlee governments.

Clement Attlee (1883–1967)
Of middle-class background, Attlee became a socialist to combat the kind of poverty that he witnessed in London's East End before the First World War. He was Chancellor of the Duchy of Lancaster and then Postmaster-General in the second Labour government, and became leader of the party in 1935. He acted as Deputy Prime Minister in Churchill's wartime coalition. In 1945 he led Labour to its first outright electoral victory, serving as Prime Minister until 1951.

Arthur Greenwood (1880–1954)
A schoolmaster by background, Greenwood was Minister of Health in the second Labour government. He was Labour's deputy leader from 1935–45 and held Cabinet posts in both the Churchill coalition and the post-war Labour government. A drink problem soured his later years and his career ended in 1947.

through in the face of trade union resistance at the 1937 conference. As Paul Adelman points out in *The Rise of the Labour Party 1880–1945* (1996), individual spokesmen who were elected to the Executive found themselves entrapped there by the trade union majority.

Perhaps the most striking feature of Labour politics in the 1930s was the further strengthening of the trade union movement's influence at the highest levels of the party. In 1934 the National Joint Council, on which the TUC, the National Executive and the Parliamentary Labour Party had enjoyed equal representation, was transformed into the National Council of Labour. On this body the TUC, whose dominant figure was the Transport Workers' chief, Ernest Bevin, secured seven of the thirteen available seats. One should not, however, exaggerate the role of this new body. As Ben Pimlott, author of a major study of *Labour and the Left in the 1930s* (1977) argues, the main function of the National Joint Council was not to determine policy but to give weight to the pronouncements of the party as a whole. The National Executive remained the most important component in the party's structure; in May 1940 it would take the crucial decision to commit Labour to membership of the wartime coalition.

One of the major themes of the decade was the failure of the left to make a lasting impact on Labour politics. Superficially the aftermath of the 1931 crisis, with the future of capitalism apparently in question, offered an unprecedented opportunity to the advocates of radical socialism. Sir Stafford Cripps, who had served as Solicitor-General under MacDonald, emerged as the champion of the left, declaring in October 1931 that 'the one thing that is not inevitable now is gradualness'. The following year the Independent Labour Party, disgusted with the ineffectual 'reformism' of the leadership, disaffiliated from the party. Some of its members formed the Socialist League, a left-wing pressure group calling for a militant response to any institutions that might try to hamper the programme of a future Labour administration.

Nevertheless the party as a whole remained firmly committed to parliamentary, rather than revolutionary, methods. In particular mainstream Labour opinion refused to be attracted by Socialist League demands for a 'united front' with other left-wing groups, including the Communist Party, to resist the growth of fascism. It was widely believed that such a strategy was 'a trap for innocents', a cover for Communist infiltration of the Labour movement. Conflict within the party came to a head in 1937, when the Socialist League agreed, under pressure from the National Executive, to dissolve itself.

In 1938, with Nazism on the march in Europe, Cripps attempted to build a wider 'popular front'. This was intended to embrace not only Socialists and Communists but also dissident Conservatives and Liberals who were opposed to the appeasement policies of the National Government. The scheme was ruined partly by the refusal of all except a handful of Conservative mavericks to rebel against their own leaders. It was also doomed by the belief of Labour Party managers, that it was simply another version of the discredited 'united front'. As Attlee later recalled, 'Labour leaders were very conscious of how many democratic socialist parties on the Continent had been given the kiss of death by the Communist Party'. Cripps' refusal to abandon the project led to his expulsion, together with that of his leading supporters, a decision that was endorsed by the Labour conference in May 1939.

At one level Labour was damaged by its absorption in internal disputes on the eve of a major international conflict. Nonetheless it is worth noting that the expulsions were a temporary disciplinary measure. Cripps had a long and respectable career ahead as a minister in the wartime coalition and as a post-war Chancellor of the Exchequer. Not for the last time in

Labour's history, a former rebel was to be transformed into a pillar of the party establishment. As Andrew Thorpe argues in *A History of the British Labour Party*, the party leadership correctly perceived that the benefits of pacts with Communists and other groups were minimal. In the political conditions of the late 1930s, Labour could not have regained power by such means. The hard left, with its ideological zeal, its underdeveloped economic ideas and ambivalence towards parliamentary government, represented a political dead end.

The formation of policy

The TUC had initiated a reappraisal of economic policy before the crisis of 1931 made such an exercise essential. Although Labour maintained its rhetorical allegiance to 'socialism', in practice the party's dominant ideas in the 1930s owed more to Keynesian concepts of managed capitalism. This was certainly the inspiration behind plans for public works, financed out of national credit and linked to proposals for a maximum working week and the raising of the school leaving age. The purpose was to revive employment by using the resources of the state to stimulate the level of demand in the economy.

By contrast with the MacDonald era, Labour paid close attention to the details of policy making. Policy committees utilised the talents of young economists such as Evan Durbin and Hugh Gaitskell, a future leader of the party. *Labour's immediate programme*, adopted in 1937, detailed a five-year-plan for state-directed investment, together with the public ownership of key industries and services. The underlying assumption was that capitalism was not, as expected earlier in the decade, doomed to final collapse in the near future. Labour's pragmatic thinkers were prepared to accept this reality, while laying plans to make the national economy work in the interests of the people as a whole. Under the influence of Herbert Morrison, the model for the new nationalised industries would be the public corporation. This meant that policy-making for each major industry would be in the hands of a board appointed by a government minister. The notion of 'workers' control' was downplayed in favour of an essentially statist approach to economic management. This concept would be the blueprint for the nationalisation programme pursued by the 1945–51 Labour governments.

By contrast it took much longer to evolve a coherent and agreed position on foreign affairs. The challenge of fascism presented Labour with a difficult set of choices. Although only a minority shared the uncompromising pacifism of Lansbury, a large section of the parliamentary party felt that a capitalist government could not be trusted with responsibility for rearmament. This meant that for much of the decade, the party maintained an illogical stance. While proclaiming its support for collective security through the agency of the League of Nations, until 1937 Labour voted annually in the Commons against the funding of rearmament. A minority, typified by Ernest Bevin and Hugh Dalton, took the straightforward view that fascism, which was responsible for the suppression of free trade unions on the Continent, must be resisted at all costs.

From 1937 the worsening of the international situation, together with the election of Bevin as chairman of the TUC General Council and of Dalton as chairman of the National Executive, served to undermine the case against rearmament. By the time of the 1938 Munich conference, Labour had at last united in opposition to the appeasement of Hitler. Even then, the conscription measures introduced by the Chamberlain administration in April 1939 met with hostility from the party. Nonetheless the party was unequivocal in its support for the declaration of war later in the year.

Electoral prospects

In a sense, the policies adopted by a party in opposition are an irrelevant issue. Elections are more commonly lost by the government of the day than won by the opposition. What, then, can be learned regarding Labour's prospects of power from the electoral record of the 1930s?

Between the general elections of 1931 and 1935, Labour made ten gains in by-elections, a development that was paralleled by a modest recovery at municipal level. In the 1935 contest Labour made a net gain of 94 seats. Tom Stannage, author of *Baldwin thwarts the opposition* (1980), a study of the election, has calculated that in the 450 constituencies where valid statistical comparison is possible, this represented a nationwide swing of 9.4 per cent in the party's favour. The swing was strongest in London and in areas such as Lancashire, west Yorkshire, north-east England and southern Scotland, where the most marginal recovery from the slump had been experienced. The limits of Labour's success are perhaps just as significant. In industrial South Wales the party won 16 seats, compared with 22 in 1929; in the Midlands, the respective figures were 11 and 35. Rising wages in many occupations, together with a drop in the cost of living and a widespread expectation of a continuing decrease in unemployment, meant that many working-class voters were generally satisfied with the National Government.

Labour fought the 1935 general election under the severe handicap of a recent change of leadership, following a public display of disunity at the party conference. Moreover, as Stannage emphasises, the party was far behind the National Government in the handling of the new media of wireless and newsreel. Ironically for the party of change, Labour seemed most at home with traditional campaigning methods, which were not best suited to courting the votes of an uncommitted mass electorate. Labour spokesmen simply could not compete with the sophisticated mastery of broadcasting technique displayed by the Prime Minister, Stanley Baldwin.

Between the 1935 general election and the outbreak of war, Labour won 13 by-elections and lost none. However, the overall impression by 1939 was one of a party that had reached, in Andrew Thorpe's words, an 'electoral plateau'. Labour failed to regain five parliamentary seats, which it had won in 1929 but had subsequently lost. In English and Welsh municipal elections, the party's gains were far from dramatic. In 1936 it lost five of its 19 Scottish burghs; by 1938 the total had recovered to a modest 14. It seems hard to escape the conclusion that, had a peacetime general election been held in 1939–40, Labour would have stood little chance of victory. The electoral hill to be climbed was simply too steep. It would take the transforming effect of the Second World War on British society to make possible the change in popular attitudes from which issued Labour's 1945 triumph.

1. Why did the Labour left fail to take control of the party's destiny in the 1930s? Use the information given in the section to answer this question.

2. Did the 1935 general election represent a significant revival for the Labour Party? Give reasons to support your answer.

Further Reading

Articles

In *Modern History Review*
'The political career of Ramsay MacDonald' by Adrian Smith (Vol. 3 No. 4)
'Perspectives: the 1931 crisis' by Andrew Thorpe and Philip Williamson (Vol. 5 No. 2)
'The challenge of Labour: class conflict in interwar Britain' by Rodney Lowe (Vol. 6 No. 1)

Texts designed specifically for AS and A2 students

Britain: Domestic Politics 1918–1939 by Robert Pearce (Access to History series, Hodder & Stoughton, 1992)

The Rise of the Labour Party 1893–1931 by Gordon Phillips (Lancaster Pamphlets, Routledge, 1992)

The Rise of the Labour Party 1880–1945 by Paul Adelman, 3rd ed., (Longman Seminar Studies, 1996) – also contains a useful selection of documentary extracts

For more advanced reading

Arthur Henderson by Chris Wrigley (University of Wales Press, 1990)

The Evolution of the Labour Party 1910–1924 by Ross McKibbin (Oxford University Press, 1974)

A History of the British Labour Party by Andrew Thorpe (Macmillan, 1997)

Labour and the Left in the 1930s by Ben Pimlott (Cambridge University Press, 1977)

Labour People: Leaders and Lieutenants: Hardie to Kinnock by Kenneth Morgan (Oxford University Press, 1987)

The Making of Modern British Politics 1867–1939 by Martin Pugh (Blackwell, 1982), see Parts 3 and 4

Politicians and the Slump: the Labour Government of 1929–1931 by Robert Skidelsky (Penguin, 1970)

Ramsay MacDonald by David Marquand (Cape, 1977)

9 British foreign and imperial policy, 1918–1939

Key Issues

- In what ways did British policy towards Europe change between 1918 and 1939?

- How was Britain able to maintain its position as a world power between 1918 and 1939?

- How did British policy towards the Empire change in the period 1918 to 1939?

9.1 What limits were there on Britain's ability to pursue an independent foreign policy between 1918 and 1939?

9.2 How did Britain deal with the problems created by the post-war settlements of 1919–20?

9.3 What problems did Britain face in the 1920s in dealing with European affairs?

9.4 What were the aims of Imperial policy between 1918 and 1939?

9.5 What were the problems facing British foreign policy during the 1930s?

9.6 Why did Britain go to war in 1939?

Framework of Events

1917	November: Balfour Declaration on the creation of a Jewish homeland in Palestine
1918	November: Germany and Austro-Hungary accept US President Wilson's Fourteen Points as a basis for an armistice
1919–1920	Paris peace conferences
1919	League of Nations Covenant is approved
	April: Amritsar massacre
	Government of India Act, introducing Montagu-Chelmsford reforms
	Introduction of Ten Year Rule
1921	Imperial Conference
1921–22	Washington Naval Conference
1922	Chanak crisis
	Genoa Conference on European economic reconstruction
1924	Dawes Plan
1925	Treaty of Locarno
1928	Kellogg-Briand Pact, outlawing war
1929	Young Plan
	New York Stock Exchange collapse
1931	Statute of Westminster
1932	Geneva Disarmament Conference
	Imperial Economic Conference, Ottawa
1933	January: Hitler becomes German Chancellor
	Germany leaves League of Nations and Disarmament Conference
1935	Stresa agreements between Britain, France and Italy
	Anglo-German naval agreement
1936	Hitler remilitarises the Rhineland and denounces Locarno Treaty
1937	Neville Chamberlain becomes Prime Minister
1938	Germany annexes Austria and declares *Anschluss*
	Munich Agreements between Britain, Germany and France on Czechoslovakia

1939 | March: Germany occupies Bohemia and Moravia in Czechoslovakia
March: Anglo-French guarantee of Poland
August: Nazi-Soviet pact
1 September: Germany invades Poland
3 September: Britain and France declare war on Germany

Overview

AFTER the First World War British governments continued to believe that they had a right to guide world affairs, preferably to the benefit of British interests. This belief derived from Britain's international role in the 19th century. Britain's security seemed assured after the First World War:

- As a victor in the First World War, Britain had a major hand in drawing up the peace settlements.
- The League of Nations appeared to provide a means of maintaining peace.
- The Royal Navy was pre-eminent in Europe, with the dismantling of the German fleet.

There were, however, problems ahead:

- Germany was politically, socially and economically unstable. Its extremist politicians were already preaching **revisionism** and **revanchism**.
- A growing fear of **Bolshevism**. This proclaimed itself in conflict with all non-Communists and posed a threat which was very well understood by Lloyd George and Winston Churchill.
- France feared renewed German aggression but at the same time was causing problems in the Near East **mandated territories**.
- Colonial nationalism threatened violent opposition to British rule, especially in India and Ireland.
- Economic difficulties created major problems and limited diplomatic and strategic options.

Britain's foreign policy in the interwar period was much concerned with attempts to deal with what were seen as Germany's legitimate complaints by revising the terms of the Versailles Treaty, but without alarming the French. The **League of Nations Covenant** was called upon to limit aggressive intent by **arbitration**, for example the French occupation of the Ruhr. Germany's problem of debt was tackled by means of the Dawes Plan of April 1924 and the Young Plan of June 1929. Germany's borders in the west were settled by the Locarno Pact of December 1925.

Additionally there were problems within the Empire. The **White Dominions** (see section 9.4) wanted complete independence. Indian Nationalists were actively agitating for the same. These problems were met by Britain as they arose and addressed in longer-term strategy, with the White Dominions' demand being granted and the Indians being given some self-government. While some of the problems of the 1920s were being settled, new ones were arising. During the 1930s the League of Nations Covenant was called upon to settle disputes, but arbitration proved unsuccessful against the increasingly bellicose 'dictators' Hitler and Mussolini, and Japanese aggression in China.

Revisionism: Seeking to revise unpopular treaty provisions, in this instance the Treaty of Versailles.

Revanchism: Policy directed towards regaining lost territory.

Bolshevism: The revolutionary communist wing of the Russian Social Democratic Party, led by Lenin, which seized power in October/November 1917.

Mandated territories: Colonies which formerly belonged to Germany and non-Turkish areas of the Ottoman empire that were administered by First World War Allies (e.g. Britain and France) on behalf of the League of Nations.

League of Nations Covenant: The constitution (the formal guiding rules and principles) of the League of Nations, adopted at the Paris Peace Conference in April 1919.

Arbitration: Settling a dispute where the parties involved agree to accept the decision of another person or organisation to act as judge.

White Dominions: Self-governing countries of the British Commonwealth: Australia, Canada, New Zealand and South Africa.

Failures of the League included:

Annexation: To take possession of a territory, particularly without right to do so.

Expansionist: Seeking to enlarge the state, not always by internationally acceptable means.

- League of Nations' condemnation of Japanese **annexation** of Manchuria provoked Japan to leave the League.
- The Geneva Disarmament Conferences were abandoned in 1933 when Hitler flatly refused to take part. Germany also left the League of Nations. His intentions were not disarmament but the strengthening of Germany's armaments to pursue his aggressive and **expansionist** foreign policy aims.
- Hitler's revisionism and revanchism aroused the envy of Mussolini. He abandoned his stance as international guarantor of peace to become Hitler's ally, and followed an expansionist foreign policy similar to Hitler's.
- The limited ability of the League of Nations to punish aggression was further demonstrated by ineffective enforcement of sanctions against Mussolini after his invasion of Abyssinia.

Ten Year Rule: The Chiefs of Staff did not anticipate Britain becoming involved in a war within ten years.

Britain could read the warning signs and abandoned the **Ten Year Rule** in 1932. The possibility of appeasing Hitler proved to be an illusion because his 'reasonable' demands grew increasingly less so, until they reached the point where they moved from Treaty revision to outright aggression. For example, in March 1939 Hitler occupied Bohemia and Moravia, the Czech part of Czechoslovakia. Slovakia became a puppet state, but was still technically independent.

Collective security: The idea was that future war could be prevented if all members of the League of Nations acted together against a potential aggressor.

Collective security proved to be unrealisable because Britain and France did not feel strong enough to oppose Hitler, but would not confront Hitler by forming an alliance with the Soviet Union because they mistrusted Bolshevism. Thus Britain's apparent security after the First World War was reversed as its position as world leader and mastery of the Empire came to be challenged by nationalism within the Empire and from Europe and the Far East.

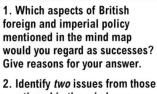

1. Which aspects of British foreign and imperial policy mentioned in the mind map would you regard as successes? Give reasons for your answer.

2. Identify *two* issues from those mentioned in the mind map which you regard as failures, giving reasons for your choice.

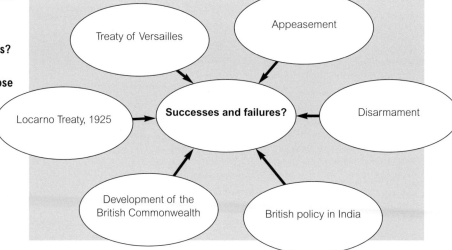

9.1 What limits were there on Britain's ability to pursue an independent foreign policy between 1918 and 1939?

Britain had run the Empire on limited means. Nevertheless, it had possessed the largest navy in the world and had widespread influence from running a large Empire. Some independence in its foreign policy direction had been maintained before the First World War. But after bearing the huge cost of the war and owing war debts to the United States, which had to be repaid, the advantages of following an independent foreign policy had to be calculated against the difficulty of finding the money to pay for it. This had the effect of limiting Britain's freedom of action.

What were Britain's main foreign policy aims between 1918 and 1939 and how far had they changed since 1900?

Britain's foreign policy aims remained broadly consistent with those followed between 1900 and 1918. What altered was how they could be achieved in the changed world circumstances after the First World War. The aims were to:

● re-establish a peace which would enable Britain to pursue the commercial interests which were essential for the health of the British economy. This was to be achieved by securing peace settlements which were not unfavourable to British interests, to be maintained through the League of Nations;

● maintain Britain's status as a world power. This would involve safeguarding economic, defence and foreign policy interests around the world;

● maintain the Empire as far as was possible, while limiting opposition;

● prevent the spread of Bolshevism (communism);

● in the 1920s, to avoid involvement in expensive continental commitments, such as guarantees of French security against Germany;

● in the 1930s, to maintain peace, in order to buy time for rearmament.

What were the limits on foreign policy?

The government had an obligation to fund social reforms at home, police the Empire and maintain a world position built on pre-war power and influence. Although far from bankrupt, Britain's financial resources had been seriously drained by the effort to achieve victory in the First World War because vital assets had to be **liquidated**. Beginning the war rich and **solvent**, during its course Britain built up enormous debts (£959 million) to the United States. These limits underpinned the formulation of British foreign, Empire and defence policies, obliging Britain to make hard budgetary choices.

Prime Minister Andrew Bonar Law, in a letter to *The Times* dated 7 October 1922, suggested that 'we cannot alone act as policeman of the world. The financial and social condition of this country makes it impossible'. If Britain were not supported, then it would be unable 'to bear the burden alone but shall have no alternative except to imitate the government of the United States and to restrict our attention to the safeguarding of the more immediate interests of the British Empire'.

The Lloyd George government of 1916 to 1922 had fed the expectation of demobilising forces that they would return to social reforms and 'homes fit for heroes' (see chapter 6). These too would have to be funded out of

Liquidated: The results of assets sold off to pay for something.

Solvent: Having sufficient assets to pay any debts.

Main Foreign Secretaries 1918–1939

Marquess Curzon	October 1919 – January 1924
Ramsey MacDonald	January – November 1924
Austen Chamberlain	November 1924 – June 1929
John Simon	November 1931 – June 1935
Samuel Hoare	June 1935 – December 1935
Anthony Eden	December 1935 – February 1938
The Earl of Halifax	February 1938 – May 1940

---

depleted resources. End-of-war exhaustion was masked by the optimism which followed the war's end, but a brief post-war boom (1919–21) was swiftly followed by an economic slump (from 1921). Unemployment increased in Britain's staple industries, coal, cotton, ship-building and engineering. Because these industries were running down, demand for materials from the Empire to feed them decreased. Without the income from export of their raw materials, the Empire could not afford to buy back finished goods, increasing the effect of the downward spiral.

With financial resources reduced by war debts and economic slump, Britain's commitment to manage and police the Empire nevertheless remained undiminished. The task was increased by responsibility for Egypt. It also involved responsibility for Palestine and Iraq, which were mandated territories, that had formerly been part of the Ottoman Empire. Additionally, the war had re-enforced the White Dominions' and India's desire for increased independence. Independence for the White Dominions was conceded during the war. Indian nationalist agitation required careful handling because the British government did not feel ready to give independence at that stage (see Section 9.4).

How did Britain deal with budgetary limitations on the formulation of defence policy?

Britain coped with this problem by cutting back on defence expenditure to balance budgets. Military commitment on the continent of Europe was potentially too costly to be considered. It was side-stepped at the Paris peace conference of 1919–20, but by doing so, Britain fed French fears about being left to meet potential German aggression alone. Savings were made by cutting the number of men in the armed forces from 3.5 million to 370,000 between the end of the war in 1918 and 1920. Defence cuts were justified by a Ten Year Rule, introduced in 1919, by which war was not foreseen for ten years ahead. Lloyd George justified cuts in defence spending when he told Service chiefs that 'they need not prepare for war as it was not foreseen for at least ten years'. The rule was renewed annually until 1932.

By 1930 British defence spending had been reduced below the level spent in 1910 and armed forces manpower was below the 1914 level, with the army bearing the brunt of the cutbacks. The army's chief role was colonial policeman, and defence responsibilities had been increased by addition of the mandates of Palestine and Iraq. Britain had therefore effectively lowered its standard of security in the Mediterranean, India and the Far East, despite the threats to stability posed by Bolshevism and unrest in Ireland, India and China.

1. What were Britain's foreign policy aims after 1918?

2. What were the factors that affected Britain's ability to pursue an independent foreign policy?

3. How effectively did Britain cope with a wide range of foreign and defence policy commitments?

9.2 How did Britain deal with the problems created by the post-war settlements of 1919–20?

What were Britain's aims in the Paris peace settlements?

Pre-1914 diplomacy: This refers to the series of treaty arrangements and secret deals which preceded the First World War and which, in effect, tripped Europe into war rather than negotiation.

At the Paris peace conference that began in January 1919, Lloyd George negotiated for Britain. He aimed to create a lasting settlement that would require no active British participation in European affairs. The British public rejected **pre-1914 diplomacy**, and the Paris peace settlements aimed to keep Britain out of entangling continental alliances. Britain refused to satisfy the French need for guarantees against future German aggression. The League of Nations was set up to contain conflict and keep the peace world-wide at low cost. Reparations (a war indemnity) were sought from Germany to finance payment of war debts to America and social reforms. But how much was to be forthcoming, given the scale of German war debts, and post-war political and economic turmoil?

Of all the settlements reached at the Paris Peace Conference, it was the Treaty of Versailles with Germany that was the most controversial and

What were the main terms of the Treaty of Versailles?

- Reparations of £6,600 million, plus interest, to be paid to the First World War victors, decided by an Inter-Allied Reparations Commission in 1921;

- Union (Anschluss) of Germany and Austria prohibited;

- Acceptance of a war guilt clause (Article 231);

- The German military to be reduced, for example the army to be limited to 100,000 men, with few military supplies (weaponry and ammunition) permitted. The navy was similarly restricted; and the air force abolished.

German territorial losses included:

- Surrender of German colonies – German East Africa (Tanganyika), German South-West Africa. The Cameroons, Togoland – to be mandates of the League of Nations (see page 161);

- Alsace-Lorraine to be returned to France;

- Eupen-Malmedy to be given to Belgium (after a plebiscite – national vote – in 1920) and Memel to Lithuania (1923);

- Northern Schleswig to Denmark (after plebiscite in 1920);

- Danzig to become a free city under League of Nations control;

- Poznan, part of Upper Silesia (after 1921 plebiscite) and parts of East Prussia to Poland;

- The Saar to enjoy special status under the control of the League of Nations for 15 years until a plebiscite to decide its future (1935) – France in the meantime to control the Saar coalmines;

- The Rhineland to be demilitarised and under Allied occupation for 15 years;

The Treaty also contained the Covenant of the League of Nations. The American Congress refused to ratify the Treaty and Germany signed it only under protest, thereby increasing Britain's difficulties.

The signing of the Treaty of Versailles, by Sir William Orpen.

Dichotomy: Separation of ideas into two mutually exclusive classes.

Weimar Republic: The German government between the abdication of the Kaiser and Hitler becoming Chancellor (1918–1933).

Fait accompli: Something that has already been done.

Diktat: A German word meaning a treaty imposed upon the defeated.

Armistice: Truce; cessation of arms for a stipulated time.

posed the greatest difficulty for Britain. Writing the peace settlements was a problem of balance, and the negotiators were faced by too many conflicting rights and demands. In his Fontainbleau memorandum of 25 March 1919 Lloyd George summed up the **dichotomy**. The twin aims of France and Britain were to crush Germany and prevent the spread of Bolshevism. But, if Germany was crushed too hard, this might encourage the spread of Bolshevism. He thought that a harsh settlement would undermine the **Weimar Republic** and possibly bring more war to Europe. But he had also to bear in mind the claims of France. A large part of French industry was located in the north-east, near the coal fields, which for four years had been the site of the battlefront. French industry had been largely destroyed and its industrial manpower seriously depleted by the enormous amount of its war dead (1,357,800 against losses of 908,371 from the British Empire, not just Britain).

The allies spent four months considering peace terms. Presented to Germany in May 1919 as a *fait accompli*, they were regarded by the Germans as a *diktat* because they considered that the **armistice** terms had entitled them to negotiate a settlement.

Why was the League of Nations formed after the First World War?

The League of Nations Covenant was signed in February 1919 to set up an international organisation that aimed to settle disputes by arbitration and so preserve the peace. It had been put forward by US President Wilson as

Fourteen Points: US President Woodrow Wilson's war aims, which were published in January 1918.

one of his **Fourteen Points**. The League's Constitution was adopted at the Paris Peace Conference and incorporated into each of the four peace treaties: Versailles with Germany, St. Germain with Austria, Sèvres with Turkey and Trianon with Hungary.

The League of Nations Covenant also provided for disarmament, but this aim was never achieved. A series of conferences were held at Geneva between 1928 and 1934. Sixty nations participated, including the United States and the Soviet Union. They failed because the French insisted that a general security scheme should come before disarmament. Before agreement on disarmament could be reached, Hitler withdrew Germany from the League in October 1933. This effectively ended plans for disarmament.

Why did Britain support the idea of the League of Nations?

The League was seen by Britain as an ideal way of achieving some of Britain's foreign policy aims. The League would spread the burden and cost of keeping world peace. Britain's defence position was undermined by spending cuts which had the effect of limiting Britain's ability to defend its world-wide interests.

The League provided Britain with an excuse to avoid giving a guarantee of security to France against German aggression. This would have bolstered French confidence and underpinned the Treaty of Versailles.

What were the problems that faced the League?

In order for the aims of the League to be achievable every state would have to either join or remain a member. But, the United States never became a member. Germany adopted membership only between 1926 and 1933. The Soviet Union was a member only between 1934 and 1940. The Japanese left the League in 1933, after the League imposed **sanctions** against them for invading Manchuria. Similarly, Italy left in 1937 after sanctions were imposed because of their invasion of Abyssinia (Ethiopia).

Arthur Balfour, chief British representative at the League of Nations in 1920, was aware of the potential weaknesses of the League. He reminded the British Cabinet that the 'chief instruments at the disposal of the League are: Public Discussion; Judicial investigation; Arbitration; and, in the last resort … some form of Compulsion. These are powerful weapons but the places where they seem least applicable are those … where nothing but force is understood …' The greatest weakness of the League lay in the fact that its only agreed method of compulsion was the imposition of sanctions. Methods of exerting compulsion by the use of force were never agreed and remained unspecified. Thus, in the last resort, the League had no method of enforcing its decisions.

Sanctions: Penalties imposed on one country by another or by a group of countries. For instance the refusal to trade.

Why was Britain involved in the Chanak crisis in 1922?

Another difficulty for Britain arising from the Paris Peace settlements was the Chanak crisis of 1922. An Allied army (which included British forces) was occupying the Straits (the Dardanelles) to safeguard the eastern Mediterranean after the end of the First World War. In 1920 the Turkish nationalist leader, Kemal Ataturk, rejected the terms of the Treaty of Sèvres of 1920 with the Ottoman (Turkish) Empire. A war began between Turkey and Greece in 1920 over Turkish territory occupied mainly by Greeks and given to Greece under the Sevres Treaty. The Chanak crisis of September–October 1922 began when it was feared that the Turks would attack the Allied army occupying the Straits. The crisis was settled by

1. In what ways did the Paris Peace Settlement meet Britain's war aims?

2. How fair were the terms of the Treaty of Versailles? Give reasons for your answer.

3. How far did the League of Nations go to meet Britain's security aims?

discussion between local commanders who agreed the terms of the Convention of Mudania of October 1922. The Convention stated that the Straits would remain neutral (to suit Britain) in return for Eastern Thrace and Adrianople being returned to Turkey. In 1923 the Treaty of Lausanne was agreed with the Turks, to replace the Treaty of Sèvres.

The crisis highlighted Dominions' discontent with the current situation concerning who should formulate their foreign policy, with the Canadians seeking first to place the problem before the Canadian Parliament rather than instantly answering Britain's appeal for support, as had Australia and New Zealand.

9.3 What problems did Britain face in the 1920s in dealing with European affairs?

The French occupation of the Ruhr

In the hope of making the Germans deliver quotas of Ruhr coal to France, as part of the reparations agreed under the Versailles treaty terms, France occupied the Ruhr from 1923 to 1925. The idea was for France to seize Ruhr coal and put pressure on the Germans to pay up.

Isolation: In diplomatic terms, isolation means not being tied into a treaty or having diplomatic obligations.

Entente Powers: Britain, France and Russia, who were allies between 1907 and 1917

Ratify: To approve a treaty.

The European foreign policy problems facing Britain in the 1920s were:

- French distrust of Germany and need for a guarantee for France against renewed German aggression;

- America's withdrawal into **isolation**, after having set the agenda at the Paris Peace Conference, and unwillingness either to take responsibility for problems caused by its withdrawal, or compound war debts until faced with the economic consequences of such refusal;

- Germany's economic crises and suspension of reparations payments;

- French occupation of the Ruhr in pursuit of financial compensation;

- Germany's aim to revise the terms of the Treaty of Versailles.

What problems for Britain and Europe arose from the American policy of isolation?

The United States of America, whose participation in the First World War had swung the balance in favour of victory for the **Entente Powers**, retired into isolationism in 1919. The United States refused to **ratify** the Treaty of Versailles and consequently did not join the League of Nations. Britain was left with the problem of maintaining peace in Europe after the Paris peace conference.

US President Wilson's Fourteen Points had provided a basis for the German agreement to an armistice in November 1918. The Fourteen Points also set the principles on which the peace negotiations were based. The British and the French believed the Americans would join with them in guaranteeing the peace settlement. The Americans did not keep their assurances to France that they, with Britain, would guarantee French security against Germany. The French therefore regarded some of terms of the Treaty of Versailles as invalidated by US non-participation and British unwillingness to give a unilateral guarantee. France was further worried by British willingness to accept the possibility that the settlement of Germany's eastern frontiers might be renegotiated at some future date.

What economic crises were caused by the issue of reparations payments?

Reparations from Germany were demanded as part of the peace settlement, in compensation for all damage to the Allied civilian population and their property, for example destruction of civilian shipping by German submarines. Lloyd George also pressed for compensation for war wounded, war widows and orphans: 'Germany must pay the cost of the war up to the limits of her capacity'.

Because of British and French war debts to America, reparations had been set too high at 50 million golden marks (£6,600 million). The justification for reparations was the decision that Germany was to blame for the First World War. Article 231 of the Treaty of Versailles assigned war guilt to Germany. However, Germany was not in a position to pay the reparations without facing social unrest in a country already affected by political extremism. John Maynard Keynes saw the potential problems, which he explained in *The Economic Consequences of the Peace* (1919), deploring the exclusion of 'provisions for the economic rehabilitation of Europe'.

The United States had emerged from the First World War richer, because the war had increased their gold reserves and industries. But they were unwilling to take on the role of world policeman. They further made it difficult to achieve fair and just peace settlements by insistence on repayment of war debts in full. Lloyd George saw that improvement in the German economy could help Britain's post-war revival. Britain had suggested that they might accept cancellation of German war debts to them, if the Americans would cancel debts owed to them by the Allies. The United States was hostile to this suggestion.

What problems arose from Franco-German distrust during the 1920s?

In the 1920s Britain was thus left to deal with two international relations problems arising from the peace settlement. On the one hand Britain sought to avoid involvement in guaranteeing French security, while at the same time calming French fears about the prospects of being at the receiving end of further German aggression. On the other hand, Britain was unwilling to make **unilateral** concessions to Germany to defuse social and political unrest, despite a growing feeling that the terms of the Treaty of Versailles were undeservedly harsh. This feeling was fostered by political agitators, such as Adolf Hitler and Wolfgang Kapp, as well as the German military High Command. They all rejected the idea that Germany had actually been defeated, instead placing the blame for accepting the armistice terms on the German civilian Social Democrat (SPD) government.

Unilateral: One sided, without anything being done in return.

Politicians in Britain realised very early in the 1920s that some of the terms of the Treaty of Versailles would probably need to be revised. Winston Churchill, for instance, saw that Britain had commercial motives for wanting to see the revival of the German economy. For this reason he was not only 'anxious to see friendship grow up and the hatred of war die' but equally 'anxious to see trade relations develop with Germany'. But he saw that 'any friendly relations which grow up in time between Britain and Germany will be terribly suspect to France' for fear 'England is more the friend of Germany than of France'. He therefore suggested that Britain should give the French a Treaty which 'bound the British Empire to protect France against unprovoked aggression by Germany. This would then give Britain 'greater freedom to establish new relations, new co-operation with Germany'.

The French desire to keep Germany down and enforce the terms of the Treaty of Versailles, especially where they concerned territory and reparations was potentially destabilising to European peace, as were German economic instability and social unrest. British diplomats recognised that the Versailles settlement was likely to provoke war unless two particular sources of German dissatisfaction were lessened: territorial losses to Poland and Czechoslovakia in the east and the economic consequences of reparations.

In 1922 France and Britain differed over reparations again. Britain was willing to agree to suspend reparations payments but France insisted on full repayment on schedule. The Germans stopped reparations payments and in 1923 France occupied the German Ruhr region, seeking to force Britain and the United States to support a new reparations scheme. But Britain could see that French actions were making German instability worse.

Under the Dawes Plan of April 1924, Germany's finances were restructured, although this involved a large US loan to Germany. At the London Reparations Conference of July and August 1924, Britain got Germany and France to accept the Dawes Plan. On that basis the Germans agreed to resume reparations payments and the French to withdraw from the Ruhr. But the incident had demonstrated an underlying weakness of post-war settlements. It showed that the reparations payments to be made by Germany had to be based on a realistic assessment of what Germany could afford to pay. To ignore this fact risked undermining the German economy and causing social and political unrest.

Why were Anglo-Soviet relations so unsatisfactory during the 1920s?

After the October/November 1917 Revolution, the Bolsheviks had announced that Communist Russia was in a state of war with every other non-communist state, including Britain. Only agreement of a Treaty of Mutual Non-Aggression between Britain and the Communist Russians could end this state of war. Anglo-Soviet hostility also derived from three other issues:

● The British resented the fact that the Bolsheviks had withdrawn from the First World War and made a separate peace treaty with the Germans at Brest-Litovsk in 1918. This meant that the Bolsheviks had freed the part of the German army that had been fighting on the Eastern front to fight on the Western Front. As a result Communist Russia was given no role at the Paris Peace Conference.

● Anglo/Russian hostility had been made worse in 1919 by British intervention in the Russian Civil War of 1918–21. Against the advice of Lloyd George, Winston Churchill had sent an expedition of British forces to Archangel (North Russia, near north Finland) to fight on behalf of the White Russians (non-communists).

● The British government also resented the activities in Britain of the Comintern (the Communist International), which the Bolsheviks had established in March 1919. The Comintern's role was to try to create political unrest and possibly Communist revolution in non-communist states. A Communist Party of Great Britain was set up in 1920. The British government was especially concerned about Communist exploitation of economic depression and unemployment in Britain in the 1920s and 1930s (see chapter 6).

How successful was Britain in attempts to improve Anglo-Soviet relations?

Lloyd George was keen to establish peace with the Bolsheviks in order to restore commercial trading relations with the new regime, but only if 'Communistic principles are abandoned'. Then he would be ready to 'assist in the economic development of Russia', which he thought would also help the British economy. When the Soviet Union abandoned the 'War Economy' of 1918–21 and embarked upon a more liberal economic policy in 1921 (the New Economic Policy) this was seen as a potential change of heart in Bolshevik political, economic and social policies. Lloyd George was unsuccessful because the Bolsheviks had not really abandoned 'communist principles'.

Lloyd George tried to get the Soviet Union diplomatically **recognised**. He was unsuccessful because mistrust of Bolshevism prevailed. Lloyd George also tried to tie the '**pariah**' nations, Germany and the Soviet Union, into the European power system. In 1922, at the Genoa conference on European Economic Reconstruction, not only was he unsuccessful in this aim, but Germany and the Soviet Union drew closer together, by means of the 'secret' Rapallo Treaty of 1922. Under its terms Germany and the Soviet Union established diplomatic relations, agreed mutual renunciation of financial claims and also agreed to co-operate on military training. This enabled the German **Reichswehr** to side-step the terms of the Treaty of Versailles by training on Soviet territory. This did not improve Anglo-Soviet relations.

In 1924 the incoming Labour government was more successful in improving Anglo-Soviet relations. It recognised the Soviet Union and attempted to establish mutually beneficial commercial relations. However, links with the Bolsheviks were seen as discrediting the Labour party, who were compromised by the '**Zinoviev Letter**', which confirmed **Reds-under-the-bed** phobia. They were further compromised by the 1926 General Strike.

In 1927 Anglo-Soviet diplomatic relations were severed, after the 'Arcos' raid on a Soviet trade mission by the British secret service. The results of the raid were inconclusive but relations were still damaged. Anglo-Soviet relations were also damaged by British fears about Soviet intentions in China, where the activities of Comintern agent Michael Borodin were encouraging Communists and Nationalists to strikes and riots which were damaging British trading privileges and interests. Fears were also raised about Soviet interests in, and intentions towards, Indian nationalists. Nevertheless, on its return to power in 1929, the Labour government succeeded in restoring diplomatic relations with the Soviet Union.

How far did Britain's foreign policy go to meet French fears and Germany's grievances in the 1920s?

It was recognised that the League of Nations could not guarantee peace and that efforts would have to be made to reconcile Franco-German distrust. Although Germany had signed the Treaty of Versailles, many Germans did not accept that they had thoroughly lost the war. The scale of Germany's defeat had little impact because German territory had not been occupied by the victors, and Germany had not been physically damaged by the war in the way that France and Belgium had suffered. The German illusion that they had not been defeated underpinned Germany's unwillingness to accept the territorial settlements imposed at Versailles and its determination to seek renegotiation of these settlements. It was this determination that made France nervous about the Franco-German borders and necessitated the meeting at Locarno in the autumn of 1925 which produced the Locarno Treaty.

A solution to the problem of French security put to Prime Minister Ramsey MacDonald in 1924, which he was willing to pursue, was a 'Geneva **protocol**'. Under this protocol the League of Nations would oversee disarmament and compulsory arbitration between disputing nations. The idea was dropped by incoming Foreign Secretary, Austen Chamberlain, who had a different agenda.

What were the main aims of the Locarno Treaty of December 1925?

Austen Chamberlain, who was Foreign Secretary from 1924 to 1929, wanted to 'remove or allay French fears' and 'bring Germany back to the

Recognise: In the diplomatic sense, to recognise signifies the establishment of formal diplomatic relations, which involves the opening of an official Embassy, staffed by accredited diplomats, with the ambassador being received by the ruler.

Pariah: Social outcast, e.g. Russia or Germany after the First World War.

Reichswehr: The German armed forces. From 1934 the word Wehrmacht is used.

Zinoviev Letter: A letter said to have been sent to British communists by Grigory Zinoviev, who was Chairman of the Comintern, pressing them to promote revolution by acts of sedition (agitation and rebellion). Published in British newspapers four days before a general election, it is credited with having persuaded middle-class opinion to vote Conservative. The Labour Party, which lost the election, considered it to be a forgery, planted for the purpose of increasing Conservative support.

Reds-under-the-bed: A term expressing the fear that Communist spies were to be found everywhere (even under your bed).

Protocol: Original draft of treaty terms forming part of a diplomatic document that has been agreed after negotiation at a conference.

Austen Chamberlain (1863–1937)
Conservative MP and son of Joseph Chamberlain and half-brother of Neville Chamberlain, he served as Chancellor of the Exchequer 1903–5, Secretary of State for India 1915–17, Minister without Portfolio 1918–19, Chancellor of the Exchequer 1919–21, Lord Privy Seal 1921–22 and Foreign Secretary 1924–29 in Baldwin's administration. Chamberlain felt that rehabilitation of Germany was the path to peace in Europe and actively engaged Britain in negotiations with France and Germany to this end. He received the 1925 Nobel Peace prize for his work on the Locarno Pact.

concert of Europe', both of which he saw as 'equally vital. Neither by itself will suffice and the first is needed to allow the second'. Chamberlain wanted to find alternatives to the Geneva Protocol binding the countries which had signed the Covenant of the League of Nations to resist aggression world-wide. He thought the Protocol would be an additional burden to Britain, given the number of existing commitments. Chamberlain recognised French fears of Germany. He also recognised that the failure of Britain and the United States to guarantee French security after the Paris peace settlements provoked France to pre-emptive acts against Germany, such as the occupation of the Ruhr.

Historian Richard Grayson argues, in *Austen Chamberlain and the Commitment to Europe: British Foreign Policy 1924–29* (1997), that Chamberlain recognised the need to stabilise Europe in order to safeguard Britain's security. Therefore he engaged Britain in a search for European stability by pacifying both France and Germany. This challenges the view that Britain was isolationist in respect of Europe and favoured France in preference to Germany. Grayson argues that Chamberlain was in favour of peace, forcing both to make concessions.

Chamberlain, French foreign minister Aristide Briand and German Foreign Minister Gustav Stresemann, together with Italian leader Mussolini, met in the autumn of 1925 at Locarno in Switzerland, near the border with Italy. They settled the following:

- Germany recognised the border with France and Belgium made in the Treaty of Versailles.

- British and French occupation troops in the Rhineland were to be reduced, the first reduction to be in January 1926 and the final in 1930. The Rhineland was to remain demilitarised.

- Britain and Italy were to act as guarantors, agreeing to act against an aggressor should the borders be violated by any party to the agreement.

However:

- Germany's eastern frontiers were not guaranteed. Chamberlain remarked that 'no British government ever will or ever can risk the bones of a British grenadier' for the Polish corridor (or any Eastern European issue considered to be outside British interests).

- Britain would not join with France in guaranteeing the '**Little Entente**', because Chamberlain did not feel that Britain had any interests to secure in Eastern Europe.

Little Entente: A series of bilateral security agreements between East European states, Yugoslavia, Czechoslovakia and Romania, mainly against Hungarian revanchism.

In 1926, resulting from the Locarno agreements, Germany rejoined the League of Nations.

How successful was Austen Chamberlain's foreign policy?

At the time, the Locarno agreements were seen as the path to lasting peace

Aristide Briand (1862–1932)
Politician of the French Third Republic and Prime Minister eleven times (briefly) between 1909 and 1929. During the 1920s he was the most influential voice in French foreign policy formulation. A strong supporter of the League of Nations, he favoured improved Franco-German relations. Briand shared with Gustav Stresemann the 1926 Nobel Peace Prize and instigated the Kellogg-Briand Pact of 1928 on the renunciation of war as an instrument of national policy.

Gustav Stresemann (1878–1929)
German Chancellor for three months in 1923 and thereafter served as Foreign Minister until his death in 1929. Stresemann believed that Germany should gain the trust of former enemies by fulfilling the Versailles peace terms, which might then be renegotiated. By this means he reduced German reparations, confirmed Franco-German borders at Locarno and gained German admission to the League of Nations and League Council in 1926.

in Europe, stabilising the continent. Chamberlain's aim was to work on both France and Germany to accept changes in the Treaty of Versailles, giving both some gains in return for some concessions.

● Chamberlain solved the major problem of the Franco-German border. By successfully reducing tensions between France and Germany, Chamberlain introduced a climate of mutual trust and co-operation. He introduced 'Geneva tea parties' (regular informal meetings of senior diplomats) outside the League of Nations to settle disputes.

● In 1927, Allied military controls in Germany were lifted. Chamberlain wanted to encourage Germans to feel trustworthy. To review German compliance with the disarmament clauses of the Treaty of Versailles, Chamberlain persuaded the French to accept regular League of Nations inspections in Germany instead of the permanent presence of the Inter-Allied Military Commission of Control (IAMC). This policy removed the ability to check German disarmament (which would prove crucial in the next decade).

● Chamberlain did not believe that Stresemann's intentions were aggressive, so he supported Stresemann in seeking some revisions of the Treaty of Versailles. Chamberlain also encouraged Stresemann to initiate discussion of the issue of German minorities in Poland, in order to satisfy German public opinion.

● In December 1927 Chamberlain encouraged informal German involvement in settling the issue of difficulties being faced by Poles living in Lithuania.

● In 1928 the Kellogg-Briand Pact, renouncing war, was signed by 65 states. Theoretically desirable, the Pact ignored the principles of **realpolitik**, but was popular at the time.

Realpolitik: Realism in politics, especially applied to international relations.

● In 1929 the Young Plan reduced German reparations by one-third of the original sum demanded. Also in 1929 the former Allies agreed to evacuate all their troops from Germany by the mid-1930s (which would prove significant in terms of Hitler's reoccupation of the Rhineland in 1936).

● Outside European affairs, Austen Chamberlain increased control of foreign policy by the Dominions.

Not all peace initiatives were successful though. For example, in 1928 preliminary discussions were held on disarmament. Britain was willing to discuss limitations on 'reduction in size and power of capital ships' and to 'establish a basis of equality between principal Air Powers of Europe'. But only if limitations on trained (manpower) reserves were agreed at the same time. France disagreed and the issue was adjourned for some months. The Foreign Office further noted in January 1928, 'it is true that we are pledged to disarm – it is not so clear that we are pledged, anywhere, to sign an agreed disarmament convention'.

1. In what ways were the security problems of the 1920s the outcome of the Paris peace settlements?

2. Were friendly relations with the Soviet Union possible?

3. Assess the achievements of Austen Chamberlain as Foreign Secretary 1924–29.

Failure to disarm was crucial because Germany was meant to be disarmed, not only as part of the Treaty of Versailles but as part of the general European movement to disarmament. The same Foreign Office memorandum suggested that 'the League has chosen to act as if it were bound to produce a general disarmament convention. The Germans have seized on this and sought to connect general disarmament with their own disarmament in such a way that they can claim to be freed from their part of the bargain if the Allied governments do not perform theirs.' It was the arrival in power of Hitler that removed any potential willingness of European powers to consider disarmament.

9.4 What were the aims of Imperial policy between 1918 and 1939?

Britain wanted to preserve as much of the Empire as circumstances and budgetary limits permitted. Britain also wanted to delay granting independence, for example to India, until such time as preparation had been adequately put into action for Indians to take over all aspects of the government of their country.

What were the problems?

● The White Dominions wanted complete independence from Britain. Especially they wanted freedom of foreign policy formulation so that they would no longer have to participate in a British war not of their making, unless they chose to do so. At the Imperial War Conference in 1917 they had demanded a post-war conference to change their constitutional relations with Britain.

● The growth of nationalism in India, in particular, giving rise to demands for independence, which were accompanied by political agitation and violence.

● There was growth of Irish Nationalism, arising from demands from the mainly Southern Irish Nationalists for complete independence. The Nationalists rejected the terms of the Government of Ireland Act of 1920, which offered only Home Rule. However, the Ulster Protestants of Northern Ireland wanted to remain part of Britain. Satisfying Ulster's demands would effectively have divided Ireland, but this was not acceptable to the Republicans. Britain became involved in a vicious conflict with the Irish Republican Army (the IRA) between 1919 and 1921 (see chapter 13).

● The 1920s saw a struggle for power in South Africa between moderate Afrikaaners, like the pro-British Jan Smuts of the Union Party, and more extreme nationalists, like General Hertzog, who had left the government in 1912 to form a National Party, with a policy of South Africa first. When it came to power in 1924, Hertzog's National Party was unwilling to make concessions to the growing force of African Nationalism, represented by the African National Congress, (founded 1912). The National Party brought in segregation of blacks and whites in their 'civilised labour' policy.

By what steps did the Dominions achieve the level of independence they wanted?

The British Empire, and especially Canada, Australia, New Zealand and South Africa, had given tremendous support, both military and economic, to Britain's war effort. Two-and-a-half million men had fought for the Empire, notably the Australians and New Zealanders at Gallipoli in 1915. The Dominions were disillusioned by lack of consultation with the British during the war and decided to seek a greater measure of independence afterwards. At the 1917 Imperial War Conference, the Dominions called for a post-war conference to settle their constitutional relations with Britain, pressing for a redefinition of Dominion status. In particular they wished to become **sovereign** nations and exercise freedom in foreign policy formulation. Moreover, they were unwilling to become involved in wars of Britain's making and the demanded reforms would provide means to refuse. Additionally they insisted on representing themselves at the Paris peace conference. These concerns were not addressed at the 1921 Imperial Conference because Britain was more involved with trying to

Sovereign: A sovereign nation has control over itself and is not ruled by the government of another nation.

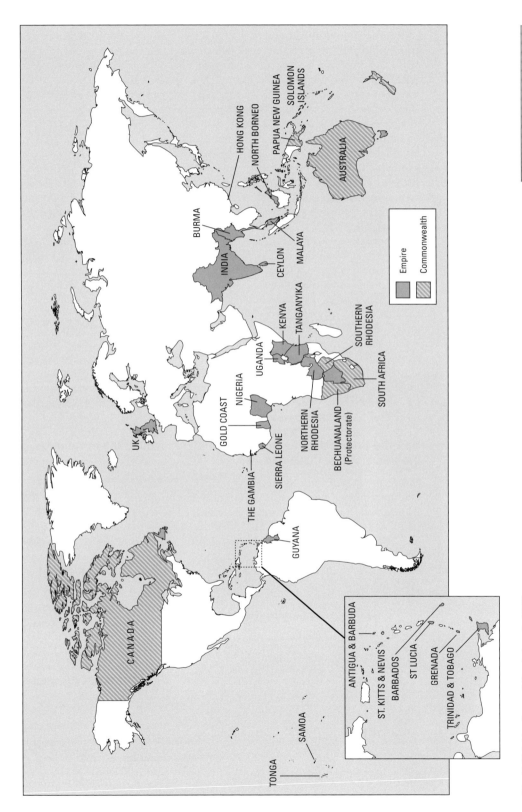

In what ways does this map show that Britain was a world power in 1939?

The British Empire and Dominions in 1939.

Autonomous communities: Self-governing communities.

Prerogative: An exclusive right or privilege.

solve other imperial dilemmas, such as producing an Irish settlement acceptable to both the Nationalists and the Ulstermen of the North. The Dominions did not support Britain in the 1922 Chanak crisis and ignored the provisions of the 1925 Locarno Pact, although Austen Chamberlain had not bound them to this anyway.

At the Imperial Conference of 1926, Arthur Balfour defined the Commonwealth as an idea developed to associate the concept of Empire with the practical reality of Dominions becoming '**autonomous communities** within the British Empire'. The White Dominions were to be 'equal in status and in no way subordinate one to another in any aspect of their domestic or external affairs'. But they were to be 'united by common allegiance to the Crown and freely associated as members of the British Commonwealth of Nations'. The significance of the Balfour Declaration lay in its provision of a means by which Britain hoped to project a semblance of Imperial unity abroad. This was important as it permitted British influence to seem undiminished. At the same time the Dominions were offered a route to achieve the level of independence they were seeking, including exercise of the **prerogative** to conduct an independent foreign policy.

A conference of constitutional experts met in 1929 to consider the problem of Westminster Parliamentary legislation being applied to the Dominions, which undermined their sovereignty. Its recommendations were considered at the Imperial Conference of 1930 and finally enacted in the 1931 Statute of Westminster. The 1931 Statute of Westminster provided a legal framework for the Dominions to be completely self-governing, confirming that they need no longer be bound by British laws if they did not so wish. Equally, the British Parliament could not invalidate Dominion legislation. The Dominions were in free association with Britain and each other within the Commonwealth, although the British monarch remained head of state, represented by a High Commissioner. The Statute covered Australia, New Zealand, Canada, South Africa, and added in the Irish Free State and Newfoundland.

How did Britain and the Commonwealth respond to the economic problems of the 1920s and 1930s?

Protectionism: Economic system of protecting home industries and commerce, usually by imposing taxes on imported goods.

While the Dominions could associate freely, there were no institutions to facilitate mutual co-operation, especially in commerce. During the 1920s Britain had clung to the ideal of free trade. The Dominions, on the other hand, favoured **protectionism**, and a system whereby they traded with each other and imposed lower or no duties on Commonwealth goods while tariffs were imposed on foreign goods. In 1924 an Empire Exhibition was held at Wembley to encourage the purchase of Empire goods and in 1926 an Empire Marketing Board was set up, but it was abandoned in 1932.

Economic problems affecting the Empire were made worse by the Depression that followed the 1929 Wall Street Crash (see chapter 6). In 1931 Britain abandoned the gold standard and set up the Sterling Area as the monetary standard throughout the Empire, with the exception of Canada, whose currency was the Canadian dollar.

Crown Colonies: Those colonies that did not have self-government.

In 1932 Britain abandoned free trade. A conference was held in Ottawa in 1932 and agreements were set up for Imperial preference, a series of bilateral agreements on tariffs between Commonwealth members. This was a revised version of tariff reform enabling the British Dominions (and in 1933 British **Crown Colonies**) to form a self-contained trading unit that was protected by high tariffs against foreign competition. It provided a means for Commonwealth countries to assist each other in the Depression (see chapter 6). Imperial preference was behind an Import Duties Act introduced in 1932 imposing first a duty of 10 per cent then 20 per cent on most foreign goods, but with exemptions on food, raw materials and Commonwealth produce. But it had only limited success because national self-interest prevailed. All Commonwealth countries wanted to sell their goods rather than to buy. They wanted to protect their own industry and agriculture against outside competition. Even so, by 1938, Commonwealth countries sold almost 50 per cent of their export goods to each other.

India

Secretaries of State for India (from 1937 Secretary of State for India and Burma)

E. Montagu	July 1917 – March 1922
V.T. Peel	March 1922 – January 1924
Earl Birkenhead	November 1924 – August 1929
S. Hoare	August 1931 – June 1935
M. Zetland	June 1935 – September 1939

What were the problems Britain had to face in India?
Large sections of the Indian people did not want to be governed by Britain. They wanted complete independence. By the outbreak of the First World War, the Morley-Minto reforms of 1909 had increased Indian representation in the administration and the legislative councils. But authority was still firmly in British hands, exercised through the **Viceroy**, and Indian nationalist aspirations for complete independence remained unsatisfied.

In 1917 Edwin Montagu, the Secretary of State for India, announced the aim of 'gradual development of self-governing institutions, with a view to

Viceroy: A ruler acting with royal authority within a colony or dependency.

Indian Councils Bill 1909 (Morley-Minto Reforms)

● Increased power of legislative councils.

● Majority of members to be elective.

● Increased Indian representation.

● Elected members given greater share in government.

● Members eligible to sit on Viceroy's Executive Council in India; and Secretary of State for India's Councils in London.

● Indians formed a majority on provincial councils, though a minority on the all-Indian legislative council.

Montagu-Chelmsford Reforms, March 1919 (formed basis of Government of India Act 1919)

● Eleven autonomous provinces created.

● Indian ministers to have control of public health, education and agriculture.

● Viceroy to be responsible for public order, finance, diplomatic relations and foreign policy.

---

progressive realisation of responsible government in India as an integral part of the British Empire', embodied in what became known as the Montagu-Chelmsford reforms. These formed the basis of the March 1919 Government of India Act.

The British government felt an obligation to give in to many nationalist demands. During the First World War India had contributed 500,000 fighting men and donated £100,000 towards the cost of the war. However Britain did not want to meet all demands for independence, feeling that India was not capable of responsible self-government. This was because there was hatred and rivalry between the many and various Indian religions and castes, which too often led to violence.

Despite the reforms begun in the 1919 Government of India Act, too much government remained in the British Viceroy's hands. This left unsatisfied demands for independence of the Indian nationalists: the Hindus in the Indian National Congress and the Muslims in the Muslim League. A civil disobedience campaign was launched by the Indian National Congress in 1919, lasting until 1922.

Anglo-Indian relations were embittered in April 1919 in what became known as the Amritsar massacre. A British army officer, Brigadier General Dyer, ordered his forces to open fire on unarmed Sikh, Hindu and Muslim demonstrators who wanted an end to Britain's special powers of imprisonment of agitators without trial, killing 379 demonstrators. It was claimed that the British authorities feared a mutiny, but the 379 deaths increased Indian nationalist fervour. In 1921 Indians boycotted the visit of the Prince of Wales to show their displeasure with the British.

Gandhi's campaign of civil disobedience continued through the 1920s. He called the British government in India 'satanic' and said that paying taxes was subsidising British repression of Nationalist agitation. The continued unrest called for a response from the British.

How did the British government deal with Indian nationalist agitation?

Large sections of the British government did not feel that India was ready for full self-government. The British government instead offered only limited self-government measures. These were unacceptable to the Indian nationalists because they fell short of the complete independence demanded. In 1927 Baldwin set up the Simon Commission to report on how the 1919 Government of India Act was working ten years on, and its prospects for the future. Gandhi and the Indian National Congress party boycotted the Commission. They saw the Commission's exclusion of

Mohandas Karamchand Gandhi (1869–1948)
Known as 'Mahatma' (Great Soul), Gandhi was an Indian nationalist and leader of the Congress movement. He was a lawyer who led a campaign of passive resistance and civil disobedience, such as boycotts, strikes and non-co-operation, in pursuit of Indian independence.

Edward Wood, Viceroy Irwin (later Earl of Halifax) (1881–1959)
Becoming Baron Irwin in 1925, he served as Viceroy of India from 1926 to 1931, during a period of increasing nationalist agitation. Nevertheless, he succeeded in winning the confidence of Gandhi. Irwin became Earl of Halifax in 1934 and served as British Foreign Secretary from 1937 to 1941.

Gandhi leading the Salt March in protest against the British government monopoly on salt production.

Indian representatives as insulting. Wherever the Commission travelled in India it was met with riots and mass demonstrations.

In October 1929, before the Simon Commission reported, Viceroy Irwin announced the intention of the British government to give Dominion status to India and speed up **devolution** of powers into Indian hands. This outcome satisfied Gandhi but not Nehru, the Congress Party leader, and his deputy, Subhas Chandra Bose, who demanded complete independence. Gandhi, not to be outdone, led 'Salt marches'. These were against the salt tax and prohibition against unlicensed manufacture of salt – but they led to violence, which Gandhi abhorred. Gandhi was gaoled, but soon released and invited to discussions with Viceroy Irwin. Beginning in 1931 three Round-Table Conferences were held, to discuss further concessions on independence. These included Indian representatives (unlike the Simon Commission). Even so, many Indians boycotted the conferences and they achieved little.

In 1935 the Government of India Act gave control of provinces to Indians, although India was still subject to the Viceroy. This was a success, but not with central government where the problem revolved around the exclusion of Muslims, who were a minority. The Congress Party participated and won eight out of the eleven provinces. However, the British had failed to satisfy the hard-line Indian nationalist demands for complete independence because the Viceroy still retained control of defence, foreign affairs, tariffs on British imports and protection of minorities.

In the 1937 provincial election the Indian National Congress Party gained power but the Muslim League received only 5 per cent of the vote. Therefore the Muslim League was regarded as not representing the Muslim vote. The Muslim leader Jinnah feared that Hindu rule would replace British rule, with Muslims still excluded from government.

Despite all the reforms enacted before the outbreak of the Second World War in 1939, the British government still had not succeeded in appeasing hardline Indian nationalist demands for full independence of central government. What they had succeeded in obtaining so far was devolved powers to the provinces.

Devolution: Formal grant of permission to rule from Parliament to the regions.

Source-based questions: Britain's policy towards India between 1918 and 1939

SOURCE A

They are autonomous Communities within the British Empire, equal in status, in no way subordinate one to another in any aspect of their domestic or external affairs, though united by a common allegiance to the Crown …

The rapid evolution of the Overseas Dominions during the last fifty years has involved many complicated adjustments of old political machinery to changing conditions. The tendency towards equality of status was both right and inevitable. Every self-governing member of the Empire is now the master of its destiny.

From The 'Balfour definition' of the Commonwealth, 1926.

SOURCE B

Whereas it is the declared policy of Parliament to provide for the increasing association of Indians in every branch of Indian administration, and for the gradual development of self-governing institutions, with a view to the progressive realisation of responsible government in British India as an integral part of the empire:

And whereas the time and manner of each advance can be determined only by Parliament, upon whom responsibility lies for the welfare and advancement of the Indian peoples:

And whereas the action of Parliament in such matters must be guided by the co-operation received from those on whom new opportunities of service will be conferred, and by the extent to which it is found that confidence can be reposed in their sense of responsibility.

From The Government of India Act 1919.

SOURCE C

His Excellency the Governor of Bengal said that in his province there is good reason to believe that the movement is definitely on the decline. Picketing is giving a certain amount of trouble … It is, however, generally recognised that the failure of the civil disobedience movement will be followed by an increase in terrorist activities. His Excellency the Governor of Bombay said … the measures so far taken by His Government have had the effect of keeping down the level of enthusiasm, but on the other hand have increased the size of the movement so far as the numbers of adherents and sympathisers is concerned …

From Report on Indian provincial governors discussion on the civil disobedience campaign, 23 July 1930.

1. Study Source A.

What does this source tell a historian about the differences in treatment by the British government of the White Dominions and India?

2. Study Source B.

How useful is this source as evidence of British policy towards India after 1918?

3. Study Sources A, B and C and use information contained in this chapter.

Using your knowledge of the political situations in the White Dominions and India in the period 1918–1939, explain the reasons for the differences in the way Britain treated them.

The Middle East

What problems did Britain face in Palestine?

In 1919 Britain and France had divided up the German and Ottoman Empires on behalf of the League of Nations. In Palestine Britain was faced with the consequences of having made promises to the Jews in the Balfour Declaration of 1917 promising a Jewish homeland in Palestine. In the course of fighting the First World War Britain had also made promises to the Arabs about an independent homeland. These promises and obligations were mutually exclusive. As a consequence, there was hostility between Jews and Arabs. They clashed in April 1919, obliging Britain to guarantee the rights of the Palestinian non-Jews.

The hostility of the Arabs grew with increased Jewish immigration into Palestine. Between 1919 and 1929 the Jewish population in Palestine had doubled and the Palestinian Arabs protested. The Jews retaliated, and in August 1929 200 people were killed in the fighting. The Arabs felt that their position in Palestine had been weakened because the Jewish population increased from 4,075 in 1931 to 61,854 in 1935, and they comprised one third of the population of Palestine. Jewish immigration, especially from Germany after 1933, sparked off an Arab Rebellion lasting from 1936 to 1939.

How did Britain try to solve the problem?

White Paper: A report published by the government on aspects of policy often with a recommendation for action.

A Labour government **White Paper** of 1930 threatening to limit Jewish immigration provoked such widespread Jewish protests that the government backed down. Following the deaths of British soldiers in the Arab Rebellion in 1936 the Peel Report was commissioned. Published in 1937, its chief recommendation was partition of Palestine into separate Jewish and Arab states. The British would supervise a corridor from Haifa inland to include Jerusalem, Bethlehem and Nazareth. Partition was rejected by most Arabs and **Zionists**. The Report's recommendations were never implemented.

Zionism: The political movement that wanted to create a separate homeland for Jews in Palestine. This new state would be called Israel.

Unable, by the terms of the mandate, to hand over to the Jews a Zionist homeland, the government were obliged both to attempt to keep the peace and find a solution acceptable to Jews and Arabs.

Iraq was the scene of a revolt in July 1919. It was crushed, but the Iraqis were given a degree of self-government, although with a British adviser and retention of a large British airfield at Habbaniya.

In 1922 Egypt was declared independent, although Britain remained in charge of foreign policy and maintained a garrison there to protect the Suez Canal. The 1936 Anglo-Egyptian Treaty gave Egypt a greater measure of independence and promised withdrawal of the British garrison in 1956.

With defence expenditure cut and force levels reduced, Britain had 'bitten off more than it could chew' by taking on administration of the Middle East mandated territories. Then why take them on? At the time, their addition to the British Empire nearly completed Curzon's hoped-for land bridge stretching from the Mediterranean to India. The effects were either unforeseen or ignored.

How successfully did Britain handle problems arising from administration of African territories?

To save the cost of administration the British government planned to incorporate Southern Rhodesia into South Africa. Frustrated by rejection of this plan in the November 1922 referendum the British government dropped it, not wishing to antagonise the settlers. Instead, in October 1923, Britain successfully saved administrative costs by handing over Southern Rhodesia to a legislative assembly. In effect Southern Rhodesia was from then governed by white settlers, but they were denied Dominion status.

In 1927 a White Paper produced by Colonial Secretary Leo Amery proposed a 'Great White Dominion' in East Africa composed of Kenya, Uganda, Tanganyika, the Rhodesias and Nyasaland, to be held in trust for Britain. Supported by white settlers, it was resisted by Indian immigrants and Africans.

A problem British administrators of African territories had to deal with was the issue of African rights conflicting with the demands of white and Indian interest groups for self-government. This problem was highlighted by the growth in organisation of African nationalist groups. In Kenya native Africans outnumbered settlers by 10,000 to one. In 1922 the Kikuyu tribe of Kenya rioted against the imposition of increased taxes and requirements for African males to carry an identity card. Twenty-five Africans died in the riots. The 1929 Young Commission Report argued for African interests to be paramount because white settlers were not the best trustees of African interests. The Labour government of 1929–31, which appointed Sidney Webb as Colonial Secretary, reasserted the Devonshire Declaration. This stated that only agents of imperial government were to act on behalf of Africans rather than white settlers. Webb argued for adequate representation for all interest groups. However, the Labour government of 1929–31 was too short-lived to achieve change in this aspect of colonial policy.

British governments were also uncertain of how to deal with colonial welfare reforms. Most colonial administrators argued that colonial policy should aim to improve the educational standards of colonial inhabitants in addition to exploiting the wealth of the colony for the benefit of Britain. However, between the wars economic and social improvements were neglected. Less than 15 per cent of black Africans in British-administered Africa went to school, health care was primitive and housing inadequate. The Labour government in 1929 introduced improvements in a Colonial Development Bill. However, with the Depression of the 1930s there was little enough government money made available for investment in social welfare programmes in Britain and even less was allocated to Colonial development. At the same time the Colonies were badly affected by the world recession, opening Colonial trade unions to targeting by the Comintern. The government could not agree on colonial policy, trying to decide whether it should deal with India or Africa first.

1. How did Britain cope with unrest in India and demands for independence?

2. Did Britain treat the White Dominions more favourably than other parts of the Empire? Explain your answer.

3. How successful were Britain's policies towards the Empire between 1918–39?

9.5 What were the problems facing British foreign policy during the 1930s?

Gunboat diplomacy: Diplomatic negotiations carried out with the backing of military action if negotiations do not progress in the right way.

Why did Britain feel unable to take too strong a line with Japanese, German and Italian aggression in the 1930s? Britain had given priority to obligations to legislate for social reforms during the 1920s, at the expense of defence requirements (under the Ten Year Rule). Budgetary limits were compounded by the Depression, which eroded the financial base that underpinned defence spending. Britain was simply unable to operate the **gunboat diplomacy** that had characterised the era of Palmerston. Thus, the British government was obliged to temporise and to negotiate agreed settlements, based on the notion of collective security through the medium of the League of Nations.

Successive governments have been blamed for seeking electoral popularity by adopting economic measures to maintain the standard of living. They did so at the cost of lowering the defence posture of a country whose overseas trade was fundamental to economic survival and whose interests must be defended and be seen to be capable of defence. Cabinet Secretary Sir Maurice Hankey believed that to safeguard trade (vital to the economy) it was necessary to 'preach to the people that they must pull in their belts and economise' as 'fighting strength has been reduced by repeated "cuts" and there has been an orgy of extravagance on social reform'.

The desire for peace was typified by the Peace Pledge Union and the East Fulham by-election results of June 1935, which portrayed the British public not only as anti-war, but willing to negotiate rather than fight, whatever the issue of principle involved. Appeasement was popular.

These were key issues in confirming Hitler's growing belief that Britain could be persuaded to allow him to go on revising the Treaty of Versailles.

How did Britain and the League of Nations deal with Japanese aggression in Manchuria?

From 1931 Britain had to deal with Japanese aggression and territorial expansion in China, which threatened British commercial interests. Attempts to solve the problem through the League of Nations failed when Japan left the League.

Japanese aggression in Manchuria

- The early 1930s saw a rise in extreme and aggressive nationalism among the Japanese military.

- They began to take control of foreign policy from the Japanese civilian government.

- The Japanese army, stationed in Manchuria (Northern China) to protect Japanese commercial interests, seized control of the South Manchuria Railway on the excuse that China was weak and unstable and that Chinese aggression posed a risk to Japanese commercial interests.

- China took the issue of Japanese aggression to the League of Nations.

- League of Nations action to sanction Japan was postponed to see if Japan and China could settle South Manchurian Railway treaty rights between themselves.

- In October 1931, the Japanese Army annexed Manchuria, after the Mukden incident.

Britain and the United States both had important commercial interests in China. They considered that the Japanese annexation of Manchuria

Open Door: A policy for economic development in China, whereby all states were to enjoy equal commercial and tariff rights and equal rights of access to commercial opportunities.

violated the Washington Nine Power Treaty of 1921, which guaranteed the 'Open Door' to trade with China. The League of Nations sent a Commission of Enquiry to Manchuria, led by Lord Lytton. The Lytton Commission reported in September 1932. The Report condemned Japanese military action as unjustifiable, but also called on China to respect Japanese and other foreign rights.

Japan withdrew from the League of Nations in March 1933 following censure of its aggression in China. Lack of a firm response from the League of Nations and failure to impose sanctions after the report of the Lytton Commission of Enquiry demonstrated the fundamental weakness of the League – its inability to punish transgressors, to a point where they desisted from aggressive behaviour, because the League lacked an agreed method and means of punishment and/or coercion.

In 1932, Japanese aggression was extended to Shanghai, threatening British commercial interests. Britain feared that the Japanese would take control of the International Settlement, making it a Japanese concession. If that happened, Britain would have to retire from the Far East because the only way to check Japan was by force. Britain's depleted defence capacity would not stretch to the defence of commercial interests in China.

Benito Mussolini (1883–1945)
Formed right-radical group which became the Italian Fascist Party and came to power in 1922 to forestall a communist revolution. As Italian Prime Minister he was also known as *Il Duce* – the Leader. During the 1920s he posed as a peacemaker but became jealous of Hitler's successes and desired to emulate him by acquiring an Italian 'empire'. Following the war with Abyssinia and imposition of League of Nations sanctions, Mussolini collaborated with Hitler, forming the Rome-Berlin Axis in 1936.

How did Britain deal with Mussolini's ambitions for an Italian Empire in 1935–36?

In the 1930s Britain and other members of the League of Nations proved as powerless to check the territorial ambitions of Mussolini as they had those of Japan. In October 1935 Mussolini invaded Abyssinia, both to avenge Italy's defeat at Adowa in 1898 and to establish an Italian 'empire' in the region. The League of Nations condemned the invasion. The British and French governments wanted to appease Mussolini's desire for African territory. This had been promised to Italy in 1915 under the terms of the Secret Treaty of London should Britain and France gain German territory in Africa. The promise was not kept. British Foreign Secretary Samuel Hoare and French Foreign Secretary Pierre Laval met in Paris in December 1935 and devised the Hoare-Laval Plan. They agreed to give Mussolini two-thirds of Abyssinia. The French were anxious to do nothing that would provoke Mussolini to leave the League. The House of Commons and the British public were enraged when these arrangements became public knowledge, believing the agreement to be a reward for aggression.

Effectively, the Stresa Front had been destroyed by Mussolini's actions and France and Britain's refusal to accommodate him. Although the League of Nations imposed oil sanctions upon Mussolini, they were neither effectively incapacitating nor properly enforced. But they provoked Mussolini to tell Hitler that he would no longer uphold the Locarno Agreements, opening the way to Germany's reoccupation of the Rhineland.

How successful was Britain's policy towards Italy in the mid-1930s?

- Britain's policy of working with Mussolini to contain Hitler through the Stresa Front failed in 1936.

- So too did Britain's policy of working through the League of Nations to contain aggression, because the League had no means to enforce punishment of aggression.

- The British government did not connive with Mussolini to permit him territory in Abyssinia, as had Laval. Their chief interest was to keep Mussolini working with Britain and France and bound by the Stresa Front agreements. But the tone of the Maffey Report of June 1935 suggested that no British interest would be served by keeping Italy out of Abyssinia.

- However this opinion was not shared by the British public, which was attached to the idea of the League of Nations and collective security. Public disgust with the terms of the leaked Hoare-Laval plan ensured that the British government would support the League of Nations' decision to impose sanctions on Italy.

- In turn, this reinforced Mussolini's desire to improve Italy's relations with Germany. The Stresa Front collapsed.

How did Britain respond to Hitler's unilateral actions to revise the Treaty of Versailles?

Appeasement: A policy of acceding to the demands of a potentially hostile nation in the hope of maintaining peace.

Britain's policy towards Hitler between 1933 and 1939 was reactive. Hitler 'made all the running' in reversing the terms of the Treaty of Versailles and Britain (and France) responded to his actions. Large numbers of British policy-makers considered that many of the Versailles Treaty terms were harsh and little was done to check Hitler until March 1939. Instead they followed a policy of gradual revision of the Versailles Treaty terms. This was known as appeasement. **Appeasement** was abandoned from March 1939, when the Germans occupied the remainder of Czechoslovakia. Britain and France then began a period of international negotiation in an effort to get together a coalition of nations willing to stand against Hitler and stop him.

The British government had some sympathy for Hitler's treaty revision ambitions. They had also approved his anti-communist stance when he first became Chancellor of Germany in 1933, elected by legitimate democratic process. But Britain and France were dismayed in October 1933 when Germany left the League of Nations and withdrew from the Geneva Disarmament Conference. This was done on the basis that, if the Allies had not disarmed (now 14 years after the Peace Conference), Germany was entitled to rearm. Furthermore, Hitler reintroduced conscription in 1934, also in contravention of the Versailles Treaty terms.

In order to get Hitler back into the Disarmament Conference, Britain wanted to negotiate with him, being willing to accept a limited German navy, airforce and military, on the basis that it was better to agree limited German rearmament than continue to argue about who was to blame for the failure of the Disarmament Conference. Britain had suggested to Hitler that a German military would be accepted if he returned to the League of Nations and agreed levels of air rearmament. The 1935 Anglo-German Naval Treaty was excused on the grounds that Hitler was going to rebuild the German navy anyway, and it would be better to agree some limitation on its size than to allow it to develop unchecked.

Early in 1934, the British government had decided that Germany was a potential enemy. In 1934 Hitler had attempted a coup to take power in Vienna, but it failed after Mussolini moved troops to the Italian borders with Austria, thereby 'dissuading' him. At that time Mussolini, one of the guarantors with Britain of the Locarno Treaty, was still posing as a peace-maker. Because Britain had run down its defence capacity, standing up to a rearming Germany seemed too risky an option. Hitler's actions and his hatred of communism persuaded the Soviet Union in 1934 to join the League of Nations, in the belief that collective security would provide protection.

In 1935, at Stresa, the Prime Ministers of Britain, Italy and France, (MacDonald, Mussolini and Flandin respectively) met to discuss a common front against German unilateral revision of the Treaty of

Versailles: the Stresa Front. Meanwhile Britain connived to allow Germany to rearm.

Britain and France were appalled in 1936 when Hitler reoccupied the Rhineland. This was in violation not only of the Treaty of Versailles but also of the Locarno Treaty. But Britain did not have troops available to tackle Hitler, because they were in India and Palestine. German military capabilities were overestimated, but even so the French were unwilling to invade the Rhineland alone, in the teeth of German opposition. Therefore, it was decided to accept the remilitarisation as a *fait accompli* and try (unsuccessfully) to negotiate with Hitler.

A German **Anschluss** with Austria in April 1938 was also seen as a legitimate revision of Versailles Treaty terms, to deal with a German grievance. After all, in terms of Wilson's Fourteen Points, Hitler was only seeking a right of **self-determination** for Germans. A similar case was put forward for the Sudeten Germans in Czechoslovakia to join Germany in September 1938.

Why did Britain rearm in the 1930s?

Britain's defence capacity had been deliberately run down to save money during the 1920s. (See section 9.2.) In 1933 Hitler left the League of Nations and the Disarmament Conference. He also began to rearm Germany. Having concluded that Hitler was potentially a major enemy, Britain decided it was imperative to rearm. However, there was a lot of lost ground to make up, based on government assumptions about Germany's superior military capability.

● 1932, the Ten Year Rule was abandoned and Baldwin expressed the fear that 'the bomber would always get through'. But in 1933, defence spending was only 3 per cent of gross national product (GNP), about £100 million. By 1939 defence spending had grown to £700 million, 18 per cent of GNP, but weapons manufacture lagged behind Germany's.

● 1936, a Joint Services Planning Committee expected that Germany's first attacks would be 'knock-out blows' and Britain should plan accordingly.

● February 1937, the Chiefs of Staff reported '… our naval, military and airforces … are still far from sufficient to meet our defensive commitments, which now extend from Western Europe through the Mediterranean to the Far East'.

● In September 1938 a record of a meeting by Defence adviser Hastings Ismay suggested that Britain's air defences were insufficient. 'If war with Germany has to come, it would be better to fight her in, say, six to twelve months time …'

● Also, the new Radar system would not be complete before 1939.

What other steps did Britain take to prepare for a possible war?

● 1935 the government took on the organisation of civil defence.

● 1936 an Air Raid Precautions Department was set up.

● 1937 Sir Thomas Inskip, the Minister for the Co-ordination of Defence, produced a major review of defence. A major rearmament programme commenced because its pessimistic view of Britain's defence capacity reinforced calls from the Chiefs of Staff for increased production of fighter aircraft and naval capability. The Munich

Anschluss: Union of Germany and Austria. In February 1938 Hitler had submitted an ultimatum to the Austrian Chancellor, demanding his resignation after he had attempted to forestall Anschluss by holding a plebiscite. His replacement, Seyss-Inquart, a Nazi, invited the German Army to occupy Austria, and proclaimed Union with Germany on 13 March 1938. A month later, on 10 April, a Nazi-controlled plebiscite voted by 99.75 per cent for Anschluss.

Self-determination: The political right of a group of people to determine the future of their own nation, through a referendum.

Agreement of September 1938 was partly inspired by Neville Chamberlain's concern for the effect on London of a bombing campaign because he thought Britain's defences insufficient to stop German bombers.

- 1937 a call for air raid wardens attracted over a million volunteers.

- 1938 an Air Raid Precautions Bill charged local authorities with drawing up detailed contingency plans, including mass evacuations from major industrial and urban centres. Fifty million gas masks were distributed.

- 1939, June, 120,000 volunteers joined the Auxiliary Fire Service.

Chamberlain and the Munich Agreement, 1938

The German annexation of the Sudetenland in Czechoslovakia was argued as another right of self-determination by Hitler, even though Czech territory was also of vital economic and strategic importance to Hitler. Czech security rested with the major European powers who met at a conference in Munich in September 1938 to solve the Sudeten Crisis. Chamberlain was eager to seek a rapprochement with Germany in order to avoid another war in Europe and – at odds with the British cabinet – agreed to Hitler's demands. Hitler pushed for further territorial gains in the hope of war, eventually backing down to the European powers and accepting the territory originally demanded.

Chamberlain was of the opinion that the resultant Munich Agreement of September 30th 1938 was a diplomatic success. However, Hitler's inevitable violation of the terms, soon after, were to give weight to the view that totalitarian states should never be appeased. The optimism of Chamberlain's "Peace in our time" speech upon his return, received a jubilant reaction in Britain, but Winston Churchill denounced the Agreement in the House of Commons. (For more on the Munich Agreement, see section 11.2.)

'Peace in our time'? Chamberlain on his return from the Munich Conference.

Why was the event in the photograph significant in Chamberlain's subsequent fall from power in May 1940?

9.6 Why did Britain go to war in 1939?

Britain went to war with Germany because Germany invaded Poland. In March 1939 Britain and France had given a guarantee that, if Poland was attacked and it fought back, Britain and France would go to war with the aggressor. However, despite having given the guarantee, both Britain and France began intensive diplomatic negotiations on ways to avoid fulfilling the obligation.

Why did Britain and France decide it was necessary to try to stop Hitler's aggression and territorial expansionism?

When Hitler occupied the Czech regions of Bohemia and Moravia in March 1939 it was apparent to the British government that:

- The policy of appeasement had failed, because Hitler would not be satisfied with revision of the Treaty of Versailles, as demonstrated by his occupation of Bohemia and Moravia, the existence of Czechoslovakia not being a term of the Treaty of Versailles;

- Hitler was therefore likely to endanger the security of other states in the path of his territorial expansionism to find 'living space' (Lebensraum), his hostility to Slavs, for example Poland, and desire to exterminate Bolshevism.

- Hitler could not be trusted because he had broken his word about Czechoslovakia. Neville Chamberlain, however, had thought he was a man 'with whom he could do business'.

- Britain must stand up to Hitler or permit him to conquer Europe unchallenged. It was feared that, once master of Europe, he would eventually pose a threat to Britain.

Why did Britain and France feel it necessary to offer a guarantee of security to Poland in March 1939?

Britain and France offered Poland a guarantee on 6 April 1939 because Poland was under threat from Hitler, who demanded the return to Germany of Danzig and a German road across the Polish corridor. Poland was chosen by Britain and France as the 'sticking point' beyond which Hitler would not be appeased. They gambled that the Poles would give in to Hitler's demands.

What was the international situation between March and September 1939?

- The Poles resisted the urgings of Britain and France to behave as the Czechs had done and refused Hitler's March 1939 demands. They also refused Hitler's invitation to join the Anti-Comintern Pact.

- After March 1939 Britain seemed to be standing alone. The Dominions did not wish to support Britain. France was weak and Eastern Europe was unstable.

- The United States was isolationist and neutral, although there was an equally appalled Anglo-American stance in the face of Japanese aggression in China from 1937.

- The British guarantee strengthened Polish resolve to hold out against Hitler over Danzig. The Poles did not want to suffer the fate of the Czechs, who had relied for security on the Western powers. They felt that, when it had come to the point, the Western Allies had not defended Czechoslovakia.

● Hitler was enraged and denounced the Anglo-German Naval Treaty of 1935 (see section 9.5) and his 1939 Non-Aggression Pact with Poland.

● A defence evaluation prepared by Defence adviser Hastings Ismay for the government suggested that Britain did not feel ready in September 1938 to oppose Hitler's demands.

Why did Britain and France fail to reach an alliance against Hitler with the Soviet Union in the summer of 1939?

Britain, France and the Soviet Union seemed to be obvious allies against Hitler, being the three strongest powers willing to stand up to him. Why did they fail to agree?

● Britain and France ignored Stalin's March 1939 proposal of a six-power conference to discuss collective action to prevent further German aggression. This was because they did not trust the Soviet Union. Britain and France were more concerned to gain Soviet help to defend Poland and Romania, than to defend the Soviet Union.

● Britain and France gave a lukewarm response to Stalin's proposal of a tripartite pact, involving an explicit military convention.

● An invitation to British Foreign Secretary Halifax to go to Moscow for negotiations was declined. Instead, negotiations commenced in June 1939 between Soviet Foreign Minister Molotov and the British Ambassador in Moscow. Molotov was empowered to make an alliance (provided Stalin agreed). The Ambassador was not so empowered to make an alliance for Britain. This could be seen as insulting to the Soviet Union.

● Britain and France dragged their feet on joint Soviet, British and French military talks. The British and French sent a low-level delegation by the slow train whereas Soviet Defence Minister Voroshilov had plans for military co-operation and was empowered to conclude an agreement.

● The Russians therefore did not believe that the British and French were serious about negotiations.

● The Russians did not trust the British, believing that they were secretly negotiating with Hitler to conclude an anti-Soviet pact with them. This view was reinforced by British and French failure to negotiate agreements with Poland and Romania for Soviet troops to cross their territory en route to Germany. German approaches to the Russians from May 1939 began to seem an attractive alternative. German Foreign Minister Ribbentrop met Molotov in Moscow on 23 August and the Nazi-Soviet Pact was negotiated and signed that day.

● On 1 September Hitler invaded Poland and on the morning of 3 September Britain and France issued an ultimatum to Hitler to depart Poland. He did not reply and on the same day Britain and France declared war on Germany.

1. Why did Britain abandon appeasement in 1939?

2. To what extent was the British government responsible for the signing of the Nazi-Soviet Pact of August 1939?

Further Reading

Texts designed specifically for AS and A2 students

Britain: Foreign and Imperial Policy 1918–1939 by Alan Farmer (Hodder & Stoughton, 1992)

British Foreign Policy in the Twentieth Century by C.J. Bartlett (British History in Perspective Series, Macmillan, 1989)

Europe 1870–1991 by Terry Morris and Derrick Murphy (Collins Educational, 2000)

The Origins of the Second World War by Richard Overy (Longman Seminar Studies, 1987)

The Origins of the Second World War by Ruth Hening (Routledge Lancaster Pamphlets, 1985)

Versailles and After by Ruth Hening (Routledge Lancaster Pamphlets, 1984)

For more advanced reading

Britain in the 20th Century, Parts One and Two by Lawrence Butler and Harriet Jones (Heinemann, 1994)

Chamberlain and Appeasement by R.A.C. Parker (Macmillan, 1993)

The Evolution of the Modern Commonwealth by Denis Judd and Peter Slinn (Macmillan, 1982)

Origins of the Second World War by Philip Bell (Longman, 1997)

10 Britain and the Second World War, 1939–1945

Key Issues

- Why was Britain victorious in the Second World War?

- How and why did Britain's position as a global empire change because of the Second World War?

- How far did the Second World War bring political, social and economic change?

10.1 What were Britain's main war aims, and how did the conduct of the military campaigns affect the international settlements at the end of the Second World War?

10.2 How did Commonwealth members respond to Britain's call to arms, and what effect did the Second World War have on Britain's relationship with the Commonwealth?

10.3 How did British politics adapt to the conditions of a world war?

10.4 Historical Interpretation: Why did the Conservative Party lose the 1945 general election?

Framework of Events

1939	September: Britain declares war on Germany
1940	May: Winston Churchill replaces Neville Chamberlain as Prime Minster
	June: evacuation of British troops from Dunkirk
	July to September: Battle of Britain
	July: beginning of Blitz
1941	March: Lend-Lease Act
	Atlantic Charter
	June: Soviet Union allies with Britain after German invasion
	Clothes rationing introduced
	December: United States allies with Britain and Soviet Union after Japanese attack on US fleet in Pearl Harbour
1942	Fall of Malaya and Singapore base to Japanese
	Beveridge Report on Social Insurance and Allied Services
1943	January: meeting of Roosevelt and Churchill at Casablanca
	Ministry of Town and Country Planning created
	November: meeting of Churchill, Roosevelt and Stalin at Tehran
1944	June: Allied invasion of Normandy, D-Day
	White Papers produced on a National Health Service, Employment Policy and Social Insurance
	Butler Education Act passed
	Moscow, 'Spheres on Influence' agreement between Churchill and Stalin
1945	February: meeting of Churchill, Roosevelt and Stalin at Yalta
	Family Allowances Act passed
	May: Victory in Europe (VE) day
	July: meeting of Churchill, Roosevelt and Stalin at Potsdam
	Attlee replaces Churchill as Prime Minister during Potsdam meeting
	August: atom bombs dropped on Hiroshima and Nagasaki
	Japan surrenders: Victory in Japan (VJ) day
	America ends Lend-Lease agreement

Overview

THE Second World War was Britain's finest hour. Britain entered the war when Germany invaded Poland in September 1939 and, as in the First World War, the decision to declare war on Germany was an attempt to preserve the European balance of power. Five years later, however, with the discovery of the Holocaust, it became clear that Britain had fought a 'moral' war. The war developed into a struggle for civilisation, with Britain representing liberal democracy and Germany represented totalitarian dictatorship. For a brief period, June 1940 to June 1941, Britain fought Germany and Italy alone. But the war soon developed into a global conflict, and from 1941 Britain was allied with the USSR and the USA in a conflict which saw British troops fight in South East Asia, North Africa, Italy and Western Europe.

In 1939 Britain was a world empire, containing one third of the world's population and covering one quarter of the world's land surface. The Second World War put great strains on the Empire, and by 1941 Britain was virtually bankrupt. In that year, however, before it had entered the conflict, the USA introduced the **Lend-Lease** programme, which provided military aid to Britain throughout the war. Without US military aid, Britain could not have continued the war beyond 1941.

The war also had a profound effect on Britain's control of India. Before 1939 Ghandi had led a campaign to gain Indian self-government within the British Empire, and during the war, in 1942, he organised the 'Quit India' campaign. By 1945 it was clear that British control over India was under severe threat, and by 1947 Britain had 'quit' its Indian Empire. This began a process of decolonisation which saw Britain retreat from the majority of its imperial possessions over the next fifteen years.

The war also had a profound effect on the Commonwealth. In 1939 all the self-governing dominions, except Eire, joined Britain in the war. However, the war caused tension between Britain and the dominions. This reached its height in early 1941 after the spectacular defeat of the British and Commonwealth armies in Malaya and Singapore at the hands of the Japanese. After the defeat, both Australia and New Zealand feared Japanese invasion. Yet Britain insisted that **ANZAC** forces still participate in the defence of Egypt, in North Africa, so from 1942 Australia and New Zealand began to look to the USA as their main protector. After the war, this led to the **ANZUS Treaty** of 1951.

The war saw British military power reach its height. With US aid, British forces fought in Europe, North Africa and Asia. In addition, Britain launched a protracted bombing campaign on Germany from 1942 to 1945. Britain's longest battle, however, was the 'Battle of the Atlantic'. From 1939 to 1945 the Royal Navy fought off relentless German attempts to starve Britain into submission by attacking British shipping in the North Atlantic. By 1945, although its power was on the wane, Britain was still seen as one of the 'Big Three' at the peace conferences of Yalta and Potsdam. After 1945, however, world power had passed to the USA and the USSR. In this new **bipolar** world of the Cold War, Britain became a junior ally of the USA.

The impact of war had a profound effect on the British economy and society.

From before the outbreak of the war the government had begun preparing for 'total war'. In April 1939, for the first time in British history, compulsory military

Lend-Lease: An American policy introduced during the Second World War where military aid was given to Britain, and other allied countries, with the aim of acquiring payment for such aid after the war.

ANZAC: The forces of Australia and New Zealand.

ANZUS Treaty: Australia, New Zealand and US treaty whereby the USA replaced Britain as the main military protector of Australia and New Zealand.

Bipolar: The split between the two superpowers the United States (capitalist) and the Soviet Union (communist). Ideologically opposed, they came to dominate Western and Eastern power blocs in world politics.

service was introduced. Also, detailed plans were drawn up to evacuate children from towns and cities as a precaution against mass aerial bombing.

From September 1939, Britain introduced rationing and placed the economy on a 'war footing'. Britain's commitment to all-out war reached a new height in 1942, when unmarried women were conscripted into the forces, the Land Army and factories. From 1940 to 1945 Britain was subjected to bombing by the Germans, with the Blitz of 1940–41 causing widespread damage to London and other major cities. From June 1944 Britain became the first country to be attacked by rockets, when the Germans launched V1 and, a few months later, V2 raids. By the end of the war virtually everyone and everywhere in Britain had been directly affected by the experience of war.

Politically, Britain was changed. In 1939 the National Government under Neville Chamberlain had declared war. In May 1940 Chamberlain resigned to be replaced by Winston Churchill. Churchill became Britain's greatest war leader, holding the country together in the dark days of 1940—41 when Britain stood alone. US journalist Ed Murrow said that Churchill even 'used the English language as a weapon' when describing Churchill's wartime speeches of that period.

From 1940 to 1945 the Labour Party joined the National Government, and Attlee, the Labour leader, became Deputy Prime Minister. Ernest Bevin, a leading Labour politician, became Minister of Labour. Attlee and Bevin were major individuals in organising the Home Front. In 1942, the Liberal, William Beveridge, produced a report suggesting the creation of a 'Welfare State' after the war. Churchill rejected the idea, but Labour supported it, and in July 1945 Labour was rewarded with a landslide victory against Churchill. Although Churchill was seen as 'the man who won the war', Labour's election victory was in recognition of its extensive plans to reshape post-war Britain.

In 1945 Britain celebrated victory over Germany in Europe on VE Day (May 8th) and victory over Japan on VJ Day (August 15th). Yet victory had come at a cost. Britain was almost completely dependent on US aid by the end of the war. For most of the post-war period Britain went into relative decline, losing out to the USA and USSR in military terms, and to the USA, Japan and Germany economically by the late 1950s. The Second World War was the major turning-point in the history of Britain in the twentieth century.

1. Explain the part played by Britain in the Second World War.

2. Why do you think the Second World War could be regarded as the major turning-point in the history of Britain in the twentieth century? Give reasons for your answer.

1. What do you regard as the most important contribution Britain made to winning the Second World War? Give a reason for your answer.

2. Place the factors mentioned in the mind map in order of importance to explain why Britain was successful in the Second World War.

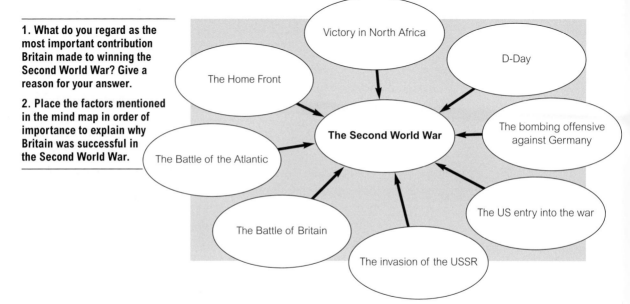

10.1 What were Britain's main war aims, and how did the conduct of the military campaigns affect the international settlements at the end of the Second World War?

What were Britain's main war aims?

The immediate cause of Britain declaring war on Germany on 3 September 1939 was Hitler's invasion of Poland on 1 September. But Britain and France had no strategy to save Poland by fighting for that country, once Hitler had invaded. They feared that they would also have to fight the Soviet Union, under the terms of the Nazi-Soviet Pact of August 1939.

At the outbreak of war, Britain and France had failed in their aim of stopping Hitler attacking Poland. They still thought it necessary to oppose him in order to prevent him from gaining mastery of Europe. Hitler made peace offers to Britain from the end of September 1939. The British government rejected them all. Hitler asked, 'Why do they fight? They have no definite objective … I want England to retain her empire and its command of the seas unimpaired. But I must have the continent. A new age is dawning in Europe.' But Hitler had not grasped the point. It was to prevent his gaining mastery of Europe and the institution of a 'new age' that Britain fought on. Hitler had broken his word so many times that his statements could not be trusted. By standing up to him, Britain aimed also to keep its Empire intact, its naval superiority (over all but for the United States navy) and preserve its status as a global power. Even so, the government understood very well from the experience of the First World War that going to war risked upsetting the status quo and would be very expensive.

- By December 1941 Roosevelt and Churchill had agreed that the defeat of Germany took precedence over defeating Japan in the Pacific war.

- At Casablanca in January 1943, Churchill and Roosevelt agreed to press for unconditional surrender of Germany and Japan. This policy was extended in May 1943 to cover the expected Italian surrender.

- As the war wore on, and Hitler's treatment of Jews, gypsies and disabled people became public knowledge, a moral dimension was added to Britain's war aims.

How was Britain involved in the early stages of the war?

The period between the start of the Second World War and the **Fall of France** is known as the 'phoney war' because very little happened to Britain. Britain and France set up a Supreme War Council, for policy co-ordination, and each agreed not to conclude a separate peace with Germany. Britain assumed the war would last three years and instituted a naval blockade in the belief that this would cause Germany to surrender. The naval blockade was completely undermined by Hitler's conquest of Eastern Europe, from which he obtained the mineral resources and agricultural produce Germany needed.

- The 'phoney war' ended in May 1940 when Hitler invaded Holland, Belgium, Luxembourg and then France. The British expeditionary force was sent to fight alongside the French, but they were encircled by the Germans and had to make a run for the coast. Although much valuable military equipment was lost, 200,000 British and 140,000 French troops escaped to the coast, at Dunkirk. Between 26 May and 6 June 1940 they were rescued by an 'armada' of mainly privately-owned

US President Franklin Delano Roosevelt (1882–1945)
Democrat President of the United States from 1932 to 1945. Roosevelt is known for his 'New Deal' programme, which drew the United States out of the Depression. He unofficially helped Britain to fight the war until December 1941 because he recognised that Hitler would eventually turn on the United States if Britain were to be defeated.

Fall of France: The surrender of France to Germany, which resulted in German domination of French strategy and diplomacy during the Second World War.

Main events and military theatres of war

1939

1 September Start of 'phoney war'. Although France and Britain had declared war on Germany, no fighting began between them.

1–27 September German conquest of Poland.

14 September Soviet occupation of Poland.

November Soviet invasion of Finland.

1940

March End of Soviet/Finnish war.

April German occupation of Norway and Denmark; a British expeditionary force sent to help failed.

May German attack on Belgium, Holland and Luxembourg. Germany attacked France, and the British Expeditionary Force in France was nearly cut off and lost. 26 May-4 June a fleet of small ships from Britain evacuated British troops cut off in France through the port of Dunkirk.

June Mussolini declared war on France and Britain. France capitulated and the northern half and western coast was occupied by Germany. The southern half was governed from Vichy (in central France) by supporters of Germany under Marshal Pétain.

July German bombing raids on Britain commenced (the Blitz).

August Battle of Britain commenced.

November Churchill and Roosevelt agreed Lend-lease scheme.

1941

March Germany invaded the Balkans to assist Italy's unsuccessful attempts at conquest.

May The Blitz ended.

June Germany invaded the Soviet Union (Operation Barbarossa).

August Churchill-Roosevelt meeting at Placentia Bay (Canada) agreeing Atlantic Charter.

December On the 7th Japan attacked the United States navy at Pearl Harbour in the Hawaiian Islands, after which Japan declared war on the United States. Germany and Italy also declared war on the United States. On the 8th Britain declared war on Japan.

1942

February The Japanese occupied Malaya, Singapore and Thailand

Spring The Japanese went on to occupy Indonesia, the Philippines, parts of Burma and New Guinea and many Pacific Islands.

June In the Far East the United States fleet destroyed the Japanese fleet at the Battle of Midway and then began to re-take all the Pacific Islands the Japanese had occupied. Germany and Italy fought British, Commonwealth and eventually United States forces for control of North Africa and the Mediterranean.

November Great Allied victory at El Alamein.

1943

January Soviet Union defeated Germany at the Battle of Stalingrad.

June Axis powers (Germany and Italy) defeated in North Africa.

July Soviet Union defeated Germany at Battle of Kursk.

August Britain and United States took Sicily and invaded Southern Italy. Italy capitulated, Mussolini was arrested and imprisoned, Germany took up the fight against United States and British forces.

1944

Germans driven out of Soviet Union.

June Normandy landings opening second front in West.

New German weapon introduced, the V1 flying bomb – an unmanned jet, known as the doodlebug.

Battle of Leyte Gulf, United States reoccupied the Philippines.

September Another new German weapon introduced, the V2, an unmanned rocket.

November Russians delayed relief of Warsaw ghetto. Poland liberated by Soviet Union. Romania and Finland surrendered.

1945

January Burma liberated and Hungary surrendered.

April Russians outside Berlin, Hitler committed suicide on 30th.

May On 7th Germany surrendered and 8th Victory in Europe (VE) day.

June United States recaptured Japanese island of Okinawa.

August United States dropped atom bombs: on Hiroshima on 6th and on Nagasaki on 9th. On 15th Japan surrendered (Victory in Japan – VJ day). Second World War officially ended.

little ships which the Royal Navy had organised to sail from Britain, with RAF cover.

The Blitz: The word by which the British public referred to the German bombing. It especially relates to the period September 1940 to May 1941.

● In July 1940 Germany launched an intensive bombing campaign from Northern France on the British mainland, known as 'the **Blitz**' (see section 11.8). The Blitz continued until May 1941.

● German Bombers flew with fighter-plane cover. British fighter-planes (Spitfires and Hurricanes) needed to destroy both German fighters and bombers to prevent their arrival over targets in Britain to release their bombs. These German attacks were countered by British fighters in aerial combat, celebrated as 'The Battle of Britain', of which Winston Churchill said 'Never in the field of human conflict has so much been owed by so many to so few'. He also said, 'The Navy can lose us the war, but the Air Force can win it'. By maintaining control of the skies over Britain, the Royal Air Force frustrated the launch of Hitler's 'Operation Sealion' to invade Britain from Northern France, for which

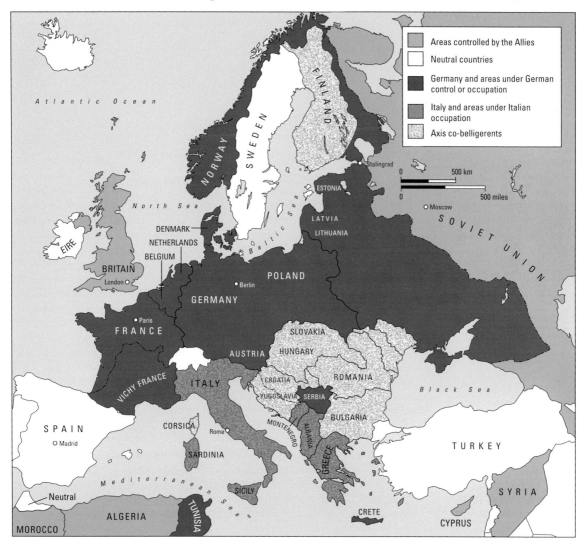

Europe in 1942, the period of Hitler's greatest expansion.

Why was Germany able to acquire so much territory in Europe by 1942?

German mastery of the skies would have been a key factor. In June 1941 Hitler turned his attention from Britain to the invasion of the Soviet Union.

Why did Britain's involvement in the war spread from Europe to North Africa?

Axis: The name given to the alliance between Germany, Italy and Japan during the Second World War.

It was Mussolini's entry into the war on 10 June 1940 which extended its geographical location. Once French defences had been put out of action, Mussolini thought it safe to enter the war on the **Axis** side. He was jealous of Hitler's conquests in Northern Europe and wanted an Empire running from the Red Sea to the Atlantic including the Mediterranean islands of Malta, Corsica, Sardinia, Crete and Cyprus. Because Britain had key interests to defend in the Eastern Mediterranean, for example, Egypt and the Suez Canal, Cyprus and Libya, the war moved to North Africa. In September 1940 the Italians invaded Egypt in an attempt to take the strategically important Suez Canal, which was a vital Allied communications and supply route. The battle for North Africa was fought between September 1940 and January 1943, principally between the Italian Army and the German Afrika Korps, commanded by General Rommel, on the one hand, and the British Eighth Army, which included Commonwealth forces, mostly Australians and New Zealanders, commanded by a succession of generals, ending with General Montgomery. The battle ended when the Germans and Italians were caught in a pincer movement between the British Eighth Army and an Anglo-American force invading Algeria (Operation Torch) under General Eisenhower. Allied forces then effectively controlled the south coast of the Mediterranean.

Why did Britain's forces move onto the European mainland?

Strategically, Britain was unwilling to open up a second front in Europe, and refused to invade France in 1942, because the British did not believe that the Allied forces were ready. Britain, with experience of fighting the Germans, believed that they needed to be worn down first before they could be defeated, otherwise deaths and casualties would be very high. The Americans thought there was no military problem that sufficient resources and men could not overcome. The British thought the Americans too rash and the Americans thought the British too cautious. This difference caused diplomatic and strategic problems between the Allies throughout the war.

The Americans had promised Stalin a second front in Europe to relieve German pressure on the Soviet Union. Churchill argued, successfully, for a Mediterranean strategy. The United States would have preferred an invasion of France. The Western Allies would not be ready to invade Northern France for another year (Operation Overlord).

The Allied forces, therefore, moved on to Italy (which Churchill called 'the soft under-belly of Europe'), taking Sicily in July 1943 and invading the Italian mainland in September 1943. Mussolini was overthrown but escaped to Northern Italy. His successor, Marshall Badoglio, surrendered, but the Germans took over the defence of Italy against the Allied forces from a line just north of Naples. Thereafter the Allied forces were bogged down, taking one year to fight their way through Italy and north of the Alps.

Josef Stalin (1879–1953). Soviet Leader from 1928. He stayed in power by operating a reign of terror. His cruelty in establishing the collectivisation programme (1931–33) and the purges (1935–38) was only exceeded by his inhumane treatment of his forces and the Soviet people during the war. However, he did drive the Red Army and the Russian people to achieve a tremendous victory over Hitler's Germany.

Why did Britain become involved in a war in the Far East?

The war in the Far Eastern theatre was fought for control of valuable resources, which the Japanese needed and the United States and Britain sought to deny them. Britain was involved because its extensive commercial

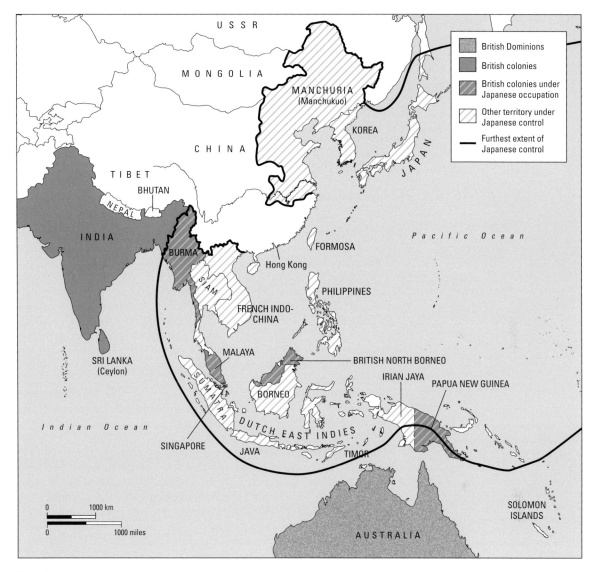

Why did Britain perform so badly in the war in the Far East until 1943?

The Far East and the Western Pacific showing the greatest extent of Japanese control

interests in China had brought it into conflict with the Japanese, who were intent on bringing China under Japanese control. Japan was seen as an aggressor nation. Germany and Italy were Japan's allies, through the 1937 Anti-Comintern Pact and the 1940 Tripartite Axis, and they were at war with Britain. Though not actually at war until 8 December 1941, Britain and Japan were nevertheless hostile to each other.

The European war was a catalyst to the outbreak of war in the Far East. German occupation of France and the Netherlands left their South-east Asian colonial territories, Indo-China and Indonesia, vulnerable to Japanese control. In 1941 the French Vichy government and the Japanese set up a joint protectorate over the whole of Indo-China, which permitted immediate Japanese occupation. In retaliation, the United States and Britain cancelled trade agreements, and the Americans stopped selling oil, copper and scrap metal to the Japanese. As the United States tightened its trade embargo, so Japan intensified its plans to seize South-east Asia to gain access to Indonesian oil and Malayan metals. Moreover, the Japanese had always maintained that they would not fight both the Royal Navy and the United States Navy simultaneously. With the fall of France, Britain had to withdraw the bulk of its ships in the Pacific region to the Mediterranean, leaving the way clear for the Japanese to take on the United States Navy. Negotiations between Japan and the United States over Japanese withdrawal from occupied territories failed. The Japanese attacked the United States fleet in Pearl Harbour, Hawaii on 7 December 1941. Japan, Germany and Italy then declared war on the United States. Britain declared war on Japan on 8 December 1941. With the United States officially in the war, Britain was no longer fighting alone.

What was the extent of Britain's involvement in the Pacific war?

Involvement in the Far Eastern theatre of war was a nightmare situation for Britain, whose Chiefs of Staff throughout the 1930s had warned that Britain would be unable to fight simultaneous wars in Europe, the Mediterranean and the Far East. Japanese forces invaded the Malayan peninsular on 7 December 1941. Non-implementation of the British defence plans permitted the Japanese to gain air superiority and by 31 January 1941 Malaya had fallen. Britain's main defences were concentrated on the Singapore naval base, which commanded strategically key sea routes through the region. Insufficiently funded to achieve its defensive purpose, Singapore fell to the Japanese on 15 February 1942. Nearly 100,000 British troops and reinforcements from Australia, New Zealand and India were captured.

Churchill's objective was to recover Burma, Malaya, Singapore and Hong Kong, but the United States and Britain had taken the decision that priority would be given to the European war. Japan's territorial expansion throughout the Pacific area was checked by the United States Navy at the Battle of Midway in June 1942. At the Casablanca meeting in January 1943 a counter-offensive was planned. Britain's role was to re-take the Burma Road to facilitate overland delivery of supplies to the Chinese ally, Chiang Kai-shek, whose Nationalist (Kuomintang) regime, based inland at Chungking in South China, was cut off by Japanese occupation of the coastal region.

Churchill was not keen for British forces to be committed to operations in conditions favourable to the Japanese. Moreover, he regarded relief of Chiang Kai-shek and the retaking of Burma as of secondary importance to European military operations. By this stage of the war, however, United States strategic planning dominated the alliance and the Americans were inclined to over-estimate the importance and capabilities of Chiang Kai-shek and his forces. Churchill's objections were over-ruled, and the first Chindit operation was launched into Burma in February 1943. British forces finally entered Rangoon on 3 May 1945 but Churchill's fears about heavy losses in jungle warfare were proved correct: combined British and Commonwealth casualties amounted to 71,244.

How did Churchill try to safeguard British interests during the Second World War?

To safeguard British interests Churchill needed allies, because Britain did not have the resources to fight alone, especially after the Fall of France. In pursuit of alliance diplomacy, Winston Churchill embarked upon a remarkable series of wartime conferences, meeting other Allied leaders to discuss war aims, strategy and the post-war settlements. These conferences involved Churchill flying several times between the United States, Canada, the Soviet Union and North Africa. By paying such close attention to wartime strategy and diplomacy Churchill was better placed to try to guard Britain's interests.

The alliance with the Soviet Union and the United States was put together over six months. Once the Germans had attacked the Soviet Union on 22 June 1941 the British signed an agreement with the Soviets on 12 July 1941. They promised to give one another material support and not to sign an armistice with Germany, except by mutual consent. The formal alliance with the United States began after the Japanese attack on the American fleet at Pearl Harbour on 7 December 1941. Britain declared war on Japan on 8 December. On 11 December Germany and Italy declared war on the United States.

Britain, the Soviet Union and the United States then came together in what Churchill called a 'Grand Alliance'.

The main meetings of the Grand Alliance

☐ **Placentia Bay, Newfoundland (Canada)** 9–14 August 1941 (Churchill and Roosevelt only)

They agreed the terms of the Atlantic Charter. This set out basic principles for the post-war world and the ideals for which Britain was fighting.

- Opposition to territorial enlargement or changes contrary to the expressed wishes of the peoples concerned.

- The right of people to select their own forms of government and the right to live without fear and want.

- Post-war collaboration: the Charter proposed that aggressor states should be disarmed pending the establishment of a security system.

The Soviet Union signed the Charter reluctantly.

☐ **Moscow, Three Power Conference**, September 1941 (Beaverbrook for Britain, Averell Harriman for the United States, and unnamed Soviet representatives)

They discussed the distribution of lend-lease military supplies to the Soviet Union from October 1941 to June 1942. Ideologically hostile to Britain and the United States, Stalin thought the offer insufficient for his needs, but took the goods anyway. As the Soviet Union was almost surrounded by Axis forces, the convoys of goods were shipped by Britain and the United States by the North Cape (Arctic) route at considerable danger to themselves, or through Iran (then called Persia).

☐ **Washington Conference**, December 1941 (Churchill, Roosevelt and their military advisers)

They hammered out military strategy and co-ordination of their war efforts, including bombing, blockade and subversion. A Combined Chiefs of Staff Committee was set up to operate from Washington. They also discussed:

- military assistance to US South-west Pacific Commander-in Chief, General MacArthur, fighting against the Japanese in the Philippines;

- the possible invasion of North Africa and conquest of the entire coastline;

- further lend-lease for the Soviet Union;

- US War Production Board manufacturing targets.

☐ **Casablanca**, January 1943 (Churchill and Roosevelt)

Stalin refused the invitation. Churchill met Roosevelt and they agreed the policy of unconditional surrender. They also decided to launch a Combined Bomber Offensive against Germany.

General de Gaulle was persuaded to work with General Giraud in opposing the French Vichy regime, leading to the formation of the French National Committee for Liberation. The Americans were pressing for a second front in France. Britain urged a Mediterranean strategy to weaken Italy believing this would draw German forces from Northern France and the Soviet Union. The Americans reluctantly agreed.

They also discussed strategy for the Pacific War. The Americans agreed to help the British attack the Japanese occupying Rangoon, in Burma, in an attempt to free up the Burma Road to assist Chiang Kai-shek. This proved impossible for another two years.

☐ **Quebec**, August 1943 (Churchill, Roosevelt and their American and British diplomatic staff)

This meeting outlined the plans for the Normandy landings, planned for 1944.

They agreed to set up South-east Asia Command, with Lord Louis Mountbatten as Supreme Commander. Brigadier Orde Wingate outlined his plans for guerrilla warfare behind Japanese lines in Burma. His men were known as Wingate's Chindits.

Churchill and Roosevelt signed the secret Quebec Agreement regulating Anglo-American co-operation in nuclear research and development (R&D). They agreed that mutual consent was required for use of the atomic bomb and for passing on details of its manufacture. (The existence of this agreement was unknown to the United States Congress, which enabled them to pass the McMahon Act of 1946 prohibiting further Anglo-United States nuclear R&D collaboration.)

☐ **Washington**, May 1943 (Churchill, Roosevelt and their military and diplomatic advisers)

In this discussion of future strategy they decided to invade France in May 1944, although Churchill had wanted to delay the invasion to maintain pressure on the Mediterranean. They also agreed that unconditional surrender should be pursued with Italy.

☐ **Tehran**, 28 November to 1 December 1943 (Churchill, Roosevelt and Stalin and their military advisers)

This was the first summit meeting of the 'Big Three', Churchill, Roosevelt and Stalin. They agreed future strategy for the conduct of the war and the political shape of post-war Europe. The meeting highlighted the growing domination of the United States and gradual eclipse of Britain as chief power-monger of the Alliance. Roosevelt made it plain to Churchill that he regarded Stalin as the key ally of the United States. It also became clear that the Soviet Union would dominate Eastern and Central Europe after the war, and that Roosevelt saw no need to adopt military strategies that might prevent it because he seemed not to share Churchill's mistrust of Stalin's intentions. In *The Turning Point* (1985), Keith Sainsbury suggests that Tehran was 'the turning point' in international relations, which foreshadowed the bipolar nature of the post-war world. The Big Three discussed:

● the opening of the second front in Europe (the Normandy landings, which had been scheduled for May 1943 but eventually took place on 6 June 1944);

- the progress of the Soviet offensive against Germany on the Eastern front;

- the possible entry of the Soviet Union into the Far Eastern war against Japan;

- the need to establish a post-war international peacekeeping organisation;

- the possibility of bringing Turkey into the war;

- the future political orientation of Poland and Finland, the post-war division of Germany and support for Yugoslavian partisans and their leader General Tito.

☐ **Quebec**, September 1944 (Churchill and Roosevelt)

- They drew up plans for the post-war division of Germany into occupation zones, and the Allied Control Commissions in Germany and Austria.

- They discussed the Morgenthau plan for the post-war de-industrialisation of Germany.

- Churchill offered Royal Naval forces to assist the United States Navy in the Pacific war.

☐ **Moscow**, October 1944 (Churchill and Stalin and their diplomatic and military advisers)

This was the conference at which the Percentages Agreement – the so-called 'naughty document' – was agreed, to settle the degree of influence the Western or Eastern blocs would have in the Balkans.

In subsequent negotiations between Sir Anthony Eden and Soviet Foreign Minister Molotov, the percentages for both Hungary and Bulgaria were amended to 80–20 per cent in favour of the Soviet Union.

☐ **Yalta**, 4 to 11 February 1945 (Churchill, Roosevelt and Stalin)

Four main issues were under discussion:

- Allied strategy to complete the defeat of Germany and the terms and ground-rules for the occupation and denazification of Germany;

- Defeat of Japan. Secret agreements between the United States and the Soviet Union covered the status quo in Mongolia, and extension of Soviet interests to cover the Kurile Islands and South Sakhalin, in return for Stalin's commitment to enter the war against Japan. Churchill was excluded from this agreement.

- The '**Declaration on Liberated Europe**' was issued to cover the future settlement in Eastern Europe concerning territory 'liberated' and/or 'occupied' by the Soviet Red Army. Agreements were reached on the constitution of a Polish Government of National Unity (a combination of the Lublin Committee of Stalin-controlled communist Poles together with the London-based Polish government-in-exile) and Polish frontiers. Britain felt a sense of obligation to Poland, arising from the failure to stop Hitler's invasion in September 1939. Stalin's failure to keep his Yalta promises on the constitution of the Polish government resulted in the new United States President Harry Truman showing his displeasure on Soviet Foreign Minister Molotov in April 1945.

- Establishment of a peaceful world order based upon the United Nations, in which both the United States and the Soviet Union would

Harry S. Truman (1884–1972)
Became United States President on the death of Roosevelt. He assumed responsibility for the final stages of the Second World War, attended the Potsdam conference, and authorised the dropping of atomic bombs on Japan. Truman soon recognised that Stalin's intentions in Eastern Europe did not accord with the Atlantic Charter. He determined that he would endeavour to stand up to the Soviet Union.

participate, and which should, therefore, be better constituted for its purpose than the League of Nations had been.

There was broad agreement between the Allies on the future of Germany, and approval was given to the plans prepared by the Three Power Commission for occupation zones, different sections in Berlin and for the setting up of the Allied Control Commission. The intention was that Germany and Austria should maintain their national unity. Reparations were to be discussed by Foreign Ministers.

☐ **San Francisco Conference**, 25 April to 26 June 1945

Molotov refused to attend this conference, which was the inaugural conference of the United Nations (United Nations Conference on International Organisation). It was attended by delegates from 50 nations, of which 45 had signed the United Nations Declaration of January 1942. Agreements were signed concerning refugees, regional collective security and the use of the veto in the United Nations Security Council, which was to comprise five permanent members: China, France, Britain, the Soviet Union and the United States, together with six temporary members. A Trusteeship Council was created to administer former Axis territories.

The Potsdam conference

The European war ended on 8 May 1945. Hitler had committed suicide on 30 April 1945 and his successor as head of state, Admiral Doenitz, offered Germany's unconditional surrender on 7 May 1945.

The Potsdam Conference (Berlin), 16 July to 2 August 1945 was the final meeting of the Grand Alliance. It was attended by Churchill, Stalin and Truman. Attlee accompanied Churchill, who left the conference on 26 July after his electoral defeat. Attlee attended all meetings, which facilitated a smooth hand-over of power on Churchill's departure. Issues covered included:

● Allied Control Commission for Germany – Germany was intended by Britain and the United States to be treated as an economic entity, meaning unified control of the German economy, with free exchange of goods and services between zones.

● Reparations – The British zone was principally industrial and could not feed itself. The Soviet zone was agricultural but the Soviets needed industrial reparations and, having stripped the Soviet Zone and wiped out German industry there, demanded more from the British and American sectors. Churchill feared that the Soviet Union might withdraw leaving Britain, after years of domestic rationing, to feed the Russian sector too.

● Poland's government and borders – Britain and the United States accepted the Western Neisse as Poland's border with Germany, (which involved the transfer of German refugees). In return they extracted pledges from the Polish government on free elections, press freedom and the repatriation of Polish forces.

● The Potsdam Declaration on surrender terms for Japan. Terms were agreed for Soviet intervention in the Pacific war.

● The existence of the atomic bomb was revealed to Stalin (who already knew, but Churchill and Truman did not know that he knew).

● Britain sought Austrian independence although the Red Army occupied Austria.

● Britain also wanted an early settlement with Italy, and to retain influence on the future of South Eastern Europe.

The Allies failed to agree at Potsdam:

● A basis for a future European peace treaty;

● An accepted settlement on the future of Poland;

● A settlement on the future of Germany.

But much was sacrificed in order to maintain a semblance of the wartime alliance.

1. Why was Britain victorious in the Second World War?

2. How did the International Conferences at

a) Placentia Bay, Newfoundland

b) Tehran

c) Yalta and

d) Potsdam

plan to deal with the post-war world?

3. Why did Britain's status as a global power change during the Second World War?

Why were two atomic bombs dropped on Japan during the Second World War?

The wartime collaboration of British, American, Canadian and European refugee scientists in nuclear research and development (R&D) was known as the Manhattan Project. They succeeded in producing an atomic bomb, which was successfully tested in the United States at Alamogordo, New Mexico on 16 July 1945 (while the Potsdam Conference was in progress). It is alleged that the allies calculated that Japan would be induced to seek an early surrender, and many allied lives would thus be saved, if an atomic bomb were to be dropped on Japan. Controversy still exists about the reasons for which the bombs were dropped. The city of Hiroshima was selected as the first target and a bomb was dropped on 6 August 1945, killing 78,000 people and injuring 90,000. A second bomb was dropped on the city of Nagasaki on 9 August 1945 and the Japanese surrendered on 14 August 1945.

An allied correspondent stands in the rubble looking to the ruins of a cinema after the bombing of Hiroshima.

Source-based questions: British war aims during the Second World War

SOURCE A

We seek no material advantage for ourselves; we desire nothing from the German people which should offend their self-respect. We are not aiming only at victory, but rather looking beyond it to the laying of a foundation of a better international system which will mean that war is not to be the inevitable lot of every succeeding generation …

The peace which we are determined to secure, however, must be a real and settled peace, not an uneasy truce interrupted by constant alarms and repeated threats.

Either the German government must give convincing proof of the sincerity of their desire for peace by definite acts and by the provision of effective guarantees of their intention to fulfil their undertakings, or we must persevere in our duty to the end.

From a speech by the Prime Minister, Neville Chamberlain to the House of Commons, 12 October 1939 on German peace proposals.

SOURCE B

The President of the United States of America and the Prime Minister, Mr Churchill … deem it right to make known certain common principles in the national policies of their respective countries …

First, their countries seek no aggrandisement, territorial or other.

Second, they desire to see no territorial changes that do not accord with the freely expressed wishes of the peoples concerned.

Third, they respect the right of all peoples to choose the form of government under which they will live; and they wish to see sovereign rights and self-government restored to those who have been forcibly deprived of them.

Fourth, they will endeavour … to further the enjoyment by all States, … of access, on equal terms, to the trade and to the raw material of the world which are needed for their economic prosperity.

From *The Atlantic Charter* 12 August 1941. The Charter was an agreement signed by Churchill for Britain, and Franklin D. Roosevelt, the President of the United States.

SOURCE C

The Premier of the USSR, the Prime Minister of the United Kingdom and the President of the USA have consulted with each other in the common interests of the peoples of their countries and those of liberated Europe. They jointly declare their mutual agreement to concert during the temporary period of instability in liberated Europe.

The establishment of order in Europe and the re-building of national economic life must be achieved by processes which will enable the liberated peoples to destroy the last vestiges of Nazism and to create democratic institutions of their own choice. This is a principle of the Atlantic Charter.

The three governments will consult the other United Nations and provisional authorities in Europe when matters of direct interest to them are under consideration.

When, in the opinion of the three governments, conditions in any European liberated state make such action necessary they will immediately consult together on the measures necessary to discharge their joint responsibilities set forth in this declaration.

By this declaration we reaffirm our faith in the principles of the Atlantic Charter, our pledge in the Declaration by the United Nations, and our determination to build in co-operation with other peace-loving nations world order under law, dedicated to peace, security, freedom and general well-being of all mankind.

From The Declaration on Liberated Europe made at the Yalta Conference in February, 1945 between Britain, the USA and USSR.

1. Study Source B.

How, by its use of language and style, does this source suggest it is an official international declaration?

2. Study Source A and use information contained within this chapter.

How reliable is this source to a historian writing about the British government's attitude towards war with Germany during 1939?

3. Study Sources B and C and use information contained within this chapter.

Of what value are these two sources to a historian writing about British war aims between 1941 and 1945?

4. Study Sources A, B and C and use information contained within this chapter.

To what extent did Britain's war aims change between 1939 and 1945?

10.2 How did Commonwealth members respond to Britain's call to arms, and what effect did the Second World War have on Britain's relationship with the Commonwealth?

How did Commonwealth countries respond to Britain's declaration of war on Germany in September 1939?

Although on the outbreak of war there was massive mobilisation of imperial resources, the response of Commonwealth countries was mixed.

Among the Dominions, Australia and New Zealand offered immediate support. Mindful of Japanese aggression in China, no doubt their decision was influenced by their reliance on the British defence system in the South Pacific and South-east Asia.

The Canadians waited until their House of Commons had had an opportunity to debate the issue, then agreed (unanimously) to enter the war.

Views in South Africa were more mixed. The South African Nationalist Prime Minister, J.B.M. Hertzog wanted to remain neutral. A resolution on neutrality was put to the South African Parliament. In response, the pro-British General Smuts put forward a pro-British and anti-German amendment, which was passed by a majority of thirteen. Failing to obtain a dissolution of parliament, Hertzog resigned. Smuts assumed the premiership and took South Africa into the war. Nevertheless, there was considerable Afrikaner opposition to supporting Britain. The Nationalists, led by Daniel Malan, were pro-Nazi and some of their extremists were interned, as were the communists.

Eire declared itself neutral. It remained neutral throughout the war, denying to the Royal Navy use of its bases. These would have been helpful in combating German U-boats in the Battle of Atlantic (see section 10.1) by reducing the distance to be travelled to reach Atlantic target zones. Thousands of Eire citizens, however, joined the UK forces. Because of Catholic and Republican sympathies in Ulster, the six northern counties did not have conscription.

In total the White Dominions spent £36,000 million on the war between them.

In India Viceroy Lord Linlithgow simply informed the people that Britain was at war with Germany. India was angered by involvement in war without prior consultation, despite the broadening of self-government implemented before the war. Congress leader Nehru and the non-violent protester Gandhi both pointed out that, if India was to fight to defend democracy, India too should have a democracy to defend. Britain did not respond to Indian demands for a statement of Britain's future plans for India. The provincial governments resigned. Section 93 of the India Act was invoked so that Britain could rule by decree, with the Indian Civil Service carrying on the administration. The Indian National Congress began a campaign of non-co-operation with the British, insisting on attainment of immediate self-government. Although anti-Nazi, they resented Britain's high-handed assumption that India would fight for a European cause which was beyond the knowledge and experience of most Indians. In contrast, the Muslim League was willing to support Britain.

In the Middle East the response to Britain's involvement in the war was also mixed. Egyptian nationalists resented the presence of a British garrison under the terms of the 1936 Anglo-Egyptian Treaty, and would have welcomed Axis forces. Nevertheless, the Egyptian government remained nominally neutral and the Suez Canal was safe for Britain's use during the war.

Zionism: The political movement that wanted to create a separate homeland for Jews in Palestine. This new state would be called Israel.

In Palestine also, response to Britain's declaration of war was mixed, with pro and anti-Nazi sympathies splitting along national lines. The Jews hated the Nazis for their anti-Semitic atrocities in Germany, and the Arabs, feeling threatened by militant **Zionism** and ever-increasing Jewish immigration into Palestine, were not completely unsympathetic to German anti-Semitism.

What effect did the Second World War have on Britain's relationship with the Commonwealth?

There was a wave of disaffection among those countries that did not share close ties with Britain.

In the British mandated territory of Iraq an anti-British regime, set up in 1941, sought to deny Britain the use of the Habbanniya Air Force base. Its position at the Eastern end of the Mediterranean gave it strategic importance for the defence of the region and the Suez Canal, which were potentially under threat from Axis presence in the Balkans and North Africa. Britain was also unwilling to relinquish an invaluable source of oil and a route for communication with its ally, the Soviet Union. In 1943 Britain invaded Iraq, and that country subsequently entered the war on the Allied side.

In the Far East and South-East Asia theatre of war (see map on page 197), the British ships *Prince of Wales* and *Repulse* were sunk by the Japanese on 10 December 1941 and Hong Kong was conquered by them on Christmas Day 1941. Singapore, and Burma fell in 1942. The loss of Singapore was both humiliating and devastating, because Britain's defence of the Pacific was based on Singapore. Moreover, by taking Burma, Japan was able to cut off the Burma Road. This was the route along which supplies were delivered to Chiang Kai-shek. The Japanese went on to take possession of British (as well as Dutch, American and French) territories and businesses in the Pacific. These events were enormously damaging to British morale and prestige. In the long term they were damaging to colonial perceptions of Britain's role at the head of the Commonwealth.

Japanese-controlled colonial inhabitants of the Far East and South-east Asia were at first inclined to listen to plans for them to become part of Japan's 'Greater East Asia Co-prosperity Sphere'. But the Japanese did not treat them well and initial enthusiasm for promises of freedom from colonial rule soon dissipated.

Although close to Britain, Australia was very worried by the loss to Japan of Singapore and the remainder of British interests in the Far East. Both Australia and India were vulnerable to Japanese penetration and the Japanese bombed the Australian mainland. Distressed by the capture and imprisonment of large numbers of Australian forces sent to defend Singapore, and losing confidence in Britain's ability to defend Australia, they looked instead to the Americans, encouraged by the British.

Canada also looked to the United States for security. The Ogdensburg Agreement was negotiated with the United States in August 1940. United States President Roosevelt and Canadian Prime Minister Mackenzie King informally agreed to form a Permanent Joint Board for Defence.

Waves of violent protest supporting demands for Indian independence were a source of ongoing concern to Britain. Churchill stood firm that the future of India would not be discussed until the war was over. Embarrassed by American criticisms of Britain's empire policy and aware of the need to keep India loyal to British interests, the government sent the Lord Privy Seal, Sir Stafford Cripps, to India to offer concessions to nationalists. He was authorised to promise self-government after the war, with the equivalent of opt-out clauses for the Muslim provinces, and immediate inclusion of nationalists on the Viceroy's Council. Rejected by Congress as too little and that little not soon enough, a widespread 'Quit India' campaign was organised, calling for the British Raj to be immediately dismantled. In 1942, in the middle of a war, this would have been an impossible step for Britain to take. A wave of protest and demonstrations provoked Britain to ban the Congress Party and detain its leaders. Not to be outdone, Jinnah's Muslim League passed a 'Divide and Quit' resolution. This was to reinforce their 1940 Lahore resolution calling for the creation of a separate state, to be named 'Pakistan', and consisting of principally Muslim provinces: Punjab, Afghania, Kashmir, Sind, Baluchistan, Bengal, Assam and the Muslim regions of the North East. Cripps supported Jinnah's secessionist scheme. So did Churchill, who saw it as a means to upset the Congress Party and reinforce the support of the large number of Muslim soldiers fighting for Britain. Nevertheless, Viceroy Linlithgow and General Wavell, the Commander-in-Chief in India, had reservations about Muslim secession from an independent India. Cripps also reported to Churchill that Hindus in particular were keen not to offend the Japanese, who might win the Pacific war, by active participation in a war effort. In 1943 Viceroy Linlithgow was replaced by Field Marshal Sir Archibald Wavell, who was much more sympathetic to the idea of Indian independence.

One extreme example of Indian anti-British resentment was Chandra Subhas Bose, a former Congress president. He supported the cause of Indian nationalism, which he thought could be served best by allying with Japan and Germany. Bose went to Germany in 1941 and offered his services. Hitler gave Bose propaganda facilities, including 'Free India' radio on which he denounced democracy. He went into exile in Singapore and proclaimed a new Indian government, the Azad Hind (Free India). Bose was also given the opportunity and the means to organise Indian, Tamil and Ghurka prisoners of war into an Indian National Army (INA) and encouraged him to co-operate with the Afghanistani Fakir of Ipi, who was anti-British. However, the INA proved to be an ineffective fighting force and Bose's propaganda equally so. The Japanese soon grew as tired of Bose as had the Germans, and while escaping to Moscow he was killed in a plane crash. Although Bose had nuisance value, he did not gather much support in India, where the most ardent nationalists could not bring themselves to ally with Britain's enemies. Even so, the government of India took the INA seriously and made Bose and his supporters the subject of surveillance, counter-intelligence and counter-propaganda initiatives.

Why did Britain undertake a major reappraisal of colonial policy during the Second World War?

The collapse of British control in Asia undermined the concept of 'trusteeship', the basic doctrine underpinning Britain's colonial administrations. The government recognised that partnership in colonial affairs should replace paternalism and that more than lip-service should be paid to the aspiration of Commonwealth members for self-government.

Debates were initiated by Lord Hailey to determine whether self-government should mean internal autonomy, with Britain controlling foreign policy and defence, or whether it should mean attainment of Dominion status. Hailey also initiated a debate to establish what were the criteria by which readiness for self-government should be determined. He recognised that some colonies were not ready for the responsibility of self-government and needed to be taught the basic principles of honest and impartial government. The idea of federation was promoted to get round this problem. Hailey wrote on imperial and commonwealth affairs. His

Lord Hailey (1872–1969)
Lord Hailey was a retired Indian civil servant. He was a former Governor of the Punjab and the United Provinces.

ideas re-awoke concern for progressive welfare reforms and were increasingly favoured by some sections of the Conservative Party.

Another idea under discussion was decolonisation. This was not meant to represent independence, but rather a change of status within the Empire. The British government felt that most of the smaller colonies would be unable to defend themselves adequately, and would need the security umbrella of the British Empire.

The British government also recognised the need to retain the loyalty of colonial subjects and humanitarian concern to rehabilitate captured peoples after the war. Plans were considered to raise colonial living standards, develop economies and social institutions and provide welfare services after the war. A Colonial Development and Welfare Act was introduced in 1940, setting aside £5,000,000 for the promotion of colonial welfare schemes. A series of colonial reforms were put in hand. Moreover, new constitutions were given to the Gold Coast and Jamaica, where the franchise was extended in preparation for post-war independence. Regional councils were set up in Northern Rhodesia and a number of universities were established in Africa, to train an elite for the administrative responsibilities of self-government.

The need for colonial welfare reforms was underpinned by raised expectations of post-war improvements among the colonial forces that were fighting for Britain. These expectations were reinforced by nationalist unrest in Africa. The Kikuyu Central Association of Kenya was banned for allegedly conspiring with the Italians. In the Northern Rhodesian copper mines there was a violent strike. In Nigeria, Nyasaland and the Cameroons, nationalist political parties were formed in 1944.

The Atlantic Charter (see section 10.1) could be read more than one way. Churchill's priority was given to the re-establishment of British control of enemy-occupied colonies. The Charter was interpreted by Roosevelt as an intention to extend American ideas of democracy and independence to the colonies of the British Empire, but Churchill had applied the terms of the Charter only to ensuring the freedom of Nazi-occupied Europe. The Americans were morally anti-imperialist. In response to sustained American criticism, Britain created a new concept of colonial rule, with the emphasis on partnership rather than domination and presented in constructive and positive terms. Roosevelt advocated that British colonies, especially those in Asia, should be placed under international control to prepare them for independence, inspiring Churchill to retort in November 1942, 'I have not become the King's First Minister to preside over the liquidation of the British Empire'. British government officials believed that the United States wanted to prise open the imperial market, which was closed to them under the terms of imperial preference. The Americans applied pressure for the elimination of imperial preferences, wanting instead a free-trading (multilateral) post-war world economic order. But Churchill was unwilling to sacrifice imperial preference, as to do so would conflict with his ideal of Empire. This attachment was shared by the British government and senior civil servants.

1. What was the impact on the Commonwealth of Britain's declaration of war on Germany?

2. How did the Second World War change Britain's relationship with the Commonwealth and Empire?

10.3 How did British politics adapt to the conditions of a world war?

For more on the impact of the Second World War on the British people and the British economy, see chapter 11.

Why did Winston Churchill replace Neville Chamberlain on 9 May 1940?

In May 1940 the National Government was in crisis. This was because the Labour and Liberal Parties and some Conservatives had lost confidence in Prime Minister Neville Chamberlain. His foreign policy was seen to have failed. He was blamed for the policy of appeasement and complacency in

**Winston Churchill
(1874–1965)**
Wartime leader famous for his inspirational, and morale-lifting, rhetoric. Preferred dealing with defence and foreign affairs, management of which he took on in the absence of Foreign Minister Sir Anthony Eden. An ardent imperialist, he was oblivious to the growth of nationalism in the Empire. Churchill is credited with forging the close wartime collaboration with the United States.

Vote of no confidence: The House of Commons is asked if it has confidence in the government. If the votes prove that it doesn't, the government falls.

believing that Hitler could be trusted to keep his word. He was also blamed for his failure to achieve an alliance with the Soviet Union during the summer of 1939. The British people had been frustrated by Britain's inability to assist Poland and resist the combined forces of Germany and the Soviet Union. The British government feared the likelihood of fighting the Soviet Union as well as Germany.

Chamberlain's leadership was fatally undermined by the Soviet attack on Finland in November 1939 and the German attacks on Norway and Denmark in April 1940. Scandinavian resources would be valuable to the Nazi war effort, but Britain's short-lived attempt to defend Norway was bungled. Additionally, Neville Chamberlain's hatred of war meant that he was seen as a man of peace. It was therefore feared that he would not wage war 100 per cent to win. Chamberlain had hoped for a short and limited war: he thought it would be possible to undermine Germany with a naval blockade. He underestimated the Nazi regime and did not appreciate the amount of public support for Hitler. This added to his unpopularity.

In the Parliamentary debate of 7 and 9 May 1940 the Labour and Liberal parties attacked Chamberlain and the National Government. The government just survived a **vote of no confidence**, but its majority fell from 200 to 81.

Chamberlain realised that he needed to create a true Coalition administration involving Conservatives, Labour and Liberals. But Labour refused to serve under him because they considered him to be discredited by the failure of appeasement and the military reverses in Norway. Alternative leaders proposed were Winston Churchill, then serving at the Admiralty, and Lord Halifax, the Foreign Secretary. But Halifax refused to compete against Churchill for the leadership. On 10 May Winston Churchill was asked to form a Coalition Government with the Labour Party, and he accepted the role the day the Germans invaded Luxembourg, Belgium and the Netherlands.

How did war affect parliamentary government?

To cope with the problems posed by the war, Leo Amery MP had suggested a change from peacetime government. He believed that wartime government would need men of resolution, daring and thrust for victory, with clear authority.

The War Cabinet in October 1941, including Winston Churchill (seated, 2nd left), Clement Attlee (seated, 2nd right), and Anthony Eden (seated, far right).

Minister without Portfolio: A minister without a specific departmental responsibility.

The adoption of Coalition government, composed of Conservative, Labour and Liberal MPs, involved setting aside confrontational Parliamentary procedures and political differences between the parties, as far as possible, to help the conduct of wartime government. In addition an all-party truce was agreed in the conduct of by-elections (see section 10.4).

Churchill set up a five-man War Cabinet, with himself as Prime Minister and Minister of Defence. Labour's Clement Attlee served as Lord Privy Seal (until 1943 when he became Lord President of the Council) and Arthur Greenwood as **Minister without Portfolio**. Neville Chamberlain served as Lord President of the Council and Lord Halifax as Foreign Secretary. Chamberlain was retained in the Cabinet because he could command a substantial number of Conservative followers in a way that Churchill could not. This was because the new prime minister had been unpopular during the 1930s when he had opposed the government's policies of appeasement and increased self-government for India. Churchill needed to minimise his unpopularity, both within the Conservative Party and within the Coalition government. In October 1940 Chamberlain resigned due to ill health. With Chamberlain out of government, Churchill's position began to strengthen. Sir Anthony Eden replaced Halifax as Foreign Secretary in December 1940.

In *The Road to 1945* (1975), historian Paul Addison saw the Second World War as a melting pot for politics. Conservatives and Labour, governing together, put together a system of wartime agreements, which formed the basis of consensus politics and the welfare state.

How did the Coalition Government tackle the problems associated with post-war reconstruction?

By late 1943, when it had become clear that the Allies would win the Second World War, the Coalition Government became concerned about examining the problems of post-war **reconstruction**. In November 1943 Lord Woolton became Chairman of the Cabinet Joint Party Reconstruction Committee. Proposals examined included:

Reconstruction: This meant both planning for the future welfare of the country after the war and the rebuilding of buildings, shipping, aircraft and other materials damaged by enemy action.

● a Town and Country Planning Act, to control how and where offices, factories and houses were built;

● post-war housing policy;

● White Papers on the principles of a national health service, post-war sickness and pension schemes, unemployment benefit, workmen's compensation.

All parties were committed to achieving and maintaining a high level of employment.

Conservative MP R. A. Butler maintained that the work of this Joint Committee laid foundations that the Labour Party had only to finalise, after they had won the 1945 election, and 'in some cases bring forward Bills already drafted' by the wartime Coalition Government.

Another issue requiring discussion was the possibility of state ownership (nationalisation). The Conservatives would have preferred to avoid discussing this subject before the election, despite Labour MP Herbert Morrison's skilful presentation of a case for electricity nationalisation.

Why did the Labour Party's approach to domestic policy gain greater public support during the war?

Contemporary commentators noticed a public swing to the left, an impatience with class privileges and a belief that statism (state control of the staple industries), the solution Labour offered, would be beneficial.

Labour sought to appear moderate in its proposals. In this they were helped by the extension of wartime controls over the economy and industry, so that Labour's nationalisation proposals did not appear so radical. The Labour Party Manifesto 'Let us Face the Future' promised to nationalise the Bank of England, fuel and power, transport, iron and steel. Labour promised to put the Beveridge Report into immediate effect (see section 11.9). It also promised economic planning and full employment. Labour was 'winning the peace' while Churchill was involved in war strategy and diplomacy.

As the Prime Minister and Minister of Defence, Churchill had overall responsibility for war strategy. He had very little time (or inclination) to concentrate on party politics or post-war domestic strategy. Other Conservatives took responsibility for foreign, imperial and defence policies, but, in the eyes of many of the public, they were responsible for failing to solve the problems of the 1930s. In contrast to Labour, the Conservative Party was seen to have reservations about implementing the Beveridge Report's proposals. The Conservative Party's manifesto incorporated the Joint Coalition Committee's plans on key issues, for example full employment and a national health service. But they refused to be explicit about policies concerning the extent of state economic controls. The Conservatives were divided between those who were cautiously enthusiastic and those who were suspicious and negative. Some saw welfare reform as creeping socialism and others recognised that it was 'an idea whose time had come' and were willing to accept it as necessary. The public were aware of these Conservative reservations and therefore preferred to vote for the party, which would bring in the reforms they wanted.

Why was the wartime Coalition abandoned?

Winston Churchill wanted to keep the Coalition going until Japan had been defeated, which was expected some time in 1946. The Labour Party felt that this was too far away. They had been ahead in the opinion polls since 1943 and in 1944 had decided not to prolong the Coalition any longer than was absolutely necessary to ensure victory in Europe and the Far East. The Conservatives too were becoming tired of Coalition government. Churchill felt that the shadow of a general election would make parliamentary government unworkable, thus making the Coalition a lame duck administration. Therefore he decided to dissolve Parliament sooner rather than later. On 23 May 1945 Parliament was dissolved and Churchill appointed a caretaker government, which took over until 26 July when the election results were known.

How successful was the Coalition Government?

The Coalition had a keen and dynamic drive to win the war, and the mixture of parties seemed to work. However, Britain *had* to win the war; the alternative was a German victory with the likely subordination of Britain's interests to those of Nazi Germany. This unacceptable alternative seemed to concentrate minds wonderfully on the job in hand.

The Coalition government successfully tackled the problems involved in gearing British society, the economy and industry to the needs of winning the war. Once victory seemed attainable, they produced White Papers to cover proposed post-war reconstruction and welfare reform legislation. The wartime Coalition gave members of all political parties experience of government; when the Labour Party won the July 1945 election, the hand-over of power was smooth because so many Labour MPs were experienced in government.

Churchill's success as wartime leader of the Coalition Government

---

1. What changes did the Second World War impose on the way Britain was governed?

2. How far was the success of the Coalition Government due to Churchill's wartime leadership?

---

resulted from his personal style of management. He was interested in many aspects of the conduct of the war. He distrusted large departments, fearing they would fail to act swiftly and effectively, preferring to establish a special relationship with a small and loyal staff. He preferred them to take personal responsibility for getting things done (and done quickly) and sent correspondence to ministers headed 'Action this day'. Moreover, Churchill's wartime leadership and his stirring speeches improved public morale.

10.4 Why did the Conservative Party lose the 1945 election?
A CASE STUDY IN HISTORICAL INTERPRETATION

The Conservative Party was in power for two-thirds of the 20th century. The Conservative-led National Government of 1931–45 was very successful, staying in power for 14 years. So what were the circumstances that led it to lose the 1945 election?

The 1945 general election

● The general election took place on 5 July 1945 but results were not available until 26 July because time was needed to collect and count votes from overseas servicemen.

● Labour was consistently in the lead from 1943 in by-elections, and opinion polls were suggesting that they had a substantial lead over the Conservatives.

● On 26 July the results showed that Labour had won 393 seats, a gain of 227. The Conservatives had won 189 seats but lost 185 to Labour.

Why did the Conservative Party lose?

Had they lost touch with the public mood for welfare reform, which Labour had understood so well? And linked to this, had their policy development section been allowed to decline during the war so that they failed to develop welfare reform policies which suited the public mood, but which were framed to be acceptable to Conservative traditional supporters?

Problems of policymaking were fundamental to the Conservatives' defeat:

● There was a lack of official policy-making on home affairs – the Conservative Party fell back on 'trust the government' and 'let's win the war first'. The Conservatives were preoccupied with Churchill, his vision of internationalism and new world order and concern for Soviet intentions, at the expense of welfare reform and reconstruction.

Collectivism: Increased involvement of the government in social and economic affairs.

● Churchill himself had no message, apart from warnings about the dangers of **collectivism**, and remained aloof from policy-making, being too concerned with wartime diplomacy and defence. This created a vacuum at the top.

● The Conservatives were not identified with welfare reforms and there was a split within the party between those who were pro- and anti-welfare reforms.

● A case in point was the party's response to the Beveridge Report. This was embraced enthusiastically by the Tory Reform Group, which favoured collectivism, but there were others who treated it with suspicion, such as Churchill, who feared an extension of state intervention and higher taxation.

- This split produced a lack of party policy-making, which did not address reconstruction, whereas the Labour Party fervently adopted the welfare reform programme outlined in the Beveridge Report.

- The 1944 Health White Paper highlighted divisions in the Coalition, which was falling apart over welfare policy, although it held up over wartime diplomacy and strategy. The Town and Country Planning Bill provided for land procurement, which was perceived by the Conservatives as robbery. But Labour would not accept any alterations to it and threatened to withdraw from the Coalition in March 1945.

Had Conservative Party organisation declined so far during the war that it proved impossible to galvanise organisers efficiently to consolidate the Conservative vote in time for the 1945 election?

- Area Offices and Constituency Associations were closed down as staff enlisted or were drafted into the forces. By 1945, 170 agents and 30 women organisers were engaged in war work.

- The co-ordination and direction of the Conservative campaign was almost non-existent in the few months before the 1945 general election. It lacked central direction and carefully composed policies. Those policies that were put together were rushed or delivered late.

- The campaign was principally based on Churchill's wartime leadership. It was not understood that the public would differentiate between Churchill as the effective wartime leader and Churchill the peacetime Prime Minister.

- Too little was spent on publicity, only £3,000. This was less than one-tenth of the £30,000 spent in 1935.

- Local Conservative Party activism was virtually non-existent up to a few months before the 1945 general election.

Were the Conservatives electorally disadvantaged supporting the 'electoral truce'?

An electoral truce had been signed by the Conservatives, Labour and the Liberals on 26 September 1939 requiring each of the parties not to 'nominate candidates at by-elections … against the candidate of the party who held the seat at the time of vacancy'.

- The Labour Party at local level did not endorse replacement Conservative candidates in accordance with the terms of the truce, and in defiance of Labour Party HQ instructions. Conservative seats were often fought by independent left-wingers who ignored the instructions of the Labour National Executive to implement the truce.

- On the other hand, the Conservatives never disobeyed party orders because there was no Party Organisation as such in existence to order conduct one way or another. Only in 1944 did Central Office propose more explicit political battle. Nevertheless, Churchill had refused to make speeches in support of Conservative candidates as being against the spirit of the truce. But even when this ruling was reversed, Conservative by-election defeats continued.

Was there a failure of leadership from Churchill?

There was a leadership vacuum because:

- Churchill was not a good party man. He had been in the political 'wilderness' until the war and had no power base within the party.

- At the time, he was identified as a war leader. This was fine for war but not for peace. He was totally involved with strategy and wartime diplomacy.

- He did not have close relations with the party organisation hierarchy and tended to listen more to his cronies, Beaverbrook and Bracken.

Conclusion

What accounted for the size of the Labour majority?

Labour strategy:

- Attlee was calm and statesmanlike. In contrast to Churchill's 'Gestapo' speech in March 1945, which warned the electorate that socialist government would lead to dictatorship.

- For sections of the electorate, the reforms promised by the White Papers were important and the Labour Party looked as if it would deliver reform pledges whereas the Conservatives did not.

- The Labour Party blamed the Conservatives for appeasement and unpreparedness for the war effort in a pamphlet entitled 'The Guilty Party', which associated the Conservatives with appeasement.

Other factors involved included:

- The British electoral system had inequalities in constituency sizes i.e. small urban electorates – which Labour won. The average Labour seat contained nearly 6,000 electors fewer than the average Conservative seat. Thus Labour received 48 per cent of the poll but two-thirds of the seats. Although the Conservatives obtained 40 per cent of the vote they were severely disadvantaged by the inequality of constituency sizes.

- The Conservatives' underestimation of lingering memories of 1930s unemployment and paying little heed to a public desire for new men and new policies.

- The National platform being seen as out of date. The public had had fourteen years of National Government and besides it could not be 'National' if it did not include Labour, so it did not ring true.

Contemporary Conservative interpretations of defeat focused on:

- Criticism of Churchill's election campaign. His campaign speeches were described as 'confused, woolly, unconstructed and wordy'.

- Lack of policy development and want of a clear policy. The Conservative Manifesto had been hurriedly produced in two or three weeks.

- The belief that the war had radicalised the forces, whose vote had gone 'en bloc' to Labour.

- The maintenance of party machinery at local level which had became divorced from central direction of National Union and Conservative Central Office.

- Failure of the Party organisation to run an effective campaign, caused by military service of party organisers and the party machine not revived in time for the election campaign. Michael Kandiah suggests in *Contemporary Record* (1995) that this last factor was central to election defeat.

Interpreting the results

What did the 12 per cent swing to Labour represent? Did Labour win or did the Conservatives lose the 1945 election?

● The scale of defeat was exaggerated by the electoral system.

● The evidence suggests that Labour was supported by new voters and benefited from Conservative abstentions. The Conservatives did not get the traditional middle-class vote or the traditional female vote.

● The Conservatives themselves agreed that the public was steadily radicalised during the war.

● Service votes were mostly pro-Labour – probably because young men were more attracted to Labour and many were worried about how long the war in the Far East would continue.

● The public was more concerned with issues of post-war reconstruction and welfare reform than theoretical socialism. Therefore Labour gathered support, and the public was not repelled by collectivist aspects of Labour's political platform. The middle classes were attracted by the health schemes and the alliance with the Soviet Union, its battle successes and the avuncular portrayals of 'Uncle Joe' Stalin inclined voters to a more favourable view of the Russians.

● There was tactical voting against the Conservatives and an anti-Conservative vote deriving from: 14 years in government, memories of Munich, unemployment and dole of the 1930s.

● Conservative Party organisation was depleted and in disarray, their election campaign was fudged and publicity and propaganda were misdirected.

1. What impact did the Second World War have on the Conservative Party?

2. Did the Labour Party win the 1945 election or did the Conservative Party lose it?

Did the Labour landslide constitute a political revolution?
On the one hand, the Conservatives and their political allies retained 40 per cent of the votes cast. On the other hand, the election gave the Labour Party a large majority for the first time and a clear mandate for them to implement considerable change, which they subsequently did.

Further Reading

Texts designed specifically for AS and A2 students

The Attlee Governments 1945 to 1951 by Kevin Jeffreys (Longman Seminar Studies, 1995), opening section on 'Labour and the Road to 1945'
The British Welfare State: A Critical History by John Brown (Historical Association Studies, Blackwell, 1995)
The Conservative Party 1902 to 1951 by Stuart Ball (Longman Seminar Studies, 1995)
Empire to Welfare State 1906–1985 by T.O. Lloyd, 3rd edn, (Oxford University Press, 1986)
The Shaping of the Welfare State by R.C. Birch (Longman Seminar Studies, 1974)
War in Europe 1939–1945 by Anthony Wood (Longman Seminar Studies, 1987)
War and Society 1899 to 1948 by Rex Pope (Longman Seminar Studies, 1991)
All the Seminar Studies books have a document section.

For more advanced reading

The Road to 1945: British Politics and the Second World War by Paul Addison (Cape, 1975)

The Churchill Coalition and Wartime Politics 1940–1945 by Kevin Jeffreys (Manchester University Press, 1991)

The People's War, by Angus Calder (Pimlico, 1992)

War and Reform: British Politics during the Second World War edited by Kevin Jeffreys, (Manchester University Press, 1994)

The Second World War by Martin Gilbert (Fontana, 1989)

The Oxford Companion to the Second World War, I.C.B. Dear (Oxford University Press, 1995) – a good book for dipping into, with short pieces on a wide variety of topics

11 Britain and the challenge of Fascism: Saving Europe at a cost? 1925–1960

Key Issues

- How successful were Britain's relations with Europe in the period 1925 to 1960?

- Was British foreign policy in the years 1937 to 1939 a triumph or a disaster for Britain?

- Was the social and economic impact of the war on Britain positive or negative in the years 1945–1960?

11.1 How successful was Britain in its dealing with Mussolini in the years 1925 to 1937?

11.2 How effectively did Britain deal with Hitler's Germany in the years 1933 to 1937?

11.3 Historical controversy: Was appeasement a success or a failure for Britain in the years 1937 to 1939?

11.4 Why was Britain able to continue fighting in the Second World War in the years 1939 to 1941?

11.5 How significant was the Battle of the Atlantic to Britain in the years 1939 to 1945?

11.6 What impact did Britain's bombing offensive have on the outcome of the Second World War?

11.7 How important was Britain to the Allied victory in the West between D-Day and VE Day?

11.8 How was the Home Front affected by the experience of war?

11.9 What was the effect of the Second World War on the British economy?

11.10 Historical Controversy: Did the impact of the Second World War have a negative impact in the years 1945 to 1960?

Framework of Events

1925	Mussolini completes the creation of a Fascist Dictatorship in Italy
1933	Hitler becomes Chancellor of Germany
1935	Anglo-German Naval Agreement
	Italy invades and conquers Abyssinia (Ethiopia)
	Hoare-Laval Pact
1936	Hitler remilitarises the Rhineland
1937	N. Chamberlain become British Prime Minister
1938	Anschluss between Germany and Austria
	Munich Agreement
1939	Germany occupies Bohemia and Moravia
	British guarantee of Poland and Romania
	Second World War begins
	Beginning of Battle of the Atlantic
1940	Blitzkrieg in the West
	Battle of Britain
	The Blitz begins
	War in North Africa begins
1941	Lend-Lease introduced
	USSR enters war
	USA enters the war
1942	Beginning of the 'bombing offensive' against Germany
1943	Turning point in Battle of the Atlantic
	War in North Africa ends
1944	D-Day

1945	Germany surrenders
	VE Day
1947	Britain forced to leave Greece
	Britain withdraws from Palestine
	Britain grants independence to India and Pakistan
1949	Britain joins NATO
1950–53	Britain fights in Korean War
1956	Suez Crisis

Overview

BRITAIN, having been victorious in the First World War, was one of the 'Big Three' powers that produced the Paris Peace Settlement of 1919–20, along with the USA and France. Britain's biggest military threat – the German Navy – had been destroyed, scuttling itself in Scapa Flow, Orkney in 1919. Britain was the world's largest empire, covering one quarter of the globe and containing one third of the world's population. But this rather rosy picture of Britain's international position was deceptive. The British Empire had lost almost a million dead in the war. It had amassed a debt to the USA of £959 million. In addition, in the 1920s and 1930s Britain faced an economic recession. Britain no longer had the financial and economic resources to maintain large armed forces and now found it difficult to maintain its global military commitments.

In the 1930s in particular, the British Empire faced major threats. In the Far East, Japan was becoming a significant naval power. It followed an aggressive foreign policy towards China, occupying Manchuria in 1931 and invading the rest of China in 1937. In the Mediterranean and East Africa, Britain faced the threat of Italy under Mussolini, who wanted to create a new Roman Empire. And in 1933, Hitler became Chancellor of Germany, with the aim of destroying the Treaty of Versailles. This raised the prospect of war in Europe by the late 1930s.

Faced with all these problems, Britain attempted to maintain international peace through diplomacy. In dealing with Mussolini and Hitler, Britain – supported by France – followed the controversial policy of appeasement. But instead of preventing a European war, it merely delayed it until 1939.

The Second World War was Britain's finest hour. Britain stood up to Hitler's aggression and, from June 1940 to June 1941, Britain stood alone against Nazi Germany and Fascist Italy. From 1941 Britain played a major role in the grand Alliance which defeated Fascist Italy and then Nazi Germany. At Yalta and Potsdam, in 1945, Britain along with the USA and USSR, decided the fate of post-war Europe.

1. What do you regard as the most important issues facing British foreign policy towards the Fascist dictators in the years 1925 to 1945?

However, victory in the Second World War came at a cost. The social, economic and military impact of the war transformed Britain and its position in the world. The war also brought enormous change to ordinary Britons. In the years after 1945 British society was changed radically under the Labour governments of 1945–1951. At the same time, Britain declined as a global power, in a world divided into two superpower blocs during the Cold War.

11.1 How successful was Britain in its dealing with Mussolini in the years 1925 to 1937?

Mussolini became Italian Prime Minister in October 1922. It took until 1925, however, for him to create a Fascist dictatorship. Mussolini succeeded in bringing political stability to Italy – but at a very high price. Independent trade unions were abolished, political parties, other than the Fascists were banned, and democracy was destroyed. Mussolini wanted Italy to play a more prominent part in international affairs. He wanted Italy to be feared and respected. In 1925 Italy signed the Locarno Treaties which were regarded as a major landmark in maintaining European peace during the 1920s. However, Mussolini aimed to create a new Roman Empire. In 1926 Italy occupied Albania. In the 1930s Mussolini's attentions spread to East Africa. In 1935 Italy invaded Abyssinia (modern-day Ethiopia) and had conquered the country by 1936. As a result of this aggressive policy, Italy was perceived as a serious threat to Britain's position in the Mediterranean and East Africa.

How did Britain react to this threat? In 1935 Britain was still in economic recession, with high levels of unemployment, and the government felt it was not in a position to deal militarily with Italy. Instead the Baldwin government of 1935–37 attempted to maintain international peace through a policy of appeasing Italy. In 1935, before the Italian invasion, a secret pact was drawn up by Britain and France to give Mussolini two-thirds of Abyssinia in return for not going to war. Both Britain and France wanted Italian support against Hitler's Germany which was in the process of rearming. In 1935, Germany reintroduced compulsory military service (conscription). To counter this move, Britain, France and Italy had formed the 'Stresa Front'. Both Britain and France were prepared to sacrifice Abyssinia for the sake of European peace. When the secret pact, known as the Hoare-Laval Pact, became public it caused outrage in the British press and parliament, and the Foreign Secretary, Sir Samuel Hoare – who had signed the Pact – was forced to resign.

However, Britain did not have an effective alternative strategy in dealing with Mussolini. As a result, in October 1935 Italy went to war with Abyssinia. Thus the first real attempt at appeasement had failed.

British and French opposition to the Italian invasion, voiced at the League of Nations, was partly responsible for Italy's decision to leave the League of Nations and become an ally of Hitler. In 1935 Italy had opposed German conscription, but in 1936 Italy signed the Rome–Berlin Axis agreement, which was the beginning of a close friendship between two aggressive right-wing dictators.

1. Explain why Britain was willing to appease Italy in the 1930s.

11.2 How effectively did Britain deal with Hitler's Germany in the years 1933 to 1937?

British policy towards Hitler was similar to its policy towards Mussolini. In 1935 Britain signed the Anglo-German Naval Agreement. This broke previous disarmament commitments made by Britain, but it helped to limit the growth of the German navy. In the following year, 1936, Hitler openly broke the Treaty of Versailles again when the German army reoccupied the demilitarised zone of the Rhineland. Britain did not possess the armed force to prevent the reoccupation, and therefore relied on the French Army to act. Unfortunately, France was unwilling to act alone. Instead, it put its faith in the defensive fortifications along the Franco-German border known as the 'Maginot Line'.

Between 1933 and 1937 Hitler had begun to rearm Germany in violation of the Treaty of Versailles. He also reoccupied the Rhineland. Britain followed a twin policy of appeasement and diplomatic action. Appeasement had taken the form of the Anglo-German Naval Agreement. Diplomatic action took the form of the Stresa Front. Neither policy had any real impact on Hitler's plans. In the mid-1930s Germany was more interested in building up its army and air force rather than its navy. The reoccupation of the Rhineland showed clearly that Hitler was unwilling to be swayed by diplomatic action.

In 1937 Baldwin resigned as prime minister to be replaced by Neville Chamberlain. But instead of abandoning appeasement, Chamberlain took the failed policy to new heights.

1. What were the main factors that determined British policy towards Germany in the years 1933 to 1937?

Why did Neville Chamberlain agree that the Sudetenland should be annexed by Germany?

Neville Chamberlain regarded the Munich Agreement of 29 September 1938 to settle the Sudeten question as a diplomatic success. He thought he had obtained 'peace in our time'. Czechoslovakia was under German threat of war over alleged mistreatment of the Sudeten Germans. Chamberlain was not interested in saving Czechoslovakia and had never given the Czechs the guarantee they desired. Czech security was based on the 1922 Little Entente alliance with France, which would hold Germany in the west and in that way divide German military efforts. But in 1938, when put under German pressure, the French decided that the alliance with Britain was more important and adopted the British line. Chamberlain reasoned that, if the French had treaty obligations to the Czechs and Britain was an ally of France, then if the French supported the Czechs, Britain was likely to be drawn into a fight in which no British interests were at stake.

Why was Czechoslovakia under threat from Germany?

● Hitler's real aim was to attack the Soviet Union. For this he would need access through Czech territory.

● Therefore he needed to cripple Czech defences by detaching the well-fortified frontier area bordering Germany.

● The Czech frontier with Germany included German Bohemians (known as Sudeten Germans). They inhabited an important economic and strategic area on the border with Germany. There was longstanding conflict between the Czechs and the Germans, which strengthened Hitler's case.

● Hitler used the Sudeten German Party (Nazis), led by Konrad Henlein, as his agents. Sudeten German Nazi agitation increased after 1935. In April 1938, under Hitler's orders, they demanded self-government for Germans in Czechoslovakia and subordination of Czech foreign policy to German interests. A German press campaign against Czechoslovakia orchestrated these demands and heightened tension.

A British mediator, Lord Runciman, was sent to Czechoslovakia in August 1938, without telling the French, to 'persuade' the Czechs to accept whatever demands were made in order to keep the peace. Runciman reported unfavourably on the Czechs. Neville Chamberlain wanted to avoid another European war at all costs. To try to avoid war, he flew to see Hitler three times during September (see page 222).

On 30 September 1938, while taking leave of Hitler, Chamberlain produced a 'piece of paper', confirming Anglo-German friendship and a determination not to go to war against each other, which Hitler signed. On

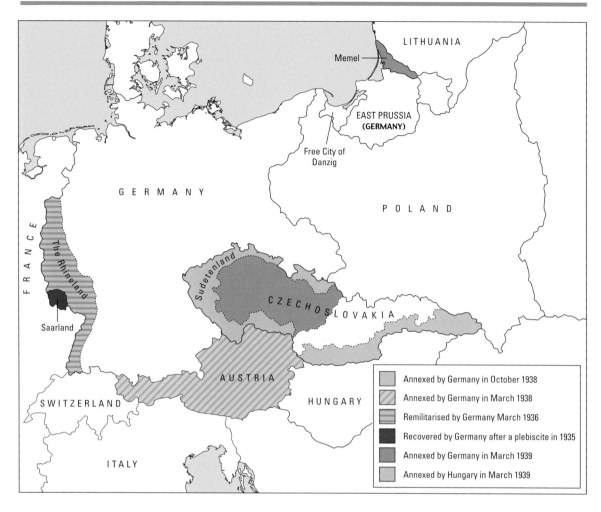

The situation in Europe after the Munich Agreement, September 1938

The terms of the Munich Agreement, 30 September 1938

- The Czechs gave 10,000 square miles of the Czech-German border to Germany, the Sudetenland;

- They gave up 5,000 square miles to Hungary on the Czech-Hungarian border;

- Later, Teschen was given to Poland;

- The Four Powers, Britain, France, Italy and Germany guaranteed the remainder of Czechoslovakia against further unprovoked aggression.

Neville Chamberlain meets Hitler, September 1938. Also pictured are French Prime Minister Daladier and Italy's Mussolini.

The Munich crisis

15 September 1938: Chamberlain and Hitler met at Berchtesgaden. They agreed that the Sudetenland should be detached from Czechoslovakia. Neither Chamberlain's Cabinet nor the French were informed of his intention to persuade Hitler to accept the territory demanded rather than go to war with the Czechs.

22 September 1938: Chamberlain flew to meet Hitler at Bad Godesberg. Hitler really wanted war with Czechoslovakia, so the territorial demands escalated to what Hitler thought would be a British, French and Czechoslovakian sticking point.

23 September 1938: Czech forces were mobilised.

23 September: Hitler's show of anger increased, because he was trying to push the British, French and Czechs to go to war.

Chamberlain attempted to persuade the British Cabinet to appease Hitler. This met with Cabinet opposition. Mobilisation of the British navy was authorised.

Mussolini convened a Four Power conference.

30 September 1938: Hitler backed down and allowed himself to be persuaded by the heads of governments of Britain, France, and Italy (Chamberlain, Daladier and Mussolini) to accept the territory demanded. Czechoslovakia was not represented at the meeting. Neither was the Soviet Union, an ally of the Czechs.

Purges: The systematic removal of an individual's or group's political enemies.

1. What circumstances persuaded the British Government to start a rearmament programme?

2. Why did Neville Chamberlain agree that the Sudetenland should be German rather than Czechoslovakian?

his return to Britain Chamberlain declared that he had secured 'peace in our time'.

Chamberlain dismissed the principle of Soviet support because British and French officials believed that the Soviet military was seriously weakened by the **purges**. He was also reluctant to involve them because he was opposed to communism. Exclusion of the Soviet Union from the Munich meeting had grave consequences. Soviet leader Stalin's belief in the value of collective security and his adherence to the League of Nations were undermined. Peter Calvocoressi and Guy Wint in *Total War* (1979) suggest that Stalin, in accordance with his treaty with the Czechs, would have mobilised and could have overflown a corner of Romania to reach Germany. Soviet mobilisation would have heartened the French and faced Hitler with war on two fronts.

How accurate is this cartoon in its portrayal of the Munich Agreement?

Soviet poster showing western powers giving Czechoslovakia to Hitler on a dish. Inscription on the flag reads 'On towards the East.'

11.3 Historical controversy: Was appeasement a success or a failure for Britain in the years 1937 to 1939?

In his *Dictionary of Political Thought* (1996) Roger Scruton defines appeasement as denoting 'policies aiming to remove by common agreement the grievances generated by the peace settlement of 1919 – especially those felt in Germany … Appeasement involves concessions in response to explicit or implied threats; it acts to the detriment of a power that doesn't threaten, and to the benefit of a state which makes non-negotiable demands.'

Appeasement began at the Paris peace conference. Lloyd George saw the Treaty of Versailles as 'a temporary measure of a nature to satisfy public

GOOD HUNTING
MUSSOLINI. "All right, Adolf – I never heard a shot"

A GREAT MEDIATOR
John Bull. "I've known many Prime Ministers in my time, Sir, but never one who worked so hard for security in the face of such terrible odds."

STILL HOPE

How useful are these cartoons in explaining events in Europe in 1938?

opinion'. He had supposed that the League of Nations would be used as the medium to renegotiate the harsher terms of the Treaty of Versailles: 'No-one supposes that the terms are eternal and immutable ... they will be sensibly modified'.

Rapprochement: Reconciliation.

Neville Chamberlain, who became Prime Minister in May 1937, was obsessed with the need to seek a **rapprochement** with Germany because he abhorred war and wanted to avoid another war in Europe. Chamberlain's views were underpinned by a movement among Liberal and Labour politicians and the British press to agree modification of the Treaty of Versailles.

But Chamberlain misread Hitler, believing that appeasement would work because Hitler was reasonable. Documents in the Public Record Office at Kew show Hitler to have been intent on attacking communism via war with the Soviet Union (not unpopular as communism was regarded as the greater menace) and regaining lost territory and uniting the German 'volk'.

Volk: The 'pure-blood' German people.

As Ruth Henig suggested in a *Modern History Review* article (Volume 10, issue 3, February 1999), many historians argue that only an alliance of Britain, France and the Soviet Union in the late 1930s could have deterred Hitler and prevented the outbreak of war, and that the only feasible alternative to appeasement was a strategy of deterrence and alliances. But deterrence by alliance was unpopular because alliances had been discredited by the outbreak of the First World War and deterrence needed rapid rearmament and accretion of trained and equipped military manpower. Chamberlain ignored the claims of the Soviet Union to be consulted at Munich as a participant in collective security, and was lukewarm about pursuit of a treaty with Stalin afterwards. The result of this was confirmation of Stalin's distrust of British and French intentions towards the Soviet Union and negotiation of the Nazi-Soviet Pact of August 1939. This became a trigger to the Second World War as it released Germany from fear of war on two fronts until it was ready.

Historiography: Different historical views by historians. Another term for historical interpretation.

Geopolitical: The political opportunities and limits determined by a nation's geographical position and natural resources.

In an article for the *Electronic Journal of International History* (2000) Patrick Finney has examined the **historiography** of appeasement and placed it in the context of Britain's **geopolitical** strategic and economic dilemmas. Britain's global strategic dilemma was too little defence and too much to defend; there were other uses for money needed to provide an adequate defence posture for all commitments. Thus Finney perceives appeasement as the outcome of decline. He divides the historiography into three periods:

The orthodox 'Guilty Men' period

The *Guilty Men* view blames Neville Chamberlain, assuming that Britain still had great power and sufficient clout and resources to take on Hitler. Therefore policy-makers were free to choose resistance and confrontation rather than appeasement.

Written in 1940 by Michael Foot (writing under the name of Cato), Peter Howard and Frank Owen, who were not in a government in power, *Guilty Men* accuses the Chamberlain Cabinet of blindly misjudging Hitler's capacity to fight by overestimating it and of appeasing him by giving in to his demands.

The problem was of gauging Hitler's intent. Winston Churchill in *The Gathering Storm* (1948), concludes that Hitler had a plan of conquest of Eastern Europe and advanced inexorably towards it. This should have been obvious and Britain lost opportunities to stop him.

The revisionist view

Revisionist: An interpretation that revises or changes a widely held point of view.

In the late 1950s and in the 1960s **revisionist** views appeared. A.J.P. Taylor's *Origins of the Second World War* (1961), exposed defects in the orthodox view. Although Taylor is ambivalent about appeasement, and his book cannot truly be considered revisionist, it did make historians re-evaluate the events of the 1920s and 1930s. Historians such as Martin Gilbert in the *Roots of Appeasement* (1966) examined the disparity between resources and commitments, suggesting that Chamberlain had little alternative. But examination of newly-opened British archives suggested that Britain was reluctant to take a stronger stance against Hitler because its defences were too weak. Additionally, the government feared to destabilise economic recovery from the Depression by embarking upon too accelerated a rearmament programme. Therefore, as Richard Overy points out, appeasement was the only rational policy in the circumstances because Britain's decline was apparent in the 1930s.

The counter-revisionist view

Counter-revisionist: Against the policy of revisionism or modification of Marxist-Leninist doctrine.

In the 1980s **counter-revisionist** interpretations appeared, admitting decline and constraint but casting doubt on Neville Chamberlain's motives. Was he driven by events or did he use events to justify his pre-determined course? R. A. C. Parker in *Chamberlain and Appeasement* (1993) suggests that the appeasers were neither fools nor cowards but misread Hitler and underestimated Nazi expansionism and its menace. Chamberlain had unreasonable hopes of satisfying Hitler. Also, the policy of appeasement was popular with the British electorate. Nevertheless Chamberlain was too conciliatory and did not apply sufficient counter-pressure.

Other views

The work of other recent historians suggests that Hitler was an opportunist. He had a programme but no detailed long-term plans of how it could be achieved. Therefore he kept pushing at the open door of appeasement, and was successful while he was revising the harsher terms of the Treaty of Versailles. But he misjudged France and Britain. Once he went beyond Treaty revision by occupying the Czech rump and demanding Polish territory, he obliged them to oppose him. With these acts of aggression Hitler had broken his promise to Neville Chamberlain, convincing him of his bad faith and incidentally turning the tide of Dominions' reluctance to stand by Britain and undermining the pacifists.

Another interpretation is offered by the Intentionalist/Functionalist view outlined by Martin Housden in *Modern History Review* (Volume 10, issue 2, November 1998). The Intentionalists believe that Hitler had a plan and some idea of how to achieve it. The Functionalists suggest that he had a plan and achieved it on an *ad hoc* basis as opportunities arose. Additionally, they suggest that much of Nazi policy was the unintentional outcome of an over-bureaucratised system, with competing departments, which was run by a lazy man (Hitler) who would not devote himself to work.

Britain and France are criticised for giving in to German demands. But there were reasons for doing so:

- There was a public dislike of war. Democratically elected politicians cannot ignore the wishes of the electorate; either they will not be voted into power or they will not remain there for more than one term. This view was reinforced by the Peace Pledge Union, set up by Dick Shepherd, Vicar of St. Martins in the Fields. Moreover, it was claimed that the East Fulham by-election of June 1935, had been lost because of pacifist votes. The League of Nations Union (a peace movement) had over 400,000 members in 1931.

- The British government believed German demands for Treaty revision were reasonable. It did not understand Hitler's intentions, especially as he could be personally charming. Neville Chamberlain believed that Hitler's territorial demands were limited and that 'he was a man who could be relied upon when he had given his word'. Therefore Chamberlain believed after Munich that he had achieved 'peace in our time'. However, others, such as Winston Churchill and Michael Foot, were less gullible.

● At the time of Munich it was not clear that the self-governing Dominions of the British Commonwealth would join Britain in a war with Germany over the Sudetenland. The Dominions had acquired control over their own foreign policy in the Statute of Westminster of 1931.The South African prime minister, Barry Hertzog, voiced his opposition to war. His concerns were echoed by the prime ministers of Canada and Australia. Therefore, an important consideration in appeasing Hitler at the time of Munich was to prevent a split in the British Commonwealth. By September 1939 it was clear that Hitler was a major menace to international peace. As a result, when Britain declared war, the majority of dominions joined her. Australia and South Africa declared war on the afternoon of 3 September 1939, and Canada declared war the following day. Only one dominion failed to join Britain in the war – Eire – which remained neutral for the entire war.

There were other reasons which made appeasement seem an attractive option:

● It had proved impossible to stop Hitler rearming. Europe did not disarm during the 1920s. This provided an excuse for German rearmament and some politicians felt it difficult to argue with.

● Unification of Germans could be interpreted as being in line with national self-determination, as per Wilson's Fourteen Points, for the Rhineland, Austrians, Sudeten Germans in Czechoslovakia, Danzig Free City – again, difficult to argue with.

● Britain and France saw themselves as being in no position to stop him anyway.

● The threat of communism was seen as a worse evil than a potentially Nazi-dominated Europe. But, having had a Mutual Assistance Treaty with Czechoslovakia, Stalin felt insulted by exclusion from the Munich settlement.

1. How far was Neville Chamberlain personally responsible for the policy of appeasement?

2. Why have historians differed in their views of appeasement? Give reasons for your answer

● Germany was seen as a buffer zone against the Soviet Union.

● The British government feared further damage to the British economy would result from engaging in another war.

● Britain had problems to deal with in the Far East, the Mediterranean and in India.

11.4 Why was Britain able to continue fighting in the Second World War in the years 1939 to 1941?

When Hitler invaded and occupied Bohemia and Moravia in April 1939 it was clear to Britain that Germany was an aggressive power which wanted to acquire non-German speaking territory in Europe. At that point, appeasement was abandoned, and from April 1939 Britain began preparations for war. For the first time in British history conscription was introduced in peacetime. In addition, Britain offered guarantees to Poland and Romania to defend their territory. When Germany invaded Poland on 1 September 1939, Britain and France declared war on Hitler two days later. The Second World War had begun.

From September 1939 to May 1940 Britain and France were engaged in a 'phoney war' against Germany. There was no land fighting between the two sides, except for the brief Norwegian campaign of April, 1940. British ineptitude in that campaign led to the resignation of Neville Chamberlain and his replacement with Winston Churchill as prime minister.

In May 1940 Germany launched its Blitzkrieg against the West. In just six weeks Germany had overrun Holland, Belgium and Luxembourg. It had also knocked France out of the war. The British Expeditionary Force (BEF) was forced to evacuate back to Britain through Dunkirk, and by the middle of June Britain stood alone against Germany. It also now faced Italy, which had declared war on Britain and France on 10 June 1940.

Britain now seemed to face impossible odds. Most of the BEF's equipment was left in France and Belgium. Germany completely dominated the European continent, so how was Britain able to continue fighting? Part of the answer was the leadership of the new prime minister, Winston Churchill. Following the fall of France, members of the British Cabinet, including Lord Halifax, considered the idea of a negotiated settlement with Hitler. Churchill refused to compromise. In a series of radio broadcasts to the British public in the summer and autumn of 1940 he adopted a patriotic, uncompromising stance. Ed Murrow, an American journalist working in London in 1940–41, stated that Churchill 'used the English language as a weapon' to wage war against Germany.

Of greater significance was the Battle of Britain. If Germany was to invade Britain, it first had to gain air superiority. From August to October 1940 the RAF fought the **Luftwaffe** for control of the skies over the Channel and southern England. By October 1940 Hitler had postponed his plans to invade Britain in 1940. Why did the RAF win the Battle of Britain?

Luftwaffe: The German air force

First, Britain had the benefit of radar, which gave prior warning of incoming Luftwaffe attacks, allowing the RAF fighters to be ready and waiting. Also, Britain had good quality fighter aircraft. The mainstay of RAF Fighter Command was the Hawker Hurricane, which was supported by the Supermarine Spitfire. Both fighters were effective at attacking, and destroying Luftwaffe bombers such as the Dornier 17 and the Heinkel 111. The Luftwaffe did possess a very effective fighter, the Messerschmidt 109, but because of its fuel limitations it could only operate over southern England for 25–30 minutes at a time. A major reason for defeat was Hitler's decision to change German tactics at the height of the battle. Initially the Luftwaffe attacked radar stations and RAF aerodromes. This tactic was having considerable success in limiting the ability of the RAF to operate. However, following an RAF bomber attack on Berlin, Hitler changed his Luftwaffe plans and ordered an all-out attack on civilian targets in London. Although this attack – the Blitz – caused considerable damage and loss of life, it gave the RAF time to recover and regroup. The decisive day of the battle was *Adlertag* (Eagle Day) on 15 September 1940 when the RAF defeated a major Luftwaffe attack on London. The failure of the Luftwaffe to win a decisive victory helped persuade Hitler to call off the invasion of Britain.

Britain also survived because of the Royal Navy's ability to maintain the sea lane link to North America. In the Battle of the Atlantic the British Merchant Navy just about maintained the flow of war supplies from the USA. Britain was aided greatly in this task by the decision of the US government in early 1941 to introduce the Lend-Lease programme, where US war supplies were given to Britain without immediate payment. Also by the autumn of 1941 the US Navy escorted British merchant shipping across the Atlantic as far as Iceland.

1. Why do you think Germany failed to knock Britain out of the war in the period 1940 to 1941?

Finally, after the fall of France, Britain quickly adapted its economy to all-out war production. This enabled Britain to rearm after Dunkirk and to maintain the Royal Navy and RAF to defend Britain and the sea lanes of the North Atlantic.

11.5 How significant was the Battle of the Atlantic to Britain in the years 1939 to 1945?

On VE Day in 1945, Winston Churchill paid specific tribute to the seamen who helped win the Battle of the Atlantic. The battle was the longest and most vital for Britain in the Second World War. If Britain lost the battle and essential war supplies and food did not reach Britain, then the war would have been lost.

Although a 'phoney war' may have existed on mainland Europe from September 1939 to May 1940, at sea the German U-boats and surface raiders attacked and sank British merchant shipping. The worst period for British losses was June 1941 to June 1942. The battle reached a turning-point, however, in 1943. From then to the end of the war Britain and the US were able to deal effectively with the German naval threat to the Atlantic sea lanes. By 1943 the main German surface raiders had been neutralised. The *Bismarck* and *Scharnhorst* had been sunk, the *Gneisenau* badly damaged, and the *Tirpitz* was forced to stay within a Norwegian fjord (and was immobilised by submarine and air attack in 1944).

1. Why was the Battle of the Atlantic so important to the British war effort in the Second World War?

2. Why do you think Britain won the Battle of the Atlantic?

Part of the British success was the capture of the German 'Enigma machine', which deciphered German naval coded transmissions. This meant that from 1942 Britain was able to successfully intercept German naval messages to and between U-boats. Also by 1943 Britain had developed effective anti-U-boat measures. The Royal Navy could use 'sonar' to track U-boats underwater, and 'asdic' to track them on the surface. Once located, the RAF and US aircraft, based on aircraft carriers and on land bases such as Iceland, could intercept and sink U-boats.

11.6 What impact did Britain's bombing offensive have on the outcome of the Second World War?

The Battle of Britain and the Battle of the Atlantic were defensive engagements to ensure that Britain was not defeated. From 1942 onwards, Britain took the war to Germany with a major bombing offensive. The architect of this strategy was the head of Bomber Command, Arthur Harris. He had the unshakeable belief that mass bombing of German cities and factories could win the war. Britain operated nightly attacks on Germany, and from the end of 1942 RAF bomber command was joined by the 8th and 9th US Army Air Forces. Stationed in Eastern England, the US by day and the RAF by night launched an almost non-stop bombing offensive against German-occupied Europe.

This policy, however, was highly controversial. The RAF heavy bombers, mainly made up of Lancasters, attacked civilian targets. An RAF report in late 1942 stated that only 10 per cent of RAF bombs got within four miles of their targets. In May 1942 the RAF launched its first thousand-bomber raid, on Cologne, losing fifty aircraft. Large numbers of German civilians were killed as a result of the bombing offensive by the RAF. A week-long raid on Hamburg in July 1943, known as Operation Gomorrah, resulted in 50,000 civilian deaths. The Nazi Propaganda Minister, Joseph Goebbels described RAF Bomber Command crews as 'Churchill's murder boys'. (The greatest loss of life, however, occurred later – in February 1945 – when a three-day combined RAF and US air force raid on Dresden resulted in as many as 80,000 deaths.)

RAF Bomber Command did achieve some spectacular public relations successes, including the destruction of the Mohne and Eder dams in the

Ruhr area in May 1943. However, the raid failed to damage the Sorpe dam, the main dam for the Ruhr industrial area.

By the end of the war the bombing offensive had devastated most German cities. But it is debatable how effective the campaign had been. It had certainly not broken the German will to fight, as Harris had claimed would happen. However, the large numbers of aircraft and anti-aircraft military personnel that were deployed to defend German cities could have been used more effectively elsewhere.

The defence of German air space involved hundreds of aircraft and more than one million military personnel, and it tied down most of the German electronics industry which was involved in aircraft detection and counter-measures.

Also the German Armaments Minister from 1943, Albert Speer, claimed that four or five bombing attacks like Operation Gomorrah could have brought German industry to a halt.

In retrospect, the most effective bombing attacks on Germany were made by 8th US Army Air Force on specific industrial targets, such as the ball-bearing works at Schweinfurt in 1943 and the Ploesti oilfields in Romania, in 1944. These attacks had a major impact on German war production. Albert Speer estimated that the bombing offensive limited German war production by 40 per cent.

An unquestioned major success for Bomber Command was its involvement in destroying much of the western European rail network in the lead up to D-Day. But the RAF bombing offensive remained controversial to the end of the war, and beyond. Churchill refused to allow Bomber Command a separate campaign medal, unlike the Battle of Britain. Also RAF bomber crews suffered the highest rate of casualties of any military service. Over 50,000 were killed and hundreds of bombers were destroyed.

1. Why do you think the RAF bombing offensive of 1942 to 1945 was a controversial aspect of Britain's war effort?

11.7 How important was Britain to the Allied victory in the West between D-Day and VE Day?

Victory in the West began on 6 June 1944 (D-Day) with the Allied invasion of France. Of the five beaches in Normandy which were attacked on the first day three were attacked by British and Canadian troops. (Also RAF Bomber Command had already caused extensive disruption to the French railway system prior to the invasion.) The Commander of all Allied ground troops in the Normandy campaign was the British general, Bernard Montgomery. Under his command, the Allies defeated the German army group in the West, liberated Paris and drove the Germans back into Holland and Germany by November 1944. However, the Allies did suffer some important reverses. Montgomery's plan to break out of Normandy through the capture of Caen (Operation Goodwood) failed. Instead it was the US Third Army, under George Patton, that won the crucial breakout at St Lo. In September 1944 Montgomery launched Operation Market Garden which was a bold attempt to end the war by Christmas 1944. British and US airborne troops attempted to capture the bridge across the rivers of Holland as a prelude to an invasion of Germany. Although partially successful, the attempt by British troops to capture the bridge at Arnhem failed. Secondly, Montgomery was taken by surprise by the German Ardennes Offensive of December 1944. Known as the 'Battle of the Bulge' the Germans almost broke the Allied front held by the Americans. The offensive failed partly because the Germans ran out of fuel for their tanks, but also because the Allies had air supremacy. By March 1945 the Allies were deep inside Germany. Operation Varsity, the crossing of the River Rhine was a complete success. It led to the rapid encirclement and total collapse of the German army in the West by April 1945.

The British contribution to victory also involved driving out the German troops from northern Italy. US forces and the British 8th Army had liberated virtually all of Italy by the time of the German surrender in May 1945.

Although the USA provided the most men and much of the war material for the Allied victory in the West, British and Canadian troops played an important role in the ground fighting. They were ably supported by the RAF, both in its role as infantry and tank support and in strategic bombing.

1. Britain's contribution to the Allied victory in the West in 1944–45 has been greatly exaggerated. How far do you agree?

2. Can you add a further important contribution of Britain to Allied victory in the blank bubble provided?

3. Place the British contributions to Allied victory in the mind map in order of importance. Give reasons for your answer.

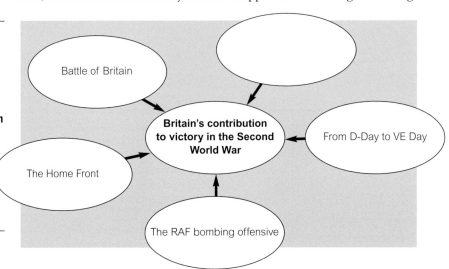

Battle of Britain

Britain's contribution to victory in the Second World War

From D-Day to VE Day

The Home Front

The RAF bombing offensive

11.8 How was the Home Front affected by the experience of war?

Food in wartime

● Meats, bacon, butter, sugar and sweets were rationed.

● People were encouraged to eat more vegetables.

● A 'Dig for victory' campaign encouraged people to grow their own vegetables; parks were turned into allotments so that people without gardens could grow their own food.

● People were also encouraged to keep rabbits and chickens to provide additional meat for the table.

In what ways did war affect people's lives?

By means of the Emergency Powers Act, introduced in May 1940, the government intervened in people's lives on an unprecedented level, mobilising the economy and population towards war production and imposing controls, such as rationing of food distribution and consumption, to ensure fair shares for all. A Ministry of Supply oversaw food distribution. An allowance of 3,000 calories per day was introduced, guaranteed to everyone, so that people were healthy and well fed. There were few consumer goods available for purchase, and clothes and household goods were also controlled. Ration books for food and coupons for clothes and consumer goods were issued.

The civilian population was involved in waging war on the home front. A call for volunteers went out in May 1940 which brought forward one-and-a-quarter million men and women by July 1940. The Local Defence Volunteer Reserve (the Home Guard) practised defensive manoeuvres designed to halt or impede invading German forces. Air Raid Protection Wardens (ARP) patrolled the streets, both to ensure that no light could be seen through blackout curtains, which could help a German bomber locate an urban or industrial centre, and to give assistance to the fire fighters and other rescue and relief services after bombing raids.

Maintenance of civilian morale was considered to be essential and the government organised the production and distribution of propaganda posters to encourage people to be sensible and cheerful about their hardships.

A Home Guard soldier stands on guard beside the wing of a German bomber which crashed near Kentish Town, north London, September 1940.

Using information in this chapter, do you think the Home Guard were an important part of Britain's defence against German invasion? Give reasons for your answer.

Upward mobility: The process of increasing personal wealth and social status, for example someone born into the working class joining the middle class.

You never know who's listening!

CARELESS TALK COSTS LIVES

Why do you think posters such as this were issued by the government during the Second World War? To what extent did they help the 'war effort'?

People's lives were not completely disrupted. Some attempts were made at maintaining normality and radio broadcasting by the British Broadcasting Corporation (BBC) assumed increased importance. Cinema attendance increased; audiences went to see films that offered them an escape from the fear and drudgery of the war. Some films were blatantly propagandist, promoting the ideals of patriotism and bravery, for example *In Which We Serve* and Laurence Oliver's *Henry V*.

In general many family incomes improved but research gives mixed results. There is little evidence of **upward mobility** based on savings and capital accumulation. Wages in key industries such as aircraft production did rise, but this was not true of all sectors of the war economy.

What was the impact of the Second World War on people's working lives?

In spite of a general public perception that everyone should pull together to win the war, this did not mean that there were no labour problems.

There was competition between employers for skilled engineers because war service depleted the work force. In June 1940 a Restriction on Engagement (Engineering) Order introduced universal recruitment of key workers through Labour Exchanges or trade unions.

In 1941 labour mobility was further limited and the government directed the labour force into war work. Training programmes were introduced to overcome skill shortages. Near full employment was achieved. Average wage rates rose and so did the tax revenue payable to the government, although this was inevitably directed to the war effort rather than to reconstruction.

Despite maintenance of morale there were increased outbreaks of industrial unrest. There was poor time keeping, absenteeism and lack of commitment. By October 1941 there had been one thousand illegal strikes, but the government feared to take harsh measures to control them at a time of national emergency. Trade union membership rose by 1.5 million and Joint Production Committees were set up in firms engaged in war production, where decision-making was based on consultation between management and employees of the firm.

How did war affect women's role in society?

Social and economic emancipation of women followed new employment opportunities arising from the need to replace men on active service or transferred to war work. Additionally, labour shortages benefited many women who were called on to supplement the workforce. Over 97 per cent of women agreed that they should undertake war work in the auxiliary services and industry, resulting in the number of women employed in commerce, industry and the armed forces, rising by almost 50 per cent to 2,250,000 between 1939 and 1943. The National Service No.2 Act of December 1941 conscripted unmarried women into women's auxiliary services such as the WAAF (Air force), WRNS (Navy) and ATS (Army). Although not allowed to engage in active service, women made very good 'backroom boys' in collating information in air force, naval or army operations rooms and in fighter control.

The war promoted a sense of independence, and many women enjoyed increased responsibility previously only accessible to men. Nevertheless the trades unions sought to maintain male privileges and pay for some manual work dropped. Even so, the number of women who remained at home, to bring up children for example, exceeded those who were employed in the forces in industry and in civil defence.

What were the effects on the British public of the German bombing campaign?

On 4 September 1940 the Blitz began on the East End of London, causing wholesale destruction of buildings and services, with over 1,000 casualties. Badly hit areas included major ports, such as Southampton, Plymouth, Liverpool, Portsmouth, together with key industrial areas, such as Coventry, Birmingham, Manchester and Newcastle. Between 1940 and 1941, 44,000 people died in bombing raids. Propaganda in the press promoted a 'Britain can take it' spirit and King George VI, Queen Elizabeth and Winston Churchill visited bombed-out areas and casualties to maintain morale. But not all was bravery and defiance. Mass Observation (an agency who surveyed and published public opinions) reported shortages of bread, milk, electricity, gas and telephones. People were disoriented by shock, discomfort, disruption, dislocation, loss of sleep and confusion. People became accustomed to hearing air raid warnings, then leaving their beds to go and sleep in an air raid shelter under the stairs of their house or in their garden. In London many families slept on platforms in Underground stations.

At the outset of the war Hitler had declared that he would not make war on women and children. His aim was to attack industrial and naval targets to disrupt imports of food supplies and British arms production. However, women and children inevitably became the victims of the Blitz because their homes were clustered around the docks and centres of industrial employment, and in the 1940s bombs could not be aimed accurately.

Over a million children were evacuated in the early stages of the war in 1939 because it was thought that a German bombing campaign would commence immediately. Evacuation brought home to the public the scale of child poverty and deprivation. It also reinforced middle-class determination to accept the potential bonus offered by the introduction of a **welfare state**. However, the culture clash between classes made many evacuees unhappy and they returned to their parents in 1941 as soon as the worst effects of the Blitz eased.

Hitler's bombing campaigns did not bring Britain to its knees because the Luftwaffe (German Air Force) lacked the capacity to mount attacks over sufficiently wide areas to knock out all major industrial centres and port

Welfare State: State provision for all citizens of a basic level of income and services through a social security system, a health service, housing, education and maintenance of full employment. This would create a new social order based on equality and a sense of community.

Attrition: Gradual wearing down, through loss of shipping.

facilities. Moreover, despite the high rate of **attrition** achieved by German U-boats (submarines) targeting the Atlantic convoys bringing goods to Britain from the United States, sufficient supplies were delivered to keep Britain going. Domestic production of coal and arms were maintained. The Minister of Food, Lord Woolton, set up a Salvage Branch. This ensured that waste food was collected regularly to feed pigs. Domestic pots and pans and iron railings were sacrificed to provide scarce minerals for weapons production. The wartime slogan 'Britain can take it' seemed appropriate.

How did the war alter public perceptions of government control of people's lives?

The difficulties and hardships of war encouraged an expectation of reduction in social inequalities and that state interference would be applied to social reform. These expectations inclined the public towards support for the Labour Party, which was seen as more likely to introduce them.

Government interference in the conduct of people's lives increased, for example, the introduction of food rationing, evacuation of children, especially from major industrial centres, and the re-housing of bombed-out families. Social legislation enacted included free milk and dinners for children at school, and nurseries for women engaged in war work

The war reinforced the debate on state provision of welfare services by highlighting the inadequacies of pre-war social welfare provision. For example, civilian casualties on the scale of occurrence arising from the Blitz could not be treated in the pre-war system of voluntary and local authority hospitals. This inspired the creation of a wartime emergency hospital service with central government funding of beds in voluntary hospitals.

Economic and industrial controls were also introduced, permitting government direction of resources to maximise the war effort. Wartime discussions about the reconstruction of Britain, at national and local level, accustomed the British public to the idea of planning for the future.

What were the main proposals of the 1942 Report on Social Insurance and Allied Services by William Beveridge?

The *Report on Social Insurance and Allied Services* was written by Sir William Beveridge, Master of University College, Oxford. It was published on 1 December 1942. In his report, Beveridge proposed the elimination of what he called the five giants: 'Want, Disease, Ignorance, Squalor and Idleness'. Beveridge's proposals were seen as a 'blue-print' for a welfare state and moved away from the principle of selectivity towards **universalism** of entitlement to national insurance.

Universalism: The paying out of government welfare assistance to everyone, regardless of need.

The Coalition government's response to Beveridge was predictable. Winston Churchill and the Conservatives, despite their reservations, thought the Report too popular to reject. The Conservative Party was alarmed by the financial implications of some sections of the Beveridge Report. They thought it would be dangerous to encourage expectations which might not be realisable, especially the commitments on post-war reconstruction. In January 1943, the Conservative Party set up a Beveridge Report Committee, which sought to scale down the extent of the proposed reforms. The Committee suggested, for example, that compulsory health insurance should not apply to the higher paid and that unemployment benefit should be less attractive than the lowest paid employment. The lukewarm Conservative response provoked the Labour Party to vote against the Coalition government for the first time. Thus, the Coalition accepted Beveridge's unified universal scheme but rejected the idea of subsistence as unworkable.

White Paper: A government document outlining proposals for changing the law.

A series of **White Papers** was issued in 1944 on provision of a National Health Service, employment policy and social insurance. A White Paper on employment policy recommended a steering committee with five subordinate working parties on manpower, investment, statistics, balance of payments and economic survey.

In 1941 the Family Means Test was abolished. A Family Allowance Act was introduced in 1945, because a quarter of all family incomes were too small. It introduced a payment of five shillings (25p) per week for the second and all following children.

The government also introduced one single universal contribution from earnings, allowing each insured worker to claim maternity, unemployment, sickness and disability benefits, old age pensions and a funeral grant, thereby providing 'cradle to grave' welfare as a right rather than as a reward for good behaviour.

How far did Beveridge's proposals build on Britain's existing welfare policies?

On the eve of the Second World War Britain was a country with the most advanced provision of social welfare services. However, the provision was patchy and many aspects of welfare were insufficiently covered or not covered at all. Pre-Beveridge welfare provision was based on a principle of **selectivity**. That is, state provision of welfare benefits was based on the means test. This identified what financial means a prospective recipient already had so that state handouts could be tailored to the recipient's needs.

Selectivity: The principle of giving government welfare assistance according to people's needs. This resulted in people being subjected to the 'means test', which wanted to know every detail of their financial circumstances. Many people considered this to be degrading.

Beveridge rejected the idea of selectivity in favour of universal entitlement. He believed that social insurance would only succeed in providing a welfare safety-net if it was part of a comprehensive social policy covering family allowances, a national health service and prevention of mass unemployment.

What were the provisions of the Education Act of 1944?

Brought in by a Conservative MP, R. A. Butler, the Act created a new Ministry of Education and 146 local education authorities. It brought in a system of secondary education for everyone based on aptitude. Pupils were sent to grammar schools, technical schools or secondary modern schools. The Act also maintained the system of grant-assisted independent schools and schools which were the responsibility of the local authority.

1. How did the Second World War change the way people lived?

2. Why was the Beveridge Report so well received when it was published in 1942?

The Act raised the school leaving age to 15 and made non-denominational worship and religious education compulsory, but with a 'conscience' clause to permit exclusion of anyone who objected on religious grounds.

11.9 What was the effect of the Second World War on the British economy?

What was the impact of the Second World War on the British economy?

The Second World War nearly bankrupted Britain. The war cost £28,000 million. Britain was obliged to borrow heavily because government revenue was inadequate to cover the cost of the war. Thus, in order to finance the war, Britain disposed of pre-war overseas assets of at least £1,000 million and lost its pre-war creditor position.

The United States provided $47 billion in Lend-Lease goods between

1941 and 1943, of which the bulk went to the UK and the Soviet Union. But, while Lend-Lease meant that no charge was levied on Britain for United States aid and goods supplied during the war, this facility ended when hostilities ceased and Britain then had to make good its promises of payment.

While UK net output rose by 20 per cent between 1938 and 1944, this did not meet the requirements of the war effort, which at its peak absorbed 50 per cent of total national income. The shortfall was made up by disposal of foreign assets, debt accumulation, capital depletion and a fall of 22 per cent in personal consumption. Britain's invisible earnings were seriously impaired through the decline in trade and shipping losses (much of them resulting from German U-boats attacking Atlantic convoys bringing food and military supplies to Britain from the United States). These losses were made good by buying American shipping, and thereby increasing Britain's indebtedness.

At the end of the war Britain's net reserves amounted to $1.8 billion, but there were overseas liabilities against these reserves of approximately $13 billion. Between 1939 and 1940, 45 per cent of public spending was on defence. By 1944–45 this had risen to 83 per cent.

War damage was another burden on the public purse. Britain lost approximately 7 per cent of pre-war housing as a result of German bombing raids.

What part did the British public play in helping to finance the war?

Post-war credits: A savings scheme introduced during the war. The public bought certificates, thereby loaning the money to the government. The government bought the certificates back after the war.

Post-war credits were launched to attract wartime earnings into savings, but purchase of these was not compulsory. The economist John Maynard Keynes had advocated the introduction of compulsory wartime savings at a time when few consumer goods were available for purchase. His idea was that, when these savings were paid back after the war, money would be released to refloat the economy and to alleviate post-war depression.

What were the principles of Lend-Lease and how was it agreed?

On 3 November 1940 United States President Roosevelt outlined a scheme which enabled Britain to acquire United States weaponry on favourable terms. Roosevelt wanted to help Britain by all means short of war and was prepared to compromise United States neutrality to do so.

The Aid to Democracies Bill was passed by Congress on 11 March 1941, enabling Roosevelt to lend or lease equipment to any nation 'whose defense the President deems vital to the defense of the United States'. The Act worked by permitting Britain to order arms and military supplies from the American government, which ordered and paid for goods from American producers. These goods were then lent or leased to Britain on promise of payment when the war was ended. The Act permitted Britain, and later China and the Soviet Union, to acquire arms, warships, military supplies and other goods immediately. The goods were brought from the United States across the Atlantic in convoys of merchant ships escorted by destroyers. These were targeted by German U-boats, which initially inflicted enormous losses on British shipping. When Britain was able to break the German codes (Ultra and Enigma) and pinpoint submarine positions, the U-boats themselves became targets. In the first half of 1943 over 100 were sunk. Britain acquired $11.3 billion worth of American goods by the end of the war, which made the United States 'the arsenal of democracy'. Without this American effort, it is doubtful that Britain could have continued to fight. It also ensured that the United States would have a predominant say in strategy once it entered the war. Lend-lease was swiftly terminated on 17 August 1945, once Japan had surrendered.

What did Britain agree to at the Bretton Woods Conference in July 1944?

An international monetary and finance conference was held at Bretton Woods in New Hampshire USA in July 1944. Twenty-eight nations, including Britain, participated and agreed to the establishment of an International Monetary Fund (IMF) and a World Bank.

The IMF was intended to operate a cash reserve system on gold and currency that member countries could draw on to meet balance of payments deficits. This was intended to ease world trade. The IMF also provided for the restoration of exchange stability with adjustments in exchange rates only occurring when there was fundamental inequality in the balance of payments. Britain wanted to establish an international currency and a variable volume of credit to facilitate the expansion of trade. Britain also wanted to underpin the IMF with larger reserves than the $25 billion with which it started. Britain's exchange rate, however, was set at too high a rate, to the detriment of the British economy in the following decades.

The World Bank was set up for the advancement of loans to finance important viable projects in the development of a country.

Britain and the United States agreed to apply the principles of free trade, no discrimination and stable rates of exchange to the international economy. It was hoped at Bretton Woods that an international trading organisation would be set up to clear tariffs and quotas. The organisation was not set up in 1944 but what evolved instead, in 1947, was the General Agreement on Tariffs and Trade.

1. What impact did the Second World War have on the British economy?

2. How did Britain cope with the economic problems posed by the Second World War?

11.10 Historical Controversy: Did the impact of the Second World War have a negative impact in the years 1945 to 1960?

In May 1945 Britain was one of the victorious Allied powers. However, the war had profoundly changed Britain and its position in the world. At home, the experience of war helped launch the Labour Party into office in the July 1945 general election. Historian Peter Hennessy entitled his study of the post-war Labour governments *Never Again*. This was a sentiment that many Britons felt. They wanted to see permanent social and economic change which would result in a fairer and more equal society. Under the post-war Labour government a 'Welfare State' was created which offered comprehensive social support for the entire population. This included universal unemployment benefit and the creation of the National Health

Nationalisation measures 1945–1951

Industry	2nd reading of bill	Vesting day	Numbers employed
Bank of England	29 October 1945	1 March 1946	6,700
Coal	29 January 1946	1 January 1947	765,000
Civil aviation	6 May 1946	1 August 1946	23,300
Cable and Wireless (telecommunications)	21 May 1945	1 January 1947	9,500
Transport (railways, canals, road haulage)	16 December 1946	1 January 1948	888,000
Electricity	3 February 1947	1 April 1948	176,000
Gas	10 February 1948	1 April 1949	143,500
Iron and steel	15 November 1948	15 February 1951	292,000

Source: Kevin Jeffrey, *The Attlee Government*, 1992.

Service in 1948. The Labour government also changed the structure of the UK economy through a programme of widespread nationalisation (see table on page 236).

By 1951 British society had been transformed. Although rationing still existed, Britain was now a fairer, more equal society. The spirit of wartime collaboration between all classes seemed to have continued into peacetime on a permanent basis.

However, the impact of war on the UK economy greatly affected Britain's ability to remain a major world power. 1945 was the beginning of the end of the British Empire. Even before 1939 the Indian nationalist movement was demanding self-government. By 1947 Britain withdrew from the Indian sub-continent, and on 15 August 1947 India and Pakistan became independent. In the following year independence was granted to Burma (Myanmar) and Ceylon (Sri Lanka). A process of decolonisation had begun which would see Britain withdraw from most of its empire by the mid-1960s.

In addition to the decline of Britain as an imperial power was the decline of Britain's role as 'the world's policeman'. British troops were stationed throughout the world after 1945 – in Germany, Austria, Japan, Palestine and South East Asia. Britain also gave military aid to the Greek Monarchists in the Greek civil war.

The year 1947 stands out as a landmark in Britain's decline in international affairs. In that year Britain announced it could no longer fulfil its military commitments to Greece or in Palestine. By 1947 the UK economy was virtually bankrupt. In the previous year, 1946, Britain had been kept going financially by a large US loan, and from 1947 to 1952 – under the US Marshall Aid plan – Britain received millions of dollars in US aid. It was clear to contemporaries that Britain could not keep going without US economic aid. It was also becoming clear that Britain would not keep going without US military support as well. This was shown in the Berlin Blockade crisis of 1948–49 when the US led the western campaign to provision West Berlin. By 1950 Britain was the home to US air bases as part of the West's response to the Cold War against the USSR. When NATO was formed in 1949, Britain was a junior partner of the USA. This junior position was reinforced in the Korean War of 1950–53 where US forces played the major role in defending South Korea.

However, Britain still maintained pretensions of Great Power status. In the early 1950s Britain became the third member of the nuclear weapons club when it successfully exploded an atomic device in the Pacific. However, these pretensions came to an abrupt end with the Suez Crisis of 1956. An Anglo-French attempt to depose Egyptian ruler, Nasser, ended in humiliating defeat when the USA and the USSR voiced their disapproval of the Anglo-French action. As result of the crisis, British Prime Minister Sir Anthony Eden was forced to resign because of ill health. Never again could Britain act independently of the USA in international affairs. In the nuclear age of the Cold War, Britain could not compete with the economic and military power of the USA or the USSR. Like France, it was losing its position as a major colonial and military power. From 1957 France saw its future within the European Economic Community which eventually became the EU. Britain, however, was still looking for a new role in 1960.

1. In what ways did the Second World War have a negative impact on Britain's position in the world?

2. 'On balance, the Second World War had more of a positive than a negative impact on Britain in the years 1945 to 1960.' Assess this view.

Further Reading

Texts designed specifically for AS and A2 students

British Foreign and Imperial Policy 1918–1939 by Alan Farmer (Hodder, 1992)
Europe 1870–1991 by D. Murphy and T. Morris (Collins, 2000)
The Origins of the Second World War by Richard Overy (Longman, 1987)
The Origins of the Second World War by Ruth Henig (Routledge, 1985)
Hitler, Chamberlain and Appeasement by Frank MacDonough (Cambridge, 2002)
Neville Chamberlain, Appeasement and the British Road to War by Frank MacDonough (New Frontiers in History, 1998)
Appeasement by Keith Robbins (Historical Association Studies, 1997)
Hitler, Appeasement and the Road to War by Graham Darby (Hodder Access to History, 2007)
Appeasement by Andrew Boxer (Collins Questions in History series, 1998)

For more advanced reading

Chamberlain and Appeasement by R.A.C Parker (Macmillan, 1993)
Origins of the Second World War by Philip Bell (Longman, 1997)
The Second World War by Martin Gilbert (Fontana, 1989)
Britain in the Second World War: A Social History by Harold Smith (Documents in Contemporary History, 1996)
Britain in the Age of Total War, 1939–1945 by Malcolm Chandler (Modern World History for Edexcel, 2002).

12 The Labour government home and abroad, 1945–1951

Key Issues

- How significant were the changes made by the Labour governments in domestic policy in the period 1945 to 1951?

- How successful was Labour foreign and imperial policy in the period 1945 to 1951?

- To what extent were the Labour governments responsible for dismantling the British Empire?

12.1 'Quite a day' – Labour and the election of 1945

12.2 'Building Jerusalem' – Labour's domestic record, 1945–1951

12.3 Historical interpretation: What caused a 'cold war' to develop after 1945?

12.4 How did British foreign policy re-adjust to the political and military realities after the Second World War?

12.5 How did the Second World War affect Britain's imperial policy?

12.6 Why did Britain have to leave India in 1947?

12.7 How did Britain attempt to make the Empire pay its way?

Framework of Events

1945	Labour wins landslide victory in general election
1945–47	Pro-Soviet regimes created in eastern and central Europe
1947	Truman Doctrine and Marshall Plan announced
	Nationalisation of the coal mines
	Partition of India into India and Pakistan
	Independence granted to India and Pakistan who both join the British Commonwealth
1948	Nationalisation of the railways
	Creation of the National Health Service
	Independence granted to Burma (Myanmar) and Ceylon (Sri Lanka)
	Burma refuses to join the Commonwealth, but Ceylon joins
	Berlin Blockade crisis begins
1949	Devaluation of the Pound
	India becomes a republic
	London Declaration allows India to remain a member of the Commonwealth
	Britain helps form NATO
1950	Outbreak of the Korean War
	Labour wins general election
1951	Festival of Britain
	Conservatives win general election. Winston Churchill becomes prime minister.

Overview

Labour's victory in the July 1945 general election brought a major change with the immediate past. From 1931 to 1945 Britain had been ruled by a National Government. Now for the first time in its history the Labour Party had a clear majority over all other parties. It also had a clear vision about what it wanted to achieve. After six years of war, rationing and privation the British electorate wanted change. They wanted a society with greater social equality. They also wanted a society that would prevent a recurrence of the 1930s with its high levels of unemployment and social privation.

Labour was led by Clement Attlee. He had been Deputy Prime Minister in the wartime coalition of 1940–45. He was completely different from his predecessor Winston Churchill. Churchill once said that Attlee was 'a modest man who has much to be modest about'! Attlee may have lacked Churchill's charisma and international stature but he was a very shrewd politician and kept the competing factions within the Labour Party in check.

From 1945 to 1951 he presided over a government which brought an economic and social transformation within Britain. Under Labour, the railways, the steel industry, gas, electricity and coal were brought under public ownership through nationalisation. By 1951 Britain had a mixed economy, with a large public as well as a private sector. The most significant long-term reform was the nationalisation of health provision, with the creation of the National Health Service. In addition, Labour introduced legislation to aid the unemployed and increased provision for housing. So great were the social reforms that, collectively, they constituted a welfare state which provided state support, free at the point of delivery, to the entire population. These changes created a post-war consensus between the major political parties. When the Conservatives regained national office in 1951 they left the welfare state intact.

The scale of Labour's achievement needs to be placed in context. The nationalisation programme and the creation of the welfare state were achieved in a country faced with severe economic problems. The Second World War had placed great strains on the UK economy. By 1945 Britain was almost bankrupt. Rationing continued into the early 1950s, and conscription remained. Even though Britain had won the war the country faced economic hardship in an age of austerity. To make matters worse, the winter of 1947 was the worst in the twentieth century, sparking off a severe energy crisis. Britain only survived economically with US aid – a large loan in 1946, then from 1947 the UK, along with the rest of western Europe, benefited from Marshall Aid. Even so, Britain still continued to have economic problems and the government had no choice but to devalue the Pound in 1949, causing a large loss in confidence in the economic management of the Labour government.

Overseas, Britain also faced major problems. British forces occupied large sections of Germany and Austria as part of the 4-Power control system, and in 1948–49 Britain participated in the Berlin Airlift. Further afield, Britain offered military aid to the Royalist faction in the Greek civil war, and British troops were fighting in Palestine against Jewish terrorists who wanted an independent state of Israel. By 1947 Britain could no longer maintain all its international commitments, and withdrew from Greece and Palestine. In August 1947 Britain gave independence to India and Pakistan. The following year independence was granted to Burma (Myanmar) and Ceylon (Sri Lanka).

Under Labour, Britain adjusted to its post-war role as a junior partner to the USA in the Cold War. It also began the process of decolonisation which led to the dismantling of the British Empire in the second half of the twentieth century.

By the time Labour left office in 1951, Britain had been transformed at home and abroad. A welfare state and mixed economy had been created which lasted under the Thatcher years of the 1980s. Britain began a process of decline in international affairs in the era of the Cold War and decolonisation. However, Britain still tried to retain an element of great power status. The Attlee government began the programme which led to the explosion of Britain's own atom bomb in the early 1950s. Also Britain was the US's major partner in the Korean War of 1950–53.

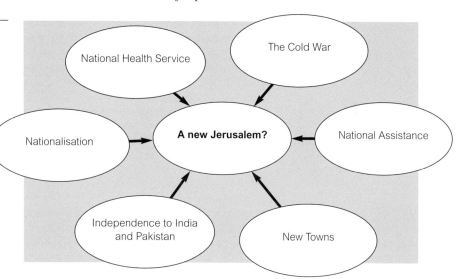

12.1 'Quite a day' – Labour and the election of 1945

The election of the Labour Government in 1945 was probably the greatest British political upset of the 20th century. Politicians of all parties and the press were united in their belief that the British people would reward Winston Churchill for his leadership during the recent war with a renewed mandate to prepare the country for the post-war world. Opinion polls, however, which politicians had yet to learn to rely on, had long told a different story.

Labour's victory was convincing. It had a majority of 146 seats over all other parties. For the first time it broke out of its industrial heartlands of the north to win seats in southern England; such as High Wycombe and Winchester, as well as suburban areas such as respectable Wimbledon. The party even won a few rural seats, mainly in Norfolk.

On the knocker: Going house to house finding out how residents would be voting at the election.

For party members the victory was an event they would always remember. Fifty years on, in 1995, Donald Matheson in Liverpool recalled: 'We went **on the knocker** and we leafleted and whatnot. We didn't expect to win. Everybody quoted Wordsworth "Bliss was it in that dawn to be alive". It was like that. It really was. We really thought "Everything is going to be all right now".' (*Generating Socialism*, 1995) Even the normally cautious Attlee, the new Prime Minister, noted in his diary that election day 'had been quite an exciting day'.

Herbert Morrison (1888–1965)
Morrison joined the wartime coalition as Home Secretary 1940–45. He served in the postwar Labour government as Deputy Prime Minister and Lord President 1945–51, and Foreign Secretary during 1951. He was Deputy Leader of the Labour Party 1951–55.

Home Front: Aspects of the Second World War that directly affected civilians.

The Labour victory was even more impressive considering the Party's dismal electoral performance since its foundation as the Labour Representation Committee in February 1900. The number of Labour MPs had risen to 154 in the 1935 general election – the last before the outbreak of war – but even so they were considerably outnumbered by the Conservatives and their allies in the National Government.

The 1930s saw a revision of Labour's aims culminating in *Labour's Immediate Programme* published in 1937. Many of the points in the Programme would find their way into the manifesto put to the country in 1945, such as the nationalisation of the Bank of England and the coal mines. Labour's leaders were also able to capitalise on the growing interest in left-wing politics, as well as concern over the appeasement policies of the Conservatives under Neville Chamberlain. In the years before the outbreak of war in 1939 the party campaigned hard against the appeasement of Nazi Germany. As a result the party attracted an increasing number of intellectuals and academics. Hugh Gaitskell, Anthony Crosland and Douglas Jay became members in the 1930s. Barbara Castle and Harold Wilson, among many others, joined during the War. They helped to ensure that for the first time the party had carefully thought-out proposals.

In the difficult days of May 1940, Labour entered the new Coalition government led by Winston Churchill. The price for their entry was full partnership in running the war. Many of the Labour's leaders became ministers: Clement Attlee became Deputy Prime Minister, Ernest Bevin Minister of Labour, and Herbert Morrison Home Secretary. Labour ministers tended to be responsible for domestic matters, as Churchill was uninterested in the **Home Front**. The effective way in which the ministers handled their responsibilities encouraged confidence in the belief that a Labour government would be run sensibly. Of the senior ministers in the first Labour Cabinet only Aneurin Bevan had not held government office before.

For many, their experiences during the war transformed their political outlook. It quickly became accepted that Britain was fighting for a better post-war world, breaking the circle of poverty and unemployment that had so blighted the inter-war period. As Queen Elizabeth, wife of George VI, wrote to her mother-in-law Queen Mary during the Blitz in October 1940, 'the destruction is so awful, and the people so wonderful – they deserve a better world'.

The most influential book published during the war was the Beveridge Report, called *Social Insurance and Allied Services* (December 1942). Steve Fielding, in *From Blitz to Blair* (1997), concludes that 'this proved to be the most significant political event of the war, establishing the parameters of the debate on post-war Britain and placing party differences in stark relief'. Beveridge prefaced his report with the statement that 'a revolutionary moment in the world's history is a time for revolution not patching'. Much of the report was, however, far from revolutionary, proposing to unify pre-war social security schemes. What it did offer was a vision of a world free from what Beveridge called the 'five giants on the road to reconstruction': Want, Disease, Ignorance, Squalor and Idleness.

Aided by careful publicity the report became astonishingly influential in thinking about the post-war world. It eventually sold some 630,000 copies. Opinion polls showed that 86 per cent of the population were in favour of the report. One worker said, 'it will make the ordinary man think that the country at last has some regard for him as he is supposed to have regard for the country'. The Conservatives, however, were distinctly cool about the proposals. Churchill himself felt that Beveridge had fostered 'a dangerous optimism' out of step with the 'hard facts of life'. The Labour Party in contrast was generally supportive, but the need to sustain the wartime coalition meant that their support was muted in public.

There were many reports and proposals published during the war years, from town and country planning to health. However, only one measure was passed, the 1944 Education Act put forward by the Conservative R. A. Butler, which raised the school leaving age to 15 and introduced secondary schooling for every child.

From the summer of 1940 the state quickly became involved in spheres of activity that would have been unthinkable a few years before. Rationing, economic controls, and the **mobilisation of labour** all became acceptable. This use of state power was very much in tune with the electorate, who had seen that life had become very much fairer, and conditions for the poorest in society improved. It became accepted that the state should play a major role in post-war reconstruction. The two main political parties had radically different views of the state, with Labour accepting that government power could be used to better the lives of the people. Douglas Jay, a senior Labour minister, wrote in 1947 that 'the gentleman in Whitehall really does know better what is good for the people than the people know themselves'.

It was clear that the electorate did not want a return to the miseries of the 1920s and 1930s. As James Callaghan, a newly-elected MP in 1945, points out, 'the pervading sentiment was no return to 1919 … it was the memory of the ex-servicemen with no legs displaying their medals on street corners, combined with unemployment in the thirties, that made us all say we are not going back there' (Election '45, 1995). The election campaign itself largely resolved round the need for reconstruction. The Conservatives fought a lack-lustre campaign around Churchill urging the electorate to 'let him finish the job'.

In contrast, Labour had a very clear idea of the post-war world that it wanted to create. In an election broadcast Clement Attlee, the Party leader, argued, 'we have to plan the broad lines of our national life so that all may have the duty and the opportunity of rendering service to the nation … and that all may help to create and share in an increasing material prosperity free from the fear of want'. Candidates stressed a better future under Labour. As Michael Foot told voters in Plymouth, 'We shall not have won the peace until every citizen in Devonport [a district of Plymouth] and every citizen of England has a good roof over his head, the chance to marry and bring up his children, safe from the fears of unemployment, sickness and worry'.

Although Labour's intentions were not as radical as commonly believed today, they were very much in tune with what voters felt needed to be done to create a new and better Britain. The title given to the manifesto said it all, 'Let us face the future'. In retirement Attlee summed up the result, 'I think the general feeling was that they [the electorate] wanted a new future. We were looking towards the future. The Tories were looking towards the past.' Kenneth O. Morgan argues, in Labour in Power, 1945–1951 (1985), that Labour's victory can be understood in the context of the war years, backed by the new realism of Labour domestic and foreign policies in the 1930s. Labour was uniquely identified with a sweeping change of mood and with the new social agenda emerging during the war years.

Mobilisation of labour: Conscription of men and women and sending them to work where there were shortages of labour.

1. How important do you think the Beveridge Report was in Labour's election victory in 1945?

2. Why do you think the Conservatives did so badly in this general election? Give reasons for your answer.

12.2 'Building Jerusalem' – Labour's domestic record, 1945–1951

Clement Attlee (1883–1967) Attlee was Leader of the Labour Party, 1935–55, Deputy Prime Minister, 1940–45, and Prime Minister 1945–51.

The Attlee administration can readily be divided into two distinct periods. The vast majority of the radical initiatives, such as the nationalisation of the coal mines and the introduction of the welfare state, were implemented before late 1947. By the end of 1947 this radicalism died away, as Britain's economic circumstances worsened and the major parts of the party's policy had been implemented. It was to be replaced by a much more cautious, pragmatic approach.

Table 1 Election results 1935–51

	1935		1945		1950		1951	
	No. seats	*% vote*	*No. seats*	*% vote*	*No. seats*	*% vote*	*No. seats*	*% vote*
Conservative	432	54	213	40	298	44	321	48
Liberal	20	6	12	9	9	9	6	3
Labour	154	38	393	48	315	46	295	49
Others	9	2	22	3	3	1	3	1
Total	615	100	640	100	625	100	625	101

Source: adapted from David and Gareth Butler, *British Political Facts 1900–1994*, 1994.

This is particularly true of Attlee's second short-lived administration between February 1950 and October 1951. The small majority – only six MPs over the other parties (see table 1) – and the illness or evident tiredness of many of the senior ministers (many of whom who had been in office continuously since 1940) led to the feeling that, in Hugh Dalton's words, Labour was in office, but was 'without authority or power'.

Historians are divided on the achievements of the 1945 government. Generally, those on the left have argued that the Labour government did not move sufficiently far down the path towards socialism. Trevor Blackwell and Jeremy Seabrook in *The Politics of Hope* (1988) wrote, 'the role of Labour was twofold. First of all to provide illusions that the new beginning actually represented a radical break from the past. The will to create a new society which would articulate the hopes and desires of their own people. And secondly, and more prosaically, to provide a scaffolding of welfare services which would both support and shroud the restoration of the old structures.'

Meanwhile, many on the right believe that Attlee should have devoted scarce resources to building up industrial recovery rather than on the welfare state – as Correlli Barnett put it in *The Audit of War* (1986), 'to them [the voters] victory in the war merited a rich reward, and they meant to have it: for the high-minded a reward in the shape of an ideal society, and for the humbler in the shape of free welfare and a secure job'.

The position lies somewhere between these two extremes. Most historians would agree with Kenneth O. Morgan's conclusion in *Labour and Power* (1984) that the Attlee government was undoubtedly the most

The Labour Cabinet 1945: Prime Minister Clement Attlee is sixth from the left in the front row. On his right is Ernest Bevin and on his left Herbert Morrison (grandfather of Peter Mandelson). On the left hand side of the back row is Aneurin Bevan.

effective of Labour governments and possibly perhaps among the most effective of all British governments.

What were the pressures on the 1945 Labour government?

Governments are subject to pressures and constraints, either of their own making – for example from party members or the resignation of ministers – or due to external forces, such as economic trends or an international incident. The Labour government of 1945 suffered as much as any other.

Internal factors

Clement Attlee was lucky in that the party was generally supportive of his administration. Unlike ministers in the Wilson and Callaghan Cabinets of the 1960s and 1970s, personal relationships were generally good. There was however deep personal animosity between Ernest Bevin and Herbert Morrison. It was once suggested to Bevin that Morrison was his own worst enemy. 'Not while I'm alive, he isn't', Bevin growled.

To an extent this unity was the result of careful party management. As Kenneth O. Morgan in *Labour in Power* argues that 'the Cabinet and leadership were in control at all levels of the party hierarchy'. Complaints from local parties, particularly about Labour's defence and foreign policies and the expulsion of MPs for Communist sympathies, such as Konni Zilliacus and John Platts-Mills, were brushed aside. Indeed these protests only came from a small number of constituencies; most members remained happy with their government's policies and achievements.

Despite some grassroots complaints about wage restraint, the trade unions remained very supportive of the government. The leaders of the big three unions, Arthur Deakin (Transport and General Workers Union), Tom Williamson (General and Municipal Workers Union), and Will Lather (National Union of Mineworkers) were all firmly on the party's right and were aggressively hostile to the left and the Communists. They ensured that the Trades Union Congress (TUC) remained supportive of the government's work.

Only during 1950 and 1951 was there a hint of the divisive left-right split which would so damage the Party in years to come. This mainly centred around the massive rearmament programme proposed by the Chancellor of the Exchequer, Hugh Gaitskell, as a result of the outbreak of the Korean War in June 1950. The programme led to the introduction of prescription charges and other cuts to the welfare state, causing the resignation of three left-wing cabinet ministers Aneurin Bevan, Harold Wilson, and John Freeman in April 1951.

For all its radicalism it should be remembered that the majority of ministers were essentially conservative figures. Paul Addison in *The Road to 1945* (1975) called them 'moderate social patriots'. They had come to political maturity in the inter-war period, and their responses were conditioned by their experiences then. This helps to explain why they were relatively uninterested in constitutional reform or in regenerating British industry, yet keen to maintain Britain's position as a great world power. They preferred to address the very real evils of poverty that they and their constituents had experienced during the 1930s, rather than plan ahead for a post-war world.

In education the ministers responsible, Ellen Wilkinson and George Tomlinson, were happy to accept the arguably socially divisive **tripartite division of secondary education** and resisted demands from teachers and educationalists for comprehensives, which indeed had been party policy since 1942. Instead Wilkinson persuaded the Cabinet to raise the school leaving age to 15 in 1944 and to maintain the expensive programme of rebuilding schools and training new teachers, undoubtedly considerable

---

Ernest Bevin (1881–1951)
A manual worker, Bevin had left school at 11. He became an official of the Dockers' Union. He organised the amalgamation of 18 unions into the Transport and General Workers Union and was its General Secretary, 1921–40. Elected to Parliament for the first time in 1940 he went straight into the Cabinet as Minister of Labour. He was Foreign Secretary from 1945 until a month before his death in 1951.

Harold Wilson (1916–1995)
Wilson was President of the Board of Trade 1947–51 in Attlee's Administration. He was Leader of the Labour Party 1963–76, during which time he served two terms as Prime Minister, 1964–70 and 1974–76.

Tripartite division of secondary education: The Education Act 1944 proposed to divide secondary education into three types of school – grammar (for academically minded children), technical (for the scientifically minded) and secondary modern (for the rest).

achievements at a time of economic difficulty. Kenneth Morgan, however, concludes that 'it is hard to avoid the view that education was an area where the Labour Government failed to provide any new ideas or inspiration'.

Economic circumstances

If Attlee was lucky in having a united party and experienced and disciplined ministers behind him, he was much less lucky with the economic circumstances. The Second World War bankrupted Britain. Victory had been achieved at enormous economic cost. In particular, Britain had become dependent on American loans to keep fighting. Within a week of the surrender of the Japanese in September 1945, the Americans abruptly ended their financial support, thereby destroying British hopes for a lengthy transition from war to peace – and putting the implementation of the policies of the new government in jeopardy. As Lord (John Maynard) Keynes, the government's financial adviser, wrote, Britain was facing an 'economic Dunkirk'. After tough negotiations a further loan of $3.75bn for five years was secured, albeit with many uncomfortable strings attached. Despite these problems the government remained committed to its programme. Hugh Dalton, the Chancellor of the Exchequer, declared in November 1945 that Labour ministers were 'determined to advance along the road to economic and social equality.'

The next economic crisis occurred two years later with a rapidly worsening **balance of payments crisis** and the outflow of British gold reserves. Eventually the introduction of import controls and other tough measures in August 1947 improved matters. Although the crisis was dangerous in the short term, it probably did most harm to the self-confidence of the government and the reputation it had built up for financial management. This reputation was to be tested again in the crisis over the devaluation of the pound sterling: in September 1949 a further 'dollar drain' from Britain forced a 30 per cent devaluation against the dollar from $4.03 to $2.80 to the pound. (The exchange rate in August 1999 was $1.60 to the pound.) This was accompanied by much dithering by ministers. The cumulative effect of these crises was pressure on social spending such as on the National Health Service, and to give credence to the accusations of incompetence levied by the Conservative opposition. However, historians such as Kenneth O. Morgan give credit to devaluation for reinvigorating the economy as devaluation meant that British goods were increasingly competitive in a world slowly recovering from the effects of the war.

Domestic circumstances

By the late 1940s British people were becoming increasingly restive. They had endured nearly a decade of rationing, shortages, and intrusive state control. This feeling is perhaps best summed up by the **Ealing Comedy** *Passport to Pimlico* released in 1949, where a London community discovers itself to be part of Burgundy, thus enabling the residents to free themselves of rationing that 'perfectly caught the public mood'. (The message of the film was, however, that they were better off as part of Britain.)

1946 saw the rise of the British Housewives League campaigning against rationing, which at its peak claimed to have 100,000 members. Although it received much attention in the newspapers the League had little effect on ministers. Indeed the League soon became discredited in the public eye because of suspected links to the Conservative Party.

Knowing the economic knife-edge on which Britain teetered the government reacted cautiously to the new mood. The new President of the Board of Trade, Harold Wilson, announced 'a bonfire of controls' in November 1948 to a broad welcome. During 1949 and 1950 rationing was gradually relaxed. Bread rationing, which had been introduced in May

Hugh Dalton (1887–1962) Dalton joined the war-time coalition as President of the Board of Trade 1942–45. Under the Labour Government he became Chancellor of the Exchequer 1945–47, and was later Minister of Town and Country Planning, 1950–51.

Balance of payments crisis: A situation when a country imports more than it can export thus causing a loss of confidence in its finances by the international markets.

Ealing Comedies: A series of films made at the Ealing Studios between 1948 and 1952. The best known films were *Kind Hearts and Coronets* and *The Man in the White Suit.*

The Festival of Britain, 1951, on the South Bank of the Thames

In what ways was the Festival of Britain similar to the Millennium Dome of 2000?

Festival of Britain: Like the Great Exhibition of 1851, the centenary of which it marked, aimed to show the world British technological and artistic skills.

1946 at the worst time in Britain's economic fortunes, was ended in July 1948. Rationing of clothes finished in March 1949, and a month later saw the freedom to buy sweets and chocolate.

The government also encouraged the **Festival of Britain**, which was held on London's South Bank in 1951 to show how the nation had recovered from the war and was ready to face the challenges of the future. Herbert Morrison sold the idea to the Cabinet by saying 'we ought to do something jolly … we need something to give Britain a lift'. Although ridiculed by the press and the Conservatives it proved immensely popular with the public and had major impact on many fields, especially design, for nearly two decades.

What were the achievements of the Attlee administration?

Despite at times desperate economic circumstances the achievements of the 1945 government are astounding. Apart from the many new initiatives, some of which are discussed below, it should not be forgotten that the government was faced with a shattered economy and in many places a physically shattered environment as well. During the war 750,000 houses were destroyed or damaged as well as hundreds of schools and hospitals. Yet the government set about with a will to repair this damage and to build new homes and schools of a quality better than anything seen before the war. It also successfully achieved the demobilisation of the armed forces and the reintegration of ex-servicemen into the economy. Indeed, the demand for labour was so great that the period saw the first arrivals of migrants from the West Indies to fill vacancies, with the arrival of the *Empire Windrush* from Jamaica in May 1948.

The welfare state
The greatest achievement of Attlee's government was undoubtedly the National Health Service, which offered free health care. Before July 1948, health care had to be paid for by individuals, private insurance or charities. About half the male workforce were entitled to free treatment through

various insurance schemes, although their wives and dependents did not qualify. Many families had no such insurance and in times of illness had to rely for support on friends and neighbours or local charities. Hospitals also varied tremendously. There were few modern hospitals. Most had begun as either Victorian workhouse infirmaries – totally unsuited for the sick – or charity hospitals, which increasingly were unable to meet needs. It was generally agreed, both before and during the war, that health provision was unsatisfactory.

Clement Attlee chose Aneurin Bevan, a leading left-wing rebel who had spent the war years on the backbenches, to be Minister of Health with responsibility for establishing the new health service. Bevan became an exceptional minister, combining considerable charm with a steely determination to succeed. His first act was to take local and charity hospitals into public ownership. This seemed a natural development, because by the end of the war, some 90 per cent of their finance came from the state. Bevan's problems, however, began when he began to establish the new National Health Service. He faced increasing opposition from the British Medical Association, representing doctors who feared that their livelihoods would be threatened by the new system. One doctor wrote in 1946 that 'I have examined the bill and it looks to me uncommonly like the first step, and a big one, towards National Socialism as practised in Germany'. As the start of the new Service approached, the doctors intensified their opposition. Eventually their fears were eased when Bevan agreed that doctors could remain outside the salaried structure of the rest of the Health Service. For the first time everybody was now entitled to free health care.

The new service was rapidly overwhelmed by the demand. The extent of health problems among the population had not been realised. It would soon have very serious consequences because the NHS budget rose from the £134 million predicted for its establishment in 1948 to £228 million in 1949, and £356 million in 1950. With increasing total NHS costs, and other demands on the national budget (such as rearmament) the principle of a free service was breached in 1949 with the introduction of a charge of one shilling (5p) per prescription. Bevan resigned from the Cabinet in 1951 over the principle of cuts to the service he had created, although by then he was no longer Minister of Health. For all the changes since 1948 it remains his memorial because as Kenneth O. Morgan says, it is the finest of monuments to his talents and his beliefs (*Labour in Power*, 1984).

Related to the National Health Service was the establishment of the welfare state to provide support to those who needed it. The minister, James Griffiths, simplified existing provisions, abolished the hated 'means testing' whereby people seeking assistance had to prove their eligibility, and introduced family allowances paying allowances for children to their mothers. The key principle of assistance for people of working age was its universality; as Griffiths later said 'it was to be all in: women from sixteen to sixty and men to sixty-five'. Pensions and allowances were also increased, in some cases for the first time in many years. In 1946 the old age pension for a single person rose to 26s (£1.30) a week, the first increase since 1920 when it had been fixed at 10s (50p).

Housing

Bevan was also responsible for housing policy. It came first among concerns of the British electorate, many of whom could remember the promise made by Lloyd George, the Prime Minister at the end of the First World War, of 'Homes fit for Heroes', which was broken in the inter-war years. This concern was not surprising because not only had some many hundreds of thousands of houses either been destroyed or damaged during the war, but many millions of people lived in slum dwellings without even

Aneurin Bevan (1897–1960)
A miner's son, Bevan was Minister of Health, 1945–51, Minister of Labour 1951. In 1959 he became Deputy Leader of Labour Party and held the post until 1960. He and his wife, Jenny Lee, (also an MP) were considered by some to be the socialist soul of Labour.

basic amenities. A White Paper published in March 1945 estimated that 750,000 new houses would be needed after the war 'to afford a separate dwelling for every family desirous of having one'. During the campaign Ernest Bevin promised 'five million homes in quick time.'

To meet Bevin's target would have required a supply and organisational miracle. Even the White Paper's estimate turned out to be beyond the reach of Attlee's administration. Raw materials were in short supply. The problem was compounded by a bureaucratic nightmare. *Picture Post* magazine in 1946 estimated that it took ten ministries in Whitehall to approve any new building project from the Ministry of Health to the Board of Trade and Ministry of Works.

Two short-term solutions were adopted to cure the housing shortage. The first was the provision of pre-fabricated houses (prefabs). By the end of 1948 nearly 125,000 had been produced largely by aircraft factories as the demand for their usual output eased. The second was squatting. Incited and encouraged by the Communists, the homeless occupied many empty properties, especially army bases. By October 1946 it was estimated that nearly 50,000 people were occupying over a thousand military properties. The authorities generally turned a blind eye, glad to have some kind of safety valve that eased the pressure on housing stock.

New council houses were slowly being built: 55,400 in 1946 rising to 217,000 in 1948. Thereafter there was a slow decline as the economic crisis further affected the provision of raw materials. Even so a million houses were built by 1951, of which four out of five were built by the state. Building private housing almost stopped as priority for scarce resources was given to council houses. Bevan insisted on good quality, well-designed houses, arguing that 'we shall be judged for a year or two by the number of houses we build. We shall be judged in ten years time by the type of house we build'. He increased the space allocated to each family from 750 square feet to 900, with lavatories upstairs as well as down.

Nationalisation

Nationalisation: The taking over and subsequent control of an industry by the state.

Some 20 per cent of British industry, much of it suffering from years of neglect and under-investment, was nationalised (see table 2). Nationalisation of the coal mines had long been a central plank of Labour's programme as the result of pressure from the mining unions, although resolutions in favour of the takeover of other industries by the state was passed at the 1944 party conference despite opposition from the leadership.

Nationalisation, however, has long been proclaimed as being one of the key successes of the Attlee government. Kenneth Morgan in *Labour in Power* argues that nationalisation was essential to sustain the morale and impetus of the 1945 Labour government. To members of the party and the movement nationalisation was the government's ultimate justification. It was a defining moment of the administration when on 1 January 1947, signs appeared outside the mines declaring, 'This colliery is now managed by the National Coal Board on behalf of the people'. In many industries – coal, electricity, gas and the railways – it made sense to establish a national monopoly rather than the patchwork of municipal and private companies that had existed before the war. Some industries, particularly coal and the railways, had suffered decades of poor management and bad labour relations. Only the nationalisation of the iron and steel industry provoked much opposition.

Yet looking at the subsequent history of these industries it is easy to query the reasons behind nationalisation. The government was often uncertain about what the nationalised industries should do, except to act as non-profit-making utilities. It was hoped that nationalisation would

Table 2 Nationalisation measures 1945–1951

Industry	2nd reading of bill	Vesting day	Numbers employed
Bank of England	29 October 1945	1 March 1946	6,700
Coal	29 January 1946	1 January 1947	765,000
Civil aviation	6 May 1946	1 August 1946	23,300
Cable and Wireless (telecommunications)	21 May 1945	1 January 1947	9,500
Transport (railways, canals, road haulage)	16 December 1946	1 January 1948	888,000
Electricity	3 February 1947	1 April 1948	176,000
Gas	10 February 1948	1 April 1949	143,500
Iron and steel	15 November 1948	15 February 1951	292,000

Source: Kevin Jeffrey, *The Attlee Government*, 1992.

encourage efficiency and investment as well as improve working conditions. Critics, such as Correlli Barnett in *The Lost Victory* (1995), have claimed that 'nationalisation turned out in all respects to be not so much a revolution as a prolonging of the *ancien regime* by bureaucratic means'.

In certain cases, particularly with the mines and railway, nationalisation was probably the only solution to the otherwise certain collapse of these industries. The record of the nationalised industries proved to be patchy, but most turned out to be competently if conservatively run.

What were the failures of the 1945 Labour government?

Certainly the 1945 'revolution' was curiously patchy, reflecting the interests of the Cabinet and to a lesser degree the wider party. In nationalising the mines, railways and other industries, the government was generally content to leave the existing managers in charge, and resisted attempts to appoint representatives of the workforce to their boards. Attempts to plan the economy were less than successful, and this from a party that had proclaimed the benefits of planning before the outbreak of the Second World War. This anomaly may be due in part to the fact that very little work had been done on the practicalities of actually implementing these measures. Planning was virtually still-born, as ministers and their advisers adopted a voluntary approach towards industry, which had been commonplace during the war, encouraging rather than directing effort.

In foreign and defence policy the Attlee administration was also very conservative. In this they received considerable criticism from the Labour Party and backbench MPs. Attlee and his ministers had grown up at a time when the British Empire was at its height. One of his colleagues described Ernest Bevin, the Foreign Secretary, as a man who 'at heart was an old-fashioned imperialist keener to expand than contract the Empire'. The departure from the Indian sub-continent, although often portrayed as a great triumph, actually came about as ministers realised that British forces could no longer control mounting communal strife, which indeed occurred with great ferocity in the months after the granting of independence to India and Pakistan in August 1947.

Closer to home the need to remain a great power distorted economic recovery. This desire persuaded the government in 1946 to build the atomic bomb. At the Cabinet meeting that decided to proceed with the development of the new weapon, Bevin exclaimed, 'we've got to have this thing over here, what ever it costs … We've got to have a bloody Union Jack flying on the top of it.' The financial crisis of 1947, caused largely by a drain on Britain's financial reserves, was in part due to the burden of a world role that in the view of many observers 'obviously exceeded the country's economic capacity'. Four years later the ambitious rearmament programme, designed to help the United Nations in Korea, derailed Britain's economic recovery, at the very time when the Germany and Japan were successfully rebuilding theirs. According to Kenneth O. Morgan the budget of April 1951, which announced this plan, was a political and economic disaster (Labour in Power, 1984). The Conservatives had to scale down the rearmament programme once they took power in October 1951 for they could see the danger it was doing to the economy.

Conclusion

There is no doubt that Attlee's administration was one of the great reforming administrations of the 20th century. It succeeded despite tremendous economic problems and an increasingly fraught international situation, not forgetting the frailties of the members of the government themselves.

The 1945 Labour government was effective in three important ways. Firstly, in contrast to Lloyd George and the Conservative administration between 1918 and 1922, it successfully saw the return of the nation to a peacetime economy with no dislocation of industry or mass unemploy-ment. Secondly, it achieved a transformation of British society which improved the lives of millions of people, male and female, young and old. For the first time the uncertainties caused by unemployment and serious illness were banished by the welfare state, and a start was made in providing decent housing and education for everyone. Thirdly, and perhaps most importantly, many of the policy assumptions, particularly the central importance of the mixed economy, containing both state controlled and privately-owned industries, and the need to maintain the welfare state and the National Health Service, were wholeheartedly adopted by politicians of all parties. Certainly Winston Churchill's incoming Conservative government in October 1951 made no attempt to reverse any of the achievements of the previous administration. With the exception of the return to the private sector of the iron and steel industry, the nationalisation of which in February 1951 had been widely opposed even within the Labour Party, they left well alone.

This 'post-war consensus' built around a shared belief in Keynesian economics, the welfare state and the mixed economy would remain until the economic difficulties of the mid-1970s forced the rethinking of ever-increasing state spending. However, it took the election of Margaret Thatcher in 1979 to rigorously challenge these beliefs by privatising the nationalised industries and shaking up the National Health Service. Even today no politician could seriously call for the National Health Service to be broken up and welfare provisions to be totally abandoned.

1. What do you think the greatest achievement of the Attlee administration was? Explain whether you think the government was successful and why.

2. What constraints were there on Attlee's government? Of these which do you think was the most important?

12.3 What caused a 'cold war' to develop after 1945?
A CASE STUDY IN HISTORICAL INTERPRETATION

The historiography of international relations in the post-war period has been largely preoccupied with the policies of the Three Big Allies towards each other. Historians have been predominantly concerned with a number of political developments, mostly in Europe, trying to assess their impor-tance in the origins of the Cold War. Two schools of thought – traditionalist and revisionist – initially offered opposing views of the causes and nature of the controversy. The former developed after the Second World War and entirely blamed the Soviet Union, which was intent on world domination and motivated by its militant Marxist-Leninist ideology. Soviet behaviour in eastern Europe and the Middle East was given as evidence. This aggressive conduct was variously explained by traditional Russian strategy, the nature of the Communist regime and even Stalin's personality. The traditionalists believed that Britain and the United States only reluctantly conceded Soviet domination over eastern Europe because they recognised their own inability to prevent such a development. The West was credited with continuing to uphold the values of democracy and human rights as outlined in the Atlantic Charter and the Yalta Declaration, even after Western recognition had been granted to the Communist governments.

The revisionists who advanced their theories in the period after the Vietnam War argue that the Soviet Union had a legitimate right to dominate the countries lying to its west. They pointed out two precedents – at the end of the war Britain and the United States did not allow equal Soviet participation in the administration of Italy, and the two also insisted on exclusive control over Japan. The revisionists also argued that the tensions between the two Western Allies and the USSR were made worse by actions such as issuing the Truman Doctrine and the Marshall Plan. These were seen not only to have condemned Soviet behaviour in eastern Europe but also to have been correctly understood by the Soviet leadership as part of a campaign to force the Soviet Union out of eastern Europe.

A later trend in historiography, called 'post-revisionism', challenged both traditionalists and revisionists. It tried to introduce new sources as well as new ideas, mainly the theory of mutual misunderstanding and misconception of each other's objectives. Influential works in this category are those of Vojtech Mastny who discussed Soviet foreign policy during 1941–47 in terms of 'the intricate relationship among Moscow's military strategy, diplomacy and management of international Communism'.

Post-Communist Russian scholars attempting to analyse newly-available documents have interestingly had the same debate. Some come to the conclusion that senior Russian diplomats were guided mostly by geo-strategic considerations rather than desire for communisation of Europe. Others claim that careful examination of the interaction between the ideas of world Communism and Russian imperialism reveals that the two were not necessarily contradictory; in fact it is even possible to perceive them as complementing each other.

As the bulk of historical literature on the Cold War originated from the United States it dealt mainly with the Soviet-US controversy and treated Britain as the junior partner in the Atlantic relationship. Such a view was reiterated by the British historian Elisabeth Barker who in *The British between the Superpowers, 1945–50* (1983) described Britain's position 'between the superpowers' as being motivated by a growing concern for its own weakness and acknowledgement of its limited ability to influence world events and pursue independent policy. In contrast, Anne Deighton in *The Impossible Peace* (1993) traced the roots of British post-war diplomacy back to the patterns of wartime thinking and planning. She claimed that it was vital for the interpretation of British policy to understand that Britain regarded itself as a Great Power able to determine the course of events in Europe. Above all Britain justified its right to do so not by its military or economic strength, but because of its expertise in international affairs.

1. What different interpretations explaining the start of the Cold War have been made by historians?

2. Explain why historians have differed in their views.

12.4 How did British foreign policy re-adjust to the political and military realities after the Second World War?

Mandate: Right or authority given to carry out specific policies.

In July 1945, even before the hostilities in Asia had ended, a general election took place in Great Britain. Returning a Labour majority to the House of Commons, the British public demonstrated a significant swing to the left that became characteristic across Europe. After the deprivations of the war, the Labour Party received an unequivocal **mandate** for a speedy economic reconstruction and above all for a welfare-oriented domestic policy. This caused both domestic and foreign observers to wonder whether the new government might not also follow a socialist foreign policy in tune with its welfare and nationalisation programmes. Stalin was shocked by the British electoral result when Churchill had to step down in the middle of the Potsdam conference of Allied leaders (17 July – 2 August 1945).

Stalin, however, could confirm his distrust of any kind of socialists as both Britain's new Prime Minister Clement Attlee and Foreign Secretary Ernest Bevin were strong opponents of communism. Bevin especially had fought the communists who had tried to overtake the Labour-dominated trade unions and was suspicious of communist methods in international affairs. Both Labour leaders had been members of the wartime National Government and were aware of the tensions rising among the Allies towards the end of the Second World War. They were convinced that Britain should preserve its Empire and the Great Power status associated with it. This belief continued to be the underpinning principle of British foreign policy.

Britain faced a number of problems as a result of the Second World War, most notably economic ones. Even though the country's share in world trade had been continuously declining since the end of the 19th century, the 30 per cent decline in the value of exports between 1938 and 1945 was unprecedented. Almost all foreign assets held in Britain by private individuals and companies had been sold off to finance the war. A debt of £365 million was owed to the Empire for materials supplied in the course of the war but it was small in comparison to the £31 billion Britain owed the United States for deliveries under the Lend-Lease agreement. Combined with the huge domestic spending necessary for the implementation of the welfare reforms all this precipitated a severe **balance of payments crisis** throughout the later 1940s.

Balance of payments crisis: When the money earned from exports is less than the money spent on imports a country has a balance of payments deficit. The size or continuation of the deficit can cause a crisis.

Demobilisation: Returning soldiers to civilian status.

This situation added to the pressures for rapid **demobilisation**. Indeed, between 1945 and 1948 the number of armed forces was cut fivefold to under 1 million. The level was well above that of the inter-war period but it had to be kept up as British troops were stationed in over 40 countries across the world. To maintain the size of the army in April 1947 the Labour government introduced 12-month national service; its length was extended to 18 months in 1948 and to two years in 1950.

Why did Britain and the Soviet Union clash over Eastern Europe?

Big Three: Winston Churchill representing the British Empire, Josef Stalin representing the U.S.S.R. and F. D.Roosevelt representing the U.S.A.

Britain's wartime dealings with either of its Allies had not been easy. Relations with the Soviet Union had never approached cordiality and there had been a lack of co-operation on anything but military matters. When as early as 1942–43 various British government departments had begun planning for the post-war reconstruction of the world, they had become deeply aware of the need to take into account the global interests of the Soviet Union. Some progress had been made at the **Big Three** conferences at Tehran, Yalta and Potsdam as well as at high-level Anglo-Soviet meetings, notably the one between Churchill and Stalin in Moscow in October 1944.

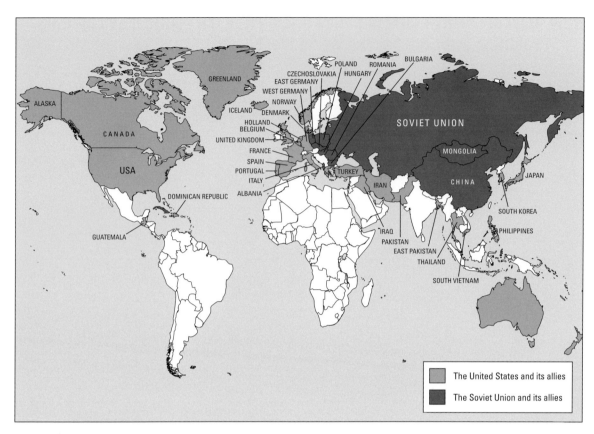

The world during the Cold War.

How does this show how the world was divided by the Cold War?

However, after the defeat of Germany, there remained a number of outstanding political questions with Soviet Russia. To those were added new spheres of friction, springing mainly from the Soviet Union's behaviour in its zones of occupation in Europe.

At Yalta (4–11 February 1945) the Allies had signed a joint declaration calling for the establishment of broadly representative governments and the conduct of free elections in all of Germany's ex-satellites. However, at the very moment he was assuring the West of his democratic intentions, Stalin was working towards the elimination of democracy in eastern Europe. One instrument for this was the Allied Control Commissions (ACC) set up to oversee the implementation of armistice terms with Bulgaria, Romania and Hungary: they were headed by high-rank Soviet commanders and used for the promotion of Soviet interests.

Throughout the war Stalin had emphasised the need for the Soviet Union to increase its security through the establishment of friendly governments in the countries along its western borders. The United States and Great Britain recognised this as a legitimate demand. They were prepared to accept an increased degree of Soviet influence over the external relations of its immediate European neighbours but did not consider this incompatible with the application of democratic principles in domestic politics. In contrast, in the view of the Soviet regime security could only result from the establishment of governments that shared its own ideological outlook. In consequence, the Soviet authorities backed the efforts of the local communist parties to secure a leading position in government. Across Eastern Europe, Communists had gained popularity due to their anti-German resistance but nowhere did they hold a parliamentary majority and so had to participate in coalition governments. In direct communication with the Central Committee of the Soviet Communist Party, east European communists used a range of violent methods to gain dominance over the other political parties and gradually eliminate them from effective government.

With practically no troops in the region the British government was reduced to watching its worst fears for eastern Europe coming true. In 1945–47 the communists were continuously strengthening their hold over such institutions as the army, the police and the justice system. Already in February 1945, a pro-Soviet **coup d'état** was carried out in Romania and in July 1945 a communist-dominated Soviet-backed government was installed in Poland with British and US recognition. The Polish question had been the subject of prolonged controversies between Stalin and Churchill, even though the latter was careful not to jeopardise Soviet-British relations during the war.

Coup d'état: An abrupt change of leadership or government, often violent or illegal.

The fact that Britain could not stand up to the Soviet Union, even when its traditional allies were involved, demonstrated Britain's declining influence in East European affairs. This was even more clearly shown by Britain's inability to secure the formation of at least broadly representative governments in the former German ex-satellites. In September 1945, Soviet Foreign Minister Molotov went as far as to insist that the Soviet Union had the right to determine unilaterally the political complexion of the post-war governments in Eastern Europe. In Britain's understanding this was a clear breach of the terms of the Yalta Declaration. However, Britain soon realised that any argument on the subject would not change the situation while also straining further overall Anglo-Soviet relations. That is why after the conclusion of the Peace Treaties in 1947, the Labour government chose to recognise the communist regimes in eastern Europe, which effectively meant that Britain was resigned to Soviet dominance in the region.

What was the nature of the Soviet threat?

From the British perspective, the consolidation of Communist power transformed eastern Europe into a Soviet stronghold, which could be used as a springboard for the extension of Soviet influence in the adjoining areas. This raised suspicions as to how far Soviet actions were due to genuine security considerations or by traditional Great Power demands for domination over foreign territories. After 1945, both opinions had supporters in the Foreign Office. Increasingly however, British foreign policy experts subscribed to the view that the Soviet Union was intent on using its strategic gains for the spread of Communism world-wide.

Proof was easily found in Soviet behaviour in the Middle East and the Eastern Mediterranean, both areas of long-term British concern. At the beginning of 1946 Soviet forces were deliberately protracting their withdrawal from the Azerbeijani province of Eastern Persia. After Persia presented the issue for discussion in the first United Nations General Assembly, Soviet troops were finally evacuated in May 1946 but the incident loomed big in British perceptions, not least because of similar Soviet actions in Greece. In that country, historically associated with British influence in the Balkans, elections had been carried out under British supervision in March 1946. The electoral success of the right-wing Populist Party spurred insurgence from Communist-led forces. As in October 1944 Churchill had obtained an undertaking from Stalin not to meddle in Greece, the Soviet Union had no direct involvement in the Greek Civil War. Nevertheless, the Soviet Union continued to voice public criticism of Britain's handling of Greek affairs and even raised the question in the United Nations General Assembly in a move mirroring that regarding Persia. Archival evidence has shown that Stalin had little hope in the victory of the Greek Communists and was therefore reluctant to associate with them.

Simultaneously, just as during the war, the Soviet Union was exerting pressure on Turkey throughout 1945. Soviet demands focused on a revision of the existing friendship treaty between the two countries that would have given the Soviet Union increased influence over the regime of the Straits not only in war but also in peacetime. When Turkey refused, the Soviet Union denounced the treaty and even prepared to invade the country but was dissuaded by the British and US support for Turkey. The Soviet move could be interpreted as nothing but a clear challenge of Britain's strategic interests. This impression was confirmed by a number of subsequent Soviet actions affecting the Eastern Mediterranean such as a demand for a share of Italy's North African territories.

How did Britain react to the Soviet challenge?

Even before the end of the Second World War the British government had realised that it had very limited means with which to counteract growing Soviet domination in Eastern Europe. Therefore, despite frequent public protests to the violent methods of the Soviet-sponsored East European Communists, the Labour government chose not to clash directly with Russia on account of the political developments in the region.

On 6 February 1946 Stalin seemed consciously to exacerbate tensions by declaring at an election rally that capitalism and communism were incompatible and therefore war between the supporters of these doctrines was inevitable. Churchill responded in his speech delivered on 5 March 1946 in Fulton, Missouri, USA, warning that 'an iron curtain' divided the European continent. Churchill's opinion was only that of the leader of the British Opposition. However, as nothing was done in London to refute Churchill's accusations against the Soviet Union, Stalin had to believe them to be also representative of British official views.

In the meantime, the British government continued to support the anti-Communist forces in Greece with measures such as the financial maintenance of the Greek Army. However, Chancellor Hugh Dalton demanded that this stop by March 1947 in view of the deteriorating economic situation at home. In the midst of an extraordinarily severe winter, the British government decided to reduce its imperial and foreign commitments, which were a drain on its limited resources. One consequence was that on 21 February 1947 the British government informed the US Department of State that British aid to Greece and Turkey would end in six weeks.

In 1945–46, the American government had itself increasingly recognised the danger to democracy and capitalist economies from the Soviet Union. However, the American demand for quick demobilisation and gradual disengagement from European affairs created uncertainty as to how far the United States would be willing to support Britain in its deepening conflict with Soviet Russia. This was all the more true for areas of traditional British strategic involvement. On the other hand, Soviet actions in eastern Europe combined with the continuing Soviet pressure in the Middle East had led a number of US diplomatic and military officers to express growing fear of the spread of communism. The announcement of Britain's ending of responsibilities alerted the American administration to the need to contain the Soviet Union within its present zone of influence. As a result, on 12 March 1947 President Truman asked the US Congress to approve $400 million in aid to Greece and Turkey and thus 'support free peoples who are resisting attempted **subjugation** by armed minorities or by outside pressures'.

Subjugation: To place under the control of someone.

What was Britain's role in the division of Germany?

Germany was another area where a major confrontation between the Soviet Union and the western Allies occurred in 1947–48. At the Potsdam Conference (17 July – 2 August 1945) the Allies had decided to share the burden of administering Germany after the war and so each of them as well as France had a separate zone of occupation. It was agreed that food deliveries would be made to the western zones from the predominantly agrarian Soviet zone in exchange for industrial goods. The Western Allies had also agreed to reduce the production levels of German industry.

Soviet policy was to extract as much reparations as possible from Germany as compensation for the huge Soviet wartime material losses. Such an approach, although also aiming at reducing Germany's long-term war potential, had the immediate effect of total disruption of what was left of the economy after the devastation of the war. Britain occupied the Ruhr which was the worst damaged part: its maintenance cost the British budget around £120 million in 1946. However reluctantly, Britain and the United States agreed that they should reintegrate their zones and encourage the regeneration of German industry so that Germany could at least partially pay for its needs. On 1 January 1947 the British and American zones were merged into what became known as bi-zonia and later in the year the French zone was added.

The Soviet Union did not approve and accused the West of not honouring its obligations for the treatment of defeated Germany. Moreover, Soviet actions in the eastern part of Germany aimed at securing a dominating role for the communists: clearly Stalin intended to follow the pattern of political developments in Eastern Europe and transform the country into another **Soviet client**.

Soviet client: A country under the influence of the USSR, e.g. East Germany or Poland.

The stalemate over Germany's settlement was a major impetus for the declaration of American economic aid to Europe by American Secretary of State General George Marshall on 5 June 1947. This became known as the 'Marshall Plan'. For Ernest Bevin this was 'like a life-line to a sinking man' and within days he had managed to co-ordinate the positive West European response to the US offer. This however accelerated problems with the Soviet Union, which after some initial hesitation decided against participation in the European recovery programme and also imposed the withdrawal from it of the eastern European countries. Eventually, when the scheme began to function in the spring of 1948, Britain received the largest single share, $3.2 billion, of the $12 billion allocated to Europe by the US Congress.

Throughout 1947 and the first half of 1948, the Soviet Union and the western Allies had continued to work at cross purposes in Germany. Each side was supervising the economy and making separate preparations for the establishment of German government while claiming to be following previous wartime agreements. On 18 June 1948 as a step towards the reconstruction of Germany a new currency was introduced in the Western zone; within four days the Soviet authorities introduced their own new German currency. Next, the Russian troops blocked land access to Berlin (itself deeply into the Soviet zone). Realising that the abandonment of West Berlin would have deep political and psychological consequences, without much initial expectation Britain and the United States hastily organised an airlift of essential supplies. It lasted until 12 May 1949 when both sides lifted the blockade.

How did the European and Atlantic circles of British policy interact?

In the final stages of the Second World War, the British Chiefs of Staff had concluded that, although not in the position to begin an immediate war,

Cominform: The Communist Bureau of Information which existed between 1947 and 1956. In addition to the Soviet Communist Party it included the Communist Parties of the USSR's Eastern European satellites except Albania and those of Italy and France. Yugoslavia was expelled in 1948. This was an instrument for the co-ordination of the domestic and foreign activities of the members and for their subjugation to Stalin's interests.

Soviet Russia was the only potential military threat for Britain. Initially this belief had not been fully shared by the Foreign Office, which worried that if the view became known to Stalin this in itself would precipitate hostility. By April 1946 the Foreign Office was convinced that the Soviet Union sought domination of Europe and would put pressure on Western governments, not least through the strong West European Communist parties. This view was sealed by every next Soviet move – the formation of the **Cominform** in September 1947, the Communist coup in Czechoslovakia in February 1948 and the events in Germany later that year.

As it had become increasingly clearer that the post-war world order would not be based on co-operation among the wartime Allies, Britain explored alternative principles for its security. One possibility was to work closer with the West European states, which in the event of Soviet aggression would provide the first line of defence. Another option would be to co-ordinate strategy primarily with the United States, which was the only power capable of facing the Soviet Union on equal terms. In the immediate post-war period the British government had some doubts about the depth of the American commitment to Europe. After the Truman Doctrine and the Marshall Plan, it became more evident that the two circles of British foreign and defence policy – the European and the Atlantic one – were not mutually exclusive. On the contrary, they influenced each other.

In March 1947 Britain signed the Dunkirk Treaty with France: the two countries pledged mutual assistance against Germany and also economic co-operation. After this Bevin continued to seek closer links between the European countries and in March 1948 Britain, France and the Benelux countries signed the Brussels Treaty committing themselves for fifty years to collective defence against any attack. Britain was convinced that the western European countries' initiative to provide for resistance to a possible Soviet attack could only be successful if underwritten by the United States. Days before the conclusion of the Brussels Treaty the US administration began negotiations with a view to placing US involvement in Europe into a definite military and political framework. The United States' growing conviction that its own interest lay in the provision of material support for any regional security organisation in the West which sought to oppose Communism culminated in the conclusion of the North Atlantic Treaty in April 1949. The new alliance, which also included the United States and Canada provided the foundation for British defence policy for the larger part of the next half a century.

British-American post-war relations were already following a particular direction before the formation of NATO. In the economic sphere they had been coloured by the abrupt termination of Lend-Lease in September 1945. However, the US government decided to demand the repayment of only about one-fiftieth of the full amount (£650 million out of £31 billion).

More controversy was caused by the US McMahon Act of August 1946 which put an end to collaboration with Britain on atomic research and development. This was a severe blow to Britain: the atomic bomb had been developed during the war as an Anglo-American project and agreement for consultation and full collaboration had been secured from both Roosevelt and Truman. After the atomic bomb had been used against Japan in August 1945, the very idea of a Great Power was inextricably bound with the possession of nuclear weapons. Immediately after the war, despite its grave economic difficulties, Britain had not lost its self-perception as a world power that had the right to a say in almost every corner of the world. Moreover, unlike the United States, Britain lay within range of Soviet bombers and this was probably the crucial factor that precipitated Britain's decision in January 1947 to develop its own bomb. The necessity for this could only be confirmed when in August 1949 the Soviet Union performed its first successful atomic explosion.

What were the causes and consequences of Britain's involvement in the Korean War?

The emphasis Britain laid on the US guarantee for the security of Europe presupposed some co-ordination on issues outside that continent. Indeed, the United States retained a generally negative attitude to Britain's ambitions to keep the Empire. In the later 1940s the doctrine of **containment** meant high level of overseas involvement by the United States and its allies. Therefore the United States agreed that Middle East was important. Britain's imperial decline should not allow its former possessions to be infiltrated by Communism: moreover, through its network of military bases from North Africa to Iraq Britain was capable of launching long-range bomb attacks on Eastern Europe and the Soviet Union itself.

Containment: A policy aiming to prevent the expansion of Communism and therefore keep Soviet influence within its current boundaries.

In contrast to this understanding was the disagreement on the treatment of China after Mao's communist victory in October 1949. The United States, following a rigid policy of anti-communism refused early diplomatic recognition of the new regime. The British Foreign Office was prepared to shelve its ideological beliefs in the name of good trade with China and also for the benefit of the British colony of Hong Kong. British attitude was additionally shaped by the consideration that normal relations with China could to a degree counter Russian influence there and therefore hinder the enlargement of the Soviet bloc. In January 1950 Britain officially recognised China.

The British-US relationship was finally tested in the Korean conflict of 1950–51. In 1945 Korea had been divided along the 38th parallel where American and Soviet forces had met at the end of the war. In the course of 1949 both the Soviet and the US occupying armies withdrew although the border situation was steadily deteriorating. Additionally, while US attention was preoccupied with developments in Europe and elsewhere in the Far East, in the beginning of 1950 both President Truman and Secretary of State Dean Acheson made speeches implying that South Korea was not included in the American defence perimeter. On 25 June 1950 with Stalin's sanction North Korea invaded the South. South Korea appealed to the UN Security Council. As this body was at the time boycotted by the Soviet Union, American troops were sent in support of the South under UN supervision. Fighting went on for a year and the **38th parallel** was twice crossed first by American and then by Chinese troops, which had entered the war on the side of the North. Although the Soviet Union had not got involved in direct action, it was actively supporting North Korea in the UN Security Council. Although fighting ended in 1951 an armistice was only reached on 27 July 1953.

38th parallel: The political border between North and South Korea.

Western governments believed that the conflict had been started by the Soviet Union and demonstrated Soviet aggressiveness and intention to uproot democratic influences from Asia. Thus, the Korean war assumed the proportions of a clash between communism and liberalism on a global level. In July 1950, British ground and naval troops were sent to Korea. By January 1951 these were more than 10,000-strong, the largest non-American element in the UN force. If Britain strove for continued US involvement in Europe it too had to back the United States in those parts of the world that mattered to the latter. Finally, the British government reasoned that its own participation would have a restraining influence on the United States. Indeed, when in October 1950 the Chinese army overran South Korea, there was a widespread fear that the United States was about to order a nuclear attack. Attlee visited Washington and received a reassurance from Truman that this would not be done without prior consultation with Britain.

The Korean war started the Labour government's plans for massive rearmament which were announced in early 1951. The Chiefs of Staff made the grim prediction of war with the Soviet Union in 1952 or even in 1951. For the first time since the end of the Second World War the total numbers of the armed forces rose. The cost of defence also increased as there was renewed emphasis on research and development, especially in air defence and anti-submarine combat. As a result, defence spending, which had constituted 8 per cent of GDP in 1950, rose to 14 per cent in 1951. This became one of a number of factors that brought a balance of payments crisis.

1. How did the Cold War develop in the years 1945 to 1953?

2. Explain how the growth and development of the Cold War affected British foreign and defence policy.

12.5 How did the Second World War affect Britain's imperial policy?

Closed economy: The deliberate protection of trade through taxation.

Free trade: A system that encourages the free flow of imports and exports.

Freely convertible: Allowing one currency to be traded for another without restrictions.

During the Second World War, it seemed possible that Britain might emerge with a much-reduced Empire. Burma, Singapore, Hong Kong and Malaya were all occupied by the Japanese in 1942, and although one of Britain's war aims was the preservation of Empire, both its principal allies, the United States and the Soviet Union, were, in principle, opposed to colonialism. The United States periodically suggested that British colonies, especially in Asia, should be placed under international control prior to independence, and was keen that the **closed imperial economy** should be opened up to **free world trade**. President Roosevelt was a committed anti-colonialist. In fact, all Britain's colonies were restored at the end of the war, and although Britain then withdrew from India and Ceylon (Sri Lanka), this was done to improve the running of the Empire as a whole and not to abandon it.

Clinging on to the Empire was intended to support both the British economy and its influence abroad, resisting American attempts to redefine Britain as a European power only. The costs of the war had left Britain dependent on loans from the United States; by the end it was overspending by £2,000 million each year and exports had lost two-thirds of their value. An American loan of $3.75 billion was made in 1945 on condition that sterling became **freely convertible** with dollars in July 1947, which would open up imperial markets to the United States. The formation of the United Nations, although Britain was a member of the security council, reflected the new situation in which the United States and the Soviet Union were the main players in world politics. Both these countries were officially opposed to colonialism.

The postwar Labour government remained committed to the Empire – in 1948 the Prime Minister, Clement Attlee, said to the House of Commons that Britain was 'not solely a European power but a member of a great Commonwealth and Empire'. Ernest Bevin, the Foreign Secretary, said in October that year, 'if we only pushed on and developed Africa, we could have the United States dependent on us and eating out of our hands in four or five years'. They saw Britain as offering a middle way between the American capitalism and Soviet communism, which were both disliked by the Labour Party. The desire to keep Britain's importance in the world is underlined by the decision in 1947 to build an independent nuclear deterrent. The development of nuclear weapons, however, was leading to a world in which possessing an empire was not the way to military greatness. This is underlined by the way that when the Soviet Union was ready to test an atomic bomb in 1949, the importance of the relationship with the United States was stressed again, and the North Atlantic Treaty Organisation was formed, linking the United States permanently with Europe.

Events in Palestine demonstrate how important US influence had become. The British, running Palestine under the UN's mandate, wanted to restrict Jewish immigration to 1,500 people a month, in order not to alienate the Arab population, thus threatening Britain's role elsewhere in the Middle East. But the Americans, responding to a strong Jewish lobby at home, suggested initially that 100,000 Jews be allowed into Palestine and then went further in support of the **Zionists**. An Anglo-American Committee of Inquiry failed to produce a solution acceptable to either Jews or Arabs, and a UN Special Committee recommended partition. In mid-1948, Britain left Palestine rather than be involved in putting the UN plan into practice; this departure was followed by the war which led to the establishment of the Jewish nation-state, Israel.

The development of the Commonwealth was one way of achieving continued British influence. Colonial policy had been redefined during the war, partly in response to American pressure, and the Colonial Office now began to talk of developing colonies' self-governing potential and guiding them along the way to independence. After independence, however, the idea was that the former colonies should join the Commonwealth and continue to co-operate with Britain in the **sterling area** and in defence.

Originally the Commonwealth (then 'the British Commonwealth') had been restricted to the 'white' Dominions – Australia, New Zealand, Canada, South Africa and the Irish Free State (Eire). These recognised the King as the head of the Commonwealth (though Eire did so only as a convenience and left the Commonwealth altogether in 1949). All except Eire fought with Britain in the Second World War. After the war the Commonwealth came to be seen as a way to set up a flexible, multi-racial community through which Britain would exercise influence. For Britain to build up a 'third force' in the world, separate from the Soviet Union and the United States, the Commonwealth needed to be as large and inclusive as possible. This meant India and Pakistan must be part of it, and since India wanted to become a republic, the Commonwealth was changed with the 1949 London Declaration to allow both Crown Dominions, which had the British monarch as their head of state, and Republican Dominions, which did not. The monarch remained the overall head of the Commonwealth. As described in a Colonial Office paper of 1950 the aim was for the new Commonwealth to be a 'circle of democratic nations exerting a powerful stabilising influence in the world'.

Within the colonies, the aim was 'to guide the colonial territories to responsible self-government within the Commonwealth in conditions that ensure to the people both a fair standard of living and freedom from oppression from any quarter' (a Colonial Office paper, May 1950). In 1946 the head of the Africa Division in the Colonial Office proposed a local government policy that would eventually transfer power to Africans, increasing democracy and bringing 'literates and illiterates together, in balanced and studied proportions, for the management of local finances and services. Failing this we shall find the masses apt to follow the leadership of **demagogues** who want to turn us right out very quickly.'

Although the United States was officially opposed to colonialism, for both ethical and economic reasons, the development of the Cold War meant it was more worried about containing Soviet influence. Protectionist policies, such as the sterling area, were accepted because they could speed European recovery, and in a healthy economy communist parties had less influence. The American military were also anxious that British withdrawal from colonies would create instability and leave those countries open to Soviet influence. As the Cold War spread to Asia, with communist China intervening in Korea in 1950, Malaya became a frontline state. The British army went in to fight during the 'Emergency' caused by a communist insurrection,

Zionists: Supporters of the creation of an independent Jewish state called Israel.

Sterling area: The group of countries that held the pound sterling as their reserve currency after the war.

Demagogue: A charismatic and authoritarian leader.

believed to be backed by the Soviet Union and China. Elsewhere, the United States and Britain co-operated in the 1953 coup in Iran that restored the Shah to power. US influence in the Middle East was increasing, but it was not particularly interested in Africa. The Bureau of African Affairs was not set up at the State Department until 1958. By the time US loans and grants were being made to African countries, British decisions on decolonisation had already been made. Nevertheless, the possibility of American intervention in colonial affairs was one of the reasons for modernising and democratising colonial government.

The British attempted to nurture moderates and create **elites** within the colonies who would work to modernise them, co-operating with the British and acting against communism. These elites would be made up of the Western-educated middle class who would, according to the plan, become involved first in local government, gradually moving towards self-government modelled on the Westminster Parliament. This was what they had attempted to do in India, where their efforts were upset by the Second World War, but they were more successful in some of the African colonies.

Such change had to happen, partly to avoid international pressure for change, partly in order to promote social and economic development, partly in response to nationalist aims stimulated by the war and partly to block Soviet imperialism. Pressure from within the colonies could produce surprisingly quick effects; in 1948 there were riots on the Gold Coast, and by 1950 there was a new constitution, guaranteeing an African majority in the legislative council. Where there was no significant group of white settlers, it was much easier to set up this system successfully.

Elites: Ruling groups or classes.

1. How did Britain attempt to restructure the Empire after 1945 and why?

2. How did the Cold War affect British colonial policy?

12.6 Why did Britain have to leave India in 1947?

The simple answer is that the Indians had been promised self-rule when the war ended. This had long been an aim – the 1935 Government of India Act had promised eventual self-government for India as a Dominion, and the new constitution, introduced in 1937, allowed the Indian National Congress, the main nationalist party (and mainly Hindu), to take control of most of the Indian provinces. Defence and foreign policies were still controlled by the Viceroy on Britain's behalf, and the army and police were still under British command.

The British government thought that India could be given self-rule as a united country, still relying on British defence co-operation and with many Britons still working there. Defence was a key issue. The Indian Army, with mainly British officers, could mobilise as many troops as the British Army and had been stationed throughout the Empire, defending the whole – so once war was declared India was vital to the British effort. After the humiliating fall of Singapore, Malaya, Hong Kong and Burma to the Japanese in early 1942, India, along with Australia, was very vulnerable to Japanese attack. At the same time the political handling of the war exposed the limits of what Britain had granted. Britain declared war with Germany on India's behalf, and the Congress Party ministers all resigned over this action being taken without consulting the wishes of the Indians. The subsequent mobilisation, shortages, inflation and disruption of trade, as well as British defeats, meant the government became more and more unpopular. Attempts to gain co-operation from Congress in 1942 failed, despite the promise of self-government immediately the war was over and instead the **Quit India** movement was started. However, the Muslim League, committed to a separate Muslim state since 1940, did work with the British government, and so became more important in Indian politics – making partition more likely.

Quit India: Led by Gandhi, this campaign of civil disruption began in 1942, and was suppressed by the British. All the Congress leaders were jailed for the rest of the war.

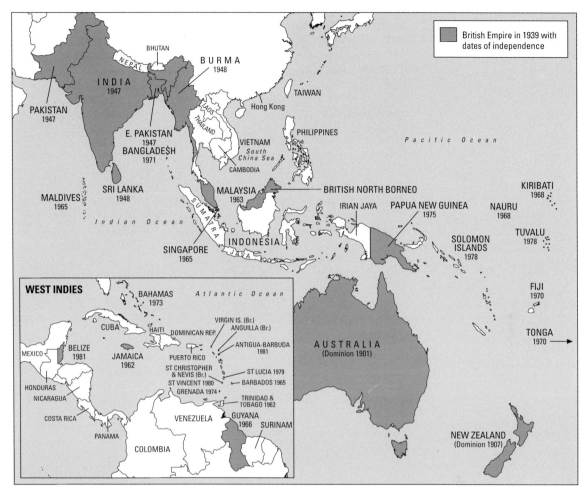

Britain's former colonies in Asia and the Pacific and the Caribbean

How does this map help show how the British Empire declined in these areas?

Visible trade: Trade in goods (e.g. cars and textiles) rather than services (e.g. insurance).

Mohammed Ali Jinnah (1876–1948)
Leader of the Muslim League and Pakistan separatist movement from 1935. Co-operated with British during the Second World War. Became Governor-General of Pakistan, 1947.

The promise of postwar independence remained, however, and the Labour government was committed to fulfilling it. American criticism of Britain's rule in the subcontinent had been very embarrassing, but in any case, by 1947 India was in deficit to the United States in **visible trade** and so did not bring additional hard currency to the sterling area. It was clear that Britain needed to focus on parts of the Empire that were likely to be assets, and withdraw from more problematic places. Africa was thought to be more adaptable than India.

At first, the British government hoped to establish a friendly government in India, co-operating with Britain in the Commonwealth. It was thought that Britain could retain access to military bases and manpower in India – as was agreed with Ceylon in 1947. Stafford Cripps proposed in 1946 that the Indian provinces should form a federation where foreign policy, defence, communications and finance were controlled by the centre. However, since 1940, the leader of the Muslim League, Jinnah, had been talking of the impossibility of Hindus and Muslims living together successfully in an independent India, and he feared that the Congress party wanted centralisation to reduce Muslim participation. The League refused to co-operate in making a constitution and decided on 'direct action' to obtain a separate Pakistan. In August 1946 over 5,000 people died in rioting in Calcutta between Hindus and Muslims. The violence

Gandhi, leader of the Indian National Congress since 1914 and of civil disobedience campaigns, with Lord Mountbatten, last Viceroy of India

continued, and in February 1947. Attlee announced that June 1948 was the date of withdrawal whether or not the League and Congress could reach any agreement, and sent Lord Louis Mountbatten to be the final Viceroy.

Mountbatten tried to get agreement from League and Congress to an all-India federation, but Nehru, the Congress president, was afraid that without a strong centre there would simply be more violence. Mountbatten then proposed partition into two separate Dominions, India and Pakistan. Congress agreed to this, but only if withdrawal was speeded up, and so India and Pakistan became independent in August 1947. They immediately began to dispute the partition of Kashmir. Britain had failed to achieve a government in India with which it would maintain defence links, nor had the rights of minorities such as the Sikhs been guaranteed, but the new Dominions were members of the Commonwealth. This did not however mean they were supporters of British policy – as leader of the Non-Aligned Movement in the 1950s, India continually criticised British imperialism, and moved away from Britain in seeking allies against China. Britain has been criticised for the speed of its withdrawal. In the violence that followed at least 250,000 people died in the Punjab alone.

1. What difference did the war make to British policy in India?

2. Why was India partitioned in 1947?

3. How did the Indian parties campaign for nationalism and respond to British policy during the Second World War and after?

12.7 How did Britain attempt to make the Empire pay its way?

The Labour government of 1945 was committed to social policies in Britain, such as the National Health Service, which would be a significant cost to the state. There were fears that continued expenditure abroad might damage Britain's economic stability – in 1946 the Chancellor of the Exchequer was warning that the balance of payments could not stand the cost of the 1.2 million British people serving abroad. In 1947 Britain's dollar reserves were reduced as US prices rose, and in June the Treasury warned that without American aid the dollar shortage combined with convertibility of sterling to dollars (promised to the Americans for July that year) could destroy the British economy. In fact, convertibility lasted just a month before the threat of a complete loss of the pound's value led to the reintroduction of exchange controls. In November 1947 the sterling area had a dollar deficit of £600–£700 million per year.

The sterling area was formed at the beginning of the war and consisted principally of the Empire/Commonwealth countries. After 1945 it was much more controlled, and discriminated against trade with 'hard currencies' – currencies like the US dollar which could be bought and sold anywhere – and became a way for Britain to earn dollars. Exports such as rubber from Malaya and cocoa from the Gold Coast brought dollars into the area. Britain then bought the dollars at a fixed exchange rate, crediting the country with a sterling balance – which could only be spent within the sterling area. Since Britain was unable to produce all the goods that a country like Malaya wanted to purchase, this led to shortages and therefore inflation in countries that earned hard currency. The Commonwealth Colombo Plan of 1950 partly hoped to address this by improving living standards in South-East Asia. This was also meant to prevent communism from being too attractive.

The colonies were vital to the sterling area since Britain had control over them, which it did not over the Crown Dominions, such as Australia. It was feared that if power were transferred to colonial nationalists, they might draw too much on their sterling balances and destabilise the British economy, which was another factor against allowing independence for many at this time.

The British economy was rescued by Marshall Aid. In fact, American assistance, first in 1945 and then in 1948, allowed Britain to postpone a serious reappraisal of its overseas commitments and ability to pay for the Empire. Instead, attempts were made to make the Empire pay. It was a source of cheap food (often bought below market rates) and raw materials, so the aim of British policy was to try to invest in the colonies to make them happy and productive, raising their living standards, benefiting Britain economically and so also presenting colonialism in a more positive way. The Empire also offered a secure outlet for British goods, and developing colonial economies would allow their consumers to buy more of these.

The Colonial Office recruited 4,100 new staff between June 1945 and September 1948; a 45 per cent increase on the whole period 1945–54. Colonial Development and Welfare Acts were passed during the war, intended to help pay for improving living standards in the colonies and developing their economies. The overseas technical departments expanded. The Act passed in 1945 provided £120 million for colonial development. The Cabinet set up a **Colonial Development Corporation** at the end of 1948. Projects such as the **East African Groundnut Scheme** were set up to attempt to exploit imperial economic resources better, and efforts were made to reform agricultural practices in Africa. These attempts, however, were often very unpopular with the local people, and the groundnut scheme was a spectacular failure. Britain never managed to turn Africa into a source of dollars.

The Middle East was of course very important economically to Britain because of oil. In May 1951 the Iranian government nationalised the Anglo-Iranian Oil Company, with its refinery at Abadan, which was owned and run by Britain. Britain would usually put pressure on Iran by threatening to intervene in south Persia, but the Americans were afraid that this would lead to the Russians attacking the north and opposed British military action. So Britain was restricted to trying to stop Iranian oil getting to the world market. Although the Iranian regime was overthrown in 1953, with secret help from the US Central Intelligence Agency (CIA), Britain only regained a 40 per cent stake in what was now an international consortium. At the time, however, this was not a disastrous economic blow,

Colonial Development Corporation (CDC): Set up 1948 to promote increased colonial production on an economic and self-supporting basis, especially of food, raw material and manufactures, which would help improve the balance of payments. It could borrow up to £100 million for investment.

East African Groundnut Scheme: In 1946 it was proposed that 1 million acres of Tanganyika be used to grow groundnuts as a solution to the shortage of edible oils and fats. The scheme was approved in January 1947 and the area increased to 3.2 million acres. By 1949 the scheme had to be closed down: almost all of the budget had been spent on clearing 1.4 per cent of the ground.

because Kuwait and other Gulf states were producing so much oil, helping the balance of payments. Attlee had contemplated withdrawing from the Middle East after the war, because of the expense of building up British bases there again, but was persuaded by the Foreign Office and the military that Britain must stay to contain the Soviet Union, and of course to protect oil interests.

Elsewhere in the Empire Britain tried to attract American investment, but although US industry needed raw materials from the Third World, it was only the Middle Eastern oil industry which attracted serious investment – where of course they were rivals to British firms. Few US companies were willing to risk their capital in an unstable and underdeveloped empire.

Despite these attempts to make the Empire pay, during the 1950s Britain was beginning to trade less with the Empire/Commonwealth and more with other industrialised nations. Economists were also beginning to question the desirability of the sterling area, and of encouraging colonies to build up large sterling balances. The various colonial loans that were floated on the Stock Market in the 1950s were all unpopular. By the end of the 1950s it was clear that the attempt to make the Empire pay had failed: in fact it had contributed to the pressure for decolonisation.

---

1. a) What was the sterling area?

b) Why was it important to British imperial policy?

2. How important was the Empire to Britain's economy in the late 1940s?

3. Could the Empire be made to pay? (Give reasons to support your answer.)

Source-based questions: Success or failure? The social reforms of Attlee's governments

SOURCE A

Clement Attlee's government enjoyed two great advantages which few other Labour governments have had. It came to power with a clear idea of what it wished to achieve and its large majority enabled it to enact its programme in full. 75 Acts of Parliament were passed in 1945–46 alone. Unquestionably its greatest achievement was the welfare state. Although many of the reforms owed a great deal to earlier schemes of state welfare, the new programme made a definite break with the past, partly because it was so comprehensive in scope and because it attempted to provide a universal level of support acceptable to the entire population.

However, the welfare state never lived up to its ideals. Poverty was far from being abolished, and as old-aged pensions were not linked to the cost of living, their value was somewhat eroded by inflation.

From: *Britain since 1789* by Martin Pugh, 1999

SOURCE B

The National Health Service was a major reform which deserved to have been introduced without the objections of the British Medical Association. The National Insurance scheme was open to criticism that it was financed by a regressive tax which took no account of the ability to pay and provided cash benefits which related only to the barest necessities of life and which, in this particular respect, gave the working class too little and the middle class virtually nothing. The National Health Service was open to no such objection. The ending of the gross social anomaly that the great hospitals of the land should depend for finance on rag days and flag days was indisputably an improvement. No longer was the community's inhumanity to be advertised publicly in the streets by the announcement: 'this hospital is maintained solely by voluntary contributions'.

From: *Post-Victorian Britain 1902–1951* by L.C.B. Seaman, 1966

SOURCE C

Labour could hardly have won the 1945 election so conclusively without a substantial accession of the middle-class voters, but they soon became disenchanted. It was for this section of society a particularly painful period. The incomes of the professional classes had not risen in proportion to those of wage earners. They felt beleaguered, bewildered, uneasy and resentful. Taxation remained very heavy. Petrol was severely rationed. Something of the bitterness of the middle classes emerges from the novels of Angela Thirkell, *Peace Breaks Out* (1946), *Love Among Ruins* (1948) and others. As novels they are not very good but as pictures of the scene from a certain social angle they deserve to be remembered by the historians of the times.

From: *The Decline from Power* by Robert Blake, 1986

SOURCE D

According to many critics, the Labour governments were, at best, heading in the wrong direction. Commentators on the political right have attacked the post-war governments for introducing too much socialism. The emphasis on welfare reform diverted attention from desperately needed industrial regeneration, and the principle of universal benefits was undesirable both financially and morally. This line of reasoning shows scant recognition of the historical context that gave rise to Attlee's administration. After six years of privation and grim resistance in wartime there was a great desire to ensure that British society was changed swiftly and radically. Against this background, the desire of the post-war government to remedy social inequality was entirely understandable.

From: *The Attlee Governments 1945 to 1951*
by Kevin Jeffreys, 1992

---

1. Study Source A

Using information contained within this chapter, explain the meaning of the term 'welfare state'.

2. Study Sources A and B

How far do these two sources agree in their views on Attlee's social reforms?

3. Study Sources B and C

Does the information in these two sources suggest that Attlee's social reforms were a success? Explain your answer.

4. Using information from this chapter and all four sources

To what extent did Attlee's reforms live up to the expectations of those who voted Labour in the 1945 general election?

Further Reading

Article

'The Cold War 1945–49', by Derrick Murphy, *Modern History Review*, Vol. No. 10, 4, April 1999

Texts designed specifically for AS and A2 students

The Attlee Government, 1945–1951 by Kevin Jeffreys (Longman Seminar Studies, 1992)
The Labour Party since 1951: 'Socialism' and Society since 1951 by Steve Fielding (Manchester University Press, 1997)
Never Again: Britain 1945–1951 by Peter Hennessy (Jonathan Cape, 1992)
The People's Peace: British History 1945–1990 by Kenneth O. Morgan (Penguin, 1990)
The Cold War by Hugh Higgins, 3rd ed., (Heinemann, 1993)
The Cold War 1945–1965 by Joseph Smith (Historical Association Studies, Blackwell, 1989)

The Cold War 1945–1991 by John W. Mason (Routledge Lancaster Pamphlets, 1996)

The Origins of the Cold War, 1941–49 by Martin Macauley, 2nd ed., (Longman Seminar Studies, 1995)

The USA and the Cold War by Oliver Edwards (Hodder & Stoughton, 1997)

The Lion's Share 1850–1995 by Bernard Porter (Macmillan, 1996)

More advanced reading

Breach of Promise: Labour in Power 1964–70 by Clive Ponting (Penguin, 1989)

The Labour Party since 1979: crisis and transformation by Eric Shaw (Routledge, 1994)

Labour in Power 1945–1951 by Kenneth O. Morgan (Oxford University Press, 1985)

Labour People: Leaders and Lieutenants Hardie to Kinnock by Kenneth O. Morgan (Oxford University Press, 1987)

Remaking the Labour Party: From Gaitskell to Blair by Tudor Jones (Routledge, 1996)

Britain and the Cold War 1945 to 1991 by Sean Greenwood (Macmillan, 2000)

Cold War Europe 1945–1989 by S. Young (Edward Arnold, 1991)

The Cold War: The Great Powers and the Allies by J. Dunbabin (Longman, 1994)

The Cold War 1947 to 1991 by S. J. Ball (Hodder Headline, 1998)

The Cold War, 1945–87, by R. Levering (Harlan Davidson, 1988)

The United States and the Cold War, 1945–53 by R. Crockatt (The British Association for the Advancement of Science, 1989)

British Decolonisation, 1946–97 by David McIntyre (St. Martin's Press, 1988)

Decolonisation and the British Empire 1775 to 1997 by D. George Boyce (Macmillan, 1999)

Decolonisation: The British Experience since 1945 by Nicholas J. White (Longman, 1999)

The Pursuit of Greatness: Britain and the World Role 1900–1970 by Robert Holland (Fontana, 1991)

13 Britain and Ireland, 1914–2007

Key Issues

- How did British policy change towards Ireland between 1914–2007?

- Why were Nationalists and Unionists in conflict in Ireland?

- Why has it been so difficult to find a permanent solution to British-Irish relations?

13.1 Why was Ireland partitioned between 1914 and 1922?

13.2 How did relations between Britain and the Irish Free State/Eire develop between 1922 and 1949?

13.3 Historical Interpretation: Why did civil and political disorder develop in Northern Ireland by 1969?

13.4 How effective was British policy towards Northern Ireland between 1969 and 1985?

13.5 Why was it so difficult to find a political solution in Northern Ireland between 1985 and 2007?

Framework of Events

1914	Home Rule becomes law but its operation is suspended for the duration of the First World War
1916	Easter Rising in Dublin
1917–1918	Irish Convention
1918	General Election: Sinn Fein wins 73 seats
1919	Dail Eireann established in Dublin
1920	Government of Ireland Act
1921	Anglo-Irish Treaty
1922	Irish Free State created
1922–3	Civil War within the Irish Free State
1926	Balfour Declaration on dominion self-government
1931	Statute of Westminster
1932	Fianna Fail win Irish Free State general election
1932–36	Fianna Fail government begins dismantling links between Irish Free State and Britain
1937	New Constitution: Irish Free State becomes Eire
1938	Anglo-Irish agreements: Treaty ports given to Eire
1939	Eire stays neutral in the Second World War
1949	Eire becomes Republic of Ireland and leaves the Commonwealth
1956–1962	IRA Border Campaign
1965	Meetings between Prime Ministers of Northern Ireland and the Republic
1968	Civil Rights Movement develops in Northern Ireland.Civil disturbances begin
1969	British government orders troops into Northern Ireland. Beginning of the 'Troubles'
1971	Northern Ireland government introduces internment
1972	'Bloody Sunday' in Londonderry. Northern Ireland government suspended
1973	Britain and the Republic of Ireland join the EEC
	Sunningdale Agreement on setting up a power sharing executive in Northern Ireland
1974	Ulster Loyalist strike against power sharing. Sunningdale Agreement collapses
1976	'Peace People' movement against violence. The two leaders Mairead Corrigan (Catholic) and Betty Williams (Protestant) win Nobel peace prize
1981	Hunger Strike by Republican prisoners. One of them, Bobby Sands, is elected MP for Fermanagh and South Tyrone. He and nine other hunger strikers die
1982	Prior's 'Rolling Devolution' Proposals

1984	Margaret Thatcher and members of the Cabinet survive Brighton Bombing by Provisional IRA
1985	Anglo-Irish Agreement: Margaret Thatcher and Garret Fitzgerald, Prime Minister of the Republic of Ireland sign agreement on Northern Ireland
1993	Downing Street Declaration
1994	IRA ceasefire
1996	IRA ceasefire collapses after failure to reach agreement on decommissioning paramilitary weapons
1998	'Good Friday Agreement'
1999	Creation of Northern Ireland Executive
	Northern Ireland Executive and Assembly suspended for first time due to Unionist claims that IRA had not decommissioned its weapons
2001	IRA offer to decommission weapons leads to reopening of Northern Ireland Assembly
2002	October: Northern Ireland Secretary, Dr John Reid suspends the Northern Ireland Executive and Assembly because of an IRA spy ring uncovered at Northern Ireland parliament. Assembly remains suspended until May 2007.
2004	Negotiations held in a bid to re-establish Assembly. Comprehensive Agreement replaces Royal Ulster Constabulary with Police Service of Northern Ireland.
2005	Sinn Fein leader Gerry Adams asks IRA to 'lay down its arms'
2006	St Andrew's Agreement leads way to elections for Northern Ireland Assembly
2007	March: Elections lead to dominance of Democratic Unionist Party in Unionist community and Sinn Fein in Nationalist/Republican community
	May: New Northern Ireland Executive formed, with Ian Paisley of DUP as First Minister and Martin McGuinness of Sinn Fein as his Deputy
	July: British army ends Operation Banner, name for its involvement in Northern Ireland which began in 1969. The 'Troubles' officially come to an end.

Overview

BRITAIN'S Irish problem, or Ireland's British problem, has been a dominant theme of United Kingdom politics between 1914–22 and since 1969. In September 1914 a political solution to British-Irish relations seemed to have been made. A Home Rule Act, granting limited self-government, was passed by the Westminster Parliament but was suspended for the duration of the First World War. However, by 1922, Ireland was partitioned between Northern Ireland and the Irish Free State. The latter was a state within the British Empire with internal self-government. These political developments occurred mainly because of the effects of a failed armed rebellion against British rule made by extreme Nationalists in Dublin in 1916.

From the founding of the Irish Free State to the creation of the Republic of Ireland in 1949, some Irish politicians attempted gradually to weaken the links with the British Empire. The most notable was Eamon de Valera. From 1932 to 1937 he severed many of these links. In 1937 he introduced a new constitution which created an independent republic 'in all but name'. In addition, he laid claim to Northern Ireland as part of a united Ireland. In 1949 Ireland became a fully independent state outside the Commonwealth.

Northern Ireland did receive Home Rule. From 1921 to 1972 it was dominated by the Ulster Unionist party. This party was predominantly Protestant. It discriminated against Catholics, who were seen as Nationalists who wanted a united Ireland. By 1968 Catholic civil rights had become a major issue in Northern Ireland politics.

It sparked off a Protestant unionist reaction which led to major sectarian violence in 1969. The British government first sent troops to Northern Ireland in 1969 in an attempt to maintain law and order. In 1972 the government suspended the Northern Ireland Parliament and ruled the area directly from London.

From 1969 to 1998 Northern Ireland was badly affected by political violence. The Provisional IRA and Loyalist paramilitary groups engaged in guerrilla warfare and sectarian murder. Successive British governments, both Labour and Conservative, had attempted to find a political solution. Attempts to involve both Nationalist and Unionists in government failed. In 1985 a new attempt was made with the Anglo-Irish (**Hillsborough**) **Agreement** which involved co-operation between the British and Irish governments. By the 1990s attempts to solve the conflict in Northern Ireland involved a fusion of previous attempts at a political solution: co-operation in government between political parties within Northern Ireland and co-operation between Britain and Ireland. A major turning-point in British-Irish relations came following the landslide victory of the Labour Party in the 1997 General Election. Under the leadership of Tony Blair, and with the support of US President, Bill Clinton, a landmark agreement was made in 1998. The Good Friday Agreement, between Britain, the Republic of Ireland and political parties in Northern Ireland offered the basis of a permanent agreement. However, there were still problems. The Democratic Unionist Party (DUP) of Ian Paisley did not sign up to the Agreement. Also, an important part of the Agreement was the **decommissioning** of IRA weapons, something the IRA were reluctant to do. However, a new Northern Ireland Executive and Parliament were chosen involving both Nationalists and Unionists. The Good Friday Agreement faced a stern test after 2000 when the UK government was forced to suspend the Northern Ireland Executive and Parliament because of disputes over decommissioning. However, by 2006, the IRA had formally renounced violence and decommissioned its weapons. Also the St Andrew's Agreement of 2006 led to the reestablishment of the Northern Ireland Executive and Parliament, this time with the historic inclusion of the DUP, working together with Sinn Fein.

Hillsborough Agreement: Hillsborough Castle is the Secretary of State for Northern Ireland's official residence.

Decommissioning: The handing in for destruction of military equipment including rifles and bomb making equipment.

Political Parties in Northern Ireland

The Ulster Unionist Party
The main party since the creation of the state in 1921. Wants to maintain the union with Britain. Moderate party, which signed the Sunningdale Agreement and the Good Friday Agreement.

The Democratic Unionist Party
Founded in 1971 by Ian Paisley. Wants the return of a Stormont-style government to Northern Ireland. Completely opposed to any involvement of the Irish Republic in Northern Ireland politics. Opposed to Sunningdale Agreement, Anglo-Irish Agreement and Good Friday Agreement all because of links with the Irish Republic.

The Social Democratic and Labour Party
Founded in 1970 by Gerry Fitt. Originated from the Civil Rights movement. Attracts about two-thirds of the Nationalist vote. In favour of a reunification of Ireland by consent. Main aim: to defend the rights of the Nationalist community.

Sinn Fein
Originally Arthur Griffith's party in 1906. Became associated with the demand for an independent Irish republic after 1916. From 1919 it opposed parliamentary representation of Ireland in the British (Westminster) Parliament. From 1922 it opposed representation in the Irish Free State, which was still part of Britain's Dominions. Present party is the political wing of the Republican movement in Northern Ireland. Initially in favour of the 'armed struggle', it moderated its views in the 1980s to support the twin policy of the political violence and democratic politics (the armalite and ballot box strategy). Received about 40 per cent of the Nationalist vote by 1990s. Now supports representation in the Northern Ireland Assembly and Dublin Parliament.

Dirty Protest: The name given to the protest by Republican prisoners when they refused to wear clothing and 'dirtied' themselves with their own excreta.

Paramilitary groups in Northern Ireland since 1969

Provisional IRA
Formed in 1970 through split with the Official IRA. Led armed struggle to expel the British from Northern Ireland since that date. In favour of a united Irish republic. Have adopted various policies such as political assassination; bombing in Northern Ireland and Britain; organising demonstrations such, as the '**Dirty Protest**' for political status in Northern Ireland's prison in late 1970s, and the Hunger Strike of 1981. Well-armed through support from Libya and money from supporters in the United States.

Irish National Liberation Army
A faction which split from the Provisional IRA in 1975. Military wing of Irish Republican Socialist Party. Engaged in campaign of violence which included the murder of Lord Mountbatten and Airey Neave. Also killed 17 people in Dropping Well pub bombing. Nearly fell apart with faction fighting in 1987.

Real IRA
Another faction which split from the Provisional IRA in November 1997. Responsible for the Omagh bombing of 1998.
UDA (The Ulster Defence Association)
Formed in 1972. Contained 40,000 members and remained legal until 1992. Sees itself as defender of Protestant working-class communities. Active in Ulster Workers' Strike of 1974. Mainly engaged in sectarian murders of Catholics.

UVF (The Ulster Volunteer Force)
Originally formed in 1912 to oppose Home Rule. Mainly engaged in sectarian murders of Catholics. For instance in 1992 11 Catholics were murdered by the UVF.

(Of the 3,600 deaths in the Northern Ireland conflict since 1969 43 per cent have been Catholic [1,548]. Most were killed by Loyalist gunmen.)

---

1. What do you regard as the political solution which has had the greatest influence on British–Irish Relations between 1914 and 2007? Give reasons for your answer.

2. What do you regard as the greatest 'missed opportunity' in bringing lasting peace in British–Irish relations in the period 1914 to 2007?

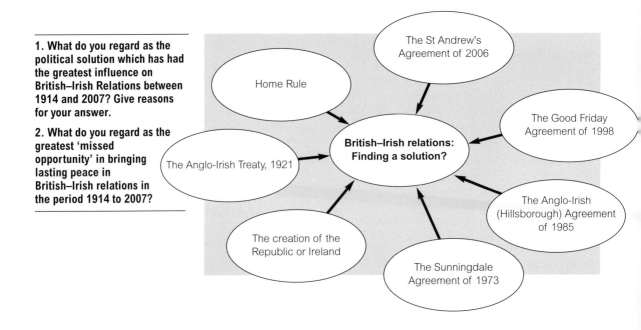

13.1 Why was Ireland partitioned between 1914 and 1922?

The Irish Question: The term given to the problem posed by Ireland to British governments.

In September 1914, it seemed that the British government had found a solution to the **Irish Question**. A Home Rule Act was passed. This granted limited self-government to Ireland within the United Kingdom and seemed to be the end of a political process, which had begun with Gladstone's conversion to Irish Home Rule in 1886.

However, within eight years Ireland was partitioned between Northern Ireland and the Irish Free State. Why did the plan to introduce Irish Home Rule fail?

The problem of Ulster

During the political crisis which led to the passage of the Home Rule Act, a political crisis occurred over Ulster. North-east Ireland contained a Protestant/Unionist majority which was opposed to Home Rule. In 1912 100,000 Ulster Unionists formed the Ulster Volunteer Force (UVF) to oppose Home Rule by force if necessary. When the First World War broke out Ireland seemed to be on the verge of civil war. In addition to the UVF, Nationalists in Ireland formed the Irish Volunteers in 1913 to defend Home Rule. It numbered 200,000 men but was not as well armed as the UVF.

The First World War prevented an armed clash. The UVF and large numbers of the Irish Volunteers volunteered for the British Army. In addition, when the Home Rule Act was passed the Prime Minister, H. H. Asquith, promised to introduce an 'Amending Bill' which would exclude the six north-eastern counties of Ireland from the operation of Home Rule for a period of time.

How did the Easter Rising of 1916 affect British-Irish Relations?

Explain the impact of the Easter Rising, 1916, on British-Irish relations.

During the early years of the war Nationalist opinion in Ireland was upset by a number of developments. At the outbreak of war the UVF were allowed to form their own division of the British Army (the 36th Division). The Irish Volunteers were not allowed the same privilege. In addition, the son of John Redmond, the leader of the Irish Nationalist Party, was denied

Edward Carson (1854–1935)
Carson was educated at Trinity College, Dublin. Irish Solicitor-General from 1892 and MP until 1918 he was a leading Irish Unionist opponent of Home Rule. Carson was a member of British Cabinet 1915–18.

Irish Republican Brotherhood: Originally founded in 1858 the IRB were once known as Fenians. They wanted to create an independent Irish Republic by violent means and engaged in an uprising in 1865–67 and bombing London in the 1880s.

Irish Citizen Army: A small group of socialist trade unionists led by James Connolly who became armed to defend trade unionists during strikes.

Dail: The Parliament of the Republic of Ireland and historically of the Irish Free State and Eire.

Guerrilla war: A plan of campaign fought against a regular army by small bands of armed men and women.

Black and Tans: Volunteers recruited by the British Government after the First World War to supplement the work of the Royal Irish Constabulary and the regular army in countering Irish republican attacks. The Black and Tans became notorious for the violence of their 'reprisals' against the nationalist population. The name is thought to derive from their dark berets and khaki tunics.

a commission to become a British army officer. When a coalition government was formed in May 1915, Sir Edward Carson, leading Irish Unionist and opponent of Home Rule, joined the Cabinet.

Of greater significance was the decision by the **Irish Republican Brotherhood** (IRB) to stage an armed uprising against British rule. Their aim was to create an independent Irish republic. The IRB had infiltrated the organisation of the Irish Volunteers. Around 11,000 men had decided to stay in Ireland and not join the British army. In league with other separatist groups, such as the **Irish Citizen Army**, an uprising involving fewer than 2,000 Volunteers occurred in Dublin at the end of April, 1916. The Rising lasted less than a week and was easily defeated by the British garrison.

Although the Easter Rising was a military failure it did have a profound effect on Irish public opinion. The decision by the British authorities to execute sixteen leaders helped turn the rebels into Nationalist martyrs. However, the Allied powers were hoping the United States would join the war on their side and Britain did not want to alienate Irish-American opinion, so in 1917 several hundred rebel prisoners were released and allowed to return to Ireland. This created a powerful Republican political force. Finally, in 1918 the British government outraged Nationalist opinion by attempting to introduce compulsory military conscription into Ireland. Irish Nationalist MPs and Republicans campaigned jointly against the plan.

British government policy to solve Irish problems came to nothing. Lloyd George, the Prime Minister, called an Irish Convention of all Irish political groups to discuss problems. It met between 1917 and 1918, but was boycotted by Republicans and Unionists opposed any attempt to introduce Home Rule. A turning-point in British-Irish relations came in the December 1918 general election. The Irish Republicans, now known as Sinn Fein, won 73 out of 106 seats in Ireland. In January 1919, instead of going to Westminster, they set up their own parliament in Dublin, **Dail** Eireann. Between 1919 and 1921 Irish Republicans attempted to create an independent state outside the United Kingdom.

Why was the Irish Free State created in 1922?

In Ireland the years 1919–21 are known as the War of Independence. Armed groups of Republicans, known as the Irish Republican Army (IRA) fought a **guerrilla war** against the armed police force, the Royal Irish Constabulary, and the British Army. IRA activity was masterminded by Michael Collins who was Minister of Finance in the Dail Government.

British policy towards this problem was two-fold. Firstly, through the Government of Ireland Act (1920), the government tried to find a political solution. Two Home Rule parliaments and governments would be established in Ireland. One would be for the six counties of the north east (Northern Ireland), the other for the remaining twenty-six counties (termed Southern Ireland). Only part of the act was implemented. In the May, 1921 elections in Ireland, Sinn Fein won an overwhelming vote in the South. They refused to accept the Act.

At the same time, the British government attempted to defeat the IRA by military means. The Royal Irish Constabulary was reinforced by two groups of volunteer forces from Britain, the Auxiliaries and the '**Black and Tans**'. These groups engaged in reprisal raids on the civilian population in retaliation for IRA attacks on British forces. This policy was unpopular in the United States and among Liberals and Labour politicians in Britain.

In the summer of 1921, Lloyd George, the Prime Minister, changed British policy. He called a ceasefire with the IRA and began political negotiations with Sinn Fein.

Michael Collins (1890–1922)
Collins was born in Clonakilty, county Cork. He took part in Easter Rising, later becoming President of the IRB. He was Minister of Finance in the Dail Government of 1919, raised the National Loan 1919–21 and organised the IRA. A member of the Irish delegation for Anglo-Irish Treaty talks, he succeeded Griffith as Prime Minister of the Irish Free State, but was assassinated a few weeks later in August 1922.

Arthur Griffith (1871–1922)
Griffith was born in Dublin, and educated by the Christian Brothers. He was a member of the IRB 1893–1910. In 1906 Griffith founded the Sinn Fein Party. He wanted internal self-government for Ireland similar to Hungary's position in Austria-Hungary, and opposed the Home Rule Bill. He didn't take part in the Easter Rising but became Vice-President of the new Sinn Fein party in 1918. He headed the Irish delegation in the Anglo-Irish Treaty talks 1921 and was elected President of the Dail [Prime Minister] in January 1922, but died seven months later.

In December 1921 an agreement was signed in London. Representatives of Sinn Fein, led by Arthur Griffith and Michael Collins, accepted the creation of a self-governing state, outside the United Kingdom but part of the British Empire. This became the Irish Free State. Initially, the six counties of Northern Ireland were to be excluded. It was agreed that a Boundary Commission would study the border between the Irish Free State and

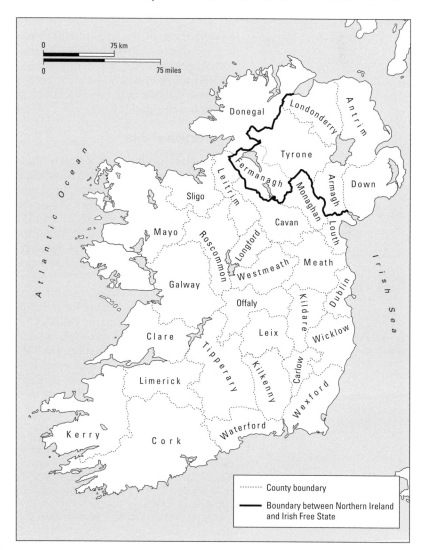

1. How did British policy towards Ireland change between 1914 and 1922?

2. Who benefited most from the Partition of Ireland and the creation of the Irish Free State?

a) The British government?

b) Irish Unionists?

c) Irish Republicans?

Give reasons to support your answer

3. How far did the political settlement of 1920–22 differ from the Home Rule Act 1914?

The partition of Ireland, 1920–21

Northern Ireland and would recommend changes. Michael Collins believed that the Boundary Commission would give the Irish Free State large parts of Northern Ireland. This would have the effect of forcing Northern Ireland into a united Irish state.

The Anglo-Irish Treaty of 1921 upset extremists on both sides. 'Die hard' Conservatives disliked the breakup of the United Kingdom. Irish republicans, led by Eamon de Valera, were opposed to staying within the British Empire. De Valera's stance seems odd because he had been notified by Lloyd George in secret negotiations in July 1921 that this was the best he could offer. It does explain why de Valera did not lead the Irish negotiating team in London in November and December 1921. The split over the Treaty led to civil war within the Irish Free State. Between June 1922 and 1923, Free State forces defeated Irish Republican forces. The main casualty was Michael Collins, then Prime Minister of the Irish Free State. He was killed in an ambush on 22 August 1922.

13.2 How did relations between Britain and the Irish Free State/Eire develop between 1922 and 1949?

In his defence of the Anglo-Irish Treaty Michael Collins claimed that it gave 'freedom to achieve freedom'. By this he meant that the creation of the Irish Free State would be the beginning of a process which would eventually lead to the creation of a completely independent Irish state. Between 1922 and 1949 the Irish Free State did follow this route. However, the chief architect of this development was Collins' political rival Eamon de Valera.

The creation of Eire

Fortunately for Irish nationalists, political developments within the British Empire assisted this change. At the Imperial Conference of 1926 the 'Balfour Declaration' gave the dominions of the British Empire full internal self-government. The dominions were Canada, Australia, New Zealand, South Africa, Southern Rhodesia, Newfoundland and the Irish Free State. By the Statute of Westminster (1931) the self-governing dominions were declared independent states within the British Commonwealth. These were all held together by common allegiance to the British monarchy.

In 1932, Eamon de Valera became Prime Minister of the Irish Free State. He used the position to sever the political links with Britain. He abolished the Oath of Allegiance to the British Crown which every Irish MP had to take. The position of **Governor-General** to Ireland was reduced to a position of political insignificance. De Valera nominated an obscure Irish politician, D. Buckley, to the post. Instead of living at the Vice-Regal Lodge, the Monarch's residence in Dublin, he was banished to a small house in the Dublin suburbs. Finally de Valera abolished the right of Irish people to send legal cases to the Judicial Committee of the Privy Council.

Governor-General: The Monarch's representative in Commonwealth countries which regard the Monarch as Head of State. Between 1939 and 1949 Britain was represented in Dublin by the UK Representative in Ireland, Sir John Maffey, later Lord Rugby.

| **Eamon de Valera (1882–1975)** De Valera was born in New York, USA and raised in County Limerick. He took a leading part in the Easter Rising but escaped execution. Elected President of Ireland in | 1919 he opposed the Anglo-Irish treaty of 1921 and sided with anti-Treaty forces in the Irish Civil War 1922–23. He founded the Fianna Fail Party in 1926. De Valera became Prime Minister of the Irish Free State in 1932. Following the | creation of Eire in 1937 he became its Prime Minister 1937–49, 1951–54 and 1957–59 and then President of the Republic of Ireland 1959–73. Throughout his life he worked to achieve a united Irish Republic. |

Political Parties in Eire/Republic of Ireland

Fianna Fail
Founded in 1926 by Eamon de Valera when he split from the IRA. Entered the Irish Parliament in 1927 and became the governing party in 1932. Has been the largest party in the Republic of Ireland since 1932. In favour of a 32-county independent Irish Republic to be achieved by democratic means. However, in 1971 two leading members of Fianna Fail, Charles Haughey (future Taoiseach) and Neil Blaney, were accused of gunrunning to the Provisional IRA.

Fine Gael
Founded in 1933. Supported the Anglo-Irish Treaty of 1921. A more pro-British party than Fianna Fail. Has taken a more conciliatory line towards cross-border security and extradition.

Prime Ministers of Irish Free State (1922–1937), Eire (1937–1948) and the Republic of Ireland (1948 onwards)

1922–32	William T. Cosgrave (Cumann na nGaedhael)
1932–48	Eamon de Valera (Fianna Fail)
1948–51	John Costello (Coalition)
1951–54	Eamon de Valera (Fianna Fail)
1954–57	John Costello (Coalition)
1957–59	Eamon de Valera (Fianna Fail)
1959–66	Sean Lemass (Fianna Fail)
1966–73	Jack Lynch (Fianna Fail)
1973–77	Liam Cosgrave (Fine Gael)
1977–79	Jack Lynch (Fianna Fail)
1979–81	Charles Haughey (Fianna Fail)
1981–82	Garret Fitzgerald (Fine Gael)
1982 (Mar–Dec)	Charles Haughey (Fianna Fail)
1982–87	Garret Fitzgerald (Fine Gael)
1987–92	Charles Haughey (Fianna Fail)
1992–94	Albert Reynolds (Fianna Fail)
1994–7	John Bruton (Fine Gael)
1997–	Bertie Ahern (Fianna Fail)

In 1937 de Valera introduced a new constitution. The Irish Free State became Eire.

The position of Governor-General was abolished. Instead Eire would have an elected President as Head of State. Eire was a 'republic in all but name'. At the Imperial Conference of 1937 it was declared that the creation of Eire did not substantially change Ireland's links with the British Commonwealth. However, the only constitutional link between Eire and Britain was the External Relations Act. This stated that Irish diplomats abroad were seen as representatives of the British Crown.

Eire and the Second World War

A major development in British-Irish relations was the Second World War. Eire was the only part of the British Empire and Commonwealth to stay neutral in the war. Given Eire's strategic position in the Battle of the Atlantic Irish neutrality created serious problems for Britain. This position had been made worse in 1938 when Neville Chamberlain had signed an Anglo-Irish Agreement with de Valera. Under the Agreement a trade war between the two states, which had existed since 1932, came to an end. Of greater significance was the British decision to hand over to Eire the 'Treaty

Ports' of Cork Harbour, Bere Haven and Lough Swilly. These ports could have provided important British naval bases during the War.

On a number of occasions Britain attempted to end Eire neutrality. In June 1940, Malcolm McDonald, former Dominions Secretary and son of Ramsay McDonald, was sent to Dublin on a secret mission. He offered de Valera the reunification of Ireland if Eire entered the War on the Allied side. De Valera refused mainly because the Northern Ireland government had not been consulted. He also believed that the British Prime Minister, Winston Churchill, did not have the political will to honour the agreement.

On two occasions the British considered military intervention to occupy Eire: in June/July 1940, shortly after the fall of France and again in the early summer of 1944, shortly before D-Day. Intervention was ruled out in 1940 because the Cabinet Committee dealing with the issue thought the action would alienate American opinion and lead to guerrilla warfare in Eire. In 1944 intervention was considered because the German and Japanese embassies were still functioning in Dublin. The Allies feared the Germans might find out about the D-Day landings because Northern Ireland was an important staging area for that operation.

By the end of the war Eire's neutrality had greatly distanced it from Britain and the Commonwealth. In his victory speech to the British Empire on V.E. Day, Winston Churchill made specific reference to the problems caused by Irish neutrality in the War. De Valera did not help matters when he signed a book of condolence at the German Embassy in Dublin on the news of Adolf Hitler's death.

The creation of the Republic of Ireland

In 1948, Costello, the Eire Prime Minister, declared, on a trip to Canada, that Eire would become an independent Republic outside the British Commonwealth. This development should have led to a widening of relations between Britain and Ireland. However, under the Ireland Act (1949) Irish citizens still retained considerable rights within the United Kingdom. Unlike any other **aliens** they could stand for the British Parliament and vote in British elections if they were resident in Britain. They could also join the British armed forces and police.

Alien: A person who is not a citizen.

The main reasons behind this British policy concerned other parts of the Commonwealth. Both Australia and New Zealand lobbied the British Government not to change the status of Irish citizens in the United Kingdom: with elections due in 1949 they feared the effects of a change in policy on the large Irish electorates in both these countries. Britain was also concerned about India's relations with the Commonwealth. India had become independent in August 1947, but remained within the Commonwealth. The British government knew that India planned to declare itself a republic. Therefore, in order to keep India, as a republic, within the Commonwealth, relations with Ireland were not changed.

There is another significant aspect of the Ireland Act. The Act stated that no attempt would be made to alter the constitutional position of Northern Ireland without the consent of the people of Northern Ireland. As Unionists had a permanent majority in Northern Ireland (they comprised about 66 per cent of the population) this declaration created the 'Unionist veto'. This had an important impact on British policy in Northern Ireland after 1969.

1. How did the Irish Free State become a completely independent state by 1949?

2. Who or what do you regard as most responsible for this political development? Give reasons for your answer.

3. How significant was the Ireland Act, 1949 to British-Irish relations?

13.3 Why did civil and political disorder develop in Northern Ireland by 1969?
A CASE STUDY IN HISTORICAL INTERPRETATION

The outbreak of widespread civil and political disorder between the Nationalist and Unionist communities in Northern Ireland was a constant feature of British politics from 1969 to 1999. The causes of this disorder, known by some as 'the Troubles', is the subject of much controversy. Both sides in Northern Ireland have widely differing interpretations of these events. Such differing perceptions are a major, if not the major reason why a political solution to Northern Ireland's problems has been so difficult to find.

The background

When Northern Ireland received Home Rule under the Government of Ireland Act, 1920, it was a political solution which Irish Unionists did not seek. They wanted to prevent any form of Home Rule for Ireland. As a result of the Irish political settlements made from 1920 to 1922 only a small number of Irish Unionists (around 100,000) lived in the Irish Free State. The majority of Irish Unionists lived in Northern Ireland.

Between 1921 and 1972 Northern Ireland politics was dominated by the Ulster Unionist Party, which held power continuously over this period. The Ulster Unionists at Westminster (there were 12 in this period) usually voted with the Conservative Party.

Nationalists, who made up around one-third of the Northern Ireland population, made very little impact on Northern Ireland politics. Some of their elected representatives abstained from attending the **Stormont** Parliament. More significantly, the electoral system ensured Unionist dominance.

Nationalists also felt discriminated against in other fields such as housing and employment. By the 1960s resentment felt against the Northern Ireland government by one-third of the population led to the creation of the Northern Ireland Civil Rights Association (NICRA) and a student organisation called People's Democracy. These groups comprised Nationalists, liberal members of the Unionist community and Churchmen. Inspired by the African American Civil Rights movement in the United States the NICRA called for 'one man one vote' and the end to discrimination in housing and employment. People's Democracy had similar aims. Its origins were similar to the student radicalism which affected much of Western Europe and North America from the mid-1960s.

These groups used similar tactics to the African American Civil Rights Movement. Demonstrations and walks were organised. In 1968 a NICRA march took place at Dungannon, County Tyrone. In October, serious rioting accompanied a Civil Rights march in Derry City. The Civil Rights movement was opposed by the Northern Ireland Government and various Unionist organisations. The latter attempted to disrupt marches and demonstrations. Following the **Apprentice Boys' March** in Derry City, in August 1969, rioting by Nationalists became so serious that the police force, the RUC, was finding it difficult to keep control. In addition, armed Unionist groups began attacking Nationalist areas in Belfast and Derry City.

Following a poor showing in the Northern Ireland general election of 1969, the Northern Ireland Prime Minister Captain Terence O'Neill resigned. He was replaced by another Unionist, Major James Chichester-Clark. Faced with ever-mounting sectarian violence, Chichester-Clark

Stormont: The site of the Northern Ireland Parliament, in a Belfast suburb. The name is also used to describe the Northern Ireland government.

Apprentice Boys' March: Celebration by a group of men of the apprentices who defended Derry from the troops of James II during the siege of 1689.

Terence O'Neill (1914–1990)
Born in London, and educated at Eton, O'Neill was a Captain in the Irish Guards 1939–45. He was leader of the Ulster Unionist Party and Prime Minister of Northern Ireland 1963–69.

James Chichester-Clark (1923–)
Eton-educated Chichester-Clark was leader of Ulster Unionist Party and Prime Minister of Northern Ireland, May 1969 to March 1971. He resigned because the Heath government would not send more troops to Ulster.

The Civil Rights March from
Coalisland to Dungannon,
Country Tyrone, in 1969

**How useful is this photograph to
a historian writing about the
Civil Rights Movement in
Northern Ireland in the late
1960s?**

requested the support of the British army to maintain peace. On 15
August 1969 British troops were sent to Northern Ireland in a 'peacekeeping role'.

The events of 1968–1969 were a turning point in British-Irish relations. Until 1968 Northern Ireland issues were rarely discussed at
Westminster. The Speaker's rules stipulated that Northern Ireland issues
be discussed by Northern Ireland ministers at Stormont not in Britain.
However, the Civil Rights Movement and the Unionist opposition to it
meant that Northern Ireland issues could no longer be ignored by a
British government. From 1968 the Northern Ireland problem has been a
major issue in British politics.

A Nationalist view of the causes of conflict in Northern Ireland

To most Nationalists, Northern Ireland is an artificial sub-state. It was
created in 1920 by Lloyd George as an attempt to solve the Irish problem
by providing a political unit within Ireland where there was a built-in
Protestant/Unionist majority. The plan was to defend British strategic
interests by preventing the unification of Ireland.

This Nationalist view is supported by the failure to create a Council of
Ireland. This body was meant to be set up under the Government of
Ireland Act. It was to contain representatives from Northern and Southern
Ireland. The aim was supposedly to create an All-Ireland political body,
which might one day lead to the end of partition. The other failure was that
of the Boundary Commission to make any significant changes to the
border between the Irish Free State and Northern Ireland. The
Commission had been created by the Anglo-Irish Treaty of 1921. When it
reported, in 1925, it left large numbers of Catholic/Nationalists within
Northern Ireland.

Northern Ireland terminology

The conflict in Northern Ireland has produced a series of inter-connected and sometimes slightly confusing titles for political groups and place names.

Nationalists are those members of the Northern Ireland community who would like to see a united Ireland. They include moderate democratic politicians and extremists.

Republicans are those members of the Nationalist community most closely associated with the idea of creating a united Irish state by force if necessary. Groups such as Sinn Fein, the Provisional IRA and INLA are republican.

Catholics: In Northern Ireland there is a very strong link between Nationalism and Catholicism. The vast majority of Catholics regard themselves as Nationalist, so much so that the terms Catholic and Nationalist are virtually interchangeable.

Unionists are those who want Northern Ireland to remain part of the United Kingdom. They include moderate democratic politicians as well as extremists who engage in sectarian violence.

Loyalists are those members of the Unionist community who engage in political violence to prevent Northern Ireland becoming part of a united Ireland. They include paramilitary groups such as the UDA, the UFF and the UVF. Most recently they have been associated with political parties such as the Ulster Democratic Party and Ulster Progressive Party.

Protestants: The link between Protestantism and Unionism is very strong; again the terms are virtually interchangeable. An important Protestant/Unionist organisation is the Orange Order. This organisation aims to defend religious liberties and the Union with Britain. It is anti-Catholic.

Place names: The most noticeable split between the Nationalist and Unionist communities is over the name of Londonderry/Derry. The former term is used by Unionists, the latter by Nationalists. Since the 1980s the official use has been Derry City for the county town and Londonderry for the county.

Prime Ministers of Northern Ireland

1921–40	Sir James Craig (Lord Craigavon)
1940–43	J. M. Andrews
1943–63	Sir Basil Brooke (Lord Brookeborough)
1963–69	Capt. Terence O'Neill
1969–71	James Chichester-Clark
1971–72	Brian Faulkner

James Craig (1871–1940)
Craig was born in Belfast. A Unionist MP for East Down, 1906, he was a leading Ulster Unionist opponent of Home Rule from 1912. He became the first Prime Minister of Northern Ireland in 1921 and held the post until his death. He was made Lord Craigavon in 1927.

British indifference to Irish Nationalism was confirmed by the failure to stop Unionist dominance of Northern Ireland. Sir James Craig, a leading Ulster Unionist, described Stormont as 'a Protestant Parliament for a Protestant people'. From the moment Northern Ireland was created, Catholics were made to feel like second-class citizens. In 1929 Nationalist fears seemed to be confirmed when the Unionist government changed the electoral system. Proportional representation was abolished. It was replaced by the 'first-past-the-post' system, which ensured Unionist dominance at Stormont.

Ian Paisley (1926–)
A founder member of Free Presbyterian Church of Ulster in 1951, Paisley was born in County Armagh, educated at Barry School of Evangelism and Bob Jones University, USA. He was imprisoned for obstructing a Civil Rights March, November 1968. In September 1971 he founded the Democratic Unionist party. He has been a European Parliament MP since 1979 and Westminster MP for North Antrim since 1970 and has opposed the Sunningdale, Anglo-Irish and Good Friday Agreements.

In local government, votes were given to rate payers rather than all adults. This discriminated against Catholics, because many did not own their own homes. In addition, **gerrymandering** took place. In Derry City, even though Catholics comprised two-thirds of the population, a Unionist city government was in control.

Discrimination against the Catholic minority was also seen in policing. The Royal Ulster Constabulary (RUC) was a predominantly Protestant force. It was supported by a part-time police force known as the 'B' specials – Protestants who harassed the local Catholic community. Both forces possessed considerable law and order powers. These were established under the Civil Authorities (Special Powers) Act, Northern Ireland (1922) and gave the police wide powers to stop, search and detain anyone they believed might be engaged in illegal political activity.

The problem also entered social and employment fields. A government Commission under Lord Cameron was set up to look into the causes of the disturbances of 1968–69. It reported in 1969 that favouritism towards Protestants in the allocation of council housing was rife in Dungannon, Armagh and, most notably, in Belfast and Derry City. In employment Protestants tended only to employ Protestants. As a result, unemployment was over twice as high among Catholics, because Protestants dominated the employer class.

The anti-Catholic/Nationalist nature of the Unionist majority was shown by the reaction to Prime Minister O'Neill's attempts to forge relations with the Republic of Ireland. In 1965, for the first time, a meeting took place between the prime ministers of Northern Ireland and the Republic. This led to opposition to O'Neill within the Unionist community. It created an opportunity for a young Presbyterian cleric, Ian Paisley, to make his political mark by opposing links with Catholics and the Republic.

In February 1969, O'Neill called a general election in Northern Ireland. He narrowly defeated Paisley in the Upper Bann constituency and the election returned a large number of anti-O'Neill Unionists. O'Neill was forced to resign.

To the Nationalists, the causes of the conflict stemmed from Britain, which had a selfish interest in maintaining control over part of Ireland. Successive British governments had allowed a Unionist-dominated government to discriminate against the Catholic minority. When Catholics engaged in legitimate political protest to highlight their grievances they were met by opposition from Unionist thugs, and the RUC and 'B' Specials.

Local government employment in County Fermanagh, March 1969

(County Fermanagh had a Catholic/Nationalist majority)

Jobs	Catholics	Protestants
County Council Administration	0	33
Housing Department	0	10
County Library	1	14
Planning and Tourism	0	5
Public Works Dept	4	60
Education Office	4	120
Health and Welfare Department	21	88
Total	30	330

Local representation in Derry City, 1966: The problem of gerrymandering

There were 24 local government councillors for Derry city. Each ward elected eight councillors.

South Ward	14,125	anti-Unionist votes	1,474	Unionist votes
North Ward	3,173	anti-Unionist votes	4,380	Unionist votes
Waterside Ward	2,804	anti-Unionist votes	4,420	Unionist votes

Both of the above inserts are from *Divided Ulster* by Liam de Paor (1971)

How useful are these two tables in explaining the degree of discrimination against Catholics in Northern Ireland in the 1960s?

A Unionist view on the causes of conflict in Northern Ireland

The majority of the population of Northern Ireland came from English and Scots stock. They had colonised the north east of Ireland from the end of the 16th century. They regard themselves as British rather than Irish. These colonists faced hostility from the Catholic Irish majority: in 1641 an Irish Rebellion led to the massacre of Protestants in Ulster. In 1688–90 the Catholic James II, in league with Louis XIV of France, attempted to force Catholicism on Britain and Ireland. He was defeated by William of Orange at the Battle of the Boyne in 1690. This victory protected the civil and religious liberties of the Protestant population of Ireland and saved Britain from absolutist government.

The link between north-east Ireland and Britain was strengthened in the 19th century by the industrial revolution. Shipbuilding and textiles industries flourished in north-east Ireland as part of an industrial British economy. The area had much more in common with central Scotland and northern England than the rest of Ireland.

As a minority in the whole of Ireland, Protestants feared domination by what they saw as an alien religion and culture. This was reinforced by the Catholic Church's insistence that in a mixed marriage between a Catholic and a Protestant, all the offspring had to be brought up as Catholics. Fear of the Catholic majority was reinforced during the political instability of 1919–22. Irish nationalists attempted to force the Unionist/Protestants of the north east into a united Ireland against their will. When Michael Collins, the Prime Minister of the Irish Free State, was shot on 22 August 1922, he was planning a major IRA campaign to destroy Northern Ireland.

From the very start of Northern Ireland's existence Catholics were seen as a dangerous **fifth column**. They supported unification with the Republic of Ireland. From 1937, under Articles 2 and 3 of the Eire constitution, the Republic claimed Northern Ireland as part of their national territory. The anti-British position of Irish Nationalists was emphasised by the neutrality of Eire during the Second World War. Between 1956 and 1962 the IRA launched a border campaign of terrorism, attacking border posts and killing RUC officers.

Fifth column: Individuals or groups within a country who support an enemy force.

Catholics had also created problems for themselves by opposing Northern Ireland from the start. Many Catholics believed that Northern Ireland wouldn't last long as a sub-state within the United Kingdom. They therefore abstained from participating in government. The Catholic Church refused to co-operate with the creation of a province-wide system of education. It insisted on running its own schools so that from an early age Catholics and Protestants were kept separate, thereby reinforcing the split within Northern Ireland society.

Unlike Nationalists, Unionists do not believe there was any historical justification for a united Ireland. Throughout history, Ulster had a separate

Sean Lemass (1899–1969)
Born in County Dublin in 1899 Lemass was in his teens when he took part in Easter Rising. He was Deputy Prime Minister 1945–49 and Taoiseach 1959–65. He re-established free trade with Britain in 1965 and was the first Irish Prime Minister to visit Belfast. He held talks with Terence O'Neill, Prime Minister of Northern Ireland on improving North–South relations in 1965.

1. What were the main grievances of the Catholic/Nationalist minority towards the Northern Ireland government by the mid-1960s?

2. To what extent are the differences between the Nationalist and Unionist views on the causes of conflict based on religion?

identity and the only time Ireland was united as one political entity was under British rule.

The disturbances which occurred in Northern Ireland had their origin in an attempt by Nationalists to push the province into the Republic of Ireland by force. The Official IRA had links with the NICRA and People's Democracy. These were seen as front organisation for this Republican plan. Attempts by the Irish Prime Minister, Sean Lemass, to meet and forge links with Captain Terence O'Neill was seen as part of a broader Nationalist conspiracy to achieve unification.

Protestant fears included the Second Vatican Council of the Catholic Church which began in 1963. Other Christian groups, including Protestants, were invited to attend as observers. This was seen as some as part of a global attempt by Catholicism to dominate Christianity. In *God Save Ulster!* (1989), S. Bruce quoted the Rev. Ian Paisley who stated: 'The aim is a super one-world Church. Rome, of course, already sees herself as that Church'.

There are important social and economic considerations in opposition to an all-Ireland state. Catholic influence in the Republic of Ireland meant that contraception was illegal. The Catholic Church also provided a form of censorship with a list of prohibited books. Northern Ireland, on the other hand, benefited from the National Health Service and the Welfare State, and the standard of living was much higher than in the Republic of Ireland.

13.4 How effective was British policy towards Northern Ireland between 1969 and 1985?

Between 1969 and 1985, British government policy was affected by a number of factors:

● high levels of political violence, which began in Northern Ireland but spread to both Britain and the Republic of Ireland. Political violence involved assassination, car bombs, and the shooting of police and soldiers. It involved paramilitary groups from the Loyalist and Republican communities (see panel on page 272), the RUC and the British army;

● attempts to find a political solution within Northern Ireland between Unionists and Nationalists;

● attempts to find a political solution between Northern Ireland and the rest of the United Kingdom;

● attempts to find a political solution which would involve the Republic of Ireland.

In trying to develop a coherent British policy, developments such as a change in government (from Labour to Conservative) or a change in the Secretary of State for Northern Ireland would have great significance. In addition, the Northern Ireland problem was affected by public opinion in the United States (in particular Irish-American opinion) and in Europe. (After January 1973 both the United Kingdom and the Republic of Ireland were part of the European Community.)

How did the policy followed by the Labour and Conservative governments towards Northern Ireland develop between 1969 and 1973?

After decades of disinterest and neglect the British government was faced with a major domestic political crisis in August 1969. Normally, the responsibility for maintaining law and order within Northern Ireland lay with the Stormont government. However, in *A House Divided* (1970) the Labour Home Secretary, James Callaghan, expressed his belief that military intervention was required by the British army to protect Catholic areas from attacks by Protestant mobs. This was most apparent in west Belfast. During the disturbances of 1968–69 Catholic areas felt that they lacked protection. Walls in these areas were daubed with slogans such as 'IRA, I ran away' condemning the IRA for its failure to defend them.

Direct British involvement under Labour was welcomed by the Catholic/Nationalist community. Their homes were now protected by the British army. A report by the Hunt Advisory Committee to the British government recommended the disarming of the RUC, the disbanding of the 'B' Specials and a transfer of council-house allocation from local authorities to the Stormont government. In April 1970 the 'B' Specials were replaced by a part-time regiment of the British Army, the Ulster Defence Regiment (UDR). Unfortunately, the UDR contained large numbers of former 'B' Specials.

The Republican reaction to the 1968–69 disturbances led to a split within the IRA. An IRA convention in 1969 saw the creation of the Provisional IRA. This group split from the Official IRA mainly because it wanted to engage in armed defence of the Catholic community. The Provisional IRA leader was Sean MacStiofain.

By the time Edward Heath became Conservative Prime Minister in June 1970 the political situation in Northern Ireland had begun to change. The continued existence of a Unionist-dominated Stormont government meant that the Catholic/Nationalist community began to regard the British Army as defenders of Unionism. This development was made worse by the decision of the Provisional IRA to go on the offensive in early 1971. The first British soldier (Gunner Curtis) was shot dead in February 1971 by the Provisional IRA.

With the escalation of political violence the British Government faced a difficult problem. British policy on the ground in Northern Ireland was determined by the senior army officer (General Officer Commanding – GOC – Northern Ireland) working with the Stormont government. A clash had occurred in October 1969 between the Chief Constable of the RUC and the GOC over security, which led to the GOC's role being restricted to co-ordination, and not overall control, of army and police. However, ultimate control lay with Westminster. In April 1971 the Northern Ireland Prime Minister, Chichester-Clark, resigned because the Heath government refused to increase troop levels in the Province.

In August 1971, the Heath government made a major tactical error by agreeing to the introduction of internment without trial, proposed by the new Northern Ireland Prime Minister, Brain Faulkner. With poor police and military intelligence about who was in the Provisional IRA, British troops and the RUC arrested large numbers of Catholic/Nationalists. They were placed mainly in an old military camp near Belfast known as Long Kesh. (It later became the Maze Prison.) The Catholic/Nationalist reaction to internment led to a large increase in support for the Provisional IRA.

The policy of using the army and police to restore law and order in the Catholic/Nationalist community reached crisis point on 30 January 1972. An illegal Civil Rights march in Derry City was stopped by the RUC and

Brian Faulkner (1921–1977)
Faulkner was born in County Down. He was leader of Ulster Unionist Party and Prime Minister of Northern Ireland March 1971 to March 1972. He introduced internment, signed Sunningdale Agreement in December 1973 and became Chief Executive of Power Sharing government January–May 1974. He founded the Unionist Party of Northern Ireland 1974.

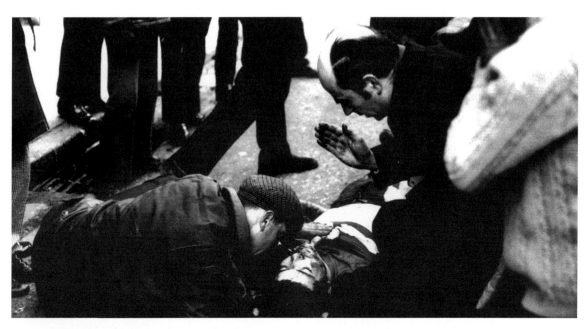

'Bloody Sunday', Derry City, January 1972

Why do you think photographs such as this helped bring about the suspension of the Stormont Government?

SDLP: The Social Democratic and Labour Party – see box on political parties in Northern Ireland, p.271.

The Alliance Party: A non-sectarian political party representing both Catholics and Protestants, and mainly supported by the middle class. It has made very little impact on the Northern Ireland political scene.

Consociational democracy: Democracy achieved by bringing together representative groups into government rather than having a ballot.

the Army. Fourteen marchers were killed by the Army, mainly by members of the Parachute Regiment. To this day the precise circumstances surrounding 'Bloody Sunday' have yet to be revealed. It was, however, a major setback for British policy. It caused uproar in the Republic of Ireland and the British Embassy was burned down. It also led directly to the Heath government's decision to suspend the Stormont government in March 1972, introducing Direct Rule from Westminster. From 1972 Northern Ireland affairs were under the responsibility of a member of the British Cabinet, the Secretary of State for Northern Ireland.

Under the first Secretary of State, William Whitelaw, the Heath government engaged in a major attempt to find a political solution within Northern Ireland. On 19 August 1969, the Labour Prime Minister, Harold Wilson, had made 'The Downing Street Declaration'. In it he declared British commitment to maintaining Northern Ireland's union with Britain as long as the majority of the Northern Ireland community agreed. Whitelaw took the bold step of opening negotiations with all sides of the conflict. In July, 1972 he even met Sean MacStiofain of the Provisional IRA but these talks came to nothing mainly because of the Provisional IRA's insistence on British withdrawal.

By the end of 1973 Whitelaw had been able to get moderate Unionists, led by Brian Faulkner, and moderate Nationalists of the **SDLP** with the **Alliance Party** to agree to the Sunningdale Agreement. The Agreement involved the passage of two acts of parliament: The Northern Ireland Assembly Act, May 1973, and the Northern Ireland Constitution Act, July 1973, and an agreement between the British and Irish governments in December 1973. Direct Rule was to be replaced by 'Power-Sharing'. The government of Northern Ireland was to contain representatives from both the Unionist and Nationalist communities. This was a version of **consociational democracy**. It was introduced because the normal operation of democracy meant that Unionists would always hold power.

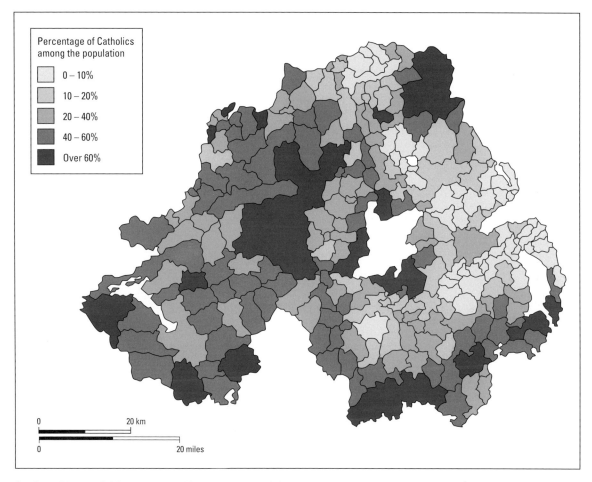

Percentage of Catholics among the population

- 0 – 10%
- 10 – 20%
- 20 – 40%
- 40 – 60%
- Over 60%

0   20 km

0   20 miles

On the evidence of this map, why do you think the partition of Northern Ireland has not been regarded as a serious political solution to the political and civil disorder since 1969?

The percentage of Catholics among the population of Northern Ireland in 1971

Taoiseach: The Prime Minister of the Republic of Ireland.

Another important feature of the Sunningdale Agreement was the inclusion of an All-Ireland dimension. Since September 1971, the **Taoiseach**, Jack Lynch, had been conducting talks with Edward Heath about Northern Ireland. Both prime ministers wanted an end to political violence. In the course of 1972 the Fianna Fail government in Dublin had introduced harsh measures against the Provisional IRA within the Republic. In December 1973 the Irish dimension of the agreement included the creation of a Council of Ireland. This would be an advisory committee involving political representatives from Northern Ireland and the Republic with limited executive power. It was a similar institution to the one proposed under the Government of Ireland Act, 1920.

The Sunningdale Agreement seemed to offer political stability for Northern Ireland. It was supported by moderate Unionists, moderate Nationalists, and the British and Irish governments. However, it was opposed by paramilitary groups on both sides, the Provisional IRA, the UDA and the UVF. It was also opposed by many Unionists. Most prominent were the Democratic Unionist Party of the Rev. Ian Paisley and the Vanguard Unionist Party of James Craig, a former Northern Ireland Home Secretary.

Secretaries of State for Northern Ireland

1972–73	William Whitelaw (Con)
1973–74	Francis Pym (Con)
1974–76	Merlyn Rees (Lab)
1976–79	Roy Mason (Lab)
1979–81	Humphrey Atkins (Con)
1981–84	James Prior (Con)
1984–85	Douglas Hurd (Con)
1985–89	Tom King (Con)
1989–92	Peter Brooke (Con)
1992–97	Sir Patrick Mayhew (Con)
1997–99	Dr Mo Mowlam (Lab)
1999–2001	Peter Mandelson
2001–2002	John Reid
2002–2005	Paul Murphy
2005–2007	Peter Hain
2007–	Shaun Woodward

Why did the Sunningdale Agreement fail?

The Power Sharing Executive operated for only four months. The collapse of the Sunningdale Agreement was brought about by a general strike organised by the Ulster Workers' Council in May 1974. This group included Unionist politicians, Loyalist paramilitaries and trade unionists. Although it lasted only 14 days, the strike brought Northern Ireland to a standstill.

One reason behind the failure was a change in government. In February 1974 Edward Heath had called a general election over the miners' strike. He was replaced by a minority Labour government under Harold Wilson which lacked the political power to act decisively.

Secondly, there was a lack of decisive leadership by the Labour Secretary of State for Northern Ireland, Merlyn Rees. He allowed the general strike to become established during the second week in May although he could, for instance, have used troops to operate power stations. Instead of supporting the Power Sharing Executive he allowed it to fail and suggested a Constitutional Convention to discuss other ways of finding a political agreement. In elections for the convention, in May 1975, anti-Power Sharing Unionists did well. By November 1975, when the Convention reported, it was split between Unionists who wanted a return of the Stormont government and a minority in favour of Power-Sharing. The Convention was dissolved, a failure, in March 1976.

Did Labour Policy towards Northern Ireland achieve anything between 1974 and 1979?

Diplock Courts: Special courts in Northern Ireland for trying terrorist cases. They were named after Lord Diplock, whose report in 1973 suggested that terrorists should not be tried by jury, because of widespread evidence of intimidation of jurors by paramilitaries.

Birmingham Pub Bombings: On 21 November 1974, the Provisional IRA placed bombs in two city centre pubs – the Tavern in the Town and the Mulberry Bush. Nineteen people were killed and 182 wounded.

Although Rees has been criticised over the failure of Power Sharing he did bring an end to internment. By 1976 the prisons contained convicted criminals, many tried by **Diplock Courts**. The Labour Government also introduced the Prevention of Terrorism Act in November 1974 following the **Birmingham Pub Bombings** by the Provisional IRA. This Act gave the British police powers of arrest and detention for anyone they suspected of terrorist offences. It also allowed the government to prevent people in Northern Ireland travelling to the mainland if they were suspected of being a security threat.

When Rees was succeeded by Roy Mason as Secretary of State in 1976, Mason abandoned attempts to find political agreement. Instead he concentrated on making Direct Rule work by attempting to reduce the level of

Deaths due to political violence and terrorism in Northern Ireland

1969–1998							
1969	13	1977	112	1985	54	1993	90
1970	25	1978	81	1986	61	1994	68
1971	174	1979	113	1987	93	1995	9
1972	467	1980	76	1988	93	1996	21
1973	250	1981	101	1989	62	1997	23
1974	216	1982	97	1990	76	1998	30
1975	247	1983	77	1991	94		
1976	297	1984	64	1992	84		

Deaths due to terrorism associated with Northern Ireland but occurring in the Republic of Ireland, Britain and Europe

1970–1992							
1970	3	1977	4	1984	6	1991	3
1971	3	1978	1	1985	4	1992	6
1972	11	1979	9	1986	0		
1973	8	1980	6	1987	6		
1974	2	1981	4	1988	9		
1975	17	1982	13	1989	16		
1976	6	1983	10	1990	6		

political violence. He gave greater responsibility to the RUC for security, and used the SAS for counter-insurgency operations against the Provisional IRA.

Unfortunately, the success of Mason's policy forced the Provisional IRA to reorganise itself into cells, a structure which was impossible for the British Army to break. A secret government report, the Glover Report, in 1968, declared that the Provisional IRA could not be defeated militarily. In his book *Final Term, the Labour Government 1974–1976* (1979) Harold Wilson declared that Labour policy seemed negative and almost defeatist in character. He declared that the political solution to Northern Ireland's problems lay within Northern Ireland. However, after Margaret Thatcher's victory in the 1979 general election British policy took a more dynamic turn.

How far did British policy change under Margaret Thatcher between 1979 and 1985?

Political violence associated with Northern Ireland reached a new intensity in 1979. Airey Neave, the Conservative Shadow spokesman on Northern Ireland, was murdered by the INLA in the House of Commons car park. In the Republic of Ireland INLA murdered Lord Mountbatten, a close relation of the Queen. At Warrenpoint, County Down, close to the border with the Republic 18 members of the Parachute Regiment were blown up by a large bomb detonated by the Provisional IRA.

However, the main problem facing the Thatcher government during its first term was the Hunger Strike by Republican prisoners in 1981. They were demanding the status of political prisoners. This crisis came to a head when a hunger-striker, Bobby Sands, was elected as MP for Fermanagh and South Tyrone. Sands' subsequent death from starvation, and the deaths of nine other hunger strikers, led to a major rise in support for the political wing of the Provisional IRA, Sinn Fein. It also gained considerable international publicity, particularly with the Irish-American community.

Garret Fitzgerald (1926–)
Fitzgerald was born in Dublin
and educated at University
College, Dublin where he was
a lecturer in Political Economy
from 1959–73. He was leader
of Fine Gael 1977–87, and
Taoiseach June 1981 – March
1982 and again December
1982 – March 1987. He signed
the Anglo-Irish Agreement of
1985.

Throughout the period 1979 to 1985 the Conservatives tried a number of political initiatives to break the political deadlock. The Secretary of State in 1982, James Prior, tried 'rolling devolution'. This meant political power would be handed back to Northern Ireland gradually if political violence subsided. More significant were the continued links between the British and Irish governments. These discussions, however, were affected by political changes in the Republic of Ireland. When the Fine Gael Taoiseach, Garret Fitzgerald, was in power relations were cordial. When Fianna Fail Taoiseach, Charles Haughey, held power relations were more difficult. These difficulties were made worse during the Falklands Conflict of 1982, when Haughey failed to support Britain. However, by 1985 a new departure in British policy occurred with the Anglo-Irish (Hillsborough) Agreement. It was jointly signed by Margaret Thatcher and Garret Fitzgerald.

To what extent was the Anglo-Irish Agreement of 1985 a turning point in British Irish relations?

The agreement established an Inter-Governmental Conference between the British and Irish governments. This would contain representatives from both governments. It would discuss Northern Ireland and the relations between Northern Ireland and the Republic of Ireland. Matters to be discussed involved cross-border security arrangements and justice. The latter involved the issue of extradition, the returning of terrorist suspects either to Britain or the Republic by the other state to face trial.

This was a major new departure. It formally involved the Republic of Ireland in the affairs of Northern Ireland for the first time. However, the Agreement also recognised that no change in the political status of Northern Ireland would occur without the consent of the majority. This meant that, for the first time, the Republic of Ireland officially recognised the existence of Northern Ireland. This went against Articles 2 and 3 of the Eire Constitution of 1937.

Why was the Anglo-Irish Agreement of 1985 significant in the development of British-Irish relations?

Margaret Thatcher and Garret Fitzgerald, the architects of the Anglo-Irish Agreement of 1985

From the British point of view this agreement was driven by increasing concerns about the growth in support for Sinn Fein. By 1985 the Republican movement had altered its strategy. It now followed a policy of 'the armalite and the ballot box'. This involved continuing the 'armed struggle' against the British but at the same time seeking election to local government and the Westminster parliament. The Anglo-Irish Agreement, by adding an 'Irish dimension', was a political strategy to stunt the growth of Sinn Fein's political power.

According to Paul Norris in 'Northern Ireland, the Long Road to Peace', published in *Talking Politics* (1998): 'The Anglo-Irish Agreement was a watershed in that it established the Irish government as a legitimate player in the internal affairs of Northern Ireland. The agreement sparked a sustained expression of a sense of absolute betrayal in the unionist community and among its political leaders. The agreement was a political boost for the SDLP who were seen to have top level access to British ministers at a time when Sinn Fein had entered politics and were capturing up to 40 per cent of the nationalist vote.'

1. What reasons can you give to explain why British policy changed towards Northern Ireland between 1969 and 1985?

2. What do you regard as the main obstacles to finding a political settlement in Northern Ireland between 1969 and 1985?

3. Who was more effective in dealing with the problems of Northern Ireland between 1969 and 1985: the Labour governments or the Conservative governments? Give reasons for your answer.

13.5 Why was it so difficult to find a political solution in Northern Ireland between 1985 and 2007?

Although the Anglo-Irish Agreement was a major new departure in Northern Ireland affairs, obstacles to peace still remained.

● The continuation of political violence. In 1987 the SAS virtually wiped out the East Tyrone Active Service Unit of the Provisional IRA at Loughgall. In November 1987 the Provisional IRA exploded a bomb at the Remembrance Day service at Enniskillen killing 11 and injuring 63. On 22 September 1989, 11 British servicemen (musicians) were killed by a the Provisional IRA bomb in Kent, England.

● The continued political success of Sinn Fein. The Agreement failed to stem the advance of Sinn Fein. They continued to win about 40 per cent of the nationalist vote. They also ended their boycott of elections in the Republic of Ireland in 1986.

● The Unionists were politically divided. Since the 1960s the once-united Unionist community had split into many factions. The largest group was the Official Unionist Party. However, Ian Paisley's Democratic Unionist Party usually represented three Westminster constituencies. Ian Paisley also topped the poll in the last three European Union elections. Other Unionist groups have appeared over the past 30 years. The UK Unionist Party held the North Down constituency in the 1997 general election. Both the DUP and the UK Unionists have been completely opposed to links with the Republic of Ireland.

● The existence of paramilitary groups on both sides. The commitment of paramilitary groups to violence created a wider gap between two communities. Any attempt by democratic politicians to exclude them from a political agreement meant that it would be difficult to find a lasting peace.

● Limited support for a lasting peace involving both communities. Between 1976 and 1977 there was a brief but popular attempt to try to bring the two communities in Northern Ireland together in a bid to create a climate for peace. It followed the deaths of three children after the Provisional IRA bank raid in August 1976. Under the cross-community leadership of Mairead Corrigan and Betty Williams, a women's movement both North and South of the border led a campaign for peace. The 'Peace People' gained international publicity and the two leaders won the Nobel Peace Prize but their movement produced nothing tangible.

What changes were made by the Downing Street Declaration of 1993?

A major move towards peace came on 15 December 1993 with a joint statement by the British and Irish governments. It declared that Britain had no selfish strategic or economic interest in Northern Ireland. It stated that a political settlement should be based on 'the right of the people on both parts of the island to exercise the right of self-determination on the basis of consent north and south to bring about a united Ireland, if that is their will'.

The declaration occurred for a number of reasons.

- Firstly, as in 1976, there was public indignation about political violence in Britain and Ireland. On 20 March 1993 two boys had been killed by a Provisional IRA bomb in Warrington, England. It was followed by bombing in both Britain and Northern Ireland.

- Secondly, the United States government was putting pressure on the British government to find a solution. The Clinton administration was sympathetic to Irish nationalist opinion in the United States. The president appointed a pro-nationalist ambassador to the Republic in 1993, Jean Kennedy-Smith. Congress had already accepted the '**MacBride Principles**' in the mid-1980s concerning trade with Northern Irish companies.

- Thirdly, Albert Reynolds had become Taoiseach in February 1991. His diplomatic skill was important in persuading the Major government to made a political statement.

- Finally, John Hume, leader of the SDLP, had several secret talks with Gerry Adams, leader of Sinn Fein. The aim was to bring Sinn Fein into the peace making process.

Following the Downing Street Declaration, the Provisional IRA declared a ceasefire on 31 August 1994, claiming that 'an opportunity to secure a just and lasting settlement had been created'.

Why did the Downing Street Declaration fail to bring an all-round peace agreement?

In 1995 and 1996 progress towards a peace agreement seemed possible. The Twin Track Initiative by the British and Irish governments on 28 November 1995 attempted a bridge-building exercise between the two communities. It established an International Commission led by ex-US Senator George Mitchell to investigate the issue of decommissioning paramilitary weapons.

The Downing Street Declaration failed to produce an all-round peace agreement in advance of the 1997 general election. The major obstacle to peace was the decommissioning of paramilitary weapons. The Conservative government was heavily dependent on Ulster Unionist support to stay in power and the Ulster Unionists demanded decommissioning before Sinn Fein should be allowed into talks.

This impasse led to the end of the Provisional IRA ceasefire with the Canary Wharf bombing of 9 February 1996. Even though elections took place for a Northern Ireland Forum to discuss peace on 30 May 1996, any genuine attempt at a peace settlement was still-born until after the election.

MacBride Principles: Passed by Congress in 1984. This was an attempt to end religious discrimination in Northern Ireland. US government firms could only agree contracts with Northern Ireland firms if the latter was proved not to discriminate against Catholics.

John Hume (1937–)
Born in Derry City, Hume was educated at Queen's University, Belfast. He was a member of the Civil Rights Association in 1968–69, founder member and Deputy Chairman of SDLP in 1970, MP for Foyle since 1983 and member of European Parliament since 1979. A major influence in the Anglo-Irish Agreement of 1985 and Good Friday Agreement of 1998, Hume received the Noble Peace Prize in 1999.

Gerry Adams (1949–)
Adams has been President of Sinn Fein since 1983. He was interned in 1971 and active in the Provisional IRA in the 1970s. He became MP for West Belfast 1983–92 and again from 1997. Adams had talks with John Hume of SDLP and with Hume and Albert Reynolds he formed a broad nationalist alliance in 1993. He signed up to the Good Friday Agreement of 1998.

Will the 'Good Friday Agreement' of 10 April 1998 bring lasting peace?

Following Blair's landslide victory in the 1997 general election the Provisional IRA announced a new ceasefire on 20 July 1997. Under the guidance of a new Secretary of State, Mo Mowlam, all sides in the Northern Ireland conflict were invited into a peace process. This included Sinn Fein and representatives of the Loyalist paramilitaries. The DUP and the UK Unionists boycotted the talks.

The Good Friday Agreement proposed change in the constitutions of Britain and the Republic of Ireland to include the principle of consent for the place of Northern Ireland within the United Kingdom. It also recognised the identity and aspirations of the Nationalist minority.

The Agreement created a Northern Ireland Assembly, a Power-Sharing Executive and a Council of Ireland between North and South. In many ways it seemed to be similar to the Sunningdale Agreement of 1973. However, this time the agreement included representatives from the paramilitaries. Sinn Fein, the Ulster Democratic Party and the Ulster Progressive Party signed up to the agreement. In return paramilitary prisoners were to be released. The Agreement was also backed by a Referendum in Northern Ireland and the Republic which supported the agreement (see table on page 294). It was also supported by the Clinton administration in the United States. However, a number of obstacles remain:

- There was opposition from within the Unionist community. Both the DUP and the UK Unionist Party opposed the Agreement. Even within the Ulster Unionist Party, David Trimble, the leader, faced criticism mainly from Jeffrey Donaldson MP.

- The Agreement and the Provisional IRA ceasefire resulted in a further split in the IRA. The Real IRA was formed in November 1997. On 15 August 1998, the worst atrocity since 1969 occurred in Omagh, County Tyrone when a car bomb planted by the Real IRA killed 29 people and wounded a further 200. Even though the Real IRA declared a ceasefire on 8 September 1998 there is still the possibility of breakaway groups within the IRA returning to political violence.

- Punishment beatings and murders continued in Republican and Loyalist areas. These were so frequent that in August 1999 Mo Mowlam investigated the possibility that the Provisional IRA had broken its ceasefire.

- One of the last acts of the Major government was to establish a Parades Commission in January 1997. This organisation had to deal with the issue of parades, usually Orange parades. Flashpoints since the Agreement were Drumcree Church, Portadown, the Lower Ormeau Road, Belfast and Derry City. The banning or rerouting of Parades caused considerable resentment in the Unionist community.

- The issue of paramilitary decommission proved to be a major problem. As part of the Mitchell Review of the Good Friday Agreement, in December 1999, the IRA appointed a go-between to discuss decommissioning with Canadian General de Chastelan.

- Linked with the decommissioning issue was the resentment felt by some members of the Northern Ireland Community about the early release of paramilitary prisoners. Many of them had been convicted of multiple murders.

David Trimble (1944–)
Trimble was the leader of the Official Unionist Party and was First Minister of Northern Ireland 1998–2002. Unionist MP for Upper Bann, he was elected leader in 1995. Trimble is a member of the Orange Order and participant at the Drumcree Marches in 1995 and 1996. Formerly a lecturer in Law at Queen's University, Belfast, he lost out to Mary McAleese (President of the Republic of Ireland) for the post of professor of Law at that university. He received the Nobel Peace Prize with John Hume in 1999.

Referendums on the Good Friday Agreement of 1997

In the Republic of Ireland

The results of the vote to change the Irish Constitution in line with the agreement were:

Votes in favour	1,442,583	(94.4%)
Votes against	85,748	(5.6%)
Electorate	2,753,127	
Turnout	1,545,395	(56%)
Valid votes	1,528,331	
Spoiled votes	17,064	

In Northern Ireland

The results of the vote on the Agreement were:

Votes in favour	676,966	(71.1%)
Votes against	274,879	(28.9%)
Electorate	1,175,403	
Turnout 9	53,583	81%)
Valid votes	951,845	
Spoiled votes	1,738	

By the end of December 1999 the prospect of permanent peace seemed possible. Former US Senator George Mitchell's review of the Good Friday Agreement had led to the creation of the Northern Ireland Executive containing members of Sinn Fein. Deputy Leader of Sinn Fein, Martin McGuinness became Minister of Education in this new Northern Ireland Government. Although two DUP members became ministers, they refused to attend meetings if Sinn Fein ministers were present.

As a result of the referendum on the Good Friday Agreement in the Republic of Ireland, the Irish government agreed to change Articles 2 and 3 of the Irish Constitution which made a claim of sovereignty over Northern Ireland. Also the 'Council of the Isles' – containing representatives of the British and Irish governments and representatives of the devolved governments of Scotland, Wales and Northern Ireland – met for the first time.

The new parliament and executive of Northern Ireland soon ran into difficulties. The key issue was IRA decommissioning. The Unionists, in particular the DUP, wanted the IRA to decommission its weapons in an open way. The Head of the Decommissioning Body, General de Chastelain, made claims that the IRA had decommissioned some of its weapons, but this did not satisfy many Unionists. One of the Ulster Unionist (UUP) MPs, Jeffrey Donaldson, defected to the DUP as a result of lack of progress on this matter. This issue was compounded by continued IRA activity, including punishment beatings in Nationalist areas and the murder of Robert MacCartney, in January 2005. This caused considerable resentment among the Nationalist community against the IRA. Meanwhile, in Colombia (South America) IRA members were arrested and accused of training anti-government guerrilla fighters.

On a number of occasions the Secretary of State for Northern Ireland had to suspend the Executive and Assembly. In 1999, the disagreement over decommissioning was the main dispute. In 2002, an IRA spy ring was uncovered working within the Northern Ireland Assembly building at Stormont. This led to a suspension which lasted until 2007.

However, elections still occurred in Northern Ireland (see tables on page 296). In the elections between 2003 and 2007 there was a drop in support for the two parties most closely associated with the Good Friday Agreement – the Ulster Unionists (UUP) and the SDLP, and the main Unionist opponents of the Good Friday Agreement, the DUP, saw major gains.

From 2004 the British and Irish governments still attempted to find a negotiated settlement based on the Good Friday Agreement. The first part of the negotiations led to the 'Comprehensive Agreement' of 2004. It was hoped that this would form the basis of a future deal between the Northern Ireland parties, including the DUP and Sinn Fein. Part of this agreement replaced the Royal Ulster Constabulary with the Police Service of Northern Ireland, which had been an important demand of Sinn Fein since 1998.

A breakthrough came in April 2005 when Sinn Fein leader, Gerry Adams, made a public appeal for the IRA to lay down their arms. This was followed in July 2005 by an announcement by the IRA that it had decommissioned all its weapons. Instead of doing so publicly, as the DUP demanded, it invited leading Catholic and Protestant clergymen to witness the event. This move was supported by General de Chastelain's Commission which confirmed, in September 2005, that the IRA had indeed completed decommissioning.

Although the IRA's decision to destroy all its weapons seemed significant at the time it paled into insignificance compared to the St Andrew's Agreement of October 2006. This agreement between the British and Irish governments and the political parties of Northern Ireland achieved the re-establishment of the Northern Ireland Executive and Assembly. In doing so, for the first time, the DUP agreed to join an Executive with Sinn Fein. In return, Sinn Fein agreed to support fully the new Police Service of Northern Ireland which it had previously boycotted. This agreement became the Northern Ireland (St Andrew's Agreement) Act of 22 November 2006.

A key part of the agreement was the decision to hold Assembly elections in March 2007, with the subsequent creation of a new Executive by May 2007.

In the March elections the DUP and Sinn Fein confirmed their positions as Northern Ireland's two major parties. As the DUP was the largest party its leader, Ian Paisley, became First Minister. Martin McGuinness of Sinn Fein became Deputy First Minister. To those who witnessed and remembered the violence and division of the 'Troubles' from 1969, the sight of the uncompromising Unionist, Ian Paisley, sitting and joking with former IRA commander Martin McGuinness was remarkable.

The achievement of peace was the work of a wide variety of people. The preliminary moves to peace had occurred under Conservative Prime Minister John Major and Irish Prime Minister Albert Reynolds in the early 1990s. However, the major breakthrough, the Good Friday Agreement, owed much to British Prime Minister, Tony Blair, Irish Prime Minister, Bertie Ahern and David Trimble and John Hume, leaders of the Ulster Unionists (UUP) and SDLP respectively. An important supporter of this process was US President Bill Clinton.

However, permanent peace was unlikely until both the DUP and Sinn Fein were willing to accept the Good Friday Agreement in full. It took a further eight years, until 2006, before all major parties within Northern Ireland were willing to accept all parts of the Good Friday Agreement.

British Prime Minister Gordon Brown (right) meets with Northern Ireland First Minister Ian Paisley, (2nd right), Deputy First Minister Martin McGuiness (2nd left) and Irish Prime Minister Bertie Ahern (left) at Stormont Parliament Buildings, in Belfast, Northern Ireland, July 2007.

Elections in Northern Ireland 2003–2007

2003 Elections to the Northern Ireland Assembly
(The Assembly was suspended at the time, and remained so until 2007)

(%)	% votes	Number of seats	Change since 1998 election
DUP	25.6	30	+7.5
UUP	22.6	27	–1
SDLP	17	18	–6
SF	24	24	+6
Other Unionist	2.5	2	–3
Alliance	3.6	4	0
Others	4.7	1	–2

2004 Elections to the European Parliament (3 MEPs)

	DUP	UUP	Others	SDLP	Sinn Fein
Seats won (2004)	1	1	0	0	1
Vote share (2004)	32.0%	16.6%	9.1%	15.9%	26.3%
Seats won (1999)	1	1	0	1	0
Vote share (1999)	28.4%	17.6%	8.5%	28.1%	17.3%

2005 Elections to the UK Parliament (18 MPs)

	DUP	UUP	Alliance	Others	SDLP	Sinn Fein
Seats won (2005)	9	1	0	0	3	5
Vote share (2005)	33.7%	17.7%	3.9%	5.1%	17.5%	24.3%
Seats won (2001)	5	6	0	0	3	4
Vote share (2001)	22.5%	26.8%	3.6%	5.1%	21.0%	21.7%

2005 Elections to the 26 Northern Ireland District Councils

	DUP	UUP	Alliance	Others	SDLP	Sinn Fein
Seats won (2005)	182	115	30	28	101	126
Vote share (2005)	29.6%	18.0%	5.0%	6.8% 17.4%	23.2%	Seats won
(2001)	131	154	28	44	117	108
Vote share (2001)	21.4%	22.9%	5.1%	10.5%	19.4%	20.7%

2007 Elections to the Northern Ireland Assembly (108 seats)
(Under the St Andrew's Agreement of November 2006)

	DUP	UUP	Alliance	OthersS	DLPSinn Fein	
Seats won (2007)	36	18	7	3	16	28
Vote share (2007)	30.1%	14.9%	5.2%	8.0%	15.2%	26.2%
Seats won (2003)	30	27	6	3	18	24
Vote share (2003)	25.6%	22.7%	3.7%	7.5%	17.0%	23.5%

1. What have been the major obstacles to finding a permanent peace in Northern Ireland since 1985?

2. To what extent is the Good Friday Agreement of 1998 different from the Sunningdale Agreement of 1973?

3. Answer using information from the whole of this chapter:

'Why has the Irish problem been such a difficult problem for British government to deal with from 1914 to 2007?'

Source-based questions: The Peace Process, 1992

SOURCE A

The problem we have to resolve in relation to Northern Ireland is the notoriously difficult one of two sets of conflicting rights. There is no argument for the self-determination of the unionist community that cannot be applied, with at least equal force, to the nationalist community in Northern Ireland. That community sees itself locked into a political entity it bitterly opposed. Its aspirations to independence were denied. It was cut off from the rest of Ireland and consigned to minority status which repeated itself at every level of politics and society. The symbols of the state, like the working of majority rule, might be neutral in Great Britain. They were, and are, both far from neutral in Northern Ireland.

From the opening statement by the Representative of the Republic of Ireland at the British-Irish Round Table talks, 6 July 1992.

SOURCE B

As to British constitutional arrangements 'Her Majesty's Government reaffirms their position that Northern Ireland's present status as part of the United Kingdom will not change without the consent of a majority of its people'.

Though perhaps not everyone will agree, I believe that the Anglo-Irish Agreement would give effect to any wish that might in future be expressed by a majority of the people of Northern Ireland for any alternative status.

As to Articles 2 and 3 of the Irish constitution, HMG fully accepts the sincerity with which the unionist delegations argue that any successful outcome from the talks process must include the repeal or amendment of those Articles.

From a statement by the Secretary of State for Northern Ireland, Sir Patrick Mayhew, on British-Irish Talks, 18 September 1992.

SOURCE C

British propaganda now claims that while 'preferring' to keep the Six County Statelet within the 'United Kingdom' it has no selfish strategic or economic reason for doing so.

British preference in relation to matters internal to Ireland holds no validity against the preference of the clear majority of the Irish people for national independence as expressed for generations.

Moreover, there are multiple democratic and practical reasons why partition should go:

It defies the wishes of the Irish people as a whole.

It rejects the wishes of the population in Britain as expressed in opinion poll after opinion poll.

It flouts international law.

It is undemocratic.

It is permanently abnormal and can only be maintained by extraordinary means.

It has created a generation of casualties in the Six Counties.

It cannot produce lasting peace.

From 'Towards a Lasting Peace in Ireland' a Sinn Fein publication, 1992.

SOURCE D

Commitment to the Army is total belief in the Army, in its aims and objects, in its style of warfare, in its methods of struggle, and in its political foundation.

Commitment to the Republican Movement is the firm belief that its struggle both military and political is morally justified, that war is morally justified and that the Army is the direct representatives of the 1918 Dail Eireann parliament, and that as such they are the legal and lawful government of the Irish Republic, which has the moral right to pass laws for the whole geographical fragment of Ireland and all its people regardless of creed or loyalty.

From 'The Green Book', the Provisional IRA Training Manual.

1. From information contained within this chapter explain the meaning of the following phrases underlined in the sources above.

a) 'Articles 2 and 3 of the Irish Constitution' (Source B)

b) The 'Republican Movement' (Source D)

2. Study Sources C and D and use information in this chapter.

How far do the points raised in these Sources reflect the view of Irish nationalists?

3. Study the Sources above and use information contained in this chapter. 'The failure to produce a lasting settlement to British-Irish relations since 1914 was the creation and maintenance of Northern Ireland within the United Kingdom.'

Assess the validity of this statement.

Further Reading

Texts designed specifically for AS and A2 students

The Irish Question in British Politics 1868–1986 by D.G. Boyce (Macmillan, 1988)
Ireland 1828–1923 by D.G. Boyce (Historical Association Studies, Blackwell, 1992)
Politics UK edited by B. Jones (Prentice Hall, 1998)
The Ulster Question 1603–1973 by T.W. Moody (Mercier, 1974)
Understanding Northern Ireland by D. Quinn (Baseline, 1993)

More advanced reading

Modern Ireland 1600–1972 by R.F. Foster (Allen Lane, 1988)
The Origins of the Present Troubles in Northern Ireland by C. Kennedy-Pipe (Longman, 1997)
The Northern Ireland Question in British Politics edited by P. Catterall and S. McDougall (Macmillan, 1996)
Northern Ireland since 1968 by P. Arthur and K. Jeffrey (Blackwell, 1988).

Index

Glossary terms

1922 Committee   130
38th parallel   259

Alien   278
Alliance Party   286
Annexation   162
Anschluss   185
ANZAC   191
ANZUS Treaty   191
Appeasement   130, 184
Apprentice Boys' March   279
Arbitration   161
Armistice   166
Attrition   233
Autonomous communities   176
Axis   196

Balance of payments   91
Balance of payments crisis   246, 253
'Balfourites'   46
Bank rate   105
Big Three   253
Bilateral   109
Bipolar   191
Birmingham Pub Bombings   288
Black and Tans   274
Blitz, The   195
Block vote   39
Bolshevism   161
Boom   89

Capitalist   142
Chain store   93
Closed economy   260
Coalition government   115
Collective security   162
Collectivism   212
Collectivist   56
Colonial Development Corporation (CDC)   265
Cominform   258
Competitiveness   107
Conservative   33
Conservative Central Office   119
Consociational democracy   286
Containment   259
Counter-revisionist   225
Coup d'etat   255
Crossed the floor   59
Crown Colonies   176

Dail   274
Decommissioning   271
Demagogue   261
Demobilisation   118, 253
Denominational schools   54
Deteriorating geological conditions   94

Devolution   179
Dichotomy   166
Diktat   166
Diplock Courts   288
Dirty Protest   272
Disarmament   126
Dreadnoughts   60

Ealing Comedies   246
East African Groundnut Scheme   265
Elites   262
Entente Powers   168
Expansionist   162

'Faddism'   35
Fait accompli   166
Fall of France   193
Festival of Britain   247
Fifth column   283
'First-past-the-post'   48
Fixed exchange rate   107
Fourteen Points   167
'Free Fooders'   46
Free trade   77, 260
Freely convertible   260

Geneva Protocol   145
Geopolitical   224
Gerrymandering   282
Gladstonian Liberalism   57
Gold standards   91
Governor-General   276
Gross domestic product (GDP)   92
Guerrilla war   274
Gunboat diplomacy   182

'Hedgers'   63
Hillsborough Agreement   271
Hire purchase   93
Historiography   224
Home Front   242
'Hotel Cecil'   34

Imperial preference   45
Independent Labour Party   139
Inflationary effect   91
Insurance principle   59
Insured population   92
Integrated works   92
Irish Citizen Army   274
Irish Question   273
Irish Republican Brotherhood   274
Isolation   168

Keynesian economic management   149

League of Nations Covenant   161
Lend-Lease   191
Liberal Nationals   129

Liquidated   163
Little Entente   172
Lock-out   96
Lord Chancellor   119
Luftwaffe   227

MacBride Principles   292
Mandate   253
Mandated territories   161
Manifesto   117
Marketing boards   109
Marxist   37, 94
Means test   102
Militant trade unionism   35
Mill, John Stuart   81
Minister without Portfolio   210
Mobilisation of labour   243
Mond-Turner talks   96

National Efficiency   54
National Executive   143
National Insurance   101
National Union   121
Nationalisation   142, 249
New Liberalism   142
Non-conformist   79

On the knocker   241
Open Door   183
Organised working class militancy   118
Overawe   96

Pacifist   142
Pariah   171
Parity of sterling   150
Party machine   120
Permissive factor   108
Philanthropist   61
Political levy   97
Poor Law   102
Populist   118
Post-war credits   235
Pre-1914 diplomacy   165
Prerogative   176
Primary producer   91
Private enterprise   94
Protectionism   176
Protocol   171
Public corporation   110
Purges   222

Quit India   262

Rapprochement   224
Ratify   168
Rationalisation   91
Real income   93
Realpolitik   173
Recognise   171